Deviance, Conformity, and Social Control in Canada

Deviance, Conformity, and Social Control in Canada

Fourth Edition

Tami M. Bereska
Grant MacEwan University

PEARSON

Toronto

Library and Archives Canada Cataloguing in Publication

Bereska, Tami M. (Tami Marie), 1968-, author
    Deviance, conformity, and social control in Canada / Tami M. Bereska.—Fourth edition.
ISBN 978-0-13-309829-7 (pbk.)
    1. Deviant behavior—Textbooks.   2. Conformity—Textbooks.   3. Social control—
Textbooks.   4. Canada—Social conditions—Textbooks.   I. Title.
HM511.B47 2014   302.5'420971   C2013-902765-3

Vice-President, Editorial Director: Gary Bennett
Editor-in-Chief: Michelle Sartor
Acquisitions Editor: Matthew Christian
Sponsoring Editor: Joel Gladstone
Marketing Manager: Lisa Gillis
Team Leader, Development: Madhu Ranadive
Developmental Editor: Louise MacKenzie
Project Manager: Susan Johnson
Production Editor: Niraj Bhatt, Aptara®, Inc.
Copy Editor: Leanne Rancourt
Proofreader: Maggie Bailey
Compositor: Aptara®, Inc.
Photo Researcher: Marta Johnson, PreMediaGlobal
Permissions Researcher: Anna Waluk, Electronic Publishing Services
Cover Designer: Karen Noferi
Cover Image: Fotolia

10   17   ISBN 978-0-13-3098297

PEARSON

Brief Contents

Contents

3   Explaining Deviance: The Perception, Reaction, and Power   66

4   Deviance 2.0: The Role of the Media   92

Preface

INTRODUCTION

The sociology of deviance is a diverse field of study, and this diversity is reflected in the content of Canadian textbooks that are available. Some books are based on theory, with separate chapters on each category of deviance theory and specific deviance examples to illustrate components of those theories. These books provide a thorough description and critical analysis of a wide range of theories, but if there is one way to make a fascinating subject like deviance rather dull in the eyes of students (as they have repeatedly pointed out to me), it is to bombard them with theory for the sake of theory. In contrast, this textbook reviews theories of deviance in two chapters, but the remaining chapters focus on substantive issues, bringing in relevant theories when doing so can meaningfully contribute to the overall "story" being told within a particular section of the chapter and within the chapter as a whole.

While some books address mainly theory, others have a criminological focus, containing extensive discussions of topics like violent crime, property crime, white-collar crime, police deviance, and sexual assault. These are all very important topics for students to be familiar with. However, students who take separate courses in criminology and in deviance frequently experience too much overlap between the course materials. In contrast, this textbook is specifically intended for courses in deviance or social control. There will still be a small amount of overlap for students taking both criminology courses and deviance courses, but that overlap is minimal. Furthermore, the material that might overlap is presented in a context very different from in a student's criminology course.

Some textbooks contain collections of readings that are based on a similar theoretical approach, such as social constructionism. These collections have the benefit of providing students with original readings; however, they lack a cohesive context to enhance student learning. This book is the kind of single-authored textbook that many professors and students prefer.

Finally, some books are characterized by what Ben-Yehuda (1990, p. 5) calls "radical phenomenalism," where countless numbers of isolated, specific phenomena (e.g., call girls, transsexualism, and marijuana use) are described in tremendous detail, but without reference to a broader social and historical structure. These phenomena are usually quite interesting to read about, but without a wider context the logic of including the various specific phenomena is unclear. To the reader, it can feel somewhat like randomly grabbing items in an all-you-can-eat buffet rather than sitting down to a four-course meal with different courses designed to complement each other. In contrast, in this textbook there is a method to the madness: The specific topics and issues addressed in each chapter have been selected as parts of a cohesive whole. Each individual topic covered is placed within a sociocultural context and contributes to a bigger picture.

FEATURES

The features of this textbook include the following:

- *Pedagogical aids for students* appear throughout every chapter. Students are asked to engage with the material as they read it. *Ask Yourself* sections ask students to think about certain questions, their own lives, or their own points of view prior to reading the next body of material. *Exercise Your Mind* sections recommend that students go beyond the textbook material to explore particular issues in more detail, by looking for critiques of theories or viewing certain movies that demonstrate a topic. *Time to Review* sections ask students to review questions at regular intervals throughout the chapters. Although formulated as pedagogical aids for students, many instructors report that they make use of these features as class activities or assignments or to stimulate class discussion.

- *Objective and subjective approaches* to deviance are integrated in the textbook, rather than only one or the other being focused on. They are also presented as complementary (rather than contradictory) approaches.

- *Two theory chapters* review those theories that are used in more objective approaches (Chapter 2) and more subjective approaches (Chapter 3).

- A *new chapter on media and deviance* (Chapter 4) introduces students to the pervasiveness of the media in our lives and the wide-ranging roles that it plays in the performance, social construction, and social control of deviance.

- The topics of the substantive chapters are *relevant to students' lives*—sexuality, youth, voluntary and involuntary physical appearance, mental disorders, religious belief systems, and scientific belief systems. The topics illustrate that the social typing and social control of deviance occurs everywhere around them, every day. They illustrate that students have experienced these processes and participate in them.

- Each of the substantive chapters incorporates material on *social typing* and *social control*.

- Each of the substantive chapters reveals the *"deviance dance."* That is, each chapter demonstrates how the social typing of deviance is not a uniform process but is characterized by *disagreement*, *debate*, and *resistance*, even for the most taken-for-granted issues (e.g., pedophilia).

- Each of the substantive chapters *tells a cohesive story*. Students are not bombarded with an assortment of cafeteria-style facts and theories; rather, they learn about the sociocultural context within which particular forms of deviance are socially typed and socially controlled.

- In the narrative of each chapter, both *criminal* and *noncriminal* forms of deviance are explored in relation to the topic at hand.

- The vital role of *power* in determining and controlling deviance is discussed in each chapter.

- In this fourth edition, more than 160 new references are included.

ORGANIZATION

The first four chapters in the book provide students with the foundation they need for a course in deviance. Chapter 1 looks at the various ways that academics, laypersons, and activists have defined deviance and how these definitions are embedded in a wider discussion of the objective/subjective dichotomy as it has traditionally been presented. From the objective perspective, various definitions are reviewed (i.e., statistical rarity, harm, normative violation, and negative societal reaction) and critiqued. From the subjective perspective, deviance is described as "anything that enough important people say it is" and is embedded in a discussion of social construction. After presenting the traditional objective and subjective points of view, this dichotomy or dualism is questioned, and material is presented showing how there is now more blending of the two perspectives in the work of many deviance scholars. Students are introduced to the concept of the social typing process, the different forms of social control, and the role of power in society. The notion of the "deviance dance"—that is, the negotiations over deviance (disagreement, debate, and resistance)—is introduced.

Chapter 2 explains that because scholars with more objective and subjective leanings shine their analytical spotlights on different aspects of deviance, different theories are more useful to each. The remainder of Chapter 2 reviews the positivist theories that are of most use to more objective researchers. This is not an exhaustive theoretical analysis, but rather a review of those theories that have been the most influential in the study of deviance. The section on functionalist theories includes Durkheim, Merton's anomie and strain theories, macro-level strain theory, differential opportunity theory, Agnew's general strain theory, and status frustration theory. The section on learning theories includes differential association theory, neutralization theory, and social learning theory. The section on social control theories reviews social bonds theory and self-control theory (also known as the general theory of crime). In the fourth edition, Durkheim's claim that deviance increases social solidarity is explored in an analysis of Virginia Polytechnic Institute before and after they experienced a mass shooting incident in 2007; Agnew's general strain theory is applied to the relationship between being victimized by bullying and self-harm or suicide ideation; principles of differential association theory are analyzed in relation to the "jamband" subculture; and the neutralization techniques used by competitive cyclists who use performance-enhancing drugs are outlined.

Chapter 3 reviews the interpretive and critical theories that are of most use to more subjective-leaning scholars. The section on interpretive theories addresses the symbolic interactionist perspective more generally, and then discusses the work of Tannenbaum, Becker, Lemert, and Goffman. The section on critical theories reviews conflict theories, power-reflexive theories, feminist theories, and postmodern theories. In this fourth edition of the textbook, an interesting addition is research illustrating that the stigma management techniques used by male sex workers in Hong Kong not only reduce the stigma of sex work, but also serve as gender strategies to negotiate respectable and responsible masculinity.

As a central pedagogical force in the twenty-first century, the media is intimately intertwined with the social processes surrounding deviance and conformity. Chapter 4 explores the nature of this relationship in some detail. First, the chapter outlines contemporary patterns of media use for both adults and children. With adults using media for more than 60 hours per week and children more than 52 hours per week, media use is so pervasive that to effectively study contemporary social life one must necessarily study the media. Research on media emerges from two distinct approaches. Administrative research on media is of greatest use to deviance scholars who lean toward the more objectivist end of the objective–subjective continuum in that it holds the individual under a microscope, trying to determine what types of media messages will result in particular outcomes in individuals. The foundational question for administrative research on media is "*Who* says *what* to *whom* and with *what effects?*" This research shows that in certain contexts, and under particular conditions, the messages that are contained in the media have some type of effects on individuals in the audience. Nowhere is this process more evident than in the world of advertising and marketing, where hundreds of billions of dollars are spent every year to maximize the impact of advertising messages on individuals' purchasing power. The chapter goes on to explore the nature of the effects of advertising on individuals and highlights the manner in which advertisers themselves use administrative research in their own work.

The question of what effects media messages have on audiences is especially profound when considering the topic of media violence—the single most researched topic in media studies. Chapter 4 reviews the research on the effects of media violence on aggression in the "real world." Although much of the research is contradictory, and therefore as a whole is somewhat inconclusive, there is evidence that at least in *some* people media violence is associated with aggressive attitudes and behaviours.

In contrast to administrative research, which proposes a relationship between media messages and individual outcomes, critical research on media emphasizes the role that the media plays in our understandings of ourselves, other people, and the world around us; critical research dominates media studies in Canada. In the first chapter of the book, the media is discussed as one of the agents of power within processes of social construction. In Chapter 4, the nature of that power is delved into more deeply, for example, by exploring the ways that ethnicity and gender are framed in the mainstream media. Frames of ethnicity exclude members of many ethnic groups from even having a presence or a voice within the media. When there is a presence, existing frames reinforce ethnic stereotypes, present some ethnic groups as being social problems, and present other ethnic groups as adornments. The chapter goes on to address the presence of these frames in Disney movies and the implications of these frames of ethnicity. Frames of gender also reinforce stereotypes of passive, vulnerable femininity and aggressive, villainous, sexually predatory masculinity. Critical research on the media also draws attention to the structure of ownership in the media industry, based on the assumption that ownership is intertwined with the nature of the media content. Growing convergence, conglomeration, and concentration in media owner-ship results in only a handful of companies in control of content, content providers, and the technical infrastructures through which content is provided. Consequently, "corporate empires control every means by which the population learns of its society" (Bagdikian, 2004, p. 4).

The latter half of Chapter 4 addresses the multifaceted relationship between the media and deviance more specifically. It explores, in some detail, five different types of relationships. First, the media can be analyzed as a cause of deviance, as illustrated in the earlier discussion of the effects of media violence on aggression in the "real world." Second, as emphasized by critical research on the media, the processes by which devi-ance and normality are socially constructed are inextricably intertwined with the media. The media affects an entire culture through its power to define boundaries, identify social problems, and shape public debates. Third, the media can be used as a *tool* for deviance. The chapter explores various forms of this relationship in some detail. Cyber-crime, and its even more malicious form, cyberterrorism, are discussed. Research on the *hacker* subculture reveals a complex normative order affecting individual identities and processes of social categorization. A comparison of contemporary cyberterrorist net-works and ancient terrorist groups shows us that despite many surface-level differences, they have important similarities as well—in communication patterns, connection and kinship webs, network structures, and obstacles faced. Another form of cybercrime—digital piracy—is also explored in terms of differential association, neutralization, and labelling theories as well as stigmatization. A form of mass-mediated deviance that has garnered considerable public attention more recently is cyberbullying. The chapter looks at the prevalence and patterns of cyberbullying as well as its implications.

The fourth relationship between the media and deviance that is addressed in Chapter 4 is the media as a site for the deviance dance. Although the media can be a tool for devi-ance, at the same time it can be a tool for the social control of deviance. Facebook tech-nology scans posts for evidence of criminal activity, online anti-bullying campaigns are pervasive, and even the Vancouver Police Department created a website to identify riot-ers following the 2011 Stanley Cup riots. The media acts as a social typer of deviance, and yet at the same time, is used by individuals and groups to resist the social typing process. Stigmatized persons can create online communities of support, and some hackers use the media to redefine their role as "hacktavists."

Finally, Chapter 4 explores the way that the media itself can be deviantized and sub-jected to measures of social control. Various examples are presented, with an emphasis on the ways that youth forms of media, in particular, seem to be targeted by social control efforts. Examples include the efforts of the PMRC in the 1980s, the deviantization of jazz music in the 1920s, and the rigorous measures of social control that the Nazi government directed at the swing music culture.

The remaining chapters in the book focus on a range of substantive issues. Chapter 5 explores sexuality. An analysis of sexual cultures in traditional and colonized Aboriginal cultures in North America, and Canadian/American society from the seventeenth century onward is particularly effective in demonstrating how conceptions of sexual deviance vary. Moving into the present day, the criteria used for evaluating people's sexuality as deviant or normal are explored. In the fourth edition, new material on the emergence of the gay rights movement and its subsequent achievements has been added. The Stonewall Inn uprising is presented as the beginning of the modern gay rights movement. The evolution of gay rights in Canadian legislation is discussed, but it is contrasted with the extensive efforts of the federal government to purge gays and lesbians from the public service. The section on the "deviance dance" in relation to sexuality in contemporary society has been expanded, with an emphasis on the debates, negotiations, struggles, and resistance surrounding the sex trade. The structure of power in the exotic dancing industry is explored. At both the individual and organizational levels in the structure of power, dancers are subjected to the power of others (i.e., customers, managers) and yet also exert their own power to control customers and maximize their incomes. However, the individual and organizational levels of power are embedded within and affected by the larger institutional level of power—a level that is increasingly controlled by organized crime and characterized by the McDonaldization of the industry.

Chapter 5 goes on to look at the question of whether pornography is "harmful," emphasizing research trends that focus on adolescents and young adults in particular. More objectively oriented research analyzes the effects of pornography consumption on negative outcomes (e.g., attitudes toward sexuality, risky sexual behaviours, etc.). These research findings are contradictory, with some studies finding more negative outcomes among youth who are greater consumers of Internet pornography, while other studies find no such effects. More subjectively oriented research focuses on the meanings and understandings that youth have of pornography. This research finds that in the Internet age, youth consider pornography use to be normal and acceptable. Yet at the same time, they also express some ambivalence, recognizing that men and women are portrayed unequally in pornography and that real relationships are better, and sometimes stating that they are just getting "tired" of it. Finally, the changing nature of the concerns surrounding prostitution is presented from a historical view, emphasizing the evolving discourses that have shaped social policy—discourses of morality, public health, victimization, and worker rights. The chapter closes by looking at contemporary debates over the decriminalization of certain forms of prostitution and recent court decisions.

Chapter 6 focuses on youth. The first section of the chapter addresses "deviant" youth—youth crime, gangs, and substance abuse (including binge drinking among college students). The concept of at-risk youth is then introduced and explored. The criticism that the concept of "at-risk" has rapidly expanded and now potentially includes all youth in society leads to the second half of the chapter. Here, the following question is asked: "Aren't all youth deviant?" That is, the issue of whether adolescence is an inherently deviant time in the life cycle is explored.

In Chapter 7, voluntary and involuntary physical appearance is examined. The first half of the chapter explores body modification. Research from a more objectivist view analyzes tattoos and piercings in the context of what body modification tells us about individuals (i.e., risk and motivation). Research from a more subjectivist view explores what body modification tells us about social interaction (e.g., impression management) and about the larger society (e.g., structures of power). The second half of the chapter looks at body size—"too fat," "too thin," and "ideal." The way these criteria are determined medically is reviewed, as are medical forms of social control. Next, the social standards that define the "ideal" body are discussed. Finally, the various means of controlling ideas of "too fat" and "too thin" through media, commercial industry, government, and medicine are reviewed, and resistance to that deviantization is addressed.

Chapter 8 is about mental illness. This chapter explores the nature and prevalence of mental illness, as well as its individual and societal costs. The contemporary and historical social control of mental illness is discussed, along with issues of mental health policy and funding and stigmatization. The impact of the deinstitutionalization movement is also presented. The chapter next moves to a more subjective look at how mental illness is determined. Criticisms of the *DSM* and the process by which it is created are presented. Rosenhan's study "Being Sane in Insane Places" is reviewed, and finally the social factors that influence diagnosis and treatment today are presented. The fourth edition includes additional critiques of the portrayal of mental illness in the media (e.g., in *Silver Linings Playbook* and the *Harry Potter* franchise), the stigma management techniques used by people with mental disorders, Parsons's concept of the sick role (and the conditions under which people with mental disorders are assigned such a role), and the guiding principles of Canada's new Mental Health Strategy.

Chapter 9 addresses religious and scientific belief systems (previously contained in two separate chapters) as two of the means by which we learn about "truth." The relationship between belief systems and deviance are twofold. First, we explore those belief systems within the context of those belief systems being socially typed as deviant and subjected to measures of social control. Religion is analyzed in this way in terms of "deviant" religions. Various churches, sects, and cults are defined and analyzed, as is the social control of sects and cults. The traditional distinction between churches, sects, and cults is then questioned, and students are presented with material demonstrating that all religious groups have been seen as deviant and made subject to social control at some time in some society.

Science is also analyzed in this way, first in terms of "deviant" acts that occur within accepted sciences—that is, acts of scientific misconduct. The prevalence of scientific misconduct, its relationship with the growing corporatization of science, and the changing discourses of its social control are explored. Science is also analyzed as being deviant itself in terms of "deviant" sciences—in other words, pseudo-sciences.

The second type of relationship that exists between belief systems and deviance is in terms of the role that belief systems play in steering the social typing process, telling us which people, behaviours, or characteristics should be considered deviant, why, and what should be done about it. With religious belief systems, this relationship is analyzed within the context of blurred boundaries between religious and political belief systems. Various instances are presented—witch persecutions, residential schooling, and the Victorian child-savers movement. When looking at scientific belief systems, we see that science can help address many problems but that there are many ways in which "scientific" claims have had negative consequences in the past. Two examples are social Darwinism, which influenced government policies regarding Aboriginal peoples, and the eugenics movement, which swept through the Western world and reached its apex in Nazi Germany.

Chapter 10 brings students full circle by reminding them of the key themes that were introduced in Chapter 1 and explored in each of the substantive chapters: the objective–subjective continuum; social typing, social control, and power; and the "deviance dance." Examples from the various chapters are reiterated to demonstrate these themes. Because of the role of subjectivity in determining and controlling deviance, some students may be left wondering if no one and nothing can ever be accurately socially typed as deviant. The notion of human rights is introduced as a possible starting point for thinking about when it is or is not appropriate to attach a deviant label and subject someone to measures of social control.

SUPPLEMENTS

The following instructor supplements are available for downloading from a password-protected section of Pearson Canada's online catalogue. Navigate to your book's catalogue page to view a list of those supplements that are available. See your local sales representative for details and access.

MyTest (978-0-13-315848-9)   The MyTest from Pearson Canada is a powerful assessment-generation program that helps instructors easily create and print quizzes, tests, exams, as well as homework or practice handouts. Questions and tests can all be authored online, allowing instructors ultimate flexibility and the ability to efficiently manage assessments at any time, from anywhere. For each of the ten chapters in the textbook, there are approximately 50 objective questions (i.e., a combination of true/false and multiple choice), 7 short answer questions, and 4 essay questions. A **Word version (ISBN 978-0-13-315847-2)** of the test bank is also available as a download from the catalogue.

Instructor's Resource Manual (978-0-13-315845-8)   Each of the chapters in this manual includes a lecture outline, teaching suggestions for active learning, video suggestions, and website suggestions.

PowerPoint Slides (978-0-13-315849-6)   The PowerPoint slides offer over 25 slides per chapter and highlight key concepts featured in the text to assist instructors.

MySearchLab® with eText

MySearchLab with eText provides access to an online interactive version of the text and contains writing and research tools—access to a variety of academic journals, Associated Press news feeds, and discipline-specific readings to help you hone your writing and research skills. Just like the printed text, you can highlight and add notes to the eText online. You can also access the eText on your iPad by downloading the free Pearson eText app. This MySearchLab also features chapter quizzes, Deviance in Print (a feature in the previous edition listing key readings), Deviance at the Movies (a feature in the previous edition listing key videos/movies), and access to videos from the Documentary and Core Concepts video series. In addition, access to MySocLibrary will reside in the Resources section of MySearchLab.

CourseSmart for Instructors (ISBN 978-0-13-315844-1)

CourseSmart goes beyond traditional expectations—providing instant, online access to the textbooks and course materials you need at a lower cost for students. And even as students save money, you can save time and hassle with a digital eTextbook that allows you to search for the most relevant content at the very moment you need it. Whether it's evaluating textbooks or creating lecture notes to help students with difficult concepts, CourseSmart can make life a little easier.

CourseSmart for Students (ISBN 978-0-13-315844-1)

CourseSmart goes beyond traditional expectations—providing instant, online access to the textbooks and course materials you need at an average savings of 60 percent. With instant access from any computer and the ability to search your text, you'll find the content you need quickly, no matter where you are. And with online tools like highlighting and note-taking, you can save time and study efficiently

Technology Specialists

Pearson's Technology Specialists work with faculty and campus course designers to ensure that Pearson technology products, assessment tools, and online course materials are tailored to meet your specific needs. This highly qualified team is dedicated to helping schools take full advantage of a wide range of educational resources by assisting in the integration of a variety of instructional materials and media formats. Your local Pearson Canada sales representative can provide you with more details on this service program.

Pearson Custom Library

Create your own textbook by choosing the chapters that best suit your own course needs to increase value for students and fit your course perfectly. With a minimum enrolment of 25 students, you can begin building your custom text. Visit www.pearsoncustomlibrary.com to get started.

peerScholar

Firmly grounded in published research, peerScholar is a powerful online pedagogical tool that helps develop students' critical and creative thinking skills through creation, evaluation, and reflection. Working in stages, students begin by submitting written assignments. *peerScholar* then circulates their work for others to review, a process that can be anonymous or not, depending on instructors' preferences. Students immediately receive peer feedback and evaluations, reinforcing their learning and driving development of higher-order thinking skills. Students can then re-submit revised work, again depending on instructors' preferences.

Contact your Pearson representative to learn more about *peerScholar* and the research behind it.

Acknowledgments

There are many people to thank for this work. Special thanks must go to those who choose to work with academics, despite our peculiarities. The entire editorial team at Pearson Canada provided welcome instruction, guidance, and tolerance. I would also like to express gratitude to my fellow academics, those reviewers whose thoughtful comments reinforce Adler and Adler's (2006) assertion that the sociology of deviance is a field that is stronger and more relevant than ever:

Lauren Barr, University of Western Ontario; Jay Clifford, St. Thomas University; Heather Angela Ford-Rosenthal, Concordia University; Shelly Ikebuch, Okanagan College; Frank Lavandier, University of Prince Edward Island; Anthony Micucci, Memorial University of Newfoundland; Karen Moreau, Niagara College; Patrik Olsson, University of Ontario Institute of Technology.

However, the most special of thanks goes to my students, who continue to inspire me with their thought-provoking ideas. It is the students who must ultimately read the books they are assigned—I have written this book for them.

Chapter 1
Determining Deviance

Learning Objectives

After reading this chapter, you should be able to

1   Describe the objective/subjective dichotomy.

2   Describe four definitions of deviance traditionally associated with the objective side of the objective/subjective dichotomy and explain their limitations.

3   Describe the definitions of deviance traditionally associated with the subjective side of the objective/subjective dichotomy and summarize the concept of social construction.

4   Explain how the study of deviance is influenced by how the researcher defines it. Depict the role of change, negotiation, opposition, and diversity in the "deviance dance" in Canadian society.

5 Outline the three components of the social typing process through which someone is defined as "deviant."

6 Explain the role of power and identify who holds this power in Canadian society.

When we think of deviance, we frequently think of negative behaviours such as crime or substance abuse. But is that necessarily the case? Might deviance actually be a good thing in some ways? Social commentator Mason Cooley (2006) writes "Conformity makes everything easier, if you can still breathe." This suggests that our lives will run more smoothly if we conform; however, it also makes the claim that conformity will constrict and limit us. Television producer David Lee (2006) goes a step further, saying that "You have to be deviant if you're going to do anything new." According to this claim, acting or thinking in a novel way is necessarily deviant, and although "thinking outside the box" is a popular corporate phrase, Lee suggests that only "deviants" will actually do so.

Taken together, the claims made in these quotations raise questions about **deviance** and **conformity**. Who are the conformists in our society and in our world? Is life easier for them? Who are the deviants? Are they really the innovators of our world, or do they represent some sort of problem that we need to control? How can we distinguish between a "deviant" and a "conformist"? These are the kinds of questions that will guide us through this textbook.

Who Is Deviant?

Who is deviant? One way to try to answer this question is by looking at the topics covered in deviance textbooks and journals. Historically, certain themes have prevailed—what have been referred to as "nuts, sluts, [and] perverts" (Liazos, 1972, p. 103). Criminality has also dominated the topics covered in some deviance textbooks. However, a growing body of recent deviance research has moved away from these tendencies toward broader notions of deviance—people who illegally download music (Hinduja & Higgins, 2011), customers in adult novelty stores (Hefley, 2007), the jamband subculture (Hunt, 2010), and people who are voluntarily childless (Park, 2002) have all been analyzed in the context of deviance. This shift in emphasis from the unusual to the mundane illustrates that "deviance is not marginal, it is central to what we do" (Adler & Adler, 2006b, p. 132).

Ask Yourself

Before going on, make a list of the types of people you consider to be deviant. We will come back to your list in a little while.

A second way to ascertain who is deviant is to ask people. As many other deviance professors have done (e.g., Goode, 1997; Herman, 1995), over several years of teaching I have conducted polls of students in my classes. Certain responses have predominated and may bear a striking resemblance to the list you created in the *Ask Yourself* exercise. For instance, people who commit crimes, especially violent crimes, are

Ask Yourself

Go back to the list you made of people you consider to be deviant. Take a look at the list. What do all of the people on your list have in common? Is there a shared characteristic that might point to how deviance can be defined or how we can recognize a deviant when we see one? This issue will be addressed in the next section of the chapter.

thought of as deviant by large numbers of students. There is also considerable consensus that those who perpetuate injustice, such as racists, are deviant as well, but once we go beyond the top three or four types of people listed, perceptions of deviance become as diverse as the students making those lists. Anyone the student dislikes or is annoyed by is added to the list—classmates who twirl their hair, people who drive SUVs, vegetarians, country singers, and professors who wear too much beige are just some of the hundreds of unique responses students have given. Although using the term "deviance" in reference to our own individual pet peeves may be common practice, the concept of deviance transcends the individual level and instead exists at the societal level. That is, "deviance" does not describe people I personally disapprove of, but rather characteristics of the broader society and sociocultural processes. Just because I might not like country singers does not mean that country singers are deviant in Canadian society.

Although each of us (along with our individual opinions) is an important participant in the social processes that occur in Canadian society, social processes constitute more than the sum of their parts, and more than the sum of each of our personal points of view. Thus, studying deviance requires you to move beyond your individual beliefs to analyze the broader social processes that occur in our society, whether or not those processes correspond to your individual beliefs or challenge them. But how is it that some people are perceived and treated as deviant while others are not?

How Can We Recognize Deviance When We See It?

Asking how we are able to determine who is deviant brings us to the issue of definitions. The dictionary tells us the following:

> Deviant: "deviating [straying] from an accepted norm." Synonyms: "abnormal, atypical, aberrant, unrepresentative." Contrasted words: "normal, natural." (Merriam-Webster, 2013)

At first glance, the dictionary seems to make the concept of deviance quite clear. Deviance involves violating norms that have been accepted in society, and apparently this is quite serious because doing so makes one abnormal and unnatural. Clearly, breaking the rules has significant consequences. Perhaps Mason Cooley, quoted at the beginning of this chapter, was correct in saying that conformity makes one's life easier.

We could stop with the dictionary definition of deviance and let that serve as the foundation for our exploration through the remainder of this book. However, the ways that the word "deviance" is used in academic research and common usage often differ from the dictionary definition—defining deviance is not as straightforward as the dictionary implies. In the academic realm, deviance is studied by **deviance specialists** who analyze criminal or noncriminal forms of deviance; those who focus exclusively on criminal forms of deviance are more specifically known as **criminologists**. Among deviance specialists (including criminologists), the study of deviance has historically been characterized by considerable disagreement over the concept of deviance, and this "problem of definition" (Ben-Yehuda, 1990, p. 4) continues to the present day. Even deviance specialists cannot entirely agree on what deviance is.

Although contradictory definitions of deviance have coexisted for many decades, some researchers suggest that a broader shift in definitions has become evident over time (Hathaway & Atkinson, 2001). Older definitions, which suggested there is an *objective* way of determining what is deviant, have shifted to more recent definitions that deconstruct the notion of objectivity and instead point out that deviance is necessarily *subjective*; in fact, some deviance specialists label the latter approach the "contemporary approach" (Herman, 1995, p. 3). **Objective** views of deviance claim that the presence of certain characteristics defines deviance; behaviours or people with those characteristics are deviant, and those lacking such characteristics are normal (Rubington & Weinberg, 2008). By looking for these characteristics, we can all identify deviance. In contrast, **subjective** views of deviance claim that there is no shared, observable characteristic that can clearly tell us who or what is deviant and who or what is normal. Instead, someone must tell us who is deviant in Canadian society (Rubington & Weinberg, 2008). Both the objective and subjective ways of defining deviance will be outlined and explored in more detail as this chapter progresses.

Proposing that there has been a shift from objective to subjective ways of defining deviance implies certain underlying assumptions. The core underlying assumption is that there is an unmistakable distinction between objective and subjective definitions of deviance—an objective definition can be clearly differentiated from a subjective definition. The distinction between objective and subjective is typically described as a dualism, or dichotomy, wherein objective and subjective represent two oppositional and mutually exclusive categories (e.g., Adler & Adler, 2003; Ben-Yehuda, 1990). These categories are analogous to the two sides of a coin that, when tossed, will show *either* heads or tails, but not both. However, the recent shifts in definitions of deviance often go beyond this notion of objective and subjective as mutually exclusive categories and instead combine aspects of both. And if it is possible to combine objective and subjective notions of deviance, this raises the question of whether the objective/subjective dichotomy that has been so frequently referred to is even a useful one to talk about in contemporary deviance research.

In the following sections the traditional objective/subjective distinction will be explored. We will look at the different objective definitions of deviance that have been used in the academic arena as well as in common usage. Subjective definitions of deviance will also be reviewed. Finally, we will look at how these two different types of definitions may not be so different after all, and how many contemporary ways of looking at deviance are blends of both objective and subjective approaches. Although this section of the chapter began with what looked like a very clear dictionary definition of deviance, when you finish reading this chapter you will see that the subject of this book—deviance—is a far more complex and multifaceted phenomenon than the dictionary definition suggests.

The Objective/Subjective Dichotomy

Objectivism: Deviance as an Act

The objective side of the dichotomy, as it has typically been depicted, emphasizes the assumption that there is something inherent in a person, behaviour, or characteristic that is necessarily deviant. All "deviants" have something in common that enables us to recognize them when we see them. However, the precise nature of that shared feature is a matter of debate. The characteristics that have been most frequently postulated include statistical rarity, harm, a negative societal reaction, and normative violation (e.g., Deutschmann, 2002; Sacco, 1992). Each of these features is emphasized by different deviance specialists, as well as by various laypersons. Each of these characteristics, when used as a defining characteristic of deviance, has also been subject to criticism by other deviance specialists, particularly those working from a subjective approach.

Statistical Rarity.   One of the definitions of deviance that has been associated with the objective side of the objective/subjective dichotomy is based on **statistical rarity**. Although this is a definition that is not commonly used in academic research, it is a definition that is "often heard in everyday conversation" (Clinard & Meier, 2001, p. 7); as a result of its popular usage, it is an important conception of deviance to analyze (Becker, 1963). According to this definition, if a behaviour or characteristic is not typical, it is deviant. Thus, because only 22.3 percent of males and 17.5 percent of females smoke, smoking may be thought of as deviant in contemporary Canada (Janz, 2012). Ex-cons may be thought of as deviant because most people have not been in prison. People with spiked green hair may be thought of as deviant because most people do not have spiked green hair.

While this definition of deviance has popular credibility, and although there are particular instances where statistical rarity can be observed, postulating statistical rarity as the defining characteristic of deviance has its limitations. First of all, how we define "rare" presents a problem. Is a behaviour rare if its prevalence is less than 50 percent? Or does it have to be less than 30 percent? The Canadian Centre on Substance Use (2011) finds that 44 percent of youth in Grade 12 have used cannabis in the previous year, and between 41 percent and 55 percent have consumed five or more drinks on one occasion within the past month. Are these behaviours rare? The difficulty in determining the criteria for rarity illustrates one of the limitations of this definition of deviance.

A second limitation is that some behaviours are not statistically rare, but are still perceived as being unacceptable in the larger society and are subjected to control efforts. For example, 61 percent of youth in Grade 10 have consumed alcohol within the last year (Canadian Centre on Substance Use, 2011). Thus, alcohol consumption among young teenagers is statistically *common* rather than rare, and yet many of us would say that it is not acceptable for 15-year-olds to drink. Furthermore, extensive efforts to prevent this behaviour are found in the school curriculum, community programs, and families, and the behaviour is, in fact, against the law.

Third, we must also consider that there are many rare behaviours or characteristics that are widely accepted in Canadian society. Left-handed people are statistically rare, but they are not treated as deviant (although they were seen that way historically) (Barsley, 1967). Sports prodigies (like Wayne Gretzky or Sidney Crosby) are statistically rare but are respected and envied. Only 7 percent of children and 15 percent of adults meet the recommended daily requirements for physical activity (Statistics Canada, 2011a), but few of us would say that people who are physically active are considered deviant in our society. This limitation, along with the previous two, suggest that it is *more than* the statistical number of people who engage in a specific behaviour that determines what is considered deviant in our society. Some deviance specialists propose that the important factor is actually harmfulness.

Harm. The second definition of deviance associated with the objective side of the objective/subjective dichotomy is based on the concept of **harm** (Deutschmann, 2002; Sacco, 1992). That is, if an action causes harm, then it is deviant. The most obvious type of harm is *physical harm*. Thus, if someone harms someone else—for example, through assault, drunk driving, or exposing others to secondhand smoke—then the perpetrator of that harm is deviant. Physical harm can also be done to oneself; for example, smoking may be considered deviant because of the harm caused to the smoker by increased risks of heart disease and various types of cancer. *Emotional harm* can be done to others (e.g., emotional abuse) and to oneself (e.g., repeatedly dating partners with addictions) as well.

Harm may also be directed not at a human being but at society itself—certain behaviours or people may constitute *social harm*, because they interfere with the smooth running of society as a whole. In this context, criminals can be considered deviant because they threaten the safety of the population at large and the social order as a whole. If everyone committed crimes, then anarchy would rule. In fact, implicit in criminal law is the assumption that certain acts must be prohibited because of their harmfulness. In Canada, *all* crimes are considered to harm society itself; the court case is between the Crown (i.e., the state) and the defendant, not the victim and the defendant.

Finally, harm may be directed at something far more abstract and ethereal than a person or society; harm may occur in the form of a *threat to the way we understand the world and our place in it*. Historically, religious belief systems have frequently provided us with this means of abstract understanding on a large scale. Even in contemporary societies, religious belief systems provide many people with a fundamental way of understanding existence. With the example of religion, we can see many instances of this more abstract notion of harm. For example, Joan of Arc was seen as deviant (Brower, 1999), in part because she claimed that she did not need the fathers of the church as a pipeline of communication to God, a claim that violated the dominant religion-based belief system of the time. In contemporary society, Muslim women who do not cover their heads may be seen by some other Muslims, who hold a particular interpretation of their religious doctrine, as threatening the fundamental assumptions upon which the religious belief system is based (Fernea, 1998; Todd, 2001).

Exercise Your Mind

Since Al-Qaeda orchestrated the attacks on the World Trade Center and the Pentagon in 2001, "terrorism" has become a word we hear daily in the media. Within the context of "harm," terrorism can be perceived as causing all four types of harm and in multiple ways. Identify the ways that terrorism causes (a) physical harm to others or to oneself, (b) emotional harm to others or to oneself, (c) harm to the social order and the smooth running of society, and (d) harm to the way people understand the world and their place in it.

At first glance, notions of physical or emotional harm to someone, harm to the social order, and harm to abstract worldviews appear to be useful in recognizing and defining deviance. Many different forms of deviance, from murder to smoking to the behaviour of persecuted historical figures such as Joan of Arc, can be seen as causing harm to someone or something. And perceptions of harm frequently do galvanize social action, such as the creation of nonsmoking bylaws. However, a more critical look at the idea of harm is useful.

The very idea of physical harm is not as clear as it might initially appear, and it has sometimes changed. Claims of physical harm can be and have been disputed. For many years, the tobacco industry claimed that smoking did not cause the harm that anti-smoking activists suggested it did. In the past, some claims of physical harm were greatly exaggerated. A century ago, doctors argued that masturbation caused hairy palms, acne, and outright insanity. For example, look at the following excerpt from a lecture by nineteenth century health reformer Sylvester Graham: "This general mental decay . . . continues with the continued abuses [of masturbation], till the wretched transgressor sinks into a miserable fatuity, and finally becomes a confirmed and degraded idiot, whose deeply sunken and vacant glassy eye, and livid, shriveled countenance, and ulcerous, toothless gums, and fetid breath, and feeble broken voice, and emaciated and dwarfish and crooked body, and almost hairless head—covered, perhaps, with suppurating blisters and running sores—denote a premature old age—a blighted body—and a mined soul" (cited in Whorton, 2001, p. 3).

Elaborate measures were taken to curb children's masturbation in orphanages, hospitals, boarding schools, and middle-class homes. This included behavioural controls, such as cold baths, intense exercise, sleeping on hard beds, and moderate eating (Hunt, 1998). It also included a wide range of anti-masturbation devices (see photograph): Bondage would prevent children from touching themselves at night; the Stephenson Spermatic Truss prevented erections from occurring; the Bowen Device would pull on the wearer's pubic hair if an erection occurred; steel armour was padlocked shut at night, and a key was

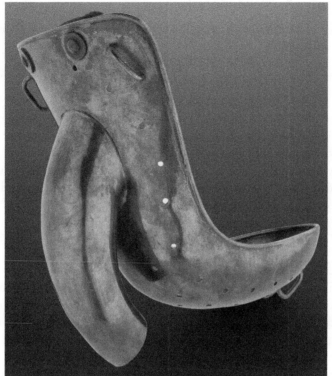

A variety of anti-masturbation devices were used on children during the Victorian era and the early twentieth century because of the harm that the behaviour was thought to cause.

required to allow trips to the bathroom; and penis-cooling devices splashed cold water on the genitals if an erection occurred (Hunt, 1998).

Exaggerated claims about the dangers of marijuana use were also common in the past. In the years leading up to the criminalization of marijuana in 1923, social activists, community leaders, and law enforcement officials spoke out about the physical harm it caused. As can be seen in Box 1.1, marijuana use was alleged to cause horrific violent crimes, murder, idiocy, and ultimately complete insanity and even death. Today, such claims are perceived as greatly exaggerated; however, debates over the physical harm caused by marijuana use continue, as do debates over the physical *benefits* for medical purposes, both of which are fundamental to debates over decriminalization and legalization.

When it comes to the idea of interfering with the current social order or threatening a belief system or worldview, the limitations of defining deviance by virtue of harm become more evident. First, whether or not society or a belief system is being *harmed* can be subjective. Are Muslim women who do not cover their heads actually a threat to the Islamic belief system? While some people would say so, these women themselves often say there is nothing in the belief system itself that requires it. What about Christian nuns who do not

Box 1.1

Emily Murphy's Marijuana Campaign

Emily Murphy, the first female judge in the British Empire and a leading Canadian suffragist in the early twentieth century, was dismayed at what she saw as the horrors of Canada's drug trade. After interviewing both drug users and law enforcement officials from across North America, in 1922 she wrote *The Black Candle*, a book about drug use. One chapter focuses specifically on the harms caused by marijuana use, quoting police officials: "[Marijuana] has the effect of driving the [user] completely insane. The addict loses all sense of moral responsibility. Addicts to this drug, while under its influence, are immune to pain... While in this condition they become raving maniacs and are liable to kill or indulge in any form of violence to other persons, using the most savage methods of cruelty ... . They are dispossessed of their natural and normal will power, and their mentality is that of idiots. If this drug is indulged in to any great extent, it ends in the untimely death of its addict" (Murphy, 1973 [1922], pp. 332–333). These types of claims are somewhat humorous to today's reader, but they had a significant influence on changing drug laws at the time.

wear habits? Historically, the habit was considered an essential component of membership in a religious order, in part symbolizing the discarding of the worldly individual and becoming part of a communal whole, a sign of one's dedication to God (Kuhns, 2003). But in contemporary society, it is relatively uncommon to see a nun wearing a habit, a fact that causes some consternation among those religious orders that perceive this change as a threat to the order, the larger religion of which it is a part, and its doctrine.

During the twentieth century, there were several times when women in North America were accused of harming the social order or abstract belief systems or both. Early feminists who fought for the right of women to vote faced such accusations, as did later groups of women in the 1960s and 1970s when they questioned the "natural" role of women as homemakers and moved outside the home into paid employment. Were these women causing harm to society or to beliefs? Because the word *harm* implies a negative impact, many would say that these women were not *harming* society—they were simply changing society. Others would say that by *changing* society they were having a negative impact on the social order of the time, and thus were technically causing harm, but that it was a social order that needed to be changed.

Indeed, there are times when the reactions cause more overt harm than the initial behaviours, characteristics, or people themselves. For instance, in 2007 Polish immigrant Robert Dziekanski arrived at the Vancouver airport. His mother was supposed to pick him up; however, due to a series of procedural problems, he ended up wandering through the airport for 10 hours, unable to speak English. He became increasingly disoriented and his behaviour came to be perceived as potentially problematic. The RCMP were called, and following a confrontation in which officers say Dziekanski raised a stapler to them in an aggressive manner they tasered him five times, which resulted in his death. Certainly in this case, the measures to control Dziekanski's behaviour were far more harmful than his behaviour was. Similarly, although Emily Murphy sought to control the "harms" of marijuana use (as well as other moral harms, such as opium use and prostitution), certain aspects of her efforts had racism as their foundation, and she was a supporter of the eugenics movement (see Chapter 9). Some would argue that both racism and the eugenics movement have caused more harm over the past century than marijuana use has.

All of the above limitations of defining deviance on the basis of harm illustrate the necessity of going beyond the idea of harm in seeking the defining characteristic of deviance. The nature of these limitations is such that this definition of deviance is rarely used in academic literature, although it does enjoy popular usage among laypersons, politicians, and social activists.

Despite the fact that academic literature rarely suggests that harm is *the* defining characteristic of deviance, some literature does acknowledge that harm, or a characteristic similar to harm (i.e., threat or dangerousness), is *one of* the characteristics of deviance. For example, Lianos (with Douglas, 2000) proposes that what is most significant to the study of deviance is not whether someone actually causes harm or is actually dangerous, but rather whether someone *seems* dangerous. Deviance specialists from the subjective side of the objective/subjective dichotomy suggest we look at the social processes that result in someone being perceived as potentially dangerous and not consider whether that person actually *is* dangerous. The *Ask Yourself* exercise has you further explore the concept of harm within the context of contemporary social debates.

Societal Reaction.   Another one of the definitions of deviance that has been associated with the objective side of the objective/subjective dichotomy is based on the nature of **societal reaction**. People may respond to others in a number of different ways. If the responses of society's "masses" are primarily negative (such as dislike, anger, hatred, stigmatization, or teasing) rather than positive (such as liking, admiration, envy, or tolerance), then the person or act being responded to is deviant. Seeing this negative societal evaluation enables us to determine who or what is deviant.

However, focusing on a negative societal reaction as the defining characteristic of deviance raises many questions. Why does society react negatively to some actions, characteristics, or people and not others? Whose reaction counts? Does my reaction, as a university professor and social scientist, count more than your reaction as a student? Does the prime minister's reaction count more than mine? How many individual negative reactions must exist before we can say that "society" is reacting negatively?

The gaps that emerge when defining deviance on the basis of societal reaction are revealed by numerous examples. For instance, Canadian surveys consistently find that "a strong majority . . . favour[s] a limited fine as the maximum penalty for cannabis possession" (i.e., decriminalization) (Fischer, Ala-Leppilampi, Single, & Robins, 2003, p. 277), and 57 percent support full legalization (Angus-Reid, 2012). However, despite this consistent data on societal reaction, since 2006 the Conservatives have explicitly stated that they will "prevent the decriminalization of marijuana" (Conservative Party of Canada, 2006, p. 25). Since that time, they have successfully done so.

In contrast, the Conservative government's position on same-sex marriage was that it would "hold a truly free vote on the definition of marriage, [and] . . . if the resolution is passed, the government [would] introduce legislation to restore the traditional definition of marriage" (Conservative Party of Canada, 2006, p. 33). On December 7, 2006, parliamentarians voted on a motion against same-sex marriage; the motion failed 175 votes to 123 votes. Elected officials in Parliament presumably consider a free vote representative of Canadian public opinion—that is, a proxy for societal reaction. The comparison of these two issues shows that the legislative action regarding one issue (i.e., same-sex marriage) is based on a representation of societal reaction, while the legislative action on another issue (i.e., the decriminalization of marijuana) is independent of societal reaction, and in fact may directly oppose public opinion. These inconsistencies reveal that the law and, more broadly, determinations of who or what is deviant in Canadian society are based upon processes that go beyond societal reaction.

Surveys of public opinion reveal diverse points of view; not everyone shares the same opinion. A large majority of Canadians (85 to 90 percent) support the full legalization of medicinal marijuana (Stein, cited in Fischer, Ala-Leppilampi, Single, & Robins, 2003), but that means 10 to 15 percent do not support it or are indifferent. These types of diverse survey results reveal that societal reactions are not uniform, and different groups of people react in various ways to the same behaviour or issue. Given the plurality of points of view on many issues, it appears that societal reaction alone does not determine how a particular behaviour is treated in Canadian society.

Normative Violation.   The dictionary, as well as many deviance specialists, suggests that recognizing deviance is quite straightforward—a behaviour or characteristic is deviant if it violates norms. In fact, this is likely the definition of deviance that was included in your introductory sociology textbook. The "general statement that deviance is focused around the violation of norms" (Ben-Yehuda, 1990, p. 4) is shared extensively among deviance specialists from both the objective and subjective sides of the objective/subjective dichotomy, as well as those who transcend this traditional dualism. However, the manner in which **normative violation** is integrated into a definition of deviance varies among deviance specialists working in the various approaches.

Among deviance specialists working in the objective side of the dichotomy, the violation of norms has been proposed to be *the* defining characteristic of deviance. Indeed, the dictionary definition of deviance makes this point quite clearly as well. Yet even among those recognized as objectivists, the nature of the normative violation seen as constituting deviance has changed. Early objectivists used what may be considered an "absolutist" conception of normative violation, wherein a particular behaviour or characteristic was perceived as being inherently and universally deviant (Adler & Adler, 2006a, p. 3).

According to this view, there are certain immutable norms and values that should be held in all cultures and at all times—norms and values that emerge from the word of God, the laws of nature, or some other unchangeable source. Because of that absolute moral order, what is considered wrong in one place should be considered wrong everywhere; cross-cultural and trans-historical norms prohibiting incest, murder, and lying are perceived as evidence of this absolute moral order.

The simplistic view of norms in the absolutist view led many objectivists to abandon the absolutist view. However, still on the objective side of the objective/subjective dichotomy, another view of normative violation has developed. Among these more modern objectivists, norms are perceived as being culturally specific rather than universal—that is, based on a given society's moral code rather than on any type of absolute moral order. This perspective is still identified as objective, in that someone who violates the norms of the society they live in is seen as deviant. From birth, we are socialized into the norms that govern the society we live in, and we learn its standards and expectations. In Canadian society, we are taught as we grow up to share with others, to be polite, to work hard, to listen to our teachers—in essence, most of us are taught by our parents, teachers, community leaders, and religious leaders to follow the rules. We learn what behaviours will be rewarded (like arriving at work on time) and what behaviours will be punished (like breaking the law). Knowing these expectations, if we then go on to violate the norms, we are "deviant." The *Ask Yourself* exercise requires you to take a closer look at some of the norms in Canadian society.

Looking at the examples in the *Ask Yourself* exercise, one can see that not all norms are the same. While violating some norms may result in prison (as for the thief), violating other norms has different (and some might say less severe) consequences. The obese person, alcoholic, social assistance recipient, or plagiarizing student will not be entered into the criminal justice system for their normative violations. These differential outcomes of normative violation emerge from the existence of various types of norms, ranging from *folkways* to *mores* to *laws* (Adler & Adler, 2006a; Kendall, Murray, & Linden, 2007; Sumner, 1906).

Norms, as standards or expectations of behaviour, can refer to informal, everyday behaviours, such as rules of etiquette, choice of clothing, and behaviour in the university classroom. These kinds of informal norms are called **folkways**, and if you violate these norms you might be considered odd (Adler & Adler, 2006a), rude, or a troublemaker. Other norms are taken more seriously. **Mores** are those standards that are often seen as the foundation of morality in a culture, such as prohibitions against incest or homosexuality. If you violate these norms you may be thought of as immoral (Adler & Adler, 2006a) or even evil. Finally, some norms are considered to be so central to the smooth running of society that they are enshrined within the legal system—for example, in Canada's Criminal Code. If you violate the Criminal Code you will be

Ask Yourself

List the norms that are being violated by each of the following people: an obese person; a student that plagiarizes by downloading a term paper from the Internet; someone on social assistance; a drug addict or alcoholic; a thief. Remember, norms refer to standards or expectations of behaviour, so ask yourself what expectations each of these people is not living up to—what "rules" of society are they breaking?

thought of as a criminal. At times, the legal system integrates mores (e.g., incest is included in the Criminal Code of Canada, and homosexual activities remain criminal offences in many parts of the world); however, other acts that are not perceived as the foundation for morality in our culture (e.g., marijuana possession) are also integrated into the legal system.

The way that norms are integrated into objectivist definitions of deviance presumes a certain level of consensus (McCaghy, Capron, & Jamieson, 2003; Miller, Wright, & Dannels, 2001; Rubington & Weinberg, 2008). Although cross-cultural variations in norms are acknowledged, it is assumed that, in a given society, the majority of citizens agree upon the norms. However, deviance specialists working in the subjective side of the objective/subjective dichotomy find this view of social norms problematic. Some have reservations about the presumption of normative consensus and question the extent to which a given expectation must be shared to be considered a "norm" and then used as an objective standard against which deviance is judged (Ward, Carter, & Perrin, 1994).

Some even question whether it is possible to determine the level of consensus that does or does not exist for a given expectation. They point out that there are countless numbers of groups in society having innumerable different sets of rules; even a single individual belongs to multiple groups having varying sets of expectations. Given the multiplicity of individuals, groups, and sets of expectations that coexist in a society, normative consensus is difficult to determine (Adler & Adler, 2003; Becker, 1963). In fact, given all of these different sets of expectations that exist in society simultaneously, which expectations are the ones that constitute society's "norms" and are then used to judge deviance and normality?

In response to these critiques, some deviance specialists have elected to focus on those norms that they suggest are characterized by some consensus, "assuming that the agreed-upon norms of a society can be found in its criminal law" (McCaghy, Capron, & Jamieson, 2003, p. 8). However, some criminologists and other deviance specialists working on the subjective side of the objective/subjective dichotomy draw our attention to the fact that law creation is a political activity, wherein those norms that are embodied in law do not necessarily reflect the opinion of the majority of citizens (Des Rosiers & Bittle, 2004). Indeed, the creation of a new law in Canada does not require the support of a majority, nor are the opinions of all Canadians sought prior to its creation. Marijuana possession remains illegal, even though since the late 1990s the courts, the Senate Special Committee on Illegal Drugs, the Canadian Centre on Substance Abuse, the Centre for Addictions and Mental Health, the Canadian Association of Chiefs of Police, and public opinion have all recommended its decriminalization (Fischer, Ala-Leppilampi, Single, & Robins, 2003). In this case, "consensus" seems to contradict the law rather than support it. The **consensual view** of law, wherein the law is perceived as arising out of social consensus and is then equally applied to all, is only one of the possible views of crime and law (Siegel & McCormick, 2003).

Critiques of the consensual view of law point to conflict and interactionist views. Criminologists who use the **conflict view** (also known as the *social power perspective*) perceive the law as a tool used by the ruling class to serve its own interests. They believe that the law is more likely to be applied to members of the powerless classes in society. For example,

Howard Becker (1963), one of the first deviance specialists to critique objectivist views of deviance, suggested that even when lower-class and middle-class youth engage in similar minor forms of law-breaking, police are more likely to enter the former into the justice system while letting middle-class youth go with a warning or into their parents' custody.

Another view of crime, the **interactionist view**, also presents a nonconsensual view of criminal law. This view suggests that society's powerful define the law at the behest of interest groups, who appeal to those with power to rectify a perceived social ill. Again, criminal law is not seen as emerging out of consensus, but rather out of the interests of certain groups in society. Looking at these different views, we can see that criminal law is based on more than a simple consensus about what society's norms are.

The normative objectivity of the law has also been critiqued on the question of the situational applicability of broad social norms. For example, in a rather objective fashion we might say that legal prohibitions against murder reflect normative clarity in society—we know that murder is wrong. However, some deviance specialists point out the many situational characteristics that can modify this abstract norm. Depending on the laws of a particular country, self-defence, capital punishment, military action in wartime, and euthanasia are all circumstances in which taking a human life may be considered acceptable.

So, is taking another human life deviant? Looking at the above, we see that the answer to this question is that taking another human life is deviant at some times but not at others. In fact, in situations where taking another human life is considered acceptable, the behaviour is not called "murder." For example, during wartime, the death of innocent civilians is not "murder," but "collateral damage." Consequently, given the situational variations in which even the most basic norms do or do not apply, some deviance specialists ask whether norms, as reflected in criminal law, are even useful in trying to define deviance (Ward, Carter, & Perrin, 1994).

Some deviance specialists step into this debate over the degree of consensus involved in social norms by proposing that there are some norms that do have higher levels of consensus. For example, despite the situational variations in prohibitions against taking another human life, it is likely that most (if not all) Canadians support the inclusion of homicide in the Criminal Code; the same can also likely be said for auto theft, sexual assault, and break-and-enter. Thio (1983) uses the concepts of **high-consensus deviance** and **low-consensus deviance** to distinguish between forms of deviance that have differential levels of support in the broader society. The norms reflected in criminal law are characterized by relatively more consensus than are society's nonlegislative norms (such as norms governing physical appearance). And within the law, certain laws are characterized by relatively more consensus than are others.

Although the dictionary defines deviance on the basis of normative violation, the limitations of that definition make it problematic. In fact, limitations are associated with each of the objectivist definitions of deviance—not only normative violation, but also statistical rarity, harm, and a negative societal reaction. Some deviance specialists suggest that these limitations have caused a large-scale shift to the subjective side of the objective/subjective dichotomy (Hathaway & Atkinson, 2001).

TIME TO REVIEW

Learning Objective 1

- What does the "problem of definition" refer to, and how is it related to the objective/subjective dichotomy?

- What is the core assumption underlying the objective side of the objective/subjective dichotomy?

Learning Objective 2

- What are the four different objective definitions of deviance? Provide examples of each.

- What are the limitations of each of the objective definitions of deviance? Provide examples of each.

- According to those who define deviance on the basis of harm, what are the different types of harm that can occur?

- How has the objectivist notion of normative violation changed over time?

- What are the different views of the role of consensus in the development of criminal law?

Subjectivism: Deviance as a Label

Having looked at the objective side of the traditional objective/subjective dichotomy, we now turn our attention to the subjective side. From this point of view, there is a very different answer to the question, "How can we recognize deviance when we see it?" While objectivists suggest that deviance can be recognized by the presence of a particular characteristic, subjectivists say that we cannot recognize deviance when we see it; we have to be taught, through processes of socialization, that a person or behaviour is deviant. There is no singular trait or characteristic that is shared by all deviant people throughout history and across cultures, other than the fact that people with some influence on society have said they are deviant (Becker, 1963).

Early subjectivism suggested deviance is anything that is identified as such—that deviance lies in people's perceptions of a behaviour rather than in any behaviour itself. Contemporary subjectivism focuses its attention on the processes by which particular people, behaviours, or characteristics come to be perceived in certain ways. The foundation for this type of analysis lies in the **dominant moral codes** (Goode, 1997, p. 29) that serve as the foundation for determining who or what is deviant in society. These are the "lists" of right/wrong, appropriate/inappropriate, moral/immoral that predominate in a particular society at a given time in history and are enforced in multiple ways (e.g., by the criminal justice system, the media, and the education system). A society's dominant moral codes are shaped by the interests and the actions of groups that hold some level of power.

However, subjective deviance specialists point to the complex nature of power relations. Social processes involve far more than simply the control and oppression of the powerless by the powerful. The use and legitimization of power interacts with negotiations about moral boundaries—negotiations in which less powerful groups in society are also able to participate. Consequently, "this process does mean that the powerless can resist deviantization" (Ben-Yehuda, 1990, p. 7) rather than simply being at the mercy of the interests of the powerful. Continual negotiations are occurring, such that the social construction of deviance and normality/conformity is in a constant state of flux (Ben-Yehuda, 1990).

Subjectivity and the "Social Construction" of Deviance

Referring to the subjective nature of deviance means focusing on deviance as a *social construction*. In other words, there is nothing inherent in a behaviour or characteristic that makes it deviant; a particular behaviour or characteristic is deviant only if the dominant moral codes of a specific society at a certain time in history *say* the behaviour is deviant. Similarly, what is considered to be normal is also socially constructed, given that notions of deviance and normality exist only in relation to each other (Freud, 1999).

Social constructionism refers to the perspective proposing that social characteristics (e.g., "thin," "delinquent") are creations or artifacts of a particular society at a specific time in history, just as objects (e.g., houses, cars) are artifacts of that society. Consequently, a person, behaviour, or characteristic that is considered "deviant" in one society may be considered "normal" in another society or at another time in history.

Social constructionism has become a dominant force in the study of deviance today. In fact, more than a decade ago Goode (1997) suggested that "most deviance specialists [today] are *constructionists*" (p. 35). However, there are different levels or different types of constructionism. One type of constructionism is labelled **radical** (Goode, 1997) or **strict** (Best, cited in Rubington & Weinberg, 2002); the other type is labelled **soft** or **contextual** (Best, cited in Rubington & Weinberg, 2002).

Radical constructionists postulate a distinct theoretical perspective claiming that the world is characterized by endless relativism, that "there is no essential reality to the social world at all, that if everything and anything is simply looked at in a certain way, that is the way it is" (Goode, 1997, p. 35). However, "most [contemporary deviance specialists] are not *radical* constructionists. What I mean by this is that most do *not* believe that *everything* is a matter of definition, that there is *no* essential reality to the social world at all. . . . Rather, most sociologists of deviance believe that there are limits to social constructionism" (Goode, 1997, p. 35). Consequently, sociologists who are soft or contextual constructionists emphasize the processes by which certain social phenomena come to be perceived and reacted to in particular ways in a given society at a specific time in history. In such cases, social construction is addressed in terms of a process rather than a theory and

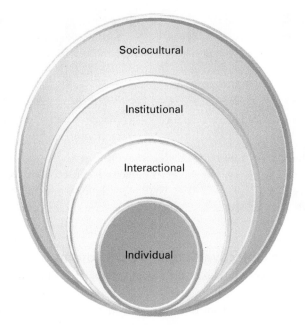

Figure 1.1 Levels of Social Construction

therefore can be combined with a number of different theoretical approaches—approaches that will be addressed in Chapter 3.

Viewing social constructionism as a process implies that what is of sociological significance is not the individual behaviour or characteristic itself, but rather (1) its place in the social order, (2) the roles assigned to people who exhibit that behaviour or characteristic, and (3) the meanings attached to that behaviour or characteristic. For example, homosexuality is "universal" in the sense that it has existed across the world and throughout history. What varies is the way that homosexuality is perceived and reacted to in particular societies; thus, while homosexuality is a part of nature, and therefore "biological," it is also "socially constructed." The way deviance is socially constructed emerges from several ongoing interconnected processes, from the macro through the micro levels (see Figure 1.1) (Nelson & Robinson, 2002).

The first process to consider is the *sociocultural* level: beliefs, ideologies, values, and systems of meaning have an influence on the path of social construction. The second is the *institutional* level: the structures of our society, such as government, the education system, and religion (among others) that affect social construction. Third is the *interactional* level: our interactions with other people influence the way we think and feel about others, thereby determining the role that each of us plays in social construction. Fourth is the *individual* level: at this level our own identities, concepts of self, and ways of understanding our own existence in the world affect the path of social construction.

Transcending the Objective/Subjective Dichotomy

The objective and subjective sides of the objective/subjective dichotomy, as it has been traditionally expressed, appear to be considerably distinct. On the objective side of the dualism, deviance specialists claim that there is a shared characteristic that all deviants have in common, a feature that enables us to recognize deviance when we see it. Although statistical rarity, harm, and a negative societal reaction have each been identified as that shared characteristic (whether by academics, laypersons, or social activists), the defining feature of deviance that is most often identified is that of normative violation. On the subjective side of the dualism, deviance specialists claim that there is no shared feature among deviants; instead, a person, behaviour, or characteristic is deviant if enough important people say so. Through the processes of social construction, which are influenced by power, a dominant moral order emerges that then serves as the standard against which deviance and normality are judged.

The conception of the objective/subjective dichotomy serves as the foundation for the claim that a shift in definitions of deviance has recently occurred, from objective to subjective (e.g., Goode, 1997; Hathaway & Atkinson, 2001). In fact, some deviance specialists suggest that using the subjective, constructionist view in exploring both legal and illegal norm-violating behaviour defines the sociology of deviance as a discipline. However, recent shifts in the study of deviance may, in fact, transcend the objective/subjective dichotomy, with elements of objectivism and subjectivism being integrated to varying degrees.

We have already seen some evidence of this in the previous discussions of the objective/subjective dualism. For example, we have seen that, over time, objective deviance specialists have changed their conceptions of norms from that of an absolute moral order to that of a culturally specific moral order. Similarly, over time, subjective deviance specialists have acknowledged the role of norms in defining deviance, but in terms of norms that may be socially constructed and determined by processes of power.

For example, Tittle and Paternoster (2000) propose that group-specific normative systems *can* be identified, such as the normative system of middle-class America. They suggest that, although this is only one of countless numbers of normative systems in society, it is the one that has come to dominate American society as a whole through the power that the middle-class holds in processes of social construction: "[T]he middle class dominates U.S. society, both by imposing its standards through the schools, the mass media, and the law and by enjoying a degree of natural hegemony in behavior styles and thinking that flows from the admiration and emulation of those with higher status" (p. 29).

Many definitions of deviance combine normative violation, negative reaction, harm, power, and/or social construction (Hathaway & Atkinson, 2001; McCaghy, Capron, & Jamieson, 2003; Ward, Carter, & Perrin, 1994). For example, Stebbins (1996) defines deviance as normative violation, but goes on to say that the nature of society's response to that violation depends on the level of perceived threat the normative violation entails, and that the structure of power relations in society influences this entire process. A retrospective look at work by earlier deviance specialists reveals that the distinction between objective and subjective has always been somewhat blurred. Even Howard Becker (1963), one of the leading proponents of the subjective view of deviance, integrated the notion of harm into his definition of deviance. He stated that deviance is that which is so labelled, but that this process of labelling depends on who has committed the act and who feels harmed by it.

The boundaries of objective and subjective become further blurred when looking at the extent to which the objective traits that have been discussed are present within processes of social construction in society at large. For instance, interest groups that are opposed to same-sex rights sometimes argue that homosexuality is statistically rare, a violation of the laws of nature or the word of God, or a threat to "the family" and to any children being raised by gay or lesbian parents. People who work toward toughening young offender legislation bring arguments of harm into their work. Those trying to decriminalize marijuana possession often refer to changing public attitudes that reflect a positive societal reaction to the issue of marijuana use. All of these groups are involved in the process of social construction in that they are attempting to influence the meanings attached to a particular behaviour, its place in the larger social order, and the roles assigned to individuals who engage in that behaviour. Yet they also draw upon objectivist concepts as a foundation for their arguments, so that objectivist traits are embedded within the subjectivist process of social construction.

Examining the complexities of the work of both past and present deviance specialists indicates that perhaps the traditional objective/subjective dichotomy that has served as the foundation for discussing definitions of deviance in the field has always been an oversimplification. The actual nature of the work done by sociologists of deviance frequently transcends the dichotomy, blending aspects of both objective and subjective. Rather than being embedded in a dichotomy, definitions of deviance and research on deviance may actually fall along more of a continuum, with more objective assumptions lying at one end of the continuum and more subjective assumptions lying at the other (see Figure 1.2).

At the extreme objective end of the continuum are those deviance specialists who have proposed an absolute moral order as the standard for determining deviance; at the

Figure 1.2 The Objective-Subjective Continuum

extreme subjective end are the most radical constructionists, who suggest that there is no reality outside of perception. The definitions and analyses of each deviance specialist fall somewhere along this continuum, with some being more objective in nature and some being more subjective in nature. Those researchers who lean toward objectivism may be more likely to study those forms of deviance that Thio (1983) referred to as high-consensus forms of deviance, such as homicide, gang membership, white-collar crime, police corruption, and prostitution. Those researchers who lean toward subjectivism may be more likely to study those forms of deviance that Thio referred to as low-consensus forms of deviance, such as marijuana use, pornography, swinging, gambling, and aspects of physical appearance (e.g., tattoos, body piercing, punk rockers, goths, and being overweight).

Studying Deviance

The way that deviance is defined along the objective–subjective continuum has implications for the way deviance is studied. That is, deviance specialists who lean more toward objectivism will study deviance in ways that those who lean more toward subjectivism will not (and vice versa).

Studying the Act: Why People Behave the Way They Do

Those who perceive more objectivity in deviance shine their analytical spotlight on a particular act or characteristic. The deviant nature of these behaviours/characteristics is, to some extent, taken for granted (because, after all, they *are* violating norms, or *are* causing harm, etc.); then the details of the deviance are studied—who the people are, how they became deviant, what their lives are like (Adler & Adler, 2006a; Rubington & Weinberg, 2008). In essence, the interest lies in explaining the person, behaviour, or characteristic in question.

Studying Social Processes: The "Deviance Dance"

Deviance specialists who focus more on the subjective aspects of deviance are less interested in shining their analytical spotlight on the "deviant" and more interested in shining it on society and social processes—the perceptions of and reactions to the act as well as the role of power in those perceptions and reactions. The focus becomes the **"deviance dance"**—the interactions, negotiations, and debates among groups with different perceptions of whether a behaviour or characteristic is deviant and needs to be socially controlled and, if so, how. The participants in this "dance" each take certain "steps" to move the dance in the direction they desire, whether that direction is the creation of a new law, the legalization of a behaviour that was previously illegal, achieving public recognition of a new social problem or one previously ignored, or changing public perceptions that will reduce the prejudices faced by certain groups.

In some cases, this "dance" may be characterized by considerable cooperation among the participants in achieving a consensual goal—analogous to a country line dance in which everyone does precisely the same steps. In other cases, it is characterized by participants taking opposing steps, but still moving together in their negotiation over the outcome—analogous to a waltz, where one partner moves backward and the other forward as they set their joint course across the dance floor. And in some cases the "dance" may look more like a mosh pit at a heavy metal or punk rock concert—with each participant moving independently of the others and in varying and often opposing directions, intentionally pushing, shoving, and ramming into other participants to move in his or her own individually desired direction.

The centrality of interactions, negotiations, debates, and resistance in the social construction and social control of deviance is illustrated by Hier (2002). In 1999, three young adults died at rave dances in Toronto following the consumption of the drug ecstasy. With widespread media attention, Toronto city council and rave organizers (i.e., the Toronto Dance Safety Committee, or TDSC) joined together in an effort to improve safety at raves; at the TDSC's request, Toronto city council passed legislation governing various safety-related measures at raves. However, as media attention continued over the next several months, some members of city council adopted a new goal—banning raves altogether. The deviance dance was played out within the media, as those in favour of banning raves used mainstream newspapers to win public favour and achieve their goal, while rave organizers, who were more concerned about threats to safety that would emerge if raves were driven underground, used a wide range of media outlets (including MuchMusic) to communicate their message to the public. What began as a cooperative effort quickly became an antagonistic debate between opposing sides.

Studying struggles and debates over deviance requires going beyond the problem of "radical phenomenalism" (Ben-Yehuda, 1990, p. 5) that some researchers see as plaguing the sociology of deviance, wherein countless numbers of specific phenomena (e.g., call girls, drug users, swingers) have been studied in tremendous detail without any attention being paid to larger social structures. Ben-Yehuda (1990) suggests that the "study of deviance should be reframed . . . within general societal processes [of change and stability], in a dynamic historical and political perspective" (p. 5). In this vein, understanding an act of deviance requires understanding its larger context in a society's value system and understanding the configuration of power relationships that influence the negotiation of moral boundaries among different groups of people.

Studying Acts and Social Processes

Both the more objective and the more subjective approaches help our understanding of deviance. The most comprehensive knowledge emerges from combining an analysis of the social processes involved in the "deviance dance" with an explication of the act or characteristic in question. For example, information about why people become overweight can be combined with knowledge of the processes by which certain people come to be perceived as "too fat" and are then made subject to various measures of social control.

Similarly, an understanding of the factors that contribute to youth smoking can be combined with knowledge of the processes by which smoking was perceived as acceptable (and even sophisticated) in the past, while in contemporary society smoking (and smokers) are subjected to widespread social control efforts. Each of these levels of understanding paints an important part of the picture of deviance that will be integrated into this text.

At various points we will analyze acts/characteristics, perceptions of and reactions to those acts, and the role played by power in these perceptions and reactions.

The Role of Powerful People

Who are the "important" people who are able to influence the dominant moral codes of society, from which emerge standards of deviance and normality? In Canadian society, some of the most powerful groups involved in this process are politicians/government, scientists, religious institutions, the media, and commercial enterprise. Each of these groups of people may act as or have a relationship with **moral entrepreneurs** (Becker, 1963), those who "manufacture public morality" (Adler & Adler, 2006a, p. 136) first by bringing a problem to public awareness and second by facilitating "moral conversion" (p. 136). For example, participants in the temperance movement, the abolitionist movement, and the "child-savers" movement all acted as moral entrepreneurs who worked to influence the development and enforcement of society's moral codes during the Victorian era.

In the early twentieth century, groups of women in the United States and Canada acted as "moral entrepreneurs" and demanded the right to vote.

In the temperance movement, members of church-based groups (frequently women's groups) throughout North America and Great Britain declared the "demon liquor" a social evil and agitated for reduced alcohol consumption ("temperance"). In Canada and the United States, groups of people acting as moral entrepreneurs sought abolition (the eradication of slavery under the law) and demanded voting rights for women. And throughout North America and Western Europe, the "child-savers" influenced child labour laws, sought the criminalization of child abuse and neglect, and encouraged compulsory education for children. During the 1950s and 1960s, North America's civil rights activists acted as moral entrepreneurs in their efforts to end segregation and gain rights for black Canadians and Americans. All of these groups had an influence on society's dominant moral codes, and thereby on perceptions of what was considered deviant and normal. In contemporary society, we continue to see groups of moral entrepreneurs, as illustrated in the *Ask Yourself* exercise.

Perhaps the most central group in society that acts as or has a relationship with moral entrepreneurs is composed of *politicians*. Politicians are the people in whom ultimate power has been vested in modern state systems—they have powers to invoke, revoke, and determine the enforcement of legislation and social policy. Interest groups, acting as moral entrepreneurs who have identified a social ill that they think must be solved in some way, often lobby the government to initiate change.

A second group, composed of *scientists*, is able to effectively make claims that influence society's moral codes. The claims made by scientists are backed by the domain that is granted perhaps the highest level of credibility in our society—that of science. As we will see in the chapter on religious and scientific belief systems later in this text, when scientists proclaim truths, many of us will believe those claims simply because scientists say so. When scientists tell us that smoking is harmful, or that having sex too frequently indicates an addiction, or that hearing voices indicates mental illness, they have a persuasive impact on what we see as "normal." When making such claims, scientists themselves may be acting as moral entrepreneurs; in addition, the claims made by scientists may be used as convincing support for the efforts of other moral entrepreneurs, such as anti-smoking activists.

Religious institutions have also played a central role in the creation of the dominant moral codes that determine deviance and normality. For example, during the Middle Ages and into the early Renaissance, the Christian church was the instigator of witch persecutions and the Spanish Inquisition, both of which resulted in countless numbers of people being tortured and killed for their deviance. In the present day, the power of religious institutions can be seen in the many nations in which religious-based governments are the source of social order. For instance, the displaced Taliban government imposed a particular and extreme interpretation of Islamic beliefs on the people of Afghanistan. Contemporary Canadian society is characterized by a separation of church and state; however, the influence of religion on perceptions of deviance and normality maintains its presence in many ways. Canadian society itself is built upon a Judeo-Christian foundation. Two of our national statutory holidays are Christian holidays—Christmas Day and Easter. Our criminal law is based on the Judeo-Christian ethic of free will—we are responsible for our own actions, and redemption can occur through punishment (Linden, 2000).

At a more individual level, many Canadians adhere to various religious belief systems. Their belief systems provide them with moral codes that subsequently affect the role individuals play in larger social processes. The Victorian prohibitionists, abolitionists, and child-savers described earlier were typically members of various Christian church-based groups.

In our twenty-first century world, the *media* serves as the central battleground in the struggles over moral codes. The media is a powerful tool used by a wide range of moral entrepreneurs. When politicians, medical doctors, or interest groups endeavour to raise awareness of an issue or sway public opinion, they turn to the media. Public service announcements, press conferences, and issue-driven advertisements all appear in the media. However, the media is not just a tool used by moral entrepreneurs; it also acts as a moral entrepreneur itself in terms of the choices made about what will and will not be included on a particular program or in a particular commercial segment. For example, when a television news program features child molesters being captured through sting operations, it contributes to the construction of pedophilia as a deviant (and criminal) activity.

Finally, in a modern capitalist economy, *commercial enterprise* has a significant level of power as well, frequently in conjunction with the use of the media; in fact, most components of the media itself are commercial enterprises driven by a profit motive. Advertisements, commercials, magazines, television programs, and movies tell us how we are and are not supposed to look: punk rock characters in a movie are the butt of the movie's jokes; magazine articles tell us we will be happier if we can just lose those 10 pounds by Labour Day; personalities on the newest popular reality TV show model the right clothes to wear. The media also tells us how we are supposed to act: beer commercials show us that drinking is the best way to have fun with friends; a fictional television show tells us that "potheads" are losers; and a nighttime news program tells us that joining a cult is problematic.

Commercial enterprise has power outside of the media as well. For example, Giesbrecht (2000) discusses the power of the alcohol industry over the content and form of alcohol policies created by government. The manner in which alcohol production, marketing, and consumption is controlled in both Canada and the United States is determined, in part, by the influence of the alcohol industry itself. A similar example can be seen in the historical development of the institution of law in modern state systems. It is the law that delineates those actions considered to require the greatest level of control by society; historically, English law developed on the basis of merchant and commercial interests. With the end of feudalism, kings had much to gain from the wealth of merchants involved in international trade. Feudal lords no longer had the means to finance the nation's warfare and colonial expansion, but merchants did. It was in the best financial interests of the king, as he oversaw the development and growth of a centralized state, to form it in accordance with commercial interests. These origins serve as the foundation for modern Canadian law, wherein most legal infractions by those involved in commercial enterprise are dealt with under the more lenient civil law rather than the more punitive criminal law (Linden, 2000).

This brief discussion of politicians, scientists, religion, the media, and commercial enterprise demonstrates the complexity of the notion of power. People are powerful for many different reasons, and their power operates in diverse ways. The moral entrepreneurship of one group of powerful people may contradict or even oppose the moral entrepreneurship of another group of powerful people; for instance, the efforts of commercial enterprise might oppose the efforts of members of a religious-based group. But whether one group's involvement in social construction contradicts or, conversely, coincides with another group's involvement in social construction, the process through which they operate is the same—that of social typing.

The Social Typing Process

As moral entrepreneurs influence the content and enforcement of society's dominant moral codes, the foundation is laid for the standards that subsequently determine deviance and normality. A closer look at the process by which some people come to be seen as deviant and others come to be seen as normal reveals what Rubington and Weinberg (2008) label **social typing**. This three-component process has the end result of changing the way society treats people who are typed or categorized as deviant.

The first component of the social typing process is **description**, wherein a label is placed on an individual because of an observed or presumed behaviour or characteristic. The exact nature of the label that is applied depends on the culture in question (Rubington & Weinberg, 2008). For example, in contemporary Canada we are more likely to label someone a "terrorist" than a "heretic"; in contrast, in Europe during the sixteenth century, people were more likely to be labelled "heretics" than "terrorists." Terrorism is a social phenomenon that has become an integral part of our worldview in the twenty-first century, while the concept of heresy reflected the religious foundations of the European worldview in the sixteenth century.

The second component of the social typing process is **evaluation**. This occurs when a judgment is attached to the individual by virtue of the label that was previously attached or the category that individual was placed in under the description component. If someone is socially typed as deviant, this judgment is characteristically negative in nature.

The third component of the social typing process is **prescription**. This is where the processes of social control or regulation emerge. Because of the label that has been given and the resulting judgment that occurs, the individual is treated in a particular way—a way she or he would not be treated if the initial label had not been applied. In other words, individuals are made subject to a range of social treatments designed to regulate or control their deviance. Just as the larger culture determines the initial label that is used, it also shapes the nature of the prescription that is used (Rubington & Weinberg, 2002). For example, a Canadian woman who violates standards of female dress is likely to be teased or stared at rather than made subject to stoning, as were women in Taliban-controlled Afghanistan.

Exercise Your Mind

Go through the three components of the social typing process, using the example of someone who is obese. What description or label is given to this person? What judgments or evaluations are attached to this person because of the label you have just given him or her? Finally, how is this person treated or socially controlled?

Forms of Social Control

As Newman (2008) points out, "all societies have ways of keeping deviants under control … . The ancient Greeks killed them; nineteenth-century societies hid them in their closets and attics, and twentieth-century societies rationalized this solution by building large institutions in which they were hidden" (p. xi). In contemporary society, we can see the regulation or social control of a person who has been subjected to the social typing process occurring at multiple levels. It may be *formal* or *informal* in nature (Becker, 1963; Edwards, 1988; Rubington & Weinberg, 2002). The informal aspect of the prescription component emerges at the level of patterns of informal social interaction—patterns of interaction with diverse people, such as family members, friends, acquaintances, colleagues, or strangers. As you go about your day seeing many different people, you react to them and interact with them in various ways. You may smile at, frown at, stare at, tease, laugh at, agree with, disagree with, talk to, avoid, ignore, criticize, applaud them, and more. These are all means by which **informal regulation** or **informal social control** can occur.

You can see one example if you think back to your adolescent years. Perhaps as you were leaving the house, your parents saw what you were wearing and clearly disapproved. They may have asked, "What do you think you're wearing?" They may have said, "In those baggy pants you look like a bum!" Or they may have even sent you back to your room to change. That is informal regulation. Alternatively, you may have noticed people staring at you and laughing when you walked down the street. Informal social controls can include staring, laughing, frowning, avoiding, shaming, and more (Braithwaite, 2000; Edwards, 1988; Goode, 1997). Informal regulation comprises much of our daily lives today, and prior to industrialization it served as the dominant way that deviance was controlled (Spector, 1981). Take a moment to look at the *Ask Yourself* exercise, and consider how informal and formal social control affects your life.

In answering the *Ask Yourself* questions, you may have referred to peer pressure—the desire to fit in with your classmates might have an effect on the clothes you wear to class, the way you style your hair, or whether you go to the library versus the bar after class. Maybe you recall a time when you were whispering to a friend during class and two of your classmates gave you a dirty look or even asked you to keep it down. When you first became a post-secondary student, perhaps an older sibling gave you advice on what it would be like and how you should act. These are all examples of informal control.

Formal regulation or **formal social control** involves processing at some type of an organizational or institutional level. Prior to industrialization in the Western world, church prohibitions served as the central means of formal social control. With industrialization and the creation of a centralized government, there was a dramatic increase in organizations and agencies involved in regulation and social control (Spector, 1981). A wide range of types of formal regulation can serve as controls for deviant behaviour—a nation's laws (such as Canada's Criminal Code), a school or work dress code, regulations governing driver's licences or hunting permits, a teacher punishing a student for misbehaviour, or the psychiatrists' handbook that lists the symptoms of various forms of mental illness.

Look at the last *Ask Yourself* question regarding formal social controls in your life. In answering it, you could have referred to registration requirements—you are permitted to take Class B only if you have already passed Class A. You could have referred to the regulations governing student conduct at your university—what behaviours are considered unacceptable and what are the consequences for those behaviours? Perhaps you referred to a course syllabus, which tells you what exams and assignments you must complete to pass a particular course. Maybe you attend a university that has a student dress code. After an outburst in class, possibly the chair of the department gave you a written reprimand or made you see a student counsellor. These are all examples of formal regulation.

Social control may be *intentional* at times, such as through the creation of rules that must be followed by a child, student, employee, or citizen of the state. At other times, regulation might be the result of a more *general influence*; for instance, professionals such as doctors and lawyers have a general influence on their clients' lives (Edwards, 1988). Social control may be either **retroactive** (treating a known deviant in a certain way) or **preventative** (trying to prevent deviance in the first place—through socialization, for example) (Edwards, 1988). Social control may be directed at an individual by someone else (e.g., a doctor, a parent, a judge), or may occur at the level of **self-regulation** or **self-control**, where people regulate their own behaviours (such as by dieting to try and conform to an idealized body image, by joining a self-help group to end an addiction, or by avoiding behaviours that they know will be stigmatized) (Foucault, 1995; Gottfredson & Hirschi, 1990).

Of course, because the social construction of deviance and normality are embedded within a bigger "dance," it means that a particular behaviour, characteristic, or person is not subjected to only one social typing process at any given moment. Multiple social typing processes may be going on simultaneously, processes that may even contradict each other. One segment of society may socially type someone as "deviant," while another segment of society may claim that same person is "normal." In some areas of society, for example, someone who is perceived as overweight is labelled "too fat," has negative judgments attached to him or her, and is then treated in particular ways as a result; however, in other areas of society that person may be seen as "normal" or "healthy."

Even if there is some agreement that a person, behaviour, or characteristic is deviant, there may be differing views on what the appropriate forms of social control are. For example, while some people suggest that addiction is a disease and should be medically regulated, other people disagree and argue that another form of social control, such as punishment, should be instituted. Thus, within these multiple social typing processes, the claims made by one group often must compete with the claims made by another; claims-makers compete with other claims-makers "in a [deviance] marketplace" (Richardson, Best, & Bromley, 1991, p. 5). But the principal role of power in this process ultimately means that some people's claims count more than other people's, and that some people's claims have a greater bearing on the society at large—its norms, its structure, its institutions, and its people.

The consequences of the social typing process, whereby a person, behaviour, or characteristic becomes typed as deviant or is **deviantized**, are far-reaching. Through this process "description becomes prescription, which is then transformed into a desirable standard of normal behaviour to be upheld and maintained by the educational system, the religious system, the legal system, and of course the psychotherapeutic system, and to which every section of the population has to measure up or be found deficient" (Freud, 1999, p. 2).

Our Journey through This Book

In the process of transcending the objective/subjective dualism and of integrating analyses of acts, perceptions/reactions, and power relations, many questions will serve as a guide in the remaining chapters of this book:

■ Where does a particular act or characteristic come from, and what is its nature?

■ What is the nature of the social typing process? What are the descriptions, evaluations, and prescriptions that are being applied to this person, behaviour, or characteristic?

■ Who has done the social typing?

■ What is the foundation for their arguments?

■ Who benefits from the deviantizing of this behaviour, characteristic, or person?

■ What larger social conditions support the social typing process?

■ How is the "deviance dance" evident?

These kinds of questions will guide us in our understanding of deviance in relation to sexuality, youth, physical appearance, mental disorder, religion, and science. The choice of these topics is intended to provide you with critical insight into some of the core processes, as well as the people, that make up the foundation of our society. Such critical insight will be based on both specific structures and processes of deviance as described in the particular topics above, as well as at a level of theoretical understanding and explanations of deviance more generally.

By the end of this book, you will see that you are not an outsider looking in at deviance in society, but instead will see that deviance is a part of *your* everyday life. And you will see that although some sociologists decried the "death of deviance" in the past (e.g., Sumner, 1994), in the twenty-first century the field may be stronger and perhaps more relevant than ever (Adler & Adler, 2006b).

CHAPTER SUMMARY

- The study of deviance is characterized by disagreement about how deviance should be defined. Some deviance specialists suggest that there has been a general shift from *objective* to *subjective* definitions, drawing upon the notion of an objective/subjective dualism or dichotomy. (1)

- The *objective* side of the dualism suggests that there is a single characteristic that distinguishes "deviant" people from "normal" people. The four different defining traits that laypersons, social activists, politicians, or academics have mentioned are *statistical rarity*, *harm*, *negative societal reaction*, and *normative violation*. (2)

- According to the subjective side of the dichotomy, the only characteristic all deviant people have in common is that *enough important people have called them deviant*. In other words, deviance is a *social construction*. (3)

- Looking at deviance from a social constructionist point of view, what is of interest are a particular behaviour's place in the social order, the roles assigned to people who exhibit that behaviour, and the societal meanings attached to it. (3)

- Recent work in the study of deviance integrates both objective and subjective components. Thus, objectivism and subjectivism may be thought of as existing along a continuum rather than as a dichotomy. (3)

- The way that deviance is defined has implications for the way it is studied. Some researchers focus their analyses on the deviant act without further contextualizing it, assuming that the act can be classified as a form of deviance, while others focus their analyses on the processes involved in the perception of and reaction to the act. (4)

- The perceptions of *powerful groups* play a central role in the creation of the *dominant moral codes* that underlie the construction of deviance. In our society, powerful groups include politicians, religious institutions, scientists, the media, and commercial enterprise. (6)

- Central to issues of deviance are the processes of *social typing*, wherein someone is labelled in a particular way, judged on the basis of that label, and subjected to measures of social control. Such treatment can occur through various levels of regulation or social control—formal, informal, preventative, retroactive, and via the self. (5)

MySearchLab®

Watch Go to MySearchLab to watch the video called "Social Norms and Conformity".

Apply What You Know: What do the two seemingly disparate topics of this video—*gender norms* and *mob-like behaviour*—tell us about the nature of social control and self-regulation in contemporary society?

MySearchLab with eText offers you access to an online interactive version of the text, extensive help with your writing and research projects, and provides round-the-clock access to credible and reliable source material.

Chapter 2

Explaining Deviance: The Act

© Jupiterimages

Learning Objectives

After reading this chapter, you should be able to

1   Explain why different theories correspond to objective and subjective views of deviance, and describe the focus of positivist, interpretive, and critical theories.

2   Describe the core motivations of positivist theories, as well as how deviance is explained by the three types of positivist theories presented in this chapter.

3   Describe the core assumptions of functionalist theories, as well as how deviance is explained by (1) Durkheim's anomie theory, (2) Merton's anomie and strain theories, (3) differential opportunity theory, (4) general strain theory, and (5) Cohen's theory of status frustration.

4 Describe the core assumptions of learning theories, as well as how deviance is explained by (1) differential association theory, (2) neutralization theory, and (3) social learning theory.

5 Describe how Hirschi's social bonds theory explains deviance and its absence. Describe Gottfredson and Hirschi's more recent self-control theory.

6 Outline the criticisms that have been directed at functionalist, learning, and social control theories, and identify any responses to those criticisms.

Theorizing Deviance

"Theory" is sometimes perceived as the flip side of the coin from "practice"; it is seen as isolated from the "real world." But in fact, "there is nothing more practical than a good theory" (Brezhnev, 2006). Theory and practice are intimately intertwined, in that ". . . theory is the central tool used in science to organize accumulated knowledge" (Hay & Meldrum, 2010). It is through theory that we come to understand the world we live in. It is through past developments in theory that those of us living in the twenty-first century can understand gravity, nuclear power, and child development. Similarly, it is through theory that we are able to try to understand the way society works, the reasons why people commit crimes, why people get tattoos, and how an underweight female body has somehow come to represent the North American cultural ideal. That is, theory provides us with the central means of explaining and understanding deviance—what could be more practical than that?

Scientific theories of crime have existed for a century. The scientific study of criminality is recognized as beginning in the early twentieth century with the work of Cesare Lombroso, who explained criminality on the basis of evolution. He suggested that criminals were **atavists**—evolutionary throwbacks whose biology prevented them from conforming to society's rules (Lombroso, 1911). Other biological theories of crime soon followed, many of which explained criminality on the basis of heredity. According to those theories, just as the colour of one's eyes is biologically inherited, so is social behaviour like criminality (e.g., Goring, 1919). By mid-century, *social* theories of crime had largely replaced biological theories, and theorizing about noncriminal forms of deviance gained prominence as well.

Deviance specialists, whether they focus on criminal or noncriminal forms of deviance, use a wide range of theories: general sociological theories (e.g., conflict theory), specific criminological theories (e.g., strain theory), and interdisciplinary theories (e.g., feminist theories). Numerous theories exist simultaneously in the social sciences, unlike in the natural sciences where more accurate theories replace older theories that have been disproven. The poem "The Blind Men and the Elephant" serves as an interesting analogy for this characteristic of sociological theory (see Box 2.1).

When American poet John Godfrey Saxe wrote this poem based on a Hindu fable more than a century ago, would he have predicted what a useful analogy it would be for

Box 2.1

The Blind Men and the Elephant

A Hindu Fable

It was six men of Indostan
To learning much inclined
Who went to see the Elephant
(Though all of them were blind),
That each by observation
Might satisfy his mind.

The *First* approached the Elephant
And happening to fall
Against his broad sturdy side
At once began to bawl:
"God bless me! but the Elephant
Is very like a wall!"

The *Second*, feeling of the tusk,
Cried, "Ho! What have we here
So very round and smooth and sharp?
To me 'tis mighty clear
This wonder of an Elephant
Is very like a spear!"

The *Third* approached the animal,
And happening to take
The squirming trunk within his hands
Thus boldly up and spake:
"I see," quoth he, "the Elephant
Is very like a snake!"

The *Fourth* reached out his eager hand,
And felt about the knee.
"What most this wondrous beast is like
Is mighty plain," quoth he; "'Tis clear

enough the Elephant
Is very like a tree!"

The *Fifth*, who chanced to touch the ear,
Said: "E'en the blindest man
Can tell what this resembles most;
Deny the fact who can,
This marvel of an Elephant
Is very like a fan!"

The *Sixth* no sooner had begun
About the beast to grope,
Then, seizing on the swinging tail
That fell within his scope,
"I see," quoth he, "the Elephant
Is very like a rope."

And so these men of Indostan
Disputed loud and long.
Each in his own opinion
Exceeding stiff and strong,
Though each was partly in the right,
And all were in the wrong!

MORAL
So oft in theologic wars,
The disputants, I ween,
Rail on in utter ignorance
Of what each other mean,
And prate about an Elephant
Not one of them has seen!

—John Godfrey Saxe (1816–1887)
(Saxe, 1873)

sociological theory? What do blind men and elephants have to do with understanding society and explaining deviance?

Just as the blind men's explanations of the nature of the elephant depended on what part of the elephant each focused on, sociologists' explanations of the nature of society depend on what aspect of society each theory focuses on. There are diverse ways of looking at the world around us, and each theoretical perspective has a different view. Each of these ways of looking at society shines a spotlight on a different aspect of the social order—some theories focus on the stability of society, some focus on conflict, some focus on interaction.

But when a spotlight is directed at one particular location, all other areas necessarily fall into the shadows, just as each blind man's hands resting on one part of the elephant mean that the rest of the elephant's body is going untouched. In other words, an area of focus within each sociological theory may be easily explainable, but areas outside of the focal range are explained to a lesser extent, if at all.

Because each theory's way of looking at the world affects its focus, the explanations provided take a particular form. Thus, certain theories may be more useful than others in coming to understand a given issue or aspect of deviance. If you are interested in deviant *acts* (as those deviance specialists who lean toward the objective side of the objective–subjective continuum are), some theories of deviance will be more useful to you than others. In contrast, if you are more interested in the *perceptions* of and *reactions* to particular acts, as well as the role that power plays in those perceptions and reactions (as those deviance specialists who lean toward the subjective side of the objective–subjective continuum are), other theories will be of more use to you.

In the previous chapter, more objective ways of recognizing deviance were addressed, including views based on normative violation, statistical rarity, harm, and societal reaction. Each of these definitions of deviance suggests that there is a trait that all deviant people share that differentiates deviants from those who are normal. Emerging from this core idea is an interest in finding out *why* people become deviant—why they violate norms, or engage in behaviours that are atypical, or cause harm, or act in ways that result in a negative societal reaction. This way of looking at deviance is intimately linked with theories of deviance that are labelled **positivist** (Ashley & Orenstein, 2001). Positivist theories will be the focus of the remainder of this chapter.

The more subjective ways of looking at deviance, which will be examined in Chapter 3, suggest that the only characteristic all deviant people have in common is that enough important people have said they are deviant. Emerging from this core idea is an interest in exploring the social typing process—the process through which deviance and normality are socially constructed. Who becomes typed as deviant, how are they treated, and what rationales are offered? In what way does power influence societal perceptions of and reactions to particular behaviours? This way of looking at deviance and the concentration on these aspects are intimately linked with theories that are labelled **interpretive** and **critical** (Ashley & Orenstein, 2001). Interpretive and critical theories will be the focus of the next chapter. Because an exhaustive analysis of theories of deviance would require a virtual library of books, this book will focus on the core assumptions of the theories that have been the most commonly used or have had the greatest impact in the sociology of deviance.

Although positivist, interpretive, and critical theories will be discussed separately, a significant trend in theorizing is that of theoretical integration—combining aspects of different theories to explain a particular phenomenon. Consequently, positivist, interpretive, and critical theories may be integrated in multiple combinations (Ashley & Orenstein, 2001). Theoretical integration is not an entirely new phenomenon; even elements of positivist Émile Durkheim's work of more than a century ago have served as a foundation for some early interpretive and critical work. However, it is a growing trend in the sociology of deviance (Kubrin, Stucky, & Krohn, 2009). As you progress through the chapter, you will see some examples of how aspects of various theories have been combined to better explain a particular phenomenon.

Why Do People Become Deviant?
Using Positivist Theories

Positivist sociological theories are fundamentally interested in explaining why people act in particular ways. They are modelled after approaches to theorizing in the natural sciences, which "seek generalizable, universally applicable laws" (Ashley & Orenstein, 2001, p. 30) that govern the environment. In pursuing the rules that govern the *social* environment, positivist sociologists seek cause-and-effect relationships in the form of statistical relationships—they look for those variables that are associated with a particular behaviour or outcome (Ashley & Orenstein, 2001). Both positivist sociological theories and theories in the natural sciences are based on a technical interest in the mastery of the environment; in the case of positivist sociological theories, this technical interest is in pursuit of planning for a better society (Ashley & Orenstein, 2001).

Thus, seeking to understand why deviant people act that way triggers subsequent attempts to prevent other people from becoming deviant. Positivist explanations of deviance are inevitably coupled with efforts at social control, efforts you might personally agree with (such as with violent crime) or disagree with (such as with homosexuality). Individual theorists may not personally seek more effective social control of particular behaviours; their interest may lie solely in explaining the variability in people's behaviours. However, positivist theorizing lays the groundwork for those individuals who are seeking more effective social control or plans for a better society (Ashley & Orenstein, 2001).

The remainder of this chapter will review some of the positivist theories that have been commonly used to explain deviant acts and that have had significant influences on the sociology of deviance as a discipline. These include functionalist theories, learning theories, and theories of social control.

TIME TO REVIEW

Learning Objective 1

■ Why do multiple theories coexist in the sociology of deviance, and how can each theory be both "partly in the right" and "partly in the wrong"?

■ What is the nature of the link between particular types of theorizing (i.e., positivist, interpretive, and critical) and the objective–subjective continuum?

Learning Objective 2

■ What are the central motivations of positivist theories?

Functionalist Theories: The Social Structure Creates Deviance

Functionalist theories, which in the past were also called *structural functionalist theories*, have their origins in the birth of the discipline of sociology itself; in fact, this theoretical perspective dominated the discipline until the mid-twentieth century. In this perspective, society is seen as comprising various structures (e.g., the family, the education system, the political system), each of which fulfills necessary functions for the smooth running of the social order. Some are **manifest functions**, which are intended and recognized; others are **latent functions**, which are unintentional and unrecognized. For example, a manifest function of post-secondary education is to train young adults for employment, but post-secondary education does more than this: its latent functions may include providing individuals with social networks and facilitating the formation of romantic relationships. The *Ask Yourself* exercise addresses manifest and latent functions in the context of your own life.

Analogous to this functionalist view of society is a pyramidal stack of cans on display in the supermarket; each can is necessary for the display as a whole to keep standing. You may be afraid of selecting one of those cans to place in your shopping cart, because if you move the wrong can, or if one of the cans is not perfectly in position, the entire display may collapse. Similarly, the smooth running of society is threatened if one of its structures has a poor fit with the other structures that make up society.

One of the core concerns in the functionalist perspective is the maintenance of the social order. This conservative focus is inherent in the perspective because of the assumption that the rules that make up the social order are consensual; in other words, the rules exist because we agree that they should exist. And we agree they should exist because they serve a useful function for society. Thus, if the rules are typically functional, and if rules exist because we agree they should, we need to figure out why some people do not follow those rules. It may be that a part of the structure of society has become dysfunctional, which is causing people to break the rules.

Ask Yourself

One of the functions of families is the socialization of children, which is accomplished, in part, by parents providing their children with specific rules. Consider an example all of us are likely familiar with—a parent requiring you to clean your room. The intended purpose of this rule (i.e., its manifest function) may be to keep the house looking nice. But what else were you learning by virtue of having to clean your room (i.e., latent functions)?

Within these broad functionalist assumptions, individual theorists have taken different paths in applying the assumptions to the study of deviance. In the remainder of this section we will look at the different ways that Émile Durkheim, Robert Merton, collaborators Cloward and Ohlin, Robert Agnew, and Albert Cohen have applied functionalist assumptions to an understanding of deviance.

Anomie Theory: The Problem of Too Much Social Change

Not only is Émile Durkheim (1933, 1951) recognized as one of the founders of the discipline of sociology, his work also defined the structural functionalist perspective itself. In his theory, the notion of deviance is addressed in two ways. First, Durkheim suggested that a certain level of deviance is actually functional for society: deviance serves a useful purpose in helping maintain society's balance or equilibrium. Second, Durkheim addressed deviance in the context of dysfunctional levels of deviance that occur when society changes too quickly and **anomie** (normlessness) emerges.

Deviance is functional in that seeing someone break the rules leads the rest of us to realize how important the rules are and the necessity of following the rules. A certain level of deviance thereby enhances social order and *increases social solidarity* among those of us who join together to fight back against those people who break the rules. Deviance is also functional in that it is through observing behaviour and its consequences that *a society determines what its moral boundaries are*, what its rules should be, and what is considered acceptable and unacceptable. Deviance can be functional in that it *tests society's boundaries* and may demonstrate when certain rules no longer work and need to be changed. Finally, deviance serves as a way of *reducing societal tensions*, which it can do in two ways. First, societal tensions can be reduced when there is some sort of scapegoat that can be blamed for a social problem, since blaming a scapegoat takes the pressure off society at large. The second way that societal tensions can be defused is when individuals engage in small acts of minor deviance that act as a safety valve and let off some steam.

Parsons and Smelser (1956) elaborate on this latter function, suggesting that letting off steam through minor acts of deviance subsequently activates social processes that return deviant actors to their acceptable roles in society. The social processes that accomplish this include *socialization* (wherein deviant actors who are letting off steam have internalized society's rules sufficiently that they return to their legitimate social roles), *profit* (which teaches citizens that there is a payoff or benefit accorded to those who conform to society's rules), *persuasion* (through advertising, the sermons of religious leaders, psychologists' advice, etc.), and *coercion* (punishment for those who do not return to their legitimate social roles).

Several researchers have explored the functionality of deviance. Kai Erikson's (1966) classic analysis of the Puritans of the Massachusetts Bay Colony reveals that acts of deviance helped to reinforce the moral boundaries of their community. As the needs of the community changed over time, the system of crimes and punishments changed as well, illustrating to citizens, for example, the power of the church (through the punishment of witchcraft) or the value of private property (through the punishment of theft). The nature of these punishments also reminded citizens of the norms and values that were considered important by authorities in that community. For example, when resident Anne Hutchinson began using Bible study classes held in her home as a forum for criticizing the minister's Sunday sermons, she was charged with heresy and disobedience to the church fathers. Her "crimes" under civil and religious law caused her to be banished from the colony and excommunicated from the Puritan church. Hutchinson's deviance reminded others of what the rules were; the severe consequences she faced by breaking those rules pointed to the importance of those rules. The entire situation reinforced the power of the civil and religious authorities in the community.

The role of deviance in testing society's boundaries and facilitating changes in outdated rules can be seen historically: Anne Hutchinson eventually came to be seen as a champion of women's rights and religious freedom (and in the 1980s the governor of Massachusetts granted her a pardon). More recently, the actions of activists on behalf of civil rights, women's rights, gay rights, and disabled rights certainly changed society in significant ways. Their efforts demonstrated to the rest of society that some of its norms were outdated and needed to be changed. That is, certain norms had become dysfunctional for society and had to be modified to maintain social order.

Does deviance increase social solidarity? Hawdon, Ryan, and Agnich (2010) had a unique opportunity to explore this question. In 2006, they conducted a comprehensive survey of students at Virginia Polytechnic Institute in the United States. The survey included questions on social solidarity. For example, students were asked the extent to which they agreed with statements such as, "People at Virginia Tech share the same values," "I trust the students/faculty/staff at Virginia Tech," and "I am proud to be a member of the Virginia Tech community." Less than a year later, in April 2007, the most deadly school shooting in American history occurred on that campus. Twenty-seven students and five faculty members were killed, and another 23 were wounded. Hawdon, Ryan, and Agnich were given the opportunity to survey the students again to see if social solidarity had changed since the previous year. They re-surveyed the students five months, nine months, and one year following the tragedy. They found that solidarity had increased significantly at five months, it showed some decline at nine months, and even further decline at one year. However, even after one year, social solidarity remained higher than it had been prior to the tragedy.

Hawdon, Ryan, and Agnich found evidence of social solidarity in the results of their surveys. We can also see social solidarity reflected in practice following this type of an event, such as in memorial services, YouTube video tributes to victims, and in physical memorials, such as the Peace Garden at Dawson College in Quebec.

Although Durkheim proposed that deviance is functional for society, he pointed out that it remains functional only up to a point. Beyond a certain level, deviance no longer enhances the social order but rather interferes with it. Living in nineteenth-century Europe, Durkheim observed that the processes of industrialization and urbanization, with their growing emphasis on individuality, were causing more deviance—wherein deviance exceeded a functional level. He noted, for example, that suicide rates were higher in more individualistic communities characterized by less **social integration** (i.e., cohesion or social bonds) and lower levels of **moral regulation** (i.e., the enforcement of society's norms).

In explaining this apparent increase in deviance, Durkheim focused on the ways that society's structures had changed with industrialization and the impact this had on people's behaviour, including deviant behaviour. Before industrialization, he theorized, society's structure was held together by **mechanical solidarity**—that is, society was bonded together by *likeness* or by a collective commitment to conformity. These societies were characterized by minimal specialization in the division of labour; people produced whatever they

The Peace Garden was created at Dawson College following a shooting in September 2006 that killed one person and injured 19 others.

needed for their survival. Interactions between individuals in this type of society were quite personal and often kin-based; everyone knew and had a personal relationship with everyone else. Each person in this society had much in common with every other person.

With industrialization, the bonding mechanism for social structure was transformed into one of **organic solidarity**—society was bonded together by *difference* or interdependence through a highly specialized division of labour. In industrial society, the tasks that keep society running smoothly are divided among different institutions. The education system fulfills certain tasks while the political system and the medical system fulfill other tasks. Interactions between people in this type of society are somewhat impersonal, based primarily on our dependence on others because of the degree of specialization in the division of labour. A collective way of thinking and interacting is replaced by individualism.

Under conditions of both mechanical and organic solidarity, social integration and moral regulation have the potential to keep deviance at a functional level and facilitate the degree of conformity necessary to maintain social order. However, when social change occurs at too rapid a pace, individualism gets out of control, and bonds between people become weaker than is necessary for the well-being of society. Traditional norms and means of social control deteriorate, creating a situation of *anomie*. The presence of anomie in modern societies opens the door for greater levels of deviance beyond the degree that is functional for society. Thus, it is the structure of society itself and its impact on individuals that contributes to harmful levels of deviance in society.

Durkheim's theory emerged during the process of industrialization, with its extensive social changes and the associated concerns about the stability of society itself. However, rapid social change is not limited to that era. The twentieth century brought possibly even greater transformation—the automobile, the airplane, immunization, the computer, the Internet, and more. Massive political and economic change occurred throughout that century and into the twenty-first century as well—change characterized by events such as World War I, World War II, the Cold War, the birth of the United Nations, the creation of human rights policies, the fall of the Iron Curtain, the "war against terrorism," various civil wars in Eastern Europe and in several countries in Africa, the growth of multinational corporations with greater wealth than most nations, and a number of natural disasters. Some might say that ongoing, rapid social change has become a way of life, with significant consequences.

McKee (2002) paints a picture of the consequences of anomie in 1930s Limerick, Ireland (as illustrated in Frank McCourt's autobiography, *Angela's Ashes*), in the outskirts of Edinburgh (as portrayed in Irvine Welsh's book *Trainspotting*), and in former Soviet-bloc countries throughout Eastern Europe. McKee states that "traditional support networks have been disrupted. Expectations have been raised, but with no obvious, legitimate means to fulfill them. These societies produce people . . . whose outlook is characterised by a sense of futility, lack of purpose, emotional emptiness and despair" (p. 456).

For example, Walberg and colleagues (cited in McKee, 2002) found that in 1990s Russia, communities with the most rapid and extensive socioeconomic change had the highest crime rates and the largest decreases in life expectancy, in large part due to alcohol abuse. Anomic disorder creates a demand for alcohol and other substances because of weakened social cohesion; in addition, it improves the supply of such substances because of diminished moral regulation in the form of police and government corruption (McKee, 2002). In those communities where people live more traditional lifestyles and have stronger family and social networks (e.g., rural areas and areas with large Muslim populations), addiction-related problems are less common (Walberg et al., cited in McKee, 2002). The contemporary world, much like Europe of the nineteenth century, is rapidly changing. With these extensive changes, anomie is becoming more common and, according to Durkheim's theory, the stage is being set for the emergence of dysfunctional levels of deviance.

Here we have seen one theorist's application of functionalist ideas to an explanation of why deviance occurs. Durkheim's approach exemplifies the central concern of both objective ways of defining deviance and the related positivist theoretical perspectives. Robert Merton, a twentieth-century functionalist theorist, both built upon and moved away from Durkheim's ideas. Looking at Merton's theory shows us another way that functionalist assumptions have been applied to the study of deviance.

Learning Objective 3

■ According to Durkheim's anomie theory, in what way is deviance functional?

■ According to Durkheim's anomie theory, why does deviance reach dysfunctional levels?

■ What historical and contemporary evidence supports Durkheim's claims?

Merton's Anomie and Strain Theories: The (North) American Dream Gone Awry

Robert Merton (1938, 1968) applied functionalist assumptions to the study of deviance in different ways, but he is best known for applying functionalist assumptions in the form of his anomie and strain theories (often labelled *classic strain theory*), which dominated "the area of deviance from the early 1950s until about 1970" (Collins, cited in Pfohl, 1994, p. 279). After two decades of being disregarded in favour of more micro-level theories, strain theories (along with other structural theories) once again came into favour (Kubrin, Stucky, & Krohn, 2009). In fact, Merton's theory of the link between anomie and strain "has been heralded as among the most significant of all major sociological theories" (Featherstone & Deflam, 2003, p. 471). Merton suggested that deviance originates not only from the individual, but also from the structure of society, which propels some people into deviance. What is it about the structure of society that creates a greater likelihood that some people, more than others, will become deviant? The *Ask Yourself* exercise will bring you closer to an answer to this question.

The *Ask Yourself* exercise asks you to think about what Merton referred to as **institutionalized goals**. In contemporary capitalist society, these are the goals that are culturally exalted, the ones that we are taught we are *supposed* to want to achieve. Merton said that in North America, the goals we are to aspire to include *wealth, status/power*, and *prestige*—the qualities that make up "success," or the "(North) American Dream." Almost everywhere we look we encounter the message that these qualities are what we should try to achieve in life. Who are the people who are admired and envied in society? We admire the wealthy: people who drive a Porsche, Jaguar, or BMW, who live in houses with indoor swimming pools, and who travel to expensive and exotic places. We admire powerful people, like Steve Jobs. We admire professional athletes (such as Sidney Crosby or Tiger Woods), famous actors (such as Julianne Moore or Johnny Depp), and famous singers and musicians (such as Kanye West, Rihanna,

> ## Ask Yourself
> As a member of Canadian society, what have you been taught that you are supposed to achieve in life to be considered "successful"? What do you see in the society around you that reinforces your belief that these are, indeed, the criteria for success?

or Steven Tyler)—people with prestige. Our society rewards those who attain wealth, power, or prestige; they have the nicest "toys," they win awards (such as a Grammy, an Oscar, or Playoff MVP), they are interviewed endlessly to share their secrets for success, and they have countless numbers of people following their every move in the daily sports section, the business news, or celebrity websites. The fact that these characteristics are culturally exalted is evident even if you think back to your childhood—it is unlikely that you aspired to grow up to be poor, powerless, and unrecognized. Of course, as adults, some of you might not personally admire people who are wealthy or famous, and you might aspire to other goals. However, even if your personal goals differ from the institutionalized goals Merton referred to, the larger issue is that our society is structured in a way that gives benefit to or rewards those who have attained these institutionalized goals.

Merton suggested that just as our culture is characterized by institutionalized goals, it is also characterized by **legitimate means** of attaining those goals. What are recognized as the legitimate ways of attaining wealth, power, and prestige? We are supposed to get a good education, find a high-paying job, and work hard; alternatively, perhaps you inherited wealth or were born into a powerful family. However, he pointed out that both *anomie* and *strain* have come to characterize American society (and presumably, North America more generally). A context of **anomie** has emerged that Merton describes as an imbalance between culturally prescribed goals and legitimate means, whereby society's emphasis on the goals of wealth, power, and prestige exceeds the emphasis on the means of achieving those goals.

This has resulted in a "deinstitutionalization of the means" (Featherstone & Deflam, 2003, p. 478). That is, simply attaining the institutionalized goals has become more important than *how* one attains them. In their *institutional anomie theory*, Messner and Rosenfeld (2001) propose that it is because of the dominance of economic institutions (with their emphasis on competition and success) that anomie characterizes North American society: as economic institutions come to dominate other institutions (e.g., family, religion), economic values come to infiltrate those institutions as well.

In addition to this cultural context of anomie in which we all live, there are also structural constraints for some people. The normative social order is such that not everyone has equal access to legitimate opportunities. A child growing up in a middle- or upper-class neighbourhood—with the best teachers and well-equipped schools, a wide range of extracurricular activities available, a home in a safe community, and middle- or upper-class parents—is likely to have assured access to the legitimate means of achieving institutionalized goals. However, consider a child growing up in an impoverished neighbourhood. The dilapidated schools, devoid of library books, have trouble attracting teachers and offer few extracurricular activities. Home is a run-down house in a disordered community. The parents live in poverty or are chronically on social assistance. Although we often perceive Canadian society as a place of equal opportunity, does this child truly have the same access to legitimate opportunities in life as the middle-class child?

The blocked opportunities that exist in some parts of the social structure create a **strain** between the goals and the means for people who live there. With this structural gap between institutionalized goals and the legitimate means of achieving those goals, individuals must find ways to adapt. According to Merton, people can adapt to the gap between goals and means in five different ways, some of which result in deviance.

The first possible mode of adaptation is **conformity**. The individual continues to accept both society's institutionalized goals and the legitimate means; this person keeps pursuing wealth, power, or prestige by going to school, finding a good job, and working hard.

The second possible mode of adaptation, **innovation**, can result in deviance. The individual accepts the institutionalized goals, but rejects the legitimate means and instead seeks alternative means of achieving those goals. For example, if you want to become wealthy, you can do so in a conforming way by pursuing a higher education and training for a high-paying career, or you can do so in an innovative way by selling drugs.

The third possible mode of adaptation is **ritualism**. The person engaging in ritualism has given up on or at least reduced the institutionalized goals but continues to engage in the legitimate means. This is someone who thinks he or she will never get anywhere in life, but still keeps going through the motions—for example, never missing a day of work. With this mode of adaptation, people are unlikely to be looked upon as deviant because, to the outside world, they appear to reliably follow the rules.

Merton's fourth mode of adaptation is **retreatism**, wherein people reject both the institutionalized goals and the legitimate means. These are people who have given up on the goals, do not even go through the motions anymore, and instead retreat into their own isolated worlds, sometimes characterized by alcohol abuse or drug addiction.

The last mode of adaptation is **rebellion**. As with retreatism, people engaged in rebellion also reject both institutionalized goals and legitimate means; however, unlike retreatists,

Louis Riel was executed for his 'rebellion,' but later came to be recognized as an initiator of important social change.

they substitute new goals and new means. These are people who have a "vision" of a different world and act to bring that vision to life.

For example, Louis Riel had a vision of a nation that would include Métis rights and culture; he fought for that vision in the Red River Rebellion (1869–1870) and the North West Rebellion (1885), eventually being executed for high treason. In his famous "I Have a Dream" speech, American civil rights leader Martin Luther King Jr. described his dream for a society based on equality for all races, religions, and creeds; King was shot and killed by a man who did not share that vision. Nelson Mandela had a vision of a different South African society, one free of apartheid, and he fought for more than 20 years for that vision; although highly celebrated throughout the world (receiving the Nobel Peace Prize in 1993), even he continues to face social typing for his rebellion, being referred to by Calgary MP Rob Anders as a "communist and terrorist" (CBC News, 2001). In the 1960s and 1970s, the hippie counterculture envisioned a society in which everyone would give up material wealth—including money—and instead seek peace and love. In pursuit of these goals, many hippies stopped working, "made love, not war," consumed a wide range of mind-altering drugs, and moved into various types of commune-like settings.

These examples illustrate how Merton's five modes of adaptation allow people to adapt to the gap between institutionalized goals and legitimate means and how some people are led into deviance—whether through rebellion, retreatism, or innovation. According to Merton, the current structure of society creates this gap, more so for some groups of people in society than for others. This is why some people engage in deviance.

Empirical research has directed its attention primarily toward innovation and retreatism by exploring the relationship between strain and criminal activity. Although early research yielded less-than-impressive results because of methodological weaknesses, more recent research finds that strain (measured by relative deprivation, perceptions of blocked opportunities, or dissatisfaction with monetary status) is associated with criminal activity (Agnew, Cullen, Burton, Evans, & Dunaway, 1996; Burton & Cullen, 1992; Burton & Dunaway, 1994). However, empirical research has largely disregarded the other modes of adaptation—conformity, ritualism, and rebellion (Kubrin, Stucky, & Krohn, 2009).

Thus far we have seen two diverse and highly influential ways that functionalist assumptions have been used to explain why people engage in deviance. As functionalist theories, both Durkheim's and Merton's approaches suggest that parts of the structure of society may become dysfunctional in some way and result in deviant behaviour on the part of some people. The next functionalist theories we will discuss are from collaborators Richard Cloward and Lloyd Ohlin, who also consider that the structure of society may lead to deviance for some people.

Differential Opportunity Theory: Access to the Illegitimate World
Cloward and Ohlin's (1960) theory extends aspects of Merton's strain theory; although their theory has received relatively little empirical attention, it has served as a foundation for social action and policy (Kubrin, Stucky, & Krohn, 2009). Like Merton, they suggest that the way society is structured results in differential access to legitimate opportunities.

However, Cloward and Ohlin go on to propose that the way society is structured also results in differential access to illegitimate opportunities—some people have more access to illegitimate opportunities than other people do by living in neighbourhoods that may have street gangs, drug dealers, or sex trade workers.

Due to the differential access to both legitimate and illegitimate opportunities that is created by the structure of society, Cloward and Ohlin suggest that some people are more likely to become participants in deviant subcultures. Some people in lower-class neighbourhoods may become part of **criminal gangs**, in which criminal behaviour is akin to a small business (e.g., the Fresh Off the Boat, or FOB, gang in Calgary, which formed in the late 1990s for the purpose of selling drugs). Other people may become part of **retreatist gangs**, which, reflecting Merton's concept of the retreatist mode of adaptation, consist of groups of people who retreat into substantial drug or alcohol use. Finally, people in these neighbourhoods may join **conflict gangs**, which fight for status and power in the neighbourhood via the use of violence against competitive gangs. For instance, although FOB formed as a criminal gang in the 1990s, a falling out among some of its members led to the creation of a new gang, the Fresh Off the Boat Killers (FK); extreme violence has now broken out between the two groups, "motivated not by battles over drug turf, but mutual hatred" (Van Rassel, 2009), resulting in dozens of deaths since 2002.

All three of these instances are a consequence of the opportunities that are available in the community. As children grow up in these neighbourhoods, they may see people making their livings through criminal involvement with similar others, people drinking and taking drugs to excess (and perhaps even trying to sell drugs and alcohol to neighbourhood children), or gang violence. Being a part of this environment makes certain illegitimate opportunities easily available.

As with Durkheim's and Merton's theories, Cloward and Ohlin see society's structure as the impetus for deviant behaviour. Robert Agnew, the next theorist to be addressed, also focuses on the roles played by structure and strain in creating deviance, but suggests that they interact with social psychological factors.

Agnew's General Strain Theory: The Effect of Negative Emotions

Robert Agnew (1992, 1998) has expanded upon the notion of strain by identifying a number of possible sources for this strain. Merton stated that strain emerges when the social structure places limitations on people's access to the means of achieving positively valued goals. However, Agnew proposes that strain can be produced by a variety of processes. While it can occur when we are unable to achieve goals (e.g., failing a course), it may also arise when valued stimuli are removed (the loss of a job or the dissolution of a marriage) or when negative stimuli are presented (being teased at school or living in a conflict-ridden family). But strain is not sufficient in itself to produce deviance; deviance emerges only when strain is accompanied by **negative affect** (negative emotions) such as anger, depression, or anxiety. Strain is especially likely to create negative affect, and subsequently deviance, if it is perceived as unjust, if it is severe, and if the individual lacks control over the situation (Agnew, 2001).

Hay and Meldrum (2010) suggest that bullying fits those three criteria. They analyzed the role that bullying plays in internalized forms of deviance on the part of the victim. They found that being victimized by either traditional bullying or cyberbullying contributed to self-harming behaviours (e.g., cutting) and suicidal thoughts. Negative emotions partially mediated this effect. Although bullying itself had a direct impact on these forms of deviance, negative emotions reduced the direct effects of bullying on self-harm by 24 to 44 percent and on suicide ideation by 30 to 41 percent. Negative emotions have also been found to play a mediating role in the use of stimulants as a "homework drug" among university students (Ford & Schroeder, 2009) and purging behaviour among young women (Sharp, Terling-Watt, Atkins, & Gillam, 2001).

Other research questions the role of negative emotions in general strain theory. One study of university students found that three particular strains—goal blockage; being harassed, embarrassed, or shamed by teachers; and racial discrimination—had a direct effect on a range of violent and nonviolent, criminal and noncriminal behaviours. The negative emotion of anger also had a direct effect on these behaviours. However, the effects of strain and anger were largely independent of each other; anger played only a minimal role in mediating the effects of strain (Moon, Hays, & Blurton, 2009).

The addition of negative emotions to notions of strain is what distinguishes Agnew's general strain theory from Merton's strain theory and from Cloward and Ohlin's differential opportunity theory. More recently, Agnew (2006) has developed a more macro-level strain theory that postulates the principles of general strain theory can be integrated with structural factors. Here he suggests deviance will be more prevalent in certain locations within the social structure (e.g., low-income neighbourhoods) because of the large number of people who are experiencing strain (because of unemployment, low wages, or low education).

The last functionalist theorist we will address is Albert Cohen, whose subcultural theory also integrates structured inequalities as the impetus for deviance.

Status Frustration Theory: The Middle-Class Classroom

Albert Cohen (1955) claims that inequalities in the structure of society are reproduced in the classroom, resulting in delinquent subcultures among lower-class boys. Just as middle-class norms dominate in society in general, they also dominate the structure and functioning of school classrooms. This creates a **middle-class measuring rod** that lower-class boys find difficult to live up to. The school's emphasis on delayed gratification, politeness, and the value of hard work does not correspond well with the lives of lower-class boys. In their homes and communities, delaying gratification may result in the object of the gratification disappearing or being taken away. Politeness may compromise safety and toughness is emphasized instead. They may see their own parents working very hard, perhaps at two or three jobs, and yet not making any progress; thus, the value of hard work may be unapparent.

When they are unable to succeed according to the standards in the classroom, they experience a situation similar to strain—**status frustration**. As a result, they join together with other lower-class boys who are having the same experience (**mutual conversion**) and develop a set of oppositional standards at which they are able to succeed (**reaction formation**). If the middle-class standard is to delay gratification, the oppositional standard is to be hedonistic. Non-utilitarian, malicious, negativistic youth gangs are the result. In support of Cohen's theory, many empirical studies have found poor school performance or early school leaving to be associated with criminal behaviour (e.g., Gomme, 1985).

TIME TO REVIEW

Learning Objective 3

■ According to Merton's concepts of anomie and strain, why does deviance emerge and what are the different modes of adaptation to strain?

■ According to Cloward and Ohlin's differential opportunity theory, how does the structure of society contribute to deviance, and what different forms does deviance take?

■ According to Agnew's general strain theory, what causes strain and what role do emotions play?

■ According to Cohen's theory of status frustration, why do lower-class boys become deviant, and what form does their deviance take?

Limitations of Functionalist Theories of Deviance

Émile Durkheim, Robert Merton, collaborators Richard Cloward and Lloyd Ohlin, Robert Agnew, and Albert Cohen have each applied functionalist assumptions to an explanation of deviance, although in slightly different ways. Durkheim's theory of society includes discussions of how deviance can be functional for society but can reach dysfunctional levels when social change occurs too rapidly and anomie is created. Merton's theory, which focuses more explicitly on explaining deviance, describes with greater specificity what it is about the normative social order that leads some people into deviance. For Merton, this is the gap between institutionalized goals and legitimate means of achieving those goals, which is experienced more by people located in certain parts of the social structure. Like Merton, Cloward and Ohlin suggest that the structure of society creates differential access to legitimate opportunities, but they extend the notion of differential access in showing how it applies to illegitimate opportunities as well. Agnew goes a step further by saying that strain must be accompanied by negative emotions for deviance to occur. Finally, Cohen suggests the reproduction of structured inequalities in the school system serves as the impetus for deviance among groups of lower-class boys.

Despite the slightly different paths that are taken by these various theorists, they all make use of functionalist assumptions—that society comprises structures that fulfill important functions for the maintenance of the social order, that the structure of society contributes to deviance in some way, and that deviance is a threat to society's equilibrium (at least at certain levels).

Functionalist theories have been subject to considerable criticism. In fact, Martins (cited in Downes & Rock, 2003) states that "every Autumn term . . . [functionalism] is ritually executed for introductory teaching purposes . . . the demolition of functionalism is almost an initiation rite of passage into sociological adulthood" (p. 81). Functionalism has been criticized on both logical and ideological or political bases. Critiques of functionalist logic suggest it is teleological and tautological.

It is **teleological** (i.e., related to goals) in that "the grounds for the existence of [a] phenomenon are simply read into the alleged function it serves" for society as a whole (Downes & Rock, 2003, p. 98). Functionalism proposes that since society has specific needs, particular institutions are created to meet those needs. However, functionalism is not able to explain *why* that specific institution, at the exclusion of others, is required to achieve particular societal goals (Ritzer & Goodman, 2004). For example, because society requires that children be socialized, the institution of family emerged—the existence of family is explained in terms of the functions it fulfills. But critics suggest that family is not *necessary* for the socialization of children; many other institutions can and do fulfill that function as well (e.g., the education system). If other institutions are able to fulfill that same function, then functionalism really has not explained the need for the family at all (Turner & Maryanski, cited in Ritzer & Goodman, 2004).

Functionalist arguments are also **tautological** (i.e., circular), where the whole is described in terms of its parts, and the parts are described in terms of the whole (Ritzer & Goodman, 2004). In a tautological argument, we would say that because we see families socializing children, the socialization of children is one of the functions of the family. The latter part of the argument merely restates the information in the former part of the argument.

Functionalist theories are also criticized at an ideological or political level. Critics claim that by determining the functions of almost any aspect of social life, functionalists ignore the social and historical circumstances from which those aspects emerge. The presumption of functionality (the idea that society's structure is somehow useful) also contributes to the critique of functionalism's conservative bias (Cohen, cited in Downes & Rock, 2003; Deutschmann, 2002; Pfohl, 1994; Ritzer & Goodman, 2004). Racial inequalities, gender inequalities, and low wages for the working class can all be justified on the basis of being "functional" for society in some way. For example, while strain theorists point out the influence of structural inequalities on deviance, they do not explicitly state that society's structure should be modified to reduce inequalities in the distribution of opportunities.

Finally, it has been suggested that functionalist theories have an **androcentric bias**, meaning that women have been addressed in functionalist theories only to a limited extent. Further, when women's experiences are addressed, a conservative bias once again becomes evident; for instance, traditional gender roles have been identified as serving important functions for society (e.g., Parsons & Bales, 1955).

Each of the specific theories reviewed thus far has also been subject to particular criticisms. Merton's theory of anomie and strain, Cloward and Ohlin's differential opportunity theory, and Cohen's theory of status frustration have traditionally focused attention on criminal behaviour, relying on official crime statistics. Because official crime statistics frequently under-represent the extent of criminal activity in the middle- and upper-classes, these theories have all been criticized for identifying deviance and criminality as lower-class phenomena. If criminal behaviour is acknowledged to be a middle- and upper-class phenomenon as well, and noncriminal forms of deviance are also analyzed (e.g., self-harm), then it becomes clear that these theorists' explanations of deviance are limited (Kitsuse & Dietrick, 1979). In that case, the very foundation of their explanations—the assumption that deviance originates from differentially structured opportunities—comes into question (Ritzer & Goodman, 2004; Downes & Rock, 2003; Ward, Carter, & Perrin, 1994; Hackler, 2000; Siegel & McCormick, 2003).

In light of these criticisms, some deviance specialists began to apply these theories to analyses of noncriminal forms of deviance. For example, Parnaby and Sacco (2004) apply Merton's strain theory to what they identify as a newly emerged institutionalized goal: the pursuit of fame and celebrity (see Box 2.2). This change eradicates the inherent link between deviance and the lower socioeconomic strata.

Merton's theory of anomie and strain and differential opportunity theory have also been criticized for failing to recognize individual differences, such as gender and cultural differences, in response to strain (Deutschmann, 2002). More recently, however, a growing body of research has been investigating strain theories within the context of gender and race. For example, Konty (2005) analyzes gender differences in deviant behaviour using the concept of **microanomie**, a state wherein an individual's self-transcendence values (the value placed on qualities such as honesty, helpfulness, equality, and social justice) are exceeded by self-enhancement values (the value placed on authority, ambition, competition, social power, and beating the system). Because females (when compared to males) are less socialized into accepting self-enhancement values, and because those values are associated with attitudes that support deviant behaviours (physical fights, stealing, marijuana use), males are more likely than females to engage in those behaviours.

Gender differences have also been analyzed in applications of Agnew's general strain theory. J. Kaufman (2009) explored gender differences in strain, emotions, and forms of deviance in more than 12 000 adolescents in Grades 7 through 12. Two particularly severe forms of strain were focused on—suicidal behaviour by a friend or family member and violent victimization. The study found that more girls had experienced the former type of strain, and more boys had experienced the latter. Some gender differences were also evident in forms of negative emotion; girls were more likely than boys to experience depressive symptoms, but there were no gender differences in anger (in the form of "bad temper"). There were gender differences in patterns of deviance as well. Girls were more likely to have had suicidal thoughts and to have run away from home at some point; boys were more likely to engage in weekly drinking and violent behaviour. There was a strong relationship between strain and negative emotions for both boys and girls. Furthermore, depression was associated with suicidal thoughts and violence in boys and with all four forms of deviance in girls.

Box 2.2

The "Strain" of Fame and Celebrity

Although Merton initially emphasized material or economic success in his theory of the relationship between anomie and strain, his more recent work uses the broader concept of *opportunity structures*, which can be generalized to goals outside of the economic realm (Merton, 1995). Using Merton's revised theoretical formulation, Parnaby and Sacco (2004) suggest that in our "mass mediated society" (p. 2), fame and celebrity status have become institutionalized goals. We have only to look at the popularity of reality shows on television, the opportunity for everyday people to become superstars on *The Voice* or *X Factor*, and the availability of celebrity-following websites like *TMZ*. Legitimate means of achieving this institutionalized goal include "individual struggle (or hard work), personal accomplishment and/or a rare talent, and . . . 'dumb luck'" (Parnaby & Sacco, 2004, p. 5). However, the opportunity structure is such that not everyone has equal access to these legitimate means. Thus, individuals who experience the strain between goals and means may use one of the four deviant *modes of adaptation* proposed by Merton.

Innovation involves continuing to pursue institutionalized goals but rejecting the legitimate means of doing so. Innovative means of pursuing fame or celebrity include the gangster celebrities of the past (e.g., Al Capone) and their contemporary equivalents—those living the "gangsta lifestyle" (p. 13). Gangsters (and gangstas) cross the line between media celebrity and criminal, a fact that has been integrated into the lyrics of some rappers themselves. The merging of fame and criminal behaviour is also evident in the news media's creation of the "killer as celebrity" (p. 14), whose picture is placed on the front page of every newspaper and news magazine and whose life is dissected and sometimes emulated. Graffiti artists use the innovative mode of adaptation as well, wherein their "tagging" is intended to both bring them recognition as artists and mark their territories.

Ritualism brings a diminishing of goals but an adherence to legitimate means. The ritualistic pursuit of celebrity is found in the workers who dress up as characters at amusement parks and people who detail every aspect of their daily lives on personal web pages or blogs. Ritualism is also evident in "the struggling actor . . . who abandons his or her dreams of mainstream Hollywood for the pornography industry" and "the cover band that dedicates itself to the remaking of songs when the multi-million dollar record deal becomes more fiction than fact . . ." (p. 16).

Retreatism leads individuals to reject both goals and means and retreat into isolation. Although somewhat difficult to apply to those in the public eye, Parnaby and Sacco suggest that this mode of adaptation is evident in those who experience extreme stage fright and people who have already achieved fame yet avoid all of its trappings by leading relatively isolated lives (e.g., Marlon Brando, who died in 2004; Johnny Depp).

Rebellion involves replacing existing goals and means with a new vision. "Culture jamming" (Adbusters, cited in Parnaby & Sacco, 2004, p. 20) works toward changing the way that the culture and consumer industries set their agendas. It is linked with critiques of globalization and resistance to corporate-driven global inequality and exploitation.

The theory of status frustration and differential opportunity theory have also faced criticism, in particular for not being able to explain why youth who are located in the same lower-class position in the social structure have different outcomes. Most lower-class youth grow up to be contributing, conforming members of society with post-secondary educations and gainful employment (Downes & Rock, 2003).

Finally, Cohen's theory of status frustration has been criticized for failing to recognize non-utilitarian, negativistic, malicious acts of deviance among middle-class suburban gangs (Kitsuse & Dietrick, 1979). This brings into question Cohen's assumption that failing to live up to the middle-class measuring rod in schools is the cause of gang behaviour (Downes & Rock, 2003). His weak treatment of female deviance has also been criticized; without any supporting empirical data, Cohen suggested that female deviance emerges from interpersonal strain rather than economic strain and is therefore more likely to be of a sexual nature.

The theorists we have discussed are certainly not the only functionalist theorists who have sought explanations for deviance. They are, however, among the most influential. Although functionalist theories no longer dominate the study of deviance, they do continue to maintain a presence (Agnew, 1992; Sharp et al., 2001; Victor, 1992).

In addition to functionalist theories, other perspectives originate from a positivist understanding of why people act in deviant ways. The next set of positivist theories we will be addressing are learning theories.

TIME TO REVIEW

Learning Objective 6

■ What are the logical and ideological/political criticisms of functionalist theories as a whole?

■ What criticisms have been directed at individual functionalist theories, and how has empirical research responded to these critiques?

Learning Theories: People Learn to Be Deviant

Learning theories, like functionalist theories, have been widely used as explanations of deviance. As the label suggests, these theories explain deviant behaviour as a result of the learning process. In other words, people *learn* to be deviant. The precise nature of this learning process is outlined in various learning theories. In this section, we will focus on differential association theory, neutralization theory, and social learning theory—all of which have had considerable influence on the way deviance has been understood over the last several decades.

Differential Association Theory: Learning from Friends and Family

Our exploration of learning theories begins with an influential theorist whose work is recognized by some people as one of the dominant explanations of deviance today (Erickson, Crosnoe, & Dornbusch, 2000; Cullen & Agnew, 1998). Edwin Sutherland

(1947), beginning with the assumption that deviant behaviour is learned, developed a theory that focuses on explaining the nature of the learning process—a process he labelled **differential association**.

Although Sutherland's theory was initially proposed as a theory of crime, it has since been successfully applied to other forms of deviance, particularly adolescent substance use (Aseltine, 1995; Elliot, Huizinga, & Ageton, 1985). Sutherland proposed that deviant behaviour is learned through the same process by which conforming behaviour is learned. Central to the learning process is the direct interaction and communication that occurs in small, intimate groups.

Deviant people act that way because that is what they learn through communication within the intimate groups of which they are a part. Intimacy is crucial to the learning of deviance, such that impersonal agents like music, television, and movies are relatively inconsequential. Within these personal groups, individuals learn both **techniques** (skills) and **motives** (reasons) for particular kinds of behaviour. If people are exposed to more deviant definitions than conforming definitions overall, they are likely to become deviant themselves; in other words, if they are learning techniques for how to engage in deviance and motives for engaging in deviance more than they are learning techniques for how to conform and motives for conforming, they are more likely to engage in deviant behaviour.

Ask Yourself

Think about the various groups that you interacted with as a child or adolescent. For each group, consider the types of techniques and motives you were exposed to. Did you learn ways to engage in what might be seen as deviant behaviour and reasons for doing so? Did you learn ways to engage in conforming behaviour and reasons for doing so? If you consider your childhood and adolescence as a whole, do you think you were exposed to more deviant definitions than conforming definitions, or vice versa?

Research finds that it is the definitions provided by *in-group* members that are especially important in influencing behaviour. Piquero, Tibbets, and Blankenship (2005) presented MBA students with a vignette in which they were responsible for making a decision as to whether the company for which they worked would continue to distribute a drug discovered to be harmful. They were also asked the extent to which they believed their co-workers, friends, business professors, and board of directors would support that decision. Some support for differential association theory was found in that the employees' decisions were associated with the corporate climate—that is, the extent to which they believed the board of directors and their closest co-workers would support that decision. Their decisions were also *negatively* associated with the extent to which they believed their business professors and friends would support those decisions. The researchers concluded that it is "somewhat disturbing" that "many of the respondents . . . essentially reported that they would take actions that would lead to injuring or killing innocent people, while knowingly disregarding the ethical responsibilities they learned from their professors and defying moral values of their closest friends" (p. 181). In this case, "the corporate environment can subvert the other associations and normative values that the individual has learned [in life]" (p. 181).

This differential exposure to deviant and conforming definitions is further complicated by the fact that not all group interactions have the same impact on our learning processes. First, the extent of group influence varies by *frequency*, in that those groups we interact with more frequently will have more of an influence on our learning. Second, interactions that are of longer *duration* have more of an influence than those of shorter duration. Third, there is a *priority* to our small group interactions; those intimate groups with which we interact earlier in life have a greater influence on our learning. Finally, interactions vary in *intensity* or in how important a particular group is to us—the more important a particular group is to us, the greater its influence on our learning processes. The frequency, duration, priority, and intensity of exposure to group interactions determine how influential the definitions of behaviour are on our learning processes.

In an analysis of the jamband subculture, Hunt (2010) finds that some of these characteristics of interactions may have more of an influence than others. The jamband subculture originated with the Grateful Dead and its fans ("Deadheads"). Musical artists considered to be "jamband" perform a blend of folk, rock, and blues and are known for improvisational jamming in their performances; this makes each individual performance completely unique. They encourage members of the audience to record their performances and share those recordings with others. Members of the jamband subculture follow bands on tour and set up temporary communities in the parking lots outside of concert venues. In these communities, the core values of the subculture are expressed: sharing, pooling resources, trading recordings, and bartering resources such as concert tickets, rides, food, and water. These prosocial behaviours are labelled "kynd" (p. 521), while threatening someone or talking down to them is labelled "unkynd." Well-established members of the subculture consistently adhere to these norms, but those who are less integrated frequently misunderstand or violate the norms. Hunt's analysis revealed that positive evaluations of kynd norms were associated with frequency (how often an individual participates in the subculture), intensity (the extent to which an individual has close friends within the subculture), and priority (the age at which an individual was first socialized into the subculture). However, duration (the length of time an individual been a part of the subculture) had no impact on support for kynd norms.

Sutherland's explanation of the learning process that leads to deviance had a substantial impact on subsequent theorizing about deviance. Gresham Sykes and David Matza's neutralization theory later highlighted and expanded upon one aspect of differential association theory.

Neutralization Theory: Rationalizing Deviance

Sykes and Matza (1957), like Sutherland, focused on criminal behaviour in the formulation of their theory, which was later appropriated for understanding the broader issue of deviance. They agreed with Edwin Sutherland's suggestion that deviance emerges as the result of a learning process in group interactions. However, the particular focus of their theory is on the nature of some of the *motives* that Sutherland referred to. According to Sykes and Matza, the most important motives that are learned, which subsequently open the door for deviant behaviour, are **techniques of neutralization**. Part of what deviant people learn are the rationalizations for the behaviour they engage in; by rationalizing their behaviour, they can convince themselves that what they are doing is not *really* wrong.

One of the techniques of neutralization is the **denial of responsibility**, which shifts the blame or responsibility off the individual and directs it elsewhere. The blame may be directed at other people, situations, or environments. Statements illustrating this technique of neutralization include "I didn't know there would be drugs there," "My father was never there for me when I was growing up," and "There's nothing else to do in a small town!"

The second technique of neutralization is the **denial of injury**. In this situation, the accused deviants express the perception that what they have done hurts or harms no one. For example, some people refer to "victimless crimes," such as drug use or prostitution. Similarly, a male cross-dresser or someone who dresses in "Goth" style may also say that what they do does not hurt anyone.

The **denial of the victim** is the third neutralization technique, where the perception is that the victim of the deviant's behaviour was somehow deserving of their fate. For example, Robin Hood was seen as a hero for robbing from the rich, who were perceived as corrupt and immoral and therefore deserved to be robbed. When Matthew Shepard, a young gay man, was murdered simply for being homosexual, protesters at his funeral carried signs saying "God hates fags." Matthew Shepard was perceived by some people as deserving his fate.

The fourth neutralization technique that Sykes and Matza refer to is **condemnation of the condemners**. This technique shifts the focus from the deviant's own behaviour to the deviant behaviour of others, especially people from the social groups that have pointed to this person's deviance. The condemners are accused of being hypocrites who are engaging in other forms of deviance, perhaps secretly. For example, although hippies in the 1960s were frequently accused of being deviant, they turned the tables on their accusers by pointing to all of the negative actions of "the establishment," such as destroying the environment for profit and being party to the Vietnam War. The condemners are thereby perceived as hypocrites who have no right to be criticizing anyone else's behaviours.

The final technique of neutralization is **appealing to higher loyalties**, where the deviant behaviour is justified as serving a higher purpose. In this situation, people acknowledge that they have violated norms, but in service of other more important norms. Someone might get into a violent fight to protect a friend. Someone might dress in punk attire in the name of individuality and freedom. A suicide bomber might walk into a shopping mall to punish evildoers and achieve spiritual salvation in the afterlife.

These five techniques of neutralization (since expanded to include a number of additional techniques), adopted through the kind of learning processes described earlier in differential association theory, are central to explaining why people engage in deviance. Only by being able to rationalize their actions do people become deviant. Techniques of neutralization have been explored in a variety of contexts. Sefiha (2012) finds that competitive cyclists who compete in events such as the Tour de France use a variety of techniques of neutralization when being accused of using performance-enhancing drugs. They

Cyclists who compete in events such as the Tour de France have long faced accusations of using performance-enhancing drugs. In 2012, Lance Armstrong was stripped of seven Tour de France titles for that reason.

condemn the condemners by pointing out that people throughout society use caffeine, aspirin, and drugs like Viagra to enhance certain types of performance. Furthermore, they accuse their condemners of being unhealthy "fat guys who watch football and smoke" (p. 227). Cyclists *appeal to higher loyalties*, indicating that performance-enhancing drugs are a necessary part of dedication to the sport; managers and teammates "would have looked at not taking drugs as a failure to give 100% to being a cyclist" (p. 231). By expressing skepticism about medical claims about the dangers of performance-enhancing drugs and by discounting those potential dangers relative to the dangerous racing conditions they always face, cyclists *deny injury* to themselves.

Techniques of neutralization have been found among numerous other groups as well, such as digital pirates (Steinmetz & Tunnell, 2013); "keener" students in university (Shoenberger, Heckert, & Heckert, 2012); the mothers of child beauty pageant contestants (Heltsley & Calhoun, 2003); and adolescents who engage in verbal/physical violence, their parents, and their school officials (Esala, 2013).

Social Learning Theory: Rewards, Punishments, and Imitation

Social learning theory highlights the role of learning processes not only in deviant behaviour but in behaviour more generally. According to these theorists (e.g., Bandura, 1986; Burgess & Akers, 1966; Akers, 1998), all of our behaviours can be explained in the same way.

In social learning theory, it is suggested that all behaviour is the result of *definitions* (attitudes about the acceptability of specific behaviours), *differential association* (with whom one associates), *imitation*, and *differential reinforcement* (rewards and punishments). It is related to the behaviourist theory of *instrumental conditioning*, which suggests that we are more likely to engage in behaviours we have been rewarded for (or that have been reinforced) in the past, and we are less likely to engage in behaviours that we have not been rewarded for or that we have been punished for in the past. Deviance first emerges from differential association and imitation, and then continues (or not) through differential reinforcement and definitions.

We can see principles of instrumental conditioning being used in parenting all the time: a child who misbehaves is spanked, is given a time out, has telephone privileges taken away, or is grounded, while a child who acts in accordance with the parents' wishes is given praise, attention, or perhaps an increase in allowance. In school, children are rewarded for behaving well and studying by getting good grades and perhaps special privileges (such as getting to help the teacher with special tasks after school).

Social learning theory goes a step further by saying that not only are our behaviours influenced by what we personally have been rewarded and punished for in the past, they are influenced by what we see other people being rewarded and punished for through the process of imitation or modelling. For example, if we hear Dad make a racist joke and see his friends laugh and show approval, we are more likely to act in similar ways and develop similar views. If Mom is bulimic and we see her rewarded with compliments on how beautiful she is, we are more likely to act in similar ways. Thus, people engage in deviance because they either have been rewarded for it in the past or have seen other people being rewarded for it (Bandura, 1986; Akers, 1977).

The role of social learning has been found with a wide range of deviant behaviours, including adolescent alcohol use (Benda, 1994), academic dishonesty among university students (Vowell & Chen, 2004), and property crime (Bruinsma, 1992). Most empirical research has directed its attention to these relatively minor acts of deviance and crime; research on more severe behaviours (e.g., violent crime) is less common and more inconsistent (Kubrin, Stucky, & Krohn, 2009). Earlier research suggested that differential reinforcement was particularly significant. However, a meta-analysis of more than 100 empirical studies of social learning finds that the effects of differential association and definitions are stronger and more consistent than the effects of differential reinforcement and imitation (Pratt et al., 2010).

Akers (1998, 2000, 2006) has recently modified his version of social learning theory to integrate structural factors as well, factors that learning theorists have been criticized for ignoring. He suggests that dimensions of the social structure create the differential contexts in which learning occurs for different people. These dimensions include *differential social organization* (a community's demographic characteristics), *differential location in the social structure* (an individual's defining characteristics such as ethnicity, gender, and educational attainment), *theoretically defined structural variables* (e.g., anomie, conflict, social disorganization), and *differential social location* (an individual's membership in different social groups, such as peer groups). He goes a step further, stating that social learning theory should be integrated with other theories that focus primarily on structural factors (Kubrin, Stucky, & Krohn, 2009). Akers's social learning theory has been extensively applied to adult and youth crime, police misconduct, and more (Chappell & Piquero, 2004).

Limitations of Learning Theories

The principles of social learning theory appeal to most of us at a common sense level; it is fairly easy for us to see reinforcement, punishment, and modelling everywhere around us and in our own lives. Like neutralization theory and differential association theory, social learning theory draws attention to processes of learning as key to explaining why people engage in deviance. Despite the differences in the way each of these theories explains the learning process that leads to deviance, they all point to learning as the answer to the question of why people act the way they do—why people become deviant.

However, learning theories have also been subjected to critique. Methodological criticisms have been directed at differential association theory, with critics pointing to the difficulties in arriving at a "tally" of the number of deviant and nondeviant associations in an individual's life. Furthermore, critics suggest that "the theory is riddled with escape clauses and qualifications that diminish its power to predict" (Downes & Rock, 2003, p. 74). Priority, intensity, frequency, and duration each have an influence on deviant or conforming outcomes. But which takes precedence—the parenting an individual received in early childhood (i.e., priority), which may have involved more "conforming" definitions, or the emotional attachment that a police officer has to the police subculture in which "deviant" definitions may contribute to police misconduct (Chappell & Piquero, 2004)?

Neutralization theory has been criticized for what it *hasn't* explored—how techniques of neutralization may vary across different types of deviant behaviours or across different normative contexts. Research using neutralization theory has responded to these critiques, finding variations in the specific neutralization techniques used by different types of white-collar or workplace criminals (Benson, 1985; Hollinger, 1991), as well as the influence of normative context on neutralization techniques. For instance, Buzzell (2005) compared the use of specific techniques of neutralization among two groups of people purchasing fireworks for Independence Day in the United States. One group lived in an area where fireworks were legal, and a second group lived in an area where fireworks were recently banned. Those living in the area where fireworks had been banned were more likely to agree with statements like, "most fireworks people use really don't hurt anyone" (denial of injury) and "if people in my neighborhood are worried about noise or harm from fireworks they should take responsibility to protect themselves or be out of town that evening" (p. 35) (denial of the victim).

Neutralization theory has also been critiqued on the basis of its reasoning and methodology. Although the theory states that techniques of neutralization are used *prior* to committing an act, most research has looked at the techniques being used by people *after* an act has occurred (e.g., convicted shoplifters). Thus, the only conclusions that can be legitimately made are that these are post-act techniques of justification rather than techniques of neutralization that contribute to the act in the first place (Piquero, Tibbets, & Blankenship, 2005; Lyman, 2000). However, Hirschi (cited in Cromwell & Thurman, 2003) suggests that a post-act technique of justification may become a pre-act technique of neutralization in the future, such that the two are not necessarily mutually exclusive. Other research attempts to overcome this critique using a vignette design: participants read about a hypothetical situation and then identify how they would act in that situation and why. For example, MBA students referred to several neutralization techniques when explaining why they would take a particular action in a hypothetical situation that involved distributing/recalling a drug being investigated by the FDA for causing harm to consumers (Piquero, Tibbets, & Blankenship, 2005). Participants who said they would continue to distribute that drug claimed that the government exaggerates the dangers (denial of injury), suggested that government regulations impede business (condemnation of the condemners), and subscribed to the expression "let the buyer beware" (denial of the victim).

The final set of positivist theories that have frequently been used to explain deviance—*social control theories*—provide yet another way of understanding the origins of deviance based on the objectivist conceptualization of the nature of deviance.

TIME TO REVIEW

Learning Objective 4

- What are the core assumptions of learning theories?

- How is deviance learned according to (1) differential association theory, (2) neutralization theory, and (3) social learning theory?

- What type of empirical support exists for each of the learning theories?

Learning Objective 6

- What criticisms have been directed at Sutherland's differential association theory and Sykes and Matza's neutralization theory?

- How have empirical researchers using these theories responded to critiques?

Social Control Theories: What Restrains Most of Us From Deviance?

Social control theories focus on a different type of question than other positivist theories. While other positivist theorists direct their attention to why some people become deviant, social control theorists direct their attention to why not all people become deviant. They suggest that deviant behaviour is inherently attractive, exciting, and appealing. Given the appeal of deviant behaviour, it is only through higher levels of social control that some of us do not become deviant.

Social Bonds Theory: Social Bonds Restrain Us

The most widely used social control theory in explanations of deviance has been Travis Hirschi's (1969) social bonds theory. His argument is that four different types of social bonds rein most of us in, restraining us from deviance.

The first bond is that of **attachment** to parents, teachers, and peers. Hirschi suggests that the greater our level of emotional attachment to others, the more bound we are to conformity. Conversely, a lack of emotional attachments leaves us freer to engage in deviance. The *type* of person to whom we are attached is not important; rather, it is the mere fact of having an emotional attachment itself that restrains us from deviance.

The second bond is **commitment** to conformity. Being committed to conventional activities like school, work, organized sports, or childrearing gives us more of a stake in the conventional world; if we were to engage in deviance, we would threaten our investments in conventionality and have too much to lose. In contrast, people who have little invested in conventional activities have less to lose by engaging in deviance.

The third social bond is **involvement** in conventional activities. In other words, people who are highly involved in such activities in terms of time simply do not have any extra time for deviance. People who have substantial unused time on their hands are more likely to be drawn to the appeal of deviance—"idle hands are the devil's workshop."

The last bond is **belief** in the norms, values, and assumptions that compose the conventional world. Holding such beliefs bonds people to the conventional world, while not holding such beliefs loosens the restraints from deviance. The interaction of these four types of social bonds determines the extent to which individuals will be restrained, or fail to be restrained, from the appeal of the deviant world.

Social bonds theory was initially applied to the study of delinquency. However, it has been successfully applied to other behaviours as well, such as the use of marijuana, cigarettes, and alcohol (Hawdon, 1996; Massey & Krohn, 1986; Marcos, Bahr, & Johnson, 1986), as well as sexual behaviours. Lauritsen (1994) finds some support for social bonds theory in the sexual behaviour of white adolescents. White females who have high educational aspirations (commitment) and who place a high value on marriage and parenthood in the future (belief) are less likely to be sexually active. White males who say they are close to their families (attachment) and who place a high value on marriage and parenthood in the future (belief) are also less likely to be sexually active. Social bonds have less of an effect on the sexual activity of black females (for whom *strain* has a greater influence), and no effect at all on the sexual activity of black males.

Life trajectories can change the nature and extent of social bonds. As one makes the transition from adolescence to adulthood, different types of social bonds can emerge,

> ### Ask Yourself
> Try to apply social bonds theory to your own life. How many people would you say you have an emotional attachment to? What might you lose from your life if you engaged in deviance? How much of your time is spent engaging in conventional activities?

which may further restrain individuals from deviance. A recent study of adults in their 20s finds that social bonds are significantly related to a lack of criminality (Salvatore & Taniguchi, 2012). Attachment, commitment, and belief were especially important. Religious participation, attachment to parents, property ownership, marriage, parenthood, and job satisfaction were all associated with lower rates of criminality. However, although job satisfaction was important, the number of hours worked per week (as a measure of involvement) was not significant.

Self-Control Theory: We Restrain Ourselves

Although Hirschi initially focused on the relationship between social bonds and deviance, more recently he has collaborated with Michael Gottfredson on what was initially called the *general theory of crime* (Gottfredson & Hirschi, 1990). Here they suggest that **self-control** is central to explaining why some people are predisposed to deviant acts while others are not.

Low self-control is characterized by impulsivity, a preference for simple tasks, risk-seeking, a preference for physical tasks, self-centredness, and a quick temper (Grasmick, Tittle, Bursik, & Arneklev, 1993). It is the result of ineffective parenting—an absence of attachment, weak supervision, and a lack of discipline when deviant behaviours occur. Although it may be ameliorated to some extent by other influences in a child's life, it remains relatively stable throughout life. Whether in childhood, adolescence, or mid-adulthood, individuals with low self-control are more likely to engage in deviant behaviours when the opportunity presents itself than are individuals with higher levels of self-control.

Although self-control theory is relatively recent, a considerable amount of research has been done testing its propositions, with mixed results (Nakhaie, Silverman, & LaGrange, 2000). Research has directed its attention primarily to criminal behaviours, as well as "analogous behaviours" (Kubrin, Stucky, & Krohn, 2009) such as substance use, risky driving, truancy/resistance to school, and adolescent sexual activity (Stylianou, 2002; Nakhaie, Silverman, & LaGrange, 2000; Hope & Chapple, 2005). More recently, some empirical research has expanded its focus to other types of behaviours, such as binging/purging, relational aggression (e.g., spreading rumours about someone), and criminal victimization (Harrison, Jones, & Sullivan, 2008; Schreck, Stewart, & Fisher, 2006).

Jones and Quisenberry (2004) have found that low self-control is related to a wide range of anti-social deviant behaviours connected to risky driving (driving above the speed limit, following vehicles too closely, driving without a seatbelt, driving while drinking) and risky sex (sex with unfamiliar partners, sex without condoms, sex without any contraception, number of sexual partners). They also found that it is related to the experience of or the intention to engage in thrill/adventure-seeking behaviours, such as rock climbing, skydiving, whitewater rafting, and more. However, they found that the same individuals did not engage in both anti-social deviant behaviours *and* thrill-seeking behaviours. Rather, low self-control led some people into risky driving and risky sex, but led others into socially acceptable forms of risk taking, which the theory is unable to explain.

Jones and Quisenberry suggest that it is necessary to integrate self-control theory with other theories to explain this phenomenon. For example, certain social bonds, such as attachment to family or commitment to conventionality, may translate low self-control into socially acceptable forms of thrill-seeking behaviour.

Other research has also integrated self-control theory with social bonds theory. Higgins, Wolfe, and Marcum (2008) found that both social bonds (in terms of commitment to school and attachment to parents) and self-control were associated with the illegal downloading of music and software among university students. Self-control has also been integrated with general strain theory. Although most research shows that self-control is not associated with deviant responses to strain in the Western world, among high school students in Hong Kong, higher levels of self-control mediate the effects of strain on a wide range of deviant behaviours—breaking curfew, truancy, smoking, drinking, gambling, property damage, gang activity, and robbery (Wai Ting Cheung & Cheung, 2010).

Limitations of Social Control Theories

Social control theories, by asking why we do not all engage in deviance instead of asking only why some people do engage in deviance, provide us with a unique standpoint from which to study deviance. However, social control theories have been subject to criticism.

Self-control theory has been criticized for the manner in which self-control is defined and measured. First, it is perceived as tautological (Akers, 1991). The origins of the tautology lie within the development of the concept itself. That is, in defining low self-control, Gottfredson and Hirschi (1990) looked to the characteristics of criminal behaviour. For instance, because they considered most criminal acts to be impulsive and resulting in some type of gain for the criminal, they concluded that low self-control includes impulsivity and self-centredness. Particular pieces of research have since been critiqued for tautology at the empirical level as well, by measuring self-control behaviourally. In one study that applied self-control theory to impaired driving (a form of "risky" driving), self-control was measured by the occurrence of other forms of risky driving (driving without a seatbelt, having driven after drinking in the past). They found that people who engage in other forms of risky driving (and who therefore are low in self-control) are more likely to drive while impaired; risky driving behaviours are treated as both the cause and the effect (Keane, Maxim, & Teevan, cited in Kubrin, Stucky, & Krohn, 2009).

In response to these perceived problems in measurement, others have measured self-control psychologically. Using this approach, low self-control is treated as a personality trait and is determined via personality inventories (e.g., Grasmick, Tittle, Bursik, & Arneklev, 1993). This has become the dominant means of defining and measuring self-control in contemporary research, although Hirschi has expressed objections about the movement away from a sociological paradigm toward a more psychological paradigm. However, the results of research applying self-control theory are similar, regardless of which type of measure is used (Kubrin, Stucky, & Krohn, 2009).

Both self-control theory and social bonds theory have been criticized for ignoring the role of peer associations in deviant outcomes. Looking at peer associations within the context of social bonds theory, Erickson, Crosnoe, and Dornbusch (2000) try to explain adolescent delinquency and substance use. They conclude that social bonds influence these behaviours via deviant peer associations and susceptibility to deviant peers; that is, adolescents who have strong social bonds are less likely to associate with deviant peers and are less susceptible to influence even if they do associate with deviant peers. Looking at peer associations within the context of self-control theory, Jones and Quisenberry (2004) suggest that associating with deviant peers may explain why some people with low self-control commit anti-social acts (e.g., risky driving), while others engage in adventure-seeking behaviours (e.g., skydiving). Longshore, Chang, Hsieh, and Messina (2004) propose a more complex relationship between self-control, social bonds, peer associations, and drug use among adults. In their final model, they conclude that low self-control results in associations with deviant peers and weakened social bonds, which result in drug use.

Although social bonds theory and self-control theory have been subjected to critique, research that integrates these theories with each other or with additional theories (e.g., general strain theory) has had some explanatory success, illustrating the role that theoretical integration can play in better explaining deviant behaviour and enhancing our understanding of deviance.

TIME TO REVIEW

Learning Objective 5

- What are the core assumptions of Hirschi's social bonds theory, and what type of support does it have?

- What are the core assumptions of Gottfredson and Hirschi's self-control theory, and what type of support does it have?

Learning Objective 6

- What criticisms have been directed at social control theories, and how have researchers responded?

The diverse positivist theories of deviance that have been addressed in this chapter share one goal: trying to explain why people act in particular ways. Functionalist theories, such as Durkheim's anomie theory, Merton's strain theory, Cloward and Ohlin's differential opportunity theory, Agnew's general strain theory, and Cohen's status frustration theory, direct their attention to the role that the structure of society itself plays in the emergence of deviance. Learning theories, such as Sutherland's differential association theory, Sykes and Matza's neutralization theory, and social learning theory point to the centrality of learning processes in the emergence of deviance. In other words, people learn to be deviant from others around them. Social control theories, like Hirschi's social bonds theory, explain why not all of us become deviant. They point to social bonds that restrain us from giving in to the appeal of deviance. Gottfredson and Hirschi's self-control theory addresses the influence that parenting patterns have on the development of self-control.

Functional, learning, and social control theories each shine a light on a particular aspect of social life in their efforts to explain deviance. Despite their differential areas of focus, and despite the diversity within each of these theories, there is a commonality: They are all positivist theories that seek to explain why some people act in deviant ways and others do not.

Positivist theories dominated academic understandings of deviance for many years. However, as more subjective views of deviance developed and become more widespread, different types of theories became useful. Just as certain types of theory correspond with more objective views of deviance, other kinds of theory correspond with more subjective ways of looking at deviance—that is, interpretive and critical theories. These theories will be addressed in the next chapter.

Exercise Your Mind

How would each of the theories in this chapter explain deviance or conformity as it exists in your own life (or the life of someone you know)? What facets of your experience are left unexplained by each theory? If you had to select the one theory that best explains deviance or conformity in your own life, which would it be? Why?

CHAPTER SUMMARY

- Many different theories are used in the sociology of deviance, corresponding to the various ways one can look at deviance. Each theory shines a spotlight on a particular aspect of deviance and provides one way of understanding it. (1)

- People with more *objective* views of deviance, who are interested in why deviant people become that way, find *positivist* theories to be the most useful. Positivist sociological theories are modelled after theories in the natural sciences as tools for mastering the natural or social environment. (1, 2)

- People with more *subjective* views of deviance find *interpretive* and *critical* theories to be the most useful for understanding societal perceptions of and reactions to particular acts, as well as the role played by power in these perceptions and reactions. (1)

- *Functionalist theories* dominated positivist understandings of deviance for many years, suggesting that problems with the social structure cause some people to become deviant. Durkheim directed his attention to *anomie* as the root cause of deviance; Merton suggested a strain between *institutionalized goals* and *legitimate means* as the cause; Cloward and Ohlin pointed to differential access to *legitimate* and *illegitimate opportunities*; Robert Agnew emphasized the relationship between strain and *negative affect*; and Albert Cohen focused on *status frustration*. (3)

- Functionalist theories have been criticized for their tautological and teleological logic, their conservative ideology, and their androcentric bias. A number of functionalist theories have also been criticized for treating deviance as a lower-class phenomenon and ignoring gender and race. Empirical and theoretical research has responded to these criticisms, exploring noncriminal forms of deviance across classes and analyzing gender and race in a variety of situations. (6)

- *Learning theories* explain deviance as a result of individual learning processes. *Differential association theory* suggests that we learn techniques and motives within intimate groups that lead us either into deviance or into conformity. According to *neutralization theory*, the key process is the learning of rationalizations that enable people to think that what they are doing is not really wrong. *Social learning theory* points to the importance of differential reinforcement in particular. (4)

- Some empirical research supports learning theories, and the principles of learning theories are easily visible to the layperson. However, learning theories have been critiqued as well. Methodological critiques are the most common, but recent empirical and theoretical research has responded to these criticisms, particularly with neutralization theory. (6)

- *Social control theories* include Hirschi's *social bonds theory*, which asks why not all of us become deviant rather than why some people do become deviant. He suggests that people with strong social bonds are restrained from deviant behaviour. Gottfredson and Hirschi's *general theory of crime* or *self-control theory* emphasizes the role of ineffective parenting in the development of low levels of *self-control*. (5)

- As the most recently developed social control theory, self-control theory has been subjected to the most criticism. It has been criticized for its measurement of self-control and its assumption that self-control remains stable throughout life. Both control theories have been criticized for ignoring the importance of peer associations, but recent research has responded to this critique by integrating social control theories with learning theories. (6)

MySearchLab®

◉─Watch Go to MySearchLab to listen to the audio clip called "Crime Study Challenges Past Assumptions (on Deviance)".

Apply What You Know: How do the findings of Dr. Earles's study on urban crime contradict sociological theories of deviance? Can you think of some explanations to account for Dr. Earles's results?

MySearchLab with eText offers you access to an online interactive version of the text, extensive help with your writing and research projects, and provides round-the-clock access to credible and reliable source material.

Chapter 3

Explaining Deviance: The Perception, Reaction, and Power

Learning Objectives

After reading this chapter, you should be able to

1   Explain how interpretive theories approach the topic of deviance, and describe how symbolic interactionism gave rise to other interpretive theories of deviance.

2   Describe such concepts as labelling, stigmatization, transition from primary to secondary deviance, the dramatization of evil, deviance as a master status, and the deviant career.

3   Identify the limitations of interpretive theories and the theoretical/empirical responses to those limitations.

4   Explain how critical theories approach the topic of deviance.

5   Describe critical theories like conflict theories, power-reflexive theories, feminist theories, and postmodern theories.

6   Identify the limitations of critical theories, and the theoretical/empirical responses to those limitations.

Nonpositivist Theorizing

Philosopher Friedrich Nietzsche (2004 [1886]) claimed that "there are no moral phenomenon [sic], but only a moral interpretation of phenomena." This claim emphasizes *interpretation* as the source of understanding, suggesting that moral codes emerge from a process of interpretation rather than from any type of absolute morality. This signals a substantial shift away from the positivist approach to theorizing that was addressed in Chapter 2. Positivist theories shine their spotlight on the actor or the act and try to explain why some people behave in deviant ways while others do not. Affiliated with more objective ways of understanding deviance, positivist theories are based on the assumption that deviance can be identified in some clear-cut way, and once identified, an explanation for that outcome can be sought. The strengths of positivist theories of deviance lie in their search for causation, which facilitates identification of the most effective means of achieving fixed ends (Ashley & Orenstein, 2001). For instance, preventing youth crime or treating alcoholism is most effective when based on an understanding of how people enter criminal activity or begin to abuse alcohol.

However, more subjective views of deviance claim that we cannot know deviance when we see it and instead must be told that a behaviour or characteristic is deviant. Consequently, the associated theories do not look at the violation of social expectations, but rather at the nature of the social expectations themselves (McCaghy, Capron, & Jamieson, 2003). The interest is not in the act, but in the perceptions of and reactions to the act as well as in the role of power in influencing these perceptions and reactions. Deviance is seen as constructed through the social typing process, whereby people have descriptive labels attached to them, are evaluated or judged on the basis of those labels, and then are treated in certain ways because of prior descriptions and evaluations (Rubington & Weinberg, 2008). When society, rather than deviant people, is held under a microscope—when the interest is in understanding social processes rather than specific people—the positivist interest in explaining the acquisition of deviant behaviour becomes less relevant. In its place, those theories that are often categorized as *interpretive* or *critical* are the ones that can best explain the social construction of deviance.

Interpretive theories explain "something that might be unique and unrepeatable" (Ashley & Orenstein, 2001, p. 31). This stands in contrast to positivist theories that seek to identify generalizable, immutable laws that govern the environment. Interpretive theorists claim that the only "reality" is that which emerges through reciprocal, intersubjective understanding between people, and as such these theorists focus on the meanings that emerge from interactions between people who are engaged in symbolic dialogue. In other words, interpretive theories emphasize how people develop understandings of the world around them, other people, and themselves. **Critical theories** have a self-reflective value-orienting foundation (Ashley & Orenstein, 2001), that is, an underlying interest in emancipation and working toward social justice. Their focus is on the power relations that underlie the creation of social rules. Taken together, critical and interpretive theories are useful in explaining those aspects of deviance that more subjective-oriented deviance specialists are interested in: the social construction of deviance.

A combination of several interpretive and critical theories is associated with the contextual social constructionism that informs more subjective understandings of deviance. One of the most well-known deviance constructionists, Joel Best (2003), claims that labelling theory (which he equates with interpretive theory more generally) and conflict theory (one of the core critical theories) make up the approach referred to as "constructionism." Other researchers suggest that elements of social learning theory (discussed in the previous chapter), symbolic interactionism, ethnomethodology, feminist theories, and postmodernist theories constitute the constructionist approach as well, even though they are all considered distinct theoretical perspectives in their own rights (Nelson & Robinson, 2002; Beaman, 2000; Peace, Beaman, & Sneddon, 2000). The boundaries among these various interpretive and critical theories are certainly more ambiguous than is the case with positivist theories, and they can be quite complementary to each other as well.

Interpretive Theories: Understandings of "Deviance" and "Normality"

As we have already noted, a wide range of specific theories are used to explain the social construction of deviance and normality. In the remainder of this chapter, the interpretive and critical theories that will be reviewed are those most commonly used to explain the construction of deviance and those that have had significant influences on the sociology of deviance as a discipline.

Symbolic Interactionism: Communication Creates Understanding

Symbolic interactionism, or what some people simply refer to as "interactionism," is the foundation for the range of interpretive theories used to study deviance; in fact, some deviance specialists (e.g., Deutschmann, 2002) equate interactionism with interpretive theories and with constructionism. This section of the chapter will begin with a broad discussion of the core assumptions of symbolic interactionism and will then progress to some of the more specific interpretive theories of deviance: labelling theories and the theory of the deviant career.

From a symbolic interactionist perspective (Blumer, 1986), society is created by social interaction, which occurs via communication through symbols. In other words, society is made up of people in constant communication with each other, and this is the source of all meaning and understanding. All communication is symbolic in nature. The symbols that constitute the English alphabet serve as the foundation for written and verbal communication in English. For example, in English, we use the symbols C-A-T to refer to a small furry creature that meows and grabs your toes under the covers when you are trying to sleep. Nonverbal communication, through avenues such as gestures and facial expressions, is symbolic as well. For example, when you have cut someone off in traffic and you are subsequently shown that person's middle finger, you know precisely what message that person is communicating to you. Clothing serves as a form of symbolic communication as well. For instance, when you are going to a job interview, do you wear sweatpants and a stained T-shirt? Why not? You probably think that would communicate the wrong message to the interviewer. All of these forms of symbolic communication constitute the basic foundation of society, according to symbolic interactionists.

However, symbolic communication is complex and nuanced, such that the same symbols may have different meanings in different contexts. The symbols C-A-T, within the context of a construction site where a new parking lot is being built, is more likely to refer to a piece of equipment that moves piles of dirt than a furry animal that meows. Add the symbols T-Y onto the end, and the message changes once again—referring to someone who says nasty things about others behind their backs and, interacting with gender stereotypes, is more likely to be used in reference to a woman than a man.

Via these avenues of communication, we create meaning in our lives and an understanding of the world around us, of other people, and of ourselves. Because each of us has a distinct set of interactions during the course of our lives, the way each of us understands the world varies to some extent. Thus, for example, my interpretation of a particular movie or novel may be different from your interpretation of that same movie or novel. Both of us may watch the same movie and, because of our different interpretations, engage in a resounding debate afterward. Similarly, the way you choose to act as a student in a university classroom may be different than the way someone else chooses to act in that same environment.

Various processes contribute to the meanings and understandings each of us creates. One of these processes is that of **role taking**. By vicariously placing ourselves in the roles of others, we try to see the world from their respective points of view and determine our own attitudes and actions accordingly. In that regard, when you are going for a job interview, you try to imagine the position of the interviewers and what they are looking for in a job candidate when you are deciding what to wear and how to answer their questions.

A second process that contributes to the way we develop meaning is through the role of the **looking-glass self**. When determining how to look or act and how we feel about ourselves, we imagine how we appear to other people and what they think of that appearance. What we imagine other people think of us influences what we think about ourselves and how we look or act. These "Others" may be *significant others* or a *generalized other*. **Significant others** are those people who are important to us—whose perceptions and reactions matter to us. What these significant others think about you has a substantial impact on your actions—you might think, "What would my grand-mother/husband/boss/favourite professor say if I did that?!" The **generalized other** refers to "other people" more generally, almost as a generic person: "What would people think if I dressed like that?!"

Through the influences of role taking, the looking-glass self, significant others, and the generalized other, we come to understand the world in particular ways, understand our places in that world, and choose our appearances and actions (see Box 3.1). The *Ask Yourself* exercise further explores these processes.

As applied to the concepts of deviance and normality, these processes contribute to our understanding of the "rules" in society, our perceptions of and reactions to ourselves and others on the basis of those rules, and whether we identify ourselves as followers of those rules or as rule breakers. It is also through these processes that individuals who share similar perceptions come together and form groups based on those shared perceptions. These groups may then attempt to influence the perceptions of deviance and normality held by others. And because meanings and understandings vary among people based on their own interactions and communications, the "deviance dance" emerges—some individuals or groups will try to socially type certain people as deviant, while other individuals or groups will argue that those same people are normal.

Deviance specialists who hold an interactionist view may focus on many different aspects of this deviance dance. What sociocultural and individual forces influence people's understandings of deviance? What leads some people to join groups that consist of others with similar understandings? How do participants in the deviance dance understand and attribute meaning to their roles in the social construction process? How do people and groups try to influence the perceptions of other people and groups? The specific questions that can be asked from within this approach are almost endless. However, what they have in common is the foundational assumption of the symbolic interactionist perspective: We develop understanding and attribute meaning to the world around us and to ourselves on the basis of interactions we have had with other people in our lives.

Labelling Theories: Becoming an Outsider

Arising from these core assumptions are a number of specific concepts and theories used to understand the social construction of deviance. **Labelling theories** all address the very same process but use slightly different language. The process they analyze is that of being labelled deviant and the consequences of that label. When individuals are "caught" at deviance and

Box 3.1

The Meaning of Being Straightedge

The emphasis on interpretation and meaning that underlies the interactionist approach is vital to researchers who study various subcultures or lifestyle groups. Research on groups such as nudists (Weinberg, 1967), gangs (Jankowski, 1991), and people with tattoos (DeMello, 2000) uses interviews with members of those groups to explore what that lifestyle means to them. Recently, the straightedge lifestyle has been the focus of this type of research attention as well (Atkinson, 2003a, 2003b; Irwin, 1999; Wood, 2001).

To the outside observer, a straightedger may look like any other punk rocker—Doc Martens boots, shaved heads, mohawk hairstyles, torn clothing. And, indeed, the straightedge movement did emerge from the punk rock scene. However, there are distinct characteristics of straightedgers that make them very different from other punk rockers and from mainstream society. The lifestyle is referred to as *straight*edge because of its ideological epicentre: a clean, straight, physically pure life. Disturbed by the hedonistic, self-indulgent nature of modern life, straightedgers developed an oppositional value system based on abstaining from alcohol, drugs, and casual (or even premarital) sex. Some members of this lifestyle group abstain from caffeine, prescription drugs, and over-the-counter medication as well. This value system does not come out of any strongly held religious belief system, as you might expect, but rather from their personal observations of where self-indulgence leads people. Straightedgers have seen how one night of "fun" can ruin people's lives—from drug overdoses, drunk driving, sexually transmitted diseases, and unwanted pregnancies to the many other "stupid" things people frequently do while intoxicated. In addition to

ruining people's lives, these hedonistic behaviours are perceived by straightedgers as holding people back from personal fulfillment and self-awareness, as well as having a negative impact on society. Controlling their bodies through physical purity and body modification (such as tattooing) is a form of resistance to the self-indulgent wider society.

© Brett Marshall/KRT/Newscom

There is, however, diversity within straightedge; the meaning of being straightedge varies somewhat among individuals and among subgroups. In the broader pursuit of physical purity and resistance to mainstream society, some individuals incorporate other behaviours—vegetarianism, anti-racist activism, militant animal rights activism, or violence directed at people who are engaging in the behaviours seen as "deviant" by straightedgers (e.g., consuming drugs). Those straightedgers who engage in violence against others to spread their message, or violence in pursuit of militant animal rights activism, face the disdain of other straightedgers—within the straightedge lifestyle itself they are socially typed as "deviant" by those who wish to distance themselves (and the larger straightedge lifestyle) from extremists.

Being straightedge has different meanings for different people, and symbolic interactionist ideas allow us to understand why.

given a deviant label, people start to treat them differently, in a way that corresponds to that label. Over time, being treated differently has an impact on how those labelled individuals perceive themselves; their own identities begin to incorporate that label. Finally, as their identities change, their subsequent behaviours and life choices are affected as well.

Tannenbaum (1938) was one of the first scholars to analyze this process, in terms of the role that **tagging** plays in the **dramatization of evil**. He suggested that as observers in society, we may initially identify a particular act as deviant or evil ("tagging") but soon come to generalize that judgment to the person as a whole ("dramatization of evil")—in other words, it is no longer just the initial act that is considered evil, but rather the person is considered evil. This process results in changes in that person's self-image and identity, whereby the identity comes to be built around the label and subsequent behaviours correspond to that label and new identity.

Lemert (1951) used the term "labelling" rather than "tagging" in what is perhaps the most well-known version of labelling theory. Lemert distinguished between **primary deviance** and **secondary deviance**. He suggested that we all engage in little acts of rule breaking that are seldom noticed and rarely caught by others (primary deviance). Even though we all engage in occasional rule breaking, few of us build a lifestyle around it (secondary deviance). Getting caught sets into motion a series of processes that result in the transition from primary deviance to secondary deviance. Someone who is not caught in an act of deviance may eventually just move on.

For instance, as a child or a teenager you may have shoplifted an item of low value from a neighbourhood convenience store, but it is likely that most of you did that only once or twice and eventually grew out of that "phase." However, Lemert suggested that the mere act of being caught changes the way others see you and subsequently changes the way you see yourself. That is, if you were caught shoplifting and then arrested, the police saw you as a "thief." If convicted in youth court, you were officially labelled a "thief" and a "delinquent." Your parents may have then considered you to be a "thief." As a result of this process of labelling, you come to understand and identify yourself as a "thief" or a "delinquent"—one who commits crimes.

Howard Becker (1963) elaborated on the processes involved in the transition to secondary deviance. He suggested that once a person is labelled deviant, that label becomes that person's master status. A **master status** is a characteristic by which others identify you. For example, you may immediately identify others on the basis of age ("teenager"), sex ("girl"), or class ("rich"). A deviant label assumes the level of master status; if you have been officially given the label of "thief," others will identify you as "that thief" rather than as "Sam."

Once a deviant label becomes a master status, implications for a person's daily life emerge. Certain life opportunities will be blocked, in that the legitimate, "normal" world will no longer be as accepting. With the conforming world no longer as accepting, the only place to turn may be the deviant world. For example, if you were convicted of theft as a youth, the way you were treated at school may have changed. Perhaps certain peer groups began to exclude you. Maybe the girl you were dating broke up with you because she did not want to tarnish her own reputation. The teacher who had offered you a baby-sitting job on Wednesday nights with her children may have revoked the offer. Soon, you began to feel like an "outsider" (which happens to be the title of Becker's 1963 book).

At that point, it may have been that only other kids who had been labelled "troublemakers" or "delinquents" were willing to spend time with you, and that became the only world in which you felt accepted. And before long, you began to see yourself as a "troublemaker"—your identity gradually changed and your behaviour soon followed. This process of exclusion from the conforming world and acceptance in the deviant world is what Becker suggested led to a lifestyle built around deviance—and what Lemert (1951) called *secondary deviance*.

Other deviance specialists have referred to this process of exclusion, of becoming an outsider, as **stigmatization** (Goffman, 1963). A proponent of the sociological school of thought known as **dramaturgy**, Goffman (1959) suggested that social life is analogous to being in the theatre. In our lives, we are all assigned or assume particular "roles" to play—university student, daughter, soccer player, smoker. When we are in front of certain groups of people, we play our roles in certain ways; we control the images that we present and the messages that we convey to the audience by bringing out our **front-stage selves**. When we leave the front stage and retreat with select groups of people who are a part of our private lives, we allow our **back-stage selves** to emerge; that is, we no longer feel like we have to play a particular role, but instead can be our true selves. If the role we have assumed is deviant in nature (i.e., we have had a deviant label attached to us), managing the impressions others have of us is that much more difficult. No matter what we try to do, others will still perceive us as deviant because we have been stigmatized—we have a **spoiled identity**.

There are a number of ways we can respond to that spoiled identity (i.e., engage in **identity management** or **impression management**). Stigma management techniques have been studied in a variety of populations, including female exotic dancers (Thompson, Harred, & Burks, 2003) and former street prostitutes and drug addicts (McCray, Wesely, & Rasche, 2011). Since 9/11, people of Middle-Eastern descent living in the United States have had to engage in greater stigma management as well (Marvasti, 2008). Some individuals use *humour*, such as when they are asked about their names (when a woman named Ladan was seriously asked by a customer about whether she was related to Bin Laden, she joked that he was, in fact, coming to dinner). Others use *educational* techniques, such as explaining to others the ways in which Islamic doctrine actually promotes peace, or answering questions about clothing. When subjected to negative treatment, some engage in *defiance*, standing up to the perpetrator. In similar situations, others will engage in *cowering*, such as agreeing to leave the elevator when challenged by a fellow passenger.

Ask Yourself

In your own life, has there ever been anything about yourself that you have tried to hide from the outside world because of your fear of stigmatization (such as a criminal past, substance abuse problem, or learning disability)? Have you ever restricted your interactions to people you knew would be accepting of you, people you knew would be able to understand you? Have you ever proudly displayed an aspect of yourself that you know many people in society consider to be deviant? What are the implications of these different approaches to stigma management?

Finally, Marvasti finds that many try to *pass* as non-Muslim (e.g., by changing clothing, accessories, or hair), or even as non-Middle-Eastern (e.g., by getting a licence plate with an Italian flag). A stigma must be managed on a daily basis, and different individuals will use diverse techniques to do so.

In an analysis of male sex workers in Hong Kong, Kong (2009) finds that stigma management techniques not only reduce the stigma of sex work, but also serve as gender strategies to negotiate respectable and responsible masculinity. Male sex workers describe the stigma they face. Sex work is perceived as immoral, the result of either a lack of choice or a bad choice, and dirty or diseased. For male sex workers, it is also perceived as demasculinizing—illustrative of female passivity rather than male agency. The men engage in a number of techniques to simultaneously reduce the stigma of their work and negotiate an acceptable hegemonic masculinity within Chinese culture. First, they reframe their job titles to reduce the stigma of immorality. They reject the title "prostitute" or "duck" in favour of "male entertainer" or someone who works in "public relations" (p. 731). Kong points out that the reframing of job titles is common when men hold traditionally feminine jobs; for example, "secretary" is reframed as "administrative assistant." Second, male sex workers reaffirm their agency, emphasizing that they made a rational choice to enter the occupation. Some made the choice to increase their incomes and achieve financial independence, while others made the choice to experiment sexually; both rationales meet the expectations of acceptable masculinity. Third, these men also emphasize the fact that success in their line of work is not only dependent on physical attractiveness, but also on quality skills such as communication and negotiation. Fourth, they point out the variety of ways in which their sex work is a better way to earn money than the regular full-time jobs they have had in office work, restaurants, or manual labour. Finally, they highlight their safe sexual practices (i.e., using condoms) as indicative of the "work ethic" all men are supposed to have in their occupations. Through these techniques, they reduce the stigma of sex work in general and of *male* sex work in particular.

Although Goffman's work on stigmatization emphasizes the negative impact of stigma, there are potentially positive consequences of stigmatization in certain situations. Braithwaite (2000) postulates that unlike **disintegrative shaming** (wherein deviantized persons are rejected by the community), **reintegrative shaming** is an effective treatment for criminal behaviour. With reintegrative shaming, the criminal is stigmatized, or shamed, for the criminal act, but it is a temporary stigma; the criminal is shown that leaving criminality behind will result in being fully accepted back into the community. Research with former psychiatric patients has also found that being labelled can have a wide range of positive consequences, including enhancing personal growth, bringing families closer together, and exempting such individuals from some of the demands and responsibilities of daily life (Herman & Miall, 1990).

Early interactionists, and particularly early labelling theorists, frequently painted a picture of the labelled deviant as a powerless, passive recipient of a socially constructed label that subsequently had irreversible consequences for the deviant's life. However, some deviance specialists have emphasized the possibility of resistance to a deviant label. Kitsuse (1980) refers to **tertiary deviance** as a stage that can potentially emerge after the transition from primary to secondary deviance. Some people who have been labelled and who then develop an identity and a lifestyle based on that label may resist the idea that the label is a "deviant" one. They may go on to try to change social norms, to show society that the behaviour they have engaged in or the characteristic they have is not "deviant" at all. They seek to redefine "normal" to include that act or characteristic. For example, some groups of gay and bisexual men who are HIV positive engage in activism to remove the stigma associated with their illness and to increase acceptance in society (Siegel, Lune, & Meyer, 1998). Similarly, some customers in an adult novelty store engaged in tertiary deviance by providing legal advice to store owners or by recruiting participants to resist conservative efforts to close down such stores in other communities (Hefley, 2007).

Whether we use the terminology of "the dramatization of evil," "tagging," "labelling," or "stigmatization," the processes of deviance being referred to are similar. Being perceived as "deviant" affects the way people treat us, which affects the way we see ourselves, which then affects the way we act in the future. But in addition to studying the processes that occur after being "caught" at deviance, some interpretive theorists are also interested in the process of living a deviant life—the deviant career.

The Deviant Career: Progressing through Deviance

In addition to the work already discussed, Howard Becker (1963) used the concept of the **deviant career** to study deviance. He postulated that deviance emerges, progresses, and changes over time, and there are stages to involvement in deviance just as there are stages in the development of a career. Thus, the concept of the "deviant career" refers not to those who make a living out of deviance, but rather the way that deviance unfolds in people's lives. Just as in the traditional notion of a "career," people enter deviance, manage their experiences of deviance, and may quit (or exit) deviance, all of which are intertwined with changes in their identities and understandings of self. Becker illustrated this sequential model of deviance with marijuana users, exploring the stages of meaning and understanding by which they became marijuana users, acted as marijuana users, and stopped using marijuana at some point. He identified three "stages" in this career: the beginner user, the occasional user, and the regular user.

A number of factors are involved in "becoming a marijuana user," such as having access to the drug, learning how to smoke correctly, and coming to perceive the effects of the drug as pleasurable. Various **career contingencies**, or what may be seen as significant *turning points*, influence the directions that people take at various points in the deviant career. For example, a lack of access to a steady supply of marijuana may lead some people to drop the habit while leading others into associations with organized groups that have a stable supply of the drug.

While Becker applied the deviant career to marijuana users, other deviance specialists have used the concept to analyze the transition from pre-mental patient to ex-mental patient (Goffman, 1959), exits from prostitution (Oselin, 2010), and becoming a confidential police informant (Miller, 2011). Particular deviance specialists may focus specifically on the entrance phases, management phases, or exit phases of the deviant career. The interactionist concepts and assumptions discussed earlier, such as role taking, meaning, understanding, and communication, lie at the core of the processes involved in deviant careers.

i believe i can fly

© neff_pad/Fotolia

Why do some people become part of cannabis subcultures, while others remain casual smokers or do not use marijuana at all?

Limitations of Interpretive Theories

Interpretive theories focus on the construction of meaning and understanding in interpersonal interactions, as well as the consequences of people's understandings for how they treat others and how they perceive themselves. These theories draw our attention to various aspects of deviance. They shine a spotlight on how someone's lifestyle and identity may come to be based on deviance, on the different ways that individuals may react once they are identified as deviant by others, and on how some people may exit deviance. They give us insight into the emergence of the "deviance dance," wherein some people will say that Group X is deviant and can be fixed in a certain way, other people will agree that Group X is deviant but can be fixed in a different way, and other people will say that Group X is not deviant at all.

The primary criticism of interpretive theories as a whole is that they fail to address the social structure and its role in the processes surrounding deviance and normality (Dennis & Martin, 2005; Downes & Rock, 2003). In order to deal with this issue, interpretive assumptions have been combined with structural approaches. A growing body of theoretical and empirical work acknowledges that the social structure provides a context in which people engage in interaction. This research suggests that interaction can result in social change (changes to the social structure), but says that the structure also places limitations on people's interactions.

For example, Solivetti (2003) found that the growing problem of drug addiction in Italy can be explained by combining functionalist and interactionist variables. Drug addiction (measured by the number of deaths from drug use and the number of people in drug treatment) shows considerable regional variation based on structural factors. That is, drug addiction is more prevalent in urban areas that have higher incomes and levels of education, a "reduced and fragile family" (p. 45) (higher rates of separation and smaller family size), and higher levels of individualism (e.g., more independent, unmarried women).

Although functionalist theories frequently associate deviance with lower socioeconomic classes, Solivetti points out that in these more affluent communities in Italy, the people who are addicted to drugs are those who experience chronic unemployment or underemployment and who have lower levels of education; thus, there is a considerable gap between their own achievements and the broader characteristics of the communities in which they live. The structural aspects of their communities (e.g., affluent) combined with the social traits of the addicted individuals (e.g., unemployed) leads those individuals into particular kinds of social interactions, where they "experiment with drugs, . . . interact with other people, . . . accept [their] own dealings with drugs, . . . [and] build up the role of addict" (p. 57). Thus, the social structure influences interactions.

Lemert's (1951) version of labelling theory in particular has faced a number of criticisms as well. Just as interpretive theories have been criticized for ignoring the role of the social structure, so has his labelling theory. But in addition to that overarching critique, three other specific criticisms have also been made. First, labelling theory has been criticized for focusing most of its attention on adolescents and not exploring the long-term effects of labelling. Second, much of the research has looked only at those who have been formally labelled in some way (e.g., through the criminal justice system), rather than comparing those who have been labelled with those who have not. Third, the specific processes involved in the transition from primary to secondary deviance have not been sufficiently addressed.

Research by Bernberg and Krohn (2003) takes all four of these criticisms into account in their analysis of crime, which integrates the assumptions of labelling theory with structural variables. They found that labelling does have a long-term effect, but the effect varies to some extent on the basis of race, which is one factor that determines an individual's location in the social structure. Bernberg and Krohn looked at young adult males who had been a part of the longitudinal Rochester Youth Development Study and compared youths who had experienced official intervention during adolescence with youths who had not. Two types of official intervention were included: *police intervention* (arrest or other contact with the police) and *juvenile justice system intervention* (formal sanctions, such as detention, probation, or community service).

The effects of both types of intervention on drug selling and other criminal behaviours at ages 19–20 were analyzed. Bernberg and Krohn found that males who had experienced police intervention during adolescence were more likely to have sold drugs or engaged in criminal behaviour in early adulthood. Intervention by the juvenile justice system had a similar effect;

however, that effect was greater for black males than for white or Hispanic males. The long-term effects of intervention by the juvenile justice system were partially mediated by educational attainment and employment. That is, high school graduation was less likely in those who were formally labelled, due to either time away from school (because of incarceration) or the harsher treatment they faced in school after being officially labelled. Those who faced official intervention were also more likely to be unemployed in early adulthood, partially because of lesser educational attainment. Thus, the authors concluded that an individual's location in the larger social structure (e.g., as influenced by race) shapes the short- and long-term effects of formal labelling, and that individuals at some locations in the social structure will have more resources to resist formal labelling than will individuals at other locations.

Research has integrated interpretive theories with other nonstructural positivist theories as well in an effort to explain particular phenomena more effectively. For instance, research on exotic dancers finds that in addition to carefully managing who is and is not aware of what they do for a living (*dividing the social world*, one of Goffman's responses to stigmatization), they also use several *techniques of neutralization* (addressed in Chapter 2) to manage the stigma. They engage in *denial of injury*, claiming that what they do does not hurt anybody. They *appeal to higher loyalties*, talking about the importance of being able to provide for their children. Finally, they *condemn the condemners* by pointing out that when the police come to give tickets to some of the dancers, they first watch the performances for an hour or two (Thompson, Harred, & Burks, 2003).

Labelling theories have been integrated with self-control theory (Gottfredson & Hirschi, 1990) and differential association theory (Sutherland, 1947) in an analysis of teenage girls who engage in high-risk sexual activity (Victor, 2004). In interviews, these girls talk about being labelled in junior high on the basis of their sexual activity (i.e., as "sluts," p. 74) and their socioeconomic status (i.e., as "welfare kids" and "white trash," p. 74). After being ostracized by their peers, those girls who had experienced inadequate parenting and subsequently developed low levels of self-control began associating with similar others. By high school, they had internalized the labels, referring to themselves as "ghetto kids" or "wiggers" (p. 76). They became part of the "marginal teen subculture" of their city, which consisted of teenagers who lived in apartments with other teenagers much or all of the time. In this environment, they learned definitions that supported risky sexual behaviours, such as unprotected sex with a high number of unfamiliar partners (see Figure 3.1).

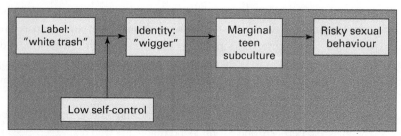

Figure 3.1 Adolescent Sexual Behaviour: The Effects of Labelling, Self-Control, and Differential Association.

The manner in which interpretive theories have been extensively integrated with a wide range of positivist theories and critical theories (to be addressed later in this chapter) provides support to those who suggest that interactionism, labelling, and stigmatization are *processes* more than they are formal *theories*. Each of the interpretive theories has, at some point, been criticized for not meeting the criteria for a formal theory, such as having concepts that can be operationalized and propositions that can be empirically tested and falsified (e.g., Downes & Rock, 2003; Ritzer & Goodman, 2004; Reid, 2003). Despite these "theoretical" shortcomings, the integration of interpretive assumptions into other theories has improved the explanatory value of those theories when analyzing particular phenomena. Interpretive concepts may be questioned as valid theories, but they nevertheless can be looked on as meaningful processes (Downes & Rock, 2003; Ritzer & Goodman, 2004).

Although interpretive assumptions provide insight into how our perceptions of and reactions to particular acts develop (including our self-perceptions and identity formation), they do not help us understand how some people are more able than others to influence what will and will not be labelled as deviant in a particular society at a particular time in history. Some interpretive theorists (e.g., Becker, 1963) have pointed out that the meanings and understandings held by some groups may be imposed on others. However, interpretive theories do not explain the precise mechanisms by which some people are more able than others to determine the direction that the "deviance dance" will take. Although different people will have varying perceptions of deviance and normality, some people's perceptions have more of an impact on the larger society; in other words, some people's perceptions count more than others. This is where critical theories of deviance step in— exploring the role of *power* in the social construction of deviance.

TIME TO REVIEW

Learning Objective 1

■ Why are interpretive and critical theories particularly useful to more subjectivist deviance specialists?

■ How can the processes described in the symbolic interactionist approach help us understand our perceptions of and reactions to particular behaviours and people?

Learning Objective 2

■ What are the core assumptions of labelling theories? What are some of

the different ways that various interpretive deviance specialists have discussed the process of labelling and responses to being labelled?

■ What do the concepts of "dramaturgy" and the "deviant career" add to our understanding of deviance?

Learning Objective 3

■ What criticisms have been directed at interpretive theories, and what have been the theoretical or empirical responses to these criticisms?

Critical Theories: Power Relations and Social Justice

The range of theories that have been categorized as **critical theories** of deviance is quite substantial—Marxist theories, non-Marxist conflict theories, nonconflict critical theories, feminist theories, postmodernist theories, discourse theories, anarchist theories, peace-making theories, radical multicultural theories, and more (Kubrin, Stucky, & Krohn, 2009; Pfohl, 1994; Deutschmann, 2002).

These theories are all both theoretical and practical in nature. At a theoretical level, they analyze "the relationship between human struggles for power in history and the ritual construction, deconstruction, and reconstruction of normative social boundaries" (Pfohl, 1994, p. 404). At a practical level, these are all theories that have an emancipatory interest—that is, an interest in working toward social justice for society's powerless. In fact, conflict theorist Karl Marx stated that social scientists have a *responsibility* to use their work in pursuit of practical, emancipatory goals, which he referred to as **praxis**. In the remainder of this chapter, a range of critical theories that have been definitive for the study of deviance will be reviewed: conflict theories, power-reflexive theories, feminist theories, and postmodern theories.

Conflict Theories: Rules Serve the Interests of the Powerful

Although conflict theories themselves are of considerable diversity, they do share some core assumptions (McCaghy, Capron, & Jamieson, 2003). First, they presume that social rules do not emerge out of consensus but rather out of conflict and serve the interests of the most influential groups in society. Second, they suggest that members of powerful groups are less likely to break the rules because the rules were created to serve their interests in the first place. Third, conflict theories propose that members of less powerful groups are more likely to act in ways that violate social rules, either because (1) their sense of oppression and alienation causes them to act out in rule-breaking ways, or (2) because social rules have defined the acts of the powerless as deviant in the first place. Precisely which groups are perceived as being in conflict varies among specific conflict theories, but all conflict theories integrate propositions about the structures of societal inequality with views about the ideologies that are used to maintain the status quo and reproduce the existing structures of inequality (Beaman, 2000).

The origins of conflict theory are typically attributed to Karl Marx, who proposed that society consists of a small group of powerful people at the top and a large group of power-less people at the bottom. He ascribed these power differentials to economic factors, specifically the relationship to the means of production. Society's powerful (the **bourgeoisie**) are those who own the means of production; society's powerless (the **proletariat**) are the wage earners who work for the people who own the means of production. The sense of alienation experienced by the proletariat because of their working conditions gives rise to deviant behaviour among some people.

Later Marxists fell into two general camps, **instrumental Marxists** and **structural Marxists**. Instrumental Marxists (e.g., Quinney, 1977) propose that institutionalized social rules, such as the law, are created by the powerful to serve the interests of the powerful—the owners of the means of production. A deviant label thereby becomes an instrument used to control the proletariat and maintain the economic structure in society. Structural Marxists (e.g., Chambliss & Seidman, 1982) propose that institutionalized social rules are created by the powerful to protect the capitalist economic system rather than to protect individual capitalists. The need to maintain the power of the economic system as a whole means that even members of the bourgeoisie may be subject to a deviant label if their behaviour threatens the fundamental principles of capitalism.

Although Marxist conflict theories are based on the presumption of economic structures of inequality, other conflict theories claim that power is based on noneconomic factors as well. *Pluralist conflict theory* focuses on multiple axes of inequality that make up the structure of society based on conflicts between various economic, religious, ethnic, political, and social groups. *Culture conflict theory* claims that in societies having multiple, diverse cultural groups, there will be multiple sets of norms that may conflict with each other (Sellin, 1938). Dominant cultural groups have the power to impose the norms that compose their culture on all other cultural groups in society, labelling the norms of conflicting cultural groups as "deviant" and in need of measures of social control.

For example, some years ago Sikh RCMP officers were not permitted to wear turbans (even those with the same patterns of coloration and having the same RCMP insignia as the hats that were a part of the uniform). Turbans are a central component of the Sikh religious and cultural belief system; however, the norms of Euro-Canadian cultural groups had been the ones integrated into the rules governing dress in the RCMP. Tremendous debate emerged among different groups of Canadians. Some groups claimed that the RCMP hat was a fundamental symbol of Canadian identity that "foreigners" had no right to tamper with. This side of the debate illustrates the notion of cultural conflict quite nicely. Other groups countered that the RCMP uniform had changed multiple times over the past century, and the hat that was part of the current uniform could not be considered a fundamental part of Canadian identity. Furthermore, they pointed out that the Canadian government had no problem with Sikh men wearing turbans when they were laying their lives on the line as Canadian soldiers during World War II. This counterargument illustrates the idea that rules are constructed by the powerful to serve their own needs at a particular time.

In *group conflict theory*, George Vold (1958) extended conflict assumptions beyond cultural groups to a wide range of other groups as well. He suggested that multiple groups are always manoeuvring for more power in society and clash with each other as a result of their simultaneous struggles for power. The norms or social rules of certain groups gain more legitimacy in society because these groups are able to get authorities on their side more effectively. In situations of conflict, crime and deviance emerge because people will commit acts they do not normally engage in (e.g., vandalism, assault) in pursuit of their higher goal—trying to attain more power for their social groups.

Austin Turk (1969) stated that the core struggle in society is more broadly between *those who are in positions of authority* and *those who are subject to authority*. Those who are in authority try to maintain their authority by convincing society's less powerful groups of the validity of the existing social rules using as much coercion as necessary if the less powerful groups refuse to be "convinced." Socially typing the norms or actions of conflicting groups as deviant is one way that positions of authority can be maintained.

Whether referring to Marxist theories, other conflict theories described above, or one of the many additional criminological conflict theories that have been proposed (e.g., Richard Quinney's radical conflict theory or Left Realism), the *theoretical* interest in exploring the struggle for power and its role in defining social norms and the *practical* interest in emancipation together define critical theories of deviance. In essence, the various conflict theories postulate that different groups in society have different interests and perceptions of what the rules should be; however, having more power and resources enables groups to pursue their own interests more effectively. Thus, the "rules" as perceived by powerful groups are imposed on all of the groups that make up society as a whole.

In this regard, it is society's powerful who are able to construct the dominant moral code by which deviance and normality are defined. Powerful groups are able to maintain their power by socially typing the interests and the perceptions of other social groups as deviant—they are able to quash the competition simply by creating rules that deviantize competitors' behaviours. For example, in an analysis of midwifery in New Orleans, Frailing and Harper (2010) point out that during the course of the 1930s, abortions (performed by midwives) became safer and more women were surviving the procedure. As more women turned to midwives instead of to physicians, the medicalization of pregnancy and childbirth was threatened. Over the course of the next two decades, midwifery was increasingly criminalized; the more powerful medical establishment was able to deviantize midwifery and thereby increase their own market share.

Of course, in contemporary democratic societies powerful groups cannot act in ways that would make them look oppressive or authoritarian. Instead, they maintain their power by convincing enough of the populace that they are responsive to the interests of the people and are working in everyone's best interests. Consequently, powerful groups must strike a balance between pursuing their own interests, integrating some of the interests of society's masses, and integrating the desires of vocal interest groups. In the end, "deviance" is a label that justifies the control efforts of powerful groups and thereby helps them to maintain their power.

Convincing society's masses that those in positions of authority are working in everyone's best interests involves manufacturing a worldview within which the actions of the powerful seem logical. Marx and other conflict theorists use the term **ideology**, in its broad sense, to refer to the worldview (a way of seeing and understanding the world) held by society's powerful groups—a worldview based on the interests and needs of the powerful.

Because the powerful control society's institutions, such as schools and the media, their ideology is taught to citizens as "common sense" via those institutions, thereby achieving what Antonio Gramsci called **hegemony** (i.e., becoming the dominant way of seeing and understanding the world). However, a later school of critical theorists that grew out of the conflict perspective, the Frankfurt School, explained that society's masses develop a **false consciousness** (originally a Marxian concept). Even though the hegemonic ideology is one that serves the interests and needs of the powerful and is imposed on everyone else through society's institutions, people come to perceive it as rational and acceptable. Consequently, they do not realize that they have been duped and come to believe that they have more freedom than they actually do. The roles of ideology, hegemony, and false consciousness are to render any alternative ways of seeing and understanding the world as outside of the realm of possibility in most people's minds, and thus the dominant view becomes "common sense."

Once a particular worldview is perceived as "common sense" by society's masses, there are implications for the structure and functioning of society. This is illustrated by Kent and Jacobs's (2004) application of conflict theory to a cross-national analysis of police presence. Economic-based conflict theory postulates a relationship between economic stratification and the need for social control. Of course, the most overt form of social control is the criminal justice system, including law enforcement. In a capitalist society, the role of law enforcement is to protect the property of the wealthy; thus, more economic stratification should be associated with greater police presence.

Kent and Jacobs compared the ratio of the number of law enforcement officers to the national population from 1975 to 1994 in 11 countries—Australia, Belgium, Canada, Denmark, France, the Republic of Ireland, Italy, Norway, Sweden, the United Kingdom, and the United States. In accordance with conflict theory, they found that nations with higher levels of economic inequality had a greater number of law enforcement officers per 100 000 people in the population. They also found that countries with higher crime rates had a higher ratio of police officers to national population—but only in recent years, once crime had become more politicized in these nations. Kent and Jacobs concluded that the economically powerful play a central role in the politicization of street crime and the corresponding public demand for more police officers; economic inequality gives "economic elites greater control over public values" (p. 357) through ownership and control of the media.

Despite the rather gloomy picture of power and control that conflict theorists paint, they do suggest that change is possible. That is, there will always be some people in society who are able to see the ideological nature of "common sense" and the hidden interests operating in the institutionalized knowledge of society. The goal of theory and action, they suggest, is to enlighten society's masses so that they too become aware of ideology, false consciousness, or hegemony. Only then can hierarchal structures of power be changed to create social justice.

Power-Reflexive Theories: Knowledge Is Power

Power-reflexive theories are built on a foundation that emphasizes the intertwining of knowledge and power. Within these theories it is proposed that all claims to knowledge are socially situated, embedded within relations of power. Multiple **discourses** (bodies of knowledge, or all that is "known" about a particular phenomenon) coexist in society; relations of power determine which claims to knowledge come to be institutionalized or perceived as "truth" within society as a whole (Foucault, 1980). For example, during the Middle Ages in Europe, the claims made by the Christian church (as a quasi-governing body in most European nations) were seen as the "truth." With the Enlightenment and the related development and growth of science, the claims made by science were accorded more "truth" than the claims of the Christian church. As we will address in a later chapter, in contemporary society, the claims made by science are granted more legitimacy in the eyes of the public than any other claims to truth being made.

Poststructuralist Michel Foucault discussed the linkages between power and knowledge (Foucault, 1980) as well as analyzing mechanisms of social control (Foucault, 1995) through his discussion of the **Panopticon**. Philosopher Jeremy Bentham designed a panoptical prison, a design that enabled guards to observe all prisoners at all times. However, the design did not allow prisoners to know for a fact whether they were currently being observed or not. They therefore lived in an environment in which they knew that the guards *might* be observing them at any given moment. The potential for constant surveillance eventually led the prisoners to regulate their own behaviour all the time, even when they were not actually being observed.

Foucault proposed that the processes of industrialization and bureaucratization have created a panoptical society as well. He suggested that bureaucratization results in the development of numerous mechanisms of social control that ensure "normal" behaviour and punish or prevent "deviant" behaviour. We accept government-sponsored surveillance because it is presented as being for our own good or for our safety and survival, as with the increased surveillance since 9/11 (Staples, cited in Robinson, 2008).

Indeed, in the twenty-first century, panoptical surveillance is not only figurative but literal—a massive increase in the number of closed-circuit television monitoring systems (CCTVs) in private (e.g., convenience stores) and public (e.g., parking lots, city intersections, highways) means that people can be "watched" by others at various points throughout the day. As part of a broader crime reduction strategy, the United Kingdom has implemented more public-space CCTVs than anywhere else in the world, covering more than 1000 towns and cities in the UK; estimates of the number of public-space cameras range from 1.5 to 4.5 million (the latter figure representing approximately one camera for every 14 people) (CCTV User Group, 2008).

Because of the pervasiveness of social control in modern society—and of the potential for constant surveillance—most of us do not need to be watched for normative transgressions; we engage in self-surveillance and regulate our own behaviours (e.g., weighing ourselves or stopping our cars when encountering a four-way stop on an abandoned road in the middle of the night). This is what Robinson (2008) refers to as "imprinting the panoptic eye in the consciousness of individuals" (p. 235). The more control becomes internalized in the form of self-control or self-regulation, the more effective it becomes.

However, Foucault pointed out that power always goes hand-in-hand with resistance. For instance, anarchist groups (which have been labelled terrorist threats since the nineteenth century) have created a "security culture" to resist their surveillance by law enforcement

© Dynamic Graphics/JupiterImages

In what ways are you monitored?

and other authorities. The security culture controls speech (what information can be shared, with whom, and in what settings), forbids speaking to the authorities, results in the wearing of black masks at demonstrations, and triggers the use of aliases (Robinson, 2008).

Feminist Theories: Deviance Is Gendered

Rather than there being a "feminist theory," there are in fact multiple forms of feminist theories and practice, often quite distinct from each other (Nelson & Robinson, 2002), ranging from those that emphasize women's experiences to those that focus on the negative impacts that patriarchy has had on both women and men. Historically, the discipline of sociology has largely been a male-oriented enterprise—male sociologists studying and theorizing about male social experiences. Mainstream sociological theories, particularly those dating from the emergence of the discipline until the mid- to late twentieth century, have often been guilty of ignoring women altogether, implicitly or explicitly assuming that the male experience can be generalized to understand the female experience or explaining female behaviour in terms of the inherent qualities of women. Mainstream theories may also treat women in a peripheral fashion—as the "Other" that stands in contrast to the normative male standard. For example, some social theorists have first developed a "theory of society" and then (usually much later) a separate "theory of women," as though women were somehow separate from or outside of "society."

In studying deviance, feminist theories in general underscore the fact that the bodies of knowledge and the norms by which we judge deviance and normality vary for women and men. That is, what are considered "normal" behaviours, appearances, or characteristics for women are quite different than for men. For example, a woman who wants to work in a daycare centre will be viewed very differently than a man who wants to work in a daycare centre; she is far more likely to be perceived as "normal" while he is far more likely to be perceived as "deviant." Similarly, a woman who dislikes being around children is more likely to be seen as abnormal than is a man who dislikes being around children. In relation to power, most feminist theories also share the assumption that historically, society has been structured in ways that serve the interests of males.

But outside of these shared basic assumptions, feminist analyses of and theories about deviance vary tremendously. For example, prostitution is addressed in very different ways by radical feminists and liberal feminists. While radical feminists see prostitution as one more example of the sexual oppression of women in patriarchy, liberal feminists are more likely to see it as an occupation in which women need to be given more control over working conditions (Larsen, 2000; Peace, Beaman, & Sneddon, 2000). The even wider range of feminist perspectives (e.g., socialist and postmodern) means there are even more varying perceptions of prostitution and ways of addressing the topic.

Feminist theorizing about deviance is perhaps most developed in the area of criminal forms of deviance. Downes and Rock (2003) suggest that feminist theorizing is so successful in this area that one can speak of *feminist criminology*. On the other hand, Reid (2003) claims that "feminist scholars are not clear on what constitutes a feminist theory in criminology" (p. 149), other than looking at how power differentials affect female crime, female victimization, and the treatment of women in the criminal justice system.

The complexities of feminist theories about deviance are further magnified when we consider the fact that not only is there a wide range of distinct "feminist theories" (such as radical feminism, cultural feminism, liberal feminism, and maternal feminism), but feminist theorizing is also done from within virtually every theoretical perspective addressed in this book. That is, there are feminist interactionist theories, feminist Marxist theories, feminist functionalist theories, feminist learning theories, and feminist social control theories. Feminist theorizing, in its diversity, is becoming fully integrated into the study of deviance as a whole. Despite the fact that feminist theorizing has been incorporated into the positivist and interpretive theories reviewed in this book (as well as into other types of critical theories), feminist theories are often categorized as inherently critical theories. This is because of their foundation in the theoretical interest in exploring power relations in society and the practical interest in emancipation—achieving equality for women in society.

Postmodern Theories: Questioning All Knowledge

If discussing "feminist theories" as a cohesive category is difficult and somewhat artificial, discussing postmodern theories as a cohesive category is perhaps even more so (Downes &

Rock, 2003). In fact, there is limited agreement about precisely what constitutes "postmodern" theorizing and whether or not it can be included in the category of "critical theories." For instance, postmodernism is sometimes equated with the power-reflexive theories addressed earlier, such as the work of Foucault (e.g., Deutschmann, 2002; Peace, Beaman, & Sneddon, 2000). Postmodern theories are broadly based on the notion of *rejection*—rejection of overarching theories of society (such as structural functionalism or symbolic interactionism), rejection of social categorization (e.g., "man," "black," "Christian"), and rejection of the possibility of "truth." **Skeptical postmodernism** (Rosenau, 1992) is solipsistic, postulating that knowledge is not possible and that only chaos and meaninglessness exist. In contrast, **affirmative postmodernism** deconstructs what are seen as master narratives, overarching theories, or "knowledge" and focuses analysis on the local and specific. This form is sometimes associated with social movements like environmental activism.

Postmodernists claim that advanced capitalist societies faced rapid social change following the end of World War II. Such societies can no longer be considered "industrial" societies, because symbols and culture (rather than products) have taken centre stage in the economy. Capitalism now exists primarily "by selling consumers new needs, new experiences, and new forms of meaning, all of which are defined exclusively by the marketplace" (Ashley & Orenstein, 2001, p. 475). Commercialism is the defining feature of society, with people pursuing "style over substance" (p. 475). Even politics has become a commercial activity—people are "consumers" rather than "citizens," becoming politically indifferent, self-absorbed, and hedonistic in their endless pursuit of personal style.

Postmodernists speak of the "end of the individual" for this very reason; the individual is no more than the style or image being pursued at a given moment in time, an image that is disjointed and constantly changing. Any notion of a dominant moral code by which we can judge deviance and normality is gradually being eroded. "The postmodern subject is besieged by an endless jumble of messages, codes, and ideas, most of which are incompatible, inconsistent, and quite infantile. Many people respond to the current cacophony of mostly commercial messages that bombard them daily by abandoning all hope that they ever could attain some kind of rational understanding of the world, [becoming] an empty shell that is incapable of exercising any kind of critical judgment" (Ashley & Orenstein, 2001, p. 476).

Although postmodern assumptions in their skeptical forms are rarely used in analyses of deviance, it is interesting to ponder the implications of the lack of a moral code and the creation of subjects that are incapable of critical judgment. Is "deviance" possible if there is no moral code that serves as the foundation for its social construction? Can anyone be socially typed as deviant if people become incapable of critical judgment? Is a populace that is incapable of critical judgment simply more susceptible to the interests and whims of those who are in authority?

In the study of deviance, postmodernism raises more questions than it answers, which some people say is the point of postmodern theories. These critical theoretical approaches do not pretend to answer questions—their goal is largely to problematize and raise questions about knowledge creation and human behaviour.

Limitations of Critical Theories

Critical theories are defined by a theoretical interest in the power struggles by which normative social boundaries are created, as well as a practical interest in the pursuit of social justice. Through their analyses, critical theorists try to determine the processes by which the views of certain groups of people come to be applied to society as a whole—how some people's "rules" become society's "rules" and thereby serve as the standard against which deviance and normality are judged.

Conflict theories focus on social structures that create an opposition between the powerful and the powerless. Power-reflexive theories emphasize the intertwining of power relations and claims to knowledge (including their own). Feminist theories focus on the gender bias embedded in most sociological knowledge claims of the past and the historical oppression of women in society. Postmodern theories, which are still rather amorphous and hard to pin down, focus on the "end of the individual" and a rejection of the possibility of "truth." They represent an important layer of recent theoretical development, although their usefulness for understanding the social construction of deviance is yet to be determined.

Each of the different bodies of critical theory has faced particular criticisms. For example, in the study of criminal forms of deviance, conflict theories have been criticized on the basis of inconsistent empirical support for the relationship between economic factors and crime and for structural bias in the criminal justice system. More broadly, conflict theories have been criticized for failing to recognize the consensus that does exist in society regarding many laws and rules (e.g., prohibitions against theft and murder). Critics suggest that a more complete theory should be able to deal with both conflict and consensus (Ritzer & Goodman, 2004).

Critical theories as a whole face an accusation similar to that levelled at interpretive theories: some theorists suggest that conflict, poststructuralist, feminist, and postmodernist assumptions may be more appropriately considered processes, perspectives, or ideologies rather than formal theories with empirically verifiable propositions. Siegel and McCormick (2003) state that research on conflict theories "places less emphasis on testing the hypotheses of a particular theory and instead attempts to show that conflict principles hold up under empirical scrutiny" (p. 238). Although they are referring specifically to conflict theories, other critical theories have been discussed in similar ways (Downes & Rock, 2003).

Some of that "empirical scrutiny" has integrated different bodies of critical theory. For example, feminist and poststructuralist perspectives have been applied to the study of Aboriginal women living in Vancouver's downtown Eastside, in conjunction with an analysis of the drug education film *Through a Blue Lens* that was filmed there (England, 2004). England explored how these women's real-world experiences are characterized by considerably more racism and sexism than is depicted in the film, particularly in the relationship between addicts and police officers.

The perspectives or assumptions of critical theories have also been combined with interpretive theories. One example of this is found in analyses of racial profiling in the criminal justice system. Many Canadians have become more aware of this topic in recent years, following extensive media attention on accusations of racial profiling by the Toronto Police Service (Wortley & Tanner, 2003; Roberts, 2003); however, the problem of racial profiling has been recognized in cities throughout North America. Gabbidon (2003) analyzes the issue of racial profiling in an American context, applying interactionist and conflict theories to shoplifting-related false arrest cases. Gabbidon's finding that members of visible minority groups are less likely than white Americans to obtain clear victories in court illustrates the conflict assumption that the law is a tool used by the powerful to oppress the powerless. Gabbidon's finding that black Americans are more likely to be falsely accused of shoplifting than are members of other visible minority groups illustrates interactionist assumptions about the effects of labelling and stigmatization. Stereotypes associate the master status of "black" with the auxiliary trait of "criminal," hence the greater likelihood of false accusations. Independently, interactionist and conflict theories are unable to explain the complete phenomenon, but when integrated they are able to explain both why black individuals are more likely than other minorities to be falsely accused of shoplifting and why members of minorities as a whole are less likely to secure clear court victories.

Taken together, critical and interpretive theories paint a picture of the social construction of deviance. Interpretive theories address the interactions between people by which diverse and even contradictory understandings of deviance and normality emerge. They also explore what happens to people once they have been labelled deviant and how people who are considered deviant attribute meaning to their own life experiences. Interpretive theories draw our attention to the many steps involved in the deviance dance.

On the other hand, critical theories address the role that power plays in the social construction of deviance, whereby the understandings of deviance held by more powerful groups in society are the understandings that become institutionalized. They draw our attention to the fact that some people, such as those of a particular sex, those with more wealth, those who control the media, or those whom we consider "scientists," are better able to determine the direction of the deviance dance—are allowed to "lead" the dance. Critical theorists look closely at various aspects of power relations, depending on the particular theory in question, and assess their relationship to how deviance is socially constructed in a particular culture at a certain time in history.

At this point in the book, we have explored what "deviance" is, as well as changing conceptions of deviance. We have also reviewed the dominant theoretical perspectives used by deviance specialists who have more objective understandings of deviance (positivist theories) and by deviance specialists who have more subjective understandings (interpretive and critical theories). Having established this foundation of knowledge about the discipline and how deviance may be studied, in the remainder of the book we will turn our attention to an exploration of several substantive topics of deviance and normality—media, sexuality, youth, voluntary and involuntary physical appearance, mental disorders, science, and religion. As you progress through these substantive topics, the concepts, ideas, and theories that have been reviewed in the first three chapters of the book—for example, normative violation or social typing—will repeatedly emerge. The application of particular concepts and theories in the discussion of concrete situations will clarify these concepts and theories.

TIME TO REVIEW

Learning Objective 4
- What are the theoretical and practical interests shared among critical theories?

Learning Objective 5
- What are the similarities and differences between the different conflict theories addressed in the chapter?
- What do power-reflexive theories tell us about *knowledge* and *social control*?
- What do feminist theories have in common, and why is it difficult to draw conclusions about what "feminist theory" tells us about deviance?
- What are the core assumptions of postmodern theory, and what questions does the theory raise about the study of deviance?

Learning Objective 6
- What criticisms have been directed at critical theories, and what have been some of the theoretical or empirical responses?

Exercise Your Mind

How would each of the theories in this chapter explain deviance or conformity as it exists in your own life (or the life of someone you know)? What facets of your experience are left unexplained by each theory? If you had to select the one theory that best explains deviance or conformity in your own life, which would it be?

CHAPTER SUMMARY

- Deviance specialists who have more subjective understandings of deviance are interested in the way particular acts are socially constructed and socially typed as deviant. *Interpretive* and *critical* theories are the most useful in understanding the social construction of deviance and normality. (1)

- *Interpretive theories*, with their emphasis on how meaning is created through social interaction and symbolic communication, draw our attention to how each of us comes to understand that certain acts are "deviant" while others are "normal." They also draw our attention to how different people develop contrasting understandings of deviance. (1)

- *Labelling theories* explain how the process of getting caught in a deviant act and subsequently being labelled as "deviant" serve as the impetus for the transition from *primary* to *secondary* deviance. A deviant label becomes a *master status* that limits opportunities in the "normal" world, opens up opportunities in the "deviant" world, and changes a person's self-perception and identity. (2)

- Different people may react to being *stigmatized* in various ways, such as by trying to hide the stigma, immersing themselves in a world of similarly stigmatized others, or proudly displaying the stigma. (2)

- The notion of the *deviant career* is another interpretive strategy for exploring people's entrance into, management of, and possible exit from deviant activities. (2)

- Interpretive theories have faced a number of criticisms, which have been responded to theoretically and empirically. (3)

- *Critical theories* share a theoretical interest in the power struggles that define normative social boundaries and a practical interest in emancipation. Diverse critical theories exist, including conflict theories, power-reflexive theories, feminist theories, and postmodern theories. (4)

- *Conflict theories* originated with the economic deterministic model of Karl Marx but have since expanded to include alternative models of power wherein powerful groups are able to impose their moral order on powerless groups. (5)

- *Power-reflexive theories* emphasize the intertwining of power relations and claims to knowledge. Some power-reflexive theorists also analyze structures of surveillance and the creation of self-surveillance, by which we regulate our own behaviours even if no one else is doing so. (5)

- *Feminist theories* suggest that deviance and normality are socially constructed in different ways for males and females in society. (5)

- *Postmodern theories* represent a recent theoretical development arising out of the social changes following the end of World War II. Their proponents propose the notion of the "end of the individual" and posit that people have become consumers rather than citizens. These theorists reject overarching theories of society and claim that the moral codes that would enable people to rationally understand society have eroded. (5)

- Critiques of critical theories have been responded to in a number of ways, such as through theoretical integration. (6)

MySearchLab®

Watch Go to MySearchLab to watch the video called "The Stanford Prison Experiment".

Apply What You Know: Consider the actions of the students who were randomly assigned to be guards and prisoners. How does their behaviour in the experiment support labelling theory? Does their behaviour tell us anything about the nature of power relations in society at large?

MySearchLab with eText offers you access to an online interactive version of the text, extensive help with your writing and research projects, and provides round-the-clock access to credible and reliable source material.

Chapter 4
Deviance 2.0: The Role of the Media

© kbuntu/Fotolia

Learning Objectives

After reading this chapter, you should be able to

1   Identify forms of media, both *traditional* and *new* or *emerging*.

2   Explain why it is important for sociologists to study media.

3   Describe patterns of media use and the nature of its impact.

4   Distinguish between *administrative* and *critical* approaches to media studies in terms of what they study and the nature of their findings.

5   Outline five different types of relationships that characterize the media–deviance nexus.

Media researcher and anti-violence educator Jackson Katz (1999) claims that the "media is the single greatest pedagogical force of our time." This suggests that the power of mass media is not limited to any particular sphere of social life, but rather permeates all aspects of life in the Western world. Indeed, it is difficult to imagine what our lives would be like without the media. As Silverstone (2007) claims, "we have become dependent on the media for the conduct of everyday life" (p. 6).

The term **media** refers to any form of communication that targets a mass audience in print or electronic format. Traditional forms of media include print (books, magazines, newspapers, comics), radio, cinema, television, and recordings. More recent forms of mass media include a broad variety of electronic communications that depend on computer technology, for example, websites, mobile computing, DVDs, CDs, blogs, smartphone apps, Twitter, and digitized forms of traditional media. These are referred to as *new* or *emerging* media.

The first three chapters of this book have already brought the role of the media in discussions of deviance to light. Several examples were evident in Chapter 1. Emily Murphy's book *The Black Candle* (a traditional form of media) had an impact on the criminalization of marijuana. The *Criminal Code of Canada* can be found on the federal government's website, and middle-class norms permeate "Married Life" chatrooms. More broadly, the media constitutes one of the five most powerful groups that are able to influence the dominant moral codes of society; it serves as a tool used by a wide range of moral entrepreneurs in their efforts to change society. Chapter 2 addressed the strain of fame and celebrity, such as the killer-as-celebrity phenomenon in the news, people who blog, and culture jamming. In Chapter 3 we explored postmodernist claims that the media has been central to societal changes in the post-World War II era, creating the *end of the individual*. This chapter explores more foundational issues related to the media: why it is important to study the media when trying to understand deviance, conformity, and social control; the different approaches that scholars have taken to studying the media that draw our attention to varying aspects of the media; and the nature of the media–deviance nexus, that is, the diverse ways in which the media and deviance are intertwined.

Why Media Matters

In the quote that opened this chapter, Jackson Katz referred to the media as the "single greatest *pedagogical* force of our time" (emphasis added). He means that in the twenty-first century, media provide the primary means by which we learn—about ourselves, about others, about the world around us. Other scholars do not consider the media to be as singularly powerful as Katz does, but rather as "part of the circle of primary and secondary definers and claimsmakers" (Tsoukala, 2008, p. 138). Although there may be some disagreement as to the magnitude of the media's power relative to other agents, there is agreement that media are powerful learning tools.

Ask Yourself

How much time do you spend each day using media? Remember, this includes reading books, magazines, newspapers, or comics; watching TV or movies; playing a game on your phone; looking at a website or updating your Facebook status; or even listening to music while you study.

Why study the media? Your responses to the *Ask Yourself* exercise may have already indicated why it is important for sociologists to do so—because so much of our everyday lives are spent using it! Sociologists also study the media because of what the media *does*—its impact on individuals and society.

Patterns of Media Use

Sociologists study everyday life, in terms of the interconnections between the micro-level of individual experiences and choices and the macro-level of broader sociocultural structures and processes. The extent of our media use means that understanding everyday life means understanding our relationship with media.

Media is so much a part of our daily lives that in some respects it is rendered almost invisible. Because it is always there, it can be difficult to actually see the extent of its pervasiveness. In 2009, the majority of Canadian adults spent at least *some* time each week using various forms of media, ranging from 99 percent of adults watching television each week to 60 percent reading a magazine. They spent more than 60 hours each week using various forms of media, an increase of 2.5 hours compared to nine years earlier (Interactive Advertising Bureau of Canada, 2011). As you can see in Figure 4.1, the greatest amount of time was spent watching television, followed by listening to the radio and using the Internet. The least amount of time was spent reading newspapers and magazines.

Children also use media extensively. Children ages 8 through 18 use media an average of 7.5 hours each day (Rideout, Foehr, & Roberts, 2009). They spend 1023 hours each year watching television alone, 123 hours more than they spend in school. Almost 98 percent

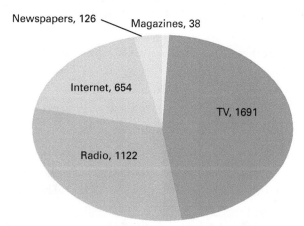

Newspapers, 126   Magazines, 38
Internet, 654
TV, 1691
Radio, 1122

Figure 4.1 Time Spent Engaged with Media, 2009 (Minutes per Week)

Source: Based on Interactive Advertising Bureau of Canada (2011). *2010 Canadian media usage trends study.* Toronto, ON.

of children under the age of six own products based on television or movie characters, and by the age of 18 they have viewed more than 200 000 acts of violence on television (Media Education Foundation, n.d.).

Use of some forms of media has been declining over the last decade, particularly radio, newspapers, and magazines. Use of other forms, however, has increased—television and especially the Internet (Interactive Advertising Bureau of Canada, 2011). Almost 80 percent of Canadian households have Internet access (Statistics Canada, 2011b), and households with children are particularly likely to be plugged in; 97 percent of children in Canada have Internet access at home, compared to 79 percent in 2001 (Zamaria & Fletcher, 2007).

In fact, Canada leads the world in online use, with adults spending an average of 45.6 hours per month online; the United States follows with 40.3 hours then the United Kingdom with 37.1 hours. The largest proportion of Internet users are between the ages of 35–54, followed by those aged 18–34 (comScore, 2012). Computers continue to be the primary means by which people access the Internet, but mobile media is becoming more common, with half of Canadian mobile users browsing the web, downloading content, or accessing apps on their smartphones (comScore, 2012). The top six iPhone and Android apps in 2010 can be seen in Figure 4.2.

The fact that YouTube and Facebook are in the top six smartphone apps on both platforms is indicative of broader patterns of online engagement overall. Going online to watch videos has become much more common, increasing by almost 60 percent between 2010 and 2011. However, the greatest share of time online is spent on social networking sites, such as Twitter, LinkedIn, and Facebook (comScore, 2012). The time spent on social networking sites ranges from 5.4 hours per month among those aged 55 and older to 10.8 hours for those aged 18–24. A recent study has found that social networking plays a role in the lives of people in all social groups, including the elderly, recent immigrants, people with disabilities, Inuit and First Nations persons, and even the homeless (Taylor, 2011).

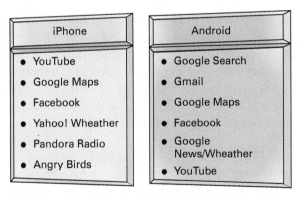

Figure 4.2 Top Six iPhone and Android Apps (2011)

Data from textual information in: comScore (2012b). 2012 *Mobile Future in Focus*. Retrieved June 7, 2012 from www.comScore.com.

Social media's primary role is a means to keep in touch with friends and family; in fact, 18 percent of Canadians say they socialize with their friends more online than in the real world (Ipsos-Reid, 2012). However, use of social media is multifaceted, ranging from playing games with others to fighting addiction to political advocacy (Taylor, 2011).

It is clear that our use of various forms of media is extensive—60 hours each week on average, and for some people even more! But so what? So what if I watch the next episode of my favourite television show, download a song from iTunes, read the front page of the *Globe and Mail* (either in hard copy or online), enter a contest on Facebook, or go see the latest action flick at the theatre? Why does it matter? Scholars suggest that it matters because the media is not innocuous—it is not merely a neutral purveyor of information or entertainment, but rather has an impact on both individuals and society. This point is of particular relevance to discussions of deviance.

The Effects of Media on Individuals and Society

Part of the media's power is its ability to define. It defines boundaries between groups and communities within those groups, thereby affecting our understandings of "us" and "them." For example, European media coverage of soccer hooliganism makes a clear distinction between irrational, animal-like soccer hooligans and authentic soccer fans (Tsoukala, 2008). The media defines social problems and shapes public debates, indicating which people and issues we should be concerned about and why. As a key site of social inclusion and exclusion, it is through the media (at least in part) that we learn who the "Other" is that we should be concerned about. Within the media, we see morality and ethics in action—the general principles that define good or bad and the application of those principles in action (Silverstone, 2007).

For example, Greer and Jewkes (2005) analyzed the "mediated constructions of otherness" (p. 20) in British newspapers. They found that newspapers placed troublesome "Others" along a continuum of stigmatized and absolute others. **Stigmatized others** are presented as threats to the way of life of decent people. People on social assistance, single mothers, or those engaged in moderately deviant behaviour "retain a degree of newsworthiness because they form part of a wider, nostalgically reactionary narrative decrying the perceived . . . collapse of discipline, the lack of respect for authority, the loss of better times, and the wistful (if hopelessly naive) call for a return to the good old days" (p. 23). **Absolute others** are presented as inherently evil and include those who commit exceptional crimes, such as suicide bombers, pedophiles who kill children, and children who commit acts of murder.

Precisely where specific others are located on this continuum is constantly changing in response to shifting public concerns and cultural sensibilities. Thus, stigmatized others can be elevated to absolute others via the media. One instance noted by Greer and Jewkes was the manner in which the newspapers came to equate "dole spongers" (people who chronically and unnecessarily rely on welfare) with "terrorists." In covering the story of one woman who was a "dole sponger," a newspaper pointed out several specific cases of

Islamic extremists who planned or engaged in terrorist acts while on social assistance: "I'm not saying that every benefit recipient is a terrorist welfare queen. I am saying that the best bet of saving the next generation of [dole spongers] is if the U.S. declares European welfare systems a national security threat'" (*The Daily Telegraph*, cited in Greer & Jewkes, 2005, p. 24). In another instance, Greer and Jewkes found that various British newspapers connected the sexual assault and murder of a 12-year-old boy by an illegal immigrant to "the complete breakdown of the immigration system" and an indication of "what can happen when the immigration and asylum system breaks down" (p. 25); "illegal immigrants" come to be equated with "pedophilic killers."

Our extensive media use and its ability to define boundaries, identify social problems, and shape public debate makes its study crucial to understanding our everyday lives and the larger society in which we live. But media scholars suggest that such understanding can also be used as a tool to help change people's behaviours, solving some social problems (e.g., violence, eating disorders, premature sexual activity) and enacting social change.

TIME TO REVIEW

Learning Objective 1

- What is *media*?
- What are the *traditional* and *new* forms of media?

Learning Objective 2

- What are the two reasons why the study of media is important?

Learning Objective 3

- How much time do adults and children spend engaged with media?

- How much online engagement is there in Canada?
- Where is the greatest share of time spent online?
- What does the media do that gives it such a powerful impact?
- Who are *stigmatized others* and *absolute others*, and how are they portrayed in newspapers?

Studying the Media

Scholars agree that studying the media is an essential component of understanding contemporary life. However, there are varying approaches to this field of study. In the 1940s, Lazarsfeld (1941) identified a distinction between administrative and critical research in media and communication studies; that distinction has continued to the present day (Shade, 2010; Hamilton, 2010).

Administrative research analyzes the effects of media messages on individuals (Hamilton, 2010). Similar to deviance scholars who lean more toward the objective end of the objective–subjective continuum, administrative research on media holds the individual under a microscope trying to determine what types of messages will result in particular outcomes in individuals. With its positivist foundation, administrative approaches to the study of media are interested in uncovering cause-and-effect relationships, knowledge that can subsequently be used in the mastery of the social environment—changing the way individuals will act.

Critical research in studies of media analyze processes of social control, structures of power, and the relationship between media and "domination, contradiction, and struggle" (Hamilton, 2010, p. 12). Similar to deviance scholars who lean toward the more subjective end of the objective–subjective continuum, critical media research holds society, rather than the individual, under a microscope, "revealing how media function in order to reproduce dominant ideology in their given social context" (Hamilton, 2010, p. 11) and how social transformation and collective emancipation can be achieved. While administrative media research largely draws on positivist theories, critical media research primarily uses interpretive and critical theories.

Because of their varying approaches, administrative and critical research may both study the same general topic (e.g., television), but then focus on very different aspects of that topic.

Media and Individuals: Administrative Research

Musician Jim Morrison stated, "Whoever controls the media controls the mind." Administrative research rests on the assumption that the media can affect people's thoughts and feelings (i.e., their minds) and their behaviour. The media itself conducts and makes use of administrative research to better influence its users. This is seen most clearly when looking at the efforts of advertisers to influence people's attitudes toward products and thus their actions as consumers. Administrative research is also used by groups and organizations that are attempting to solve particular social problems that they believe are influenced by the media; one area that has been thoroughly explored is the effect depictions of violence in the media have on the behaviour of those who view it.

Advertising

From commercials on television and radio, to advertisements placed in magazines or on your Facebook page, to product placements in television episodes, movies, and video games, advertising permeates all forms of media. In fact, it can be considered a form of media itself, being found on billboards, the sides of public transit buses, the bulletin boards at your campus, and even inside the doors of bathroom stalls. Advertising is everywhere. It has been estimated that while the average person in North America encountered 500 advertisements daily in the 1970s, now we are encountering up to 5000 per day (Johnson, 2009).

Does advertising work? Does it actually affect people's behaviour as consumers? Most people think that advertising does have an influence on people, although interestingly they tend to think it influences *other people* more than it influences themselves (Wilson & Brekke, 1994). Research finds that, indeed, advertising does work. Desmond and Carveth

(2007) found that when people are repeatedly exposed to particular advertisements, their brand recognition increases, they develop positive associations with those brands, and they subsequently wish to purchase those specific products. Of course, given that hundreds of billions of dollars are spent by companies on advertising each year, this finding may not come as a big surprise; for instance, an estimated $60 billion was spent on television advertising in the United States alone in 2011 (Investopedia, 2011).

Advertising's effectiveness lies in its ability to persuade people—that is, to change their attitudes about a particular product. Research into the process of persuasion studies *who* says *what* to *whom* and with what *effects*. This research finds that characteristics of the source of the communication (e.g., the model featured in an advertisement), characteristics of the message itself (e.g., the language used in the advertisement), and characteristics of the audience (e.g., the individual looking at the advertisement) all have an impact on the effectiveness of the attempt at persuasion (Aronson, Wilson, Akert, & Fehr, 2013).

Furthermore, different types of advertisements are more effective for different types of products. Some products tend to be associated with cognitively based attitudes, wherein our attitudes about the product are based on *what we think* about it—its features, strengths, and weaknesses. In contrast, other products tend to be associated with affectively based attitudes, wherein our attitudes about the product are based on how that product *makes us feel*. For example, attitudes about computer printers are more likely to be cognitively based, while attitudes about beer are affectively based. Advertisements for cognitively based

© yanlev/Fotolia

Would this photo have a greater effect on consumers in an advertisement for a computer printer or beer?

products are more effective if they stimulate people's thoughts, such as by providing utilitarian information about features and value. Advertisements for affectively based products are more effective if they stimulate people's emotions, such as by using attractive models and pleasing settings (Shavitt, 1990).

Attitudes toward products can also be affected by a more subtle form of advertising known as "product placement". This refers to inserting brand name products into television shows, movies, or video games. For example, the judges on *American Idol* drink from Coke cups to raise the profile of that brand. A more recent trend has been digitally inserting products into reruns of television shows; this enables different products to be placed in the show in different broadcasts or in different geographical regions. The first instance of digital product placement to reach widespread public attention was when a DVD of the recently released movie *Zookeeper* was placed in a rerun of the hit television show *How I Met Your Mother*. Sometimes product placement is initiated not by a company spending its advertising dollars to promote a specific product, but rather by the creators of the television show or movie. For instance, during its first season the characters on the hit television show *Mad Men* were repeatedly shown drinking *Canadian Club* whisky. Sales for the whisky climbed 8 percent over the next year after many years of a sales plateau (Krashinsky, 2012). The company that owns this brand quickly took advantage of the opportunity, shifting a larger percentage of its advertising dollars to the *Canadian Club* brand and creating an advertising campaign that dovetailed into the retro nature of the show *Mad Men*: "Damn Right Your Dad Drank It."

Administrative research on the effects of media messages on individuals can provide valuable information to the media itself, enabling it to attract audiences and in the case of advertising affect people's behaviour as consumers. But administrative approaches to media research are also of value to groups or organizations that are concerned about the media's potential to contribute to social problems, such as violence in society.

Violence in the Media

Violence permeates the media, whether in the news, movies, the latest video game, children's cartoons, professional sports, or music lyrics. Its pervasiveness has made violence the most-researched topic in media studies. Research in the mid-twentieth century demonstrated that children who witnessed adults (in person) acting aggressively with a doll also behaved more aggressively when they were given the opportunity to play with that doll (Bandura, Ross, & Ross, 1961). The same researchers found similar effects when children watched a film of adults abusing the doll (Bandura, Ross, & Ross, 1963). Does this mean that exposure to violence in the media makes people violent in the real world? Two types of research methods have been used to explore this issue: correlational research and experimental research.

Correlational studies have found a small but statistically significant association between the amount of violent media consumed and people's level of aggressiveness. For example, one study followed children from ages 8 through 18 and found that those who spent more time watching violent television programs were higher in aggression in their daily lives (Eron et al., 1996). Another study found that adolescents and young adults who watched more television (and therefore presumably more television violence) were also more aggressive, even in terms of their likelihood of having committed violent crimes (Johnson et al., 2002). However, as you most likely learned in your introductory sociology class, correlational research is not able to determine whether violent television *causes* aggression in viewers; it may be that individuals who are more aggressive to begin with choose to engage with more violent media.

Experimental research attempts to determine causation. In a typical study, individuals are exposed to forms of media with varying levels of violence and are then placed in situations where they have the opportunity to act aggressively toward someone (e.g., administering a noxious sound). This type of research does find that, at least in the short term, exposure to media violence increases levels of aggression in people. For example, Fischer and Greitemeyer (2006) had research participants listen either to songs containing violent, misogynistic lyrics (e.g., Dr. Dre's "Bitches Ain't Shit") or to more innocuous pop songs (e.g., Miley Cyrus's "The Climb"). Afterwards, when given the opportunity to pour measures of hot sauce that other participants were supposedly going to be forced to drink (although no one actually did have to drink it), those who listened to the violent songs poured larger amounts of hot sauce, especially when they were pouring it for a female. In another study, boys watched films that either portrayed a bike race or police violence. When playing a floor hockey game after watching the films, the boys who watched the film containing police violence played the game more aggressively as evidenced by behaviours such as body checking, high sticking, and name calling (Josephson, 1987).

Ask Yourself

Do you think different types of media violence have varying effects on people's aggression? Consider, for example, the violence in a children's cartoon compared to a video game (e.g., Call of Duty) or a song.

Although experimental research does find that exposure to media violence increases aggression in the short term, whether it results in aggression over the long term remains unknown. It may be that media violence affects some individuals more than others. After all, we are all exposed to considerable media violence and yet most of us do not engage in acts of violence. Indeed, Josephson (1987) found that even in the short term, film violence seemed to have its greatest impact on the boys who were more aggressive to start with. Similarly, in addressing the relationship between violence in video games and levels of aggression, Gackenbach and Snyder (2012) state, "violent videogames + violent douchebags = high probability of increased violence" (p. 43).

But why is it that violence in the media affects people (or at least some people)? Some scholars suggest the pervasiveness of violence throughout all forms of media desensitizes people, lessening the emotional impact of violent acts and making people more tolerant or accepting of aggression. Other scholars suggest that a steady diet of media violence stimulates feelings of vulnerability in people, making them think that their neighbourhoods, their cities, and society as a whole are more dangerous than they actually are. Because of their fear, people begin to use aggression as a wall of protection (Gerbner, Gross, Morgan, Signorielli, & Shanahan, et al., 2002).

So does the media control the mind, as musician Jim Morrison claimed? Administrative approaches to media research suggest that in some cases it does. Effective advertising campaigns do affect the way individuals think and feel about specific products and thereby influence their behaviours as consumers. Similarly, the wealth of research on media violence suggests that some type of relationship likely exists between violence in the media and people's levels of aggression, although the precise nature of that relationship and its magnitude remain unclear.

Because of the media's ability to affect individuals' thoughts, feelings, and behaviours—and potentially in negative ways, such as through aggression—administrative research frequently serves as the foundation for demands to change the content or to more stringently regulate various forms of media. Thus, some media becomes deviantized and subjected to measures of social control, a topic that will be addressed later in this chapter.

TIME TO REVIEW

Learning Objective 4

- How do administrative and critical approaches to media research differ?
- In what way does the media itself make use of administrative research?
- How effective is advertising?
- What three sets of characteristics affect the effectiveness of a persuasive attempt?
- What types of advertisements are most effective for cognitively based attitudes and for affectively based attitudes?

- What type of relationship has correlational research found between media violence and aggression in the real world?
- What has experimental research regarding the effects of media violence on individuals' levels of aggression found?
- Does the media have an impact on individuals' thoughts, feelings, and behaviours?

Media and Society: Critical Research

In the previous section, Jim Morrison stated that the media controls the *mind*. But Allan Ginsberg, a poet and leader of the Beat movement in the 1950s, had a different point of view, claiming that "whoever controls the media, the images, controls the *culture* [emphasis added]." This small difference in their respective statements captures the distinction between administrative and critical approaches to media studies. While administrative research analyzes the effects of media messages on individuals' thoughts, feelings, and behaviours, critical research studies the media's relationship to the broader society—structures of power, processes of social control, and patterns of struggle and resistance. The critical approach to media studies, rather than the administrative approach, "predominates in Canadian research Canadian research?" (Hamilton, 2010; Shade, 2010).

According to critical researchers, the media constructs reality, or at least a portion of it. Media show and tell us the way things are, the way they can be, and the way they should be (Macnamara, 2006). The media doesn't just have an impact on individuals but rather on the entire society—interpersonal relationships, social institutions, and societal norms, values, and beliefs. Thus, critical researchers claim that the media is intertwined with all four levels of social construction (see Chapter 1): individual, interpersonal, institutional, and sociocultural. Critical research has emphasized how media socially construct events, issues, and identities, and how those constructions may be affected by changing structures of media ownership.

The Media Frames Society

Two key topics that have been studied extensively are the media's framing of race/ethnicity and of gender. In media studies, **framing** refers to the way that the media "select some aspects of a perceived reality and make them more salient in a communication text in such a way as to promote a particular problem definition, causal interpretation, moral evaluation, and/or treatment recommendation" (Entman, 1993, p. 52). In other words, framing refers to the overall way that an issue is depicted in the media, and therefore what we notice about reality. For example, the news media comprises three generic frames: the **conflict frame**, which emphasizes conflicts between nations, institutions, groups, or individuals; the **human interest frame**, which focuses on human life stories and emotions; and the **economic consequences frame**, which highlights material costs and benefits for countries, regions, groups, or individuals (Price, Tewkesbury, & Powers, 1997). Framing provides a cognitive framework that helps us understand and interpret what we are seeing. However, it also serves as a metaphorical picture frame, which determines what we are able (and conversely unable) to see.

Exercise Your Mind

Consider your three favourite television shows—the ones that you watch the most regularly. What frames of race/ethnicity, gender, and socioeconomic status would you say are present in those shows? What races and ethnicities, genders, and socioeconomic statuses do you see in the shows? How are they presented? What groups do you *not* see represented in the shows? Why do you think they aren't represented? What messages does their absence give to viewers of the shows?

Framing Race, Ethnicity, and Gender.   Historically, the media has been characterized by a lack of diversity, presenting primarily people who are white and middle-class. Fleras and Kunz (2001) find that ethnic minorities (and especially visible minorities) tend to be portrayed in one of five interrelated ways. First, they are most typically *invisible*, in that minorities are under-represented in the media. Second, when minorities are represented they are often portrayed in ways that support existing stereotypes; these stereotypes are a foundation for the remaining frames. Third, some minorities are represented as social problems; for example, Jamaican-Canadians are frequently presented as criminals, Asian-Canadians as gangbangers, and Aboriginals as alcoholics. Fourth, some ethnic minorities are represented as adornments, such as the "noble savage" uncorrupted by civilization (e.g., Tonto, the Lone Ranger's loyal companion). Finally, minorities are represented as white-washed, their experiences identical to the ethnic majority. These frames are even found in children's media, including Disney films (see Box 4.1).

Box 4.1

Disney's Frames of Race and Ethnicity

Disney has been the subject of controversy several times for the way racial and ethnic minorities have been presented in their films. The movie *Aladdin* (1992) was criticized for its portrayal of Arabs and the Middle East more generally. In the opening song, the lyrics state "where they cut off your ear if they don't like your face, . . . it's barbaric, but hey, it's home" (James, 2009). In response to the pressures of a number of activist groups, Disney promised to remove the offending lyrics in the future DVD releases of the movie and CD releases of the soundtrack, but then did not do so.

More recently, Disney's portrayal of a black princess in *The Princess and the Frog* (2009) used the stereotype frame (Stephey, 2009; Ofori-Atta, 2012). Originally, the princess was going to be named "Maddy" and work as a maid for a white family, both drawing upon longstanding stereotypes of black Americans. In response to pressure, Disney renamed the princess a more ethnically typical "Tiana" and made her a head chef instead of a maid—but she still worked for a white family. A Haitian character in the movie was portrayed as a medicine man practising voodoo. Even cross-promotional activities between Disney and the candy Dig 'n Dips included the stereotype frame, in that Princess Tiana was used to promote a watermelon-flavoured candy.

On the pop culture website Cracked. com, you can find a story on "The 9 Most Racist Disney Characters." It includes a discussion of the manner in which stereotyping is present in portrayals of each of the characters, as well as relevant clips from each of the movies.

Critical researchers point out that framing racial and ethnic minorities has implications at the individual, interpersonal, institutional, and sociocultural levels (Jiwani, 2010). First, given the way that media permeates the lives of virtually all people in the developed (and increasingly in the developing) world, when certain communities are not represented in the media they become symbolically annihilated, erased from public consciousness. Second, the media is a public sphere in which important issues are discussed; however, a community must have access to traditional media if their voices are to be heard. Third, well-known media scholar Stuart Hall (2009) pointed out that media representations are not something *outside of* audience members, but rather that representations and individuals become intertwined; that is, identity is formed *within* media representations. Thus, the media is an important agent of socialization: the frames used to present minorities may become integrated into the identities of children of those minorities. Finally, media framing has an impact on social policy: "[If] particular groups are consistently under represented, or represented as criminals, as unassailable immigrants, or as simply not belonging, then measures may be enacted that effectively curtail their rights" (Jiwani, 2010, p. 271).

The framing of gender has received a considerable amount of attention in critical research as well. Just as the media frequently frames racial and ethnic minorities in negative ways, femininity and masculinity also tend to be framed in negative ways. Early research on representations of women in the media pointed to their relative absence— their symbolic annihilation. Renowned sociologist Erving Goffman (1979) found that in advertising, certain codes of gender governed portrayals of women. Advertisements that included women were characterized by the **feminine touch** (i.e., caressing or stroking an object, person, or themselves), the **ritualization of subordination** (i.e., lying on a bed, off-balance, or beneath men), **licensed withdrawal** (i.e., not paying attention, eyes glazed over), and **infantilization** (i.e., in little-girl poses, such as peeking from behind an object). But those representations did not end in the 1970s, when Goffman was writing. In the documentary *Codes of Gender*, writer and director Sut Jhally (2009) found that twenty-first-century advertising continues to be governed by these codes. Even when women in nontraditional roles are featured in advertisements (e.g., race-car driver Danica Patrick), they are framed in terms of their sexuality, such as stretched out across a bed in a revealing outfit. In commercials, women are less likely to do voiceovers, and when females are speaking in commercials they are frequently speaking to children or animals rather than to other adults (Ross, 2010). Across various forms of media, women continue to be framed in terms of subservience, attractiveness, dependence on men, and being outside of the workplace (Ross, 2010).

Although women tend to be represented in the media as less powerful than men, masculinity tends to be framed in a number of negative ways as well. Macnamara (2006) conducted an analysis of the framing of masculinity in the Australian media—in 650 newspapers, 100 magazines, and 330 hours of television. He found that more than 80 percent of portrayals of men were framed in negative rather than positive ways (see Table 4.1). Three-quarters of media portrayals framed men as villains, aggressors, perverts, or philanderers.

The media frames issues, events, people, and identities in particular ways, which provides us with a cognitive framework by which to understand what we are seeing and also places boundaries around what we can (and cannot) see. The media constructs a world for us to see, but at the same time it is also constructed within and by that world (Silverstone, 2007, p. 6). Media content is shaped by external forces that are increasingly global in nature. One of those global forces that critical researchers have paid particular attention to is the structure of ownership in the media industry.

Table 4.1 Most Common Negative and Positive Representations of Men in the Media

Negative Representations		Positive Representations	
Frame	% of Media Portrayals	Frame	% of Media Portrayals
Villain	37.7	Good father	4.8
Aggressor	23.8	Hero	3.1
Pervert	8.3	Protector	2.6
Philanderer	6.0	Leader	2.5

Adapted from Macnamara, J. R. (2006). *Media and male identity: The making and remaking of men.* New York, NY: Palgrave MacMillan.

Media Ownership

In Chapter 3, we saw that conflict theorists claim that powerful groups in society are able to perpetuate a dominant ideology and establish hegemony, thereby controlling how the "masses" think about the world and their place in it. Marxist theorists, in particular, state that power is determined by economic means—by owning the means of production. Critical researchers of media draw our attention to the structure of ownership in the media industry based on this assumption that ownership of the means is intertwined with the nature of the content.

Of greatest concern within this approach are the trends toward media convergence, conglomeration, and concentration (Shade & Lithgow, 2010). **Convergence** refers to media companies owning multiple forms of media. For instance, a single corporation may own not only a number of television stations, but also the cable companies that deliver the service; not only websites, but also the Internet service providers. **Conglomeration** refers to the trend toward media companies merging, or some companies purchasing other companies to form large multinational conglomerates—companies own other companies that own yet other companies. Because of convergence and conglomeration, the structure of media ownership is characterized by **concentration**, where a small number of corporations control the majority of media products.

In 1983, approximately 50 companies owned and operated the media in most parts of the world. By 2003, a small fraction of those companies controlled most of the global media (Bagdikian, 2004). In 2011, six corporations held most of the power: Time Warner, The Walt Disney Company, News Corporation, CBS, Viacom, and General Electric (Free Press, 2011; Symbaluk & Bereska, 2013). Time Warner owns television channels, movie studios, magazines, comic books, and video game developers. Disney owns television networks, television programming, radio stations, music studios, magazines, publishers, comic books, movie studios, Internet sites, and theme parks. News Corporation owns television channels, magazines, newspapers, publishers, movie studios, and Internet sites. CBS owns

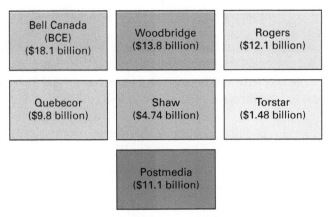

Figure 4.3 Canada's Seven Media Giants (With Annual Revenue Shown in Parentheses)

Data from Tencer, D. (2012, March 16). Concentration of media ownership in Canada: Bell Astral deal raises concerns among consumer advocates. *Huffington Post Canada*. Retrieved June 12, 2012 from www.huffingtonpost.ca.

television networks, radio stations, publishers, and Internet sites. Viacom owns television channels, radio stations, magazines, movie studios, Internet sites, and video games. General Electric owns television channels, movie studios, magazines, Internet sites, and theme parks. These six corporations (known as "The Big Six") own and control virtually all of American media, as well as much of the global media.

Media convergence, conglomeration, and concentration exist within Canada as well (see Figure 4.3). Canadian media are owned and controlled by seven media giants, which have combined annual revenues of more than $70 billion. Bell Canada (BCE) alone controls 118 radio stations, 54 cable channels, CTV, a wireless network, satellite/digital television infrastructure, and even an outdoor advertising business (billboards).

From the perspective of critical researchers, concentration within the structure of media ownership means that "corporate empires control every means by which the population learns of its society" (Bagdikian, 2004, p. 4).

Media Research and Deviance Research

In contemporary society, the media matters more than ever. Administrative research demonstrates that media messages have an effect on the behaviours of individuals, whether through the purchases they make or the acts of aggression they perpetrate. For deviance scholars, this approach to media studies is of greatest value to those who lean toward the more objective end of the objective–subjective continuum. It enables these deviance scholars to analyze the influence that certain media messages may have on specific deviant behaviours, such as crime, gang activity, substance use, premature sexual activity, and eating disorders.

Critical research shows that the impact of media goes beyond the minds of certain individuals whose behaviour may be affected by particular media messages. Media are intertwined with broader structures of power and social control and therefore affects individuals, interpersonal interactions, societal institutions, and cultural norms, values, and beliefs. For deviance scholars, this approach to media studies is of greatest value to those on the more subjective end of the objective–subjective continuum. It enables them to explore the role of media within broader patterns of the social construction of deviance—the role the media plays in our perceptions of and reactions to deviance, and who it is that has the power to determine the nature of that role.

TIME TO REVIEW

Learning Objective 4

- What do critical approaches to media studies focus their attention on?

- In the context of media studies, what is *framing*?

- What three generic frames are present in the news media?

- What five frames predominate in the framing of racial and ethnic minorities in the media, and how are they evident in Disney films?

- What are the consequences of the media's framing of racial and ethnic minorities?

- What four *codes of gender* govern women in advertisements, and how are women framed in the media overall?

- What negative and positive frames represent men in the media, and which are more common?

- In what ways is the structure of media ownership characterized by convergence, conglomeration, and concentration?

The Media–Deviance Nexus

The components of the media–deviance nexus, or the types of relationships that can exist between the media and deviance, are multifaceted. Five different relationships exist: (1) the media as a cause of deviance, (2) the media as socially constructing deviance and normality, (3) the media as a tool used to commit acts of deviance, (4) the media as a site where the deviance dance is played out—a site of debate, struggle, and resistance, and (5) the media as deviantized itself and subjected to measures of social control.

The Media Causes Deviance

The administrative approach to media studies points to one of the relationships that exists between media and deviance. Administrative research rests on the assumption that the content of media messages has an effect on individuals' thoughts, feelings, and behaviours—although its precise impact may vary across individuals. Thus, specific media messages may propel certain individuals into various forms of deviant behaviour. For example, violence in the media has been found to have some impact on aggressive behaviour in the real world, at least in some people (Josephson, 1987; Gackenbach & Snyder, 2012; Gerbner et al., 2002).

The view that the media may be a *cause* of deviance, such as aggressive behaviour, is reflected in various areas in the remainder of this book as well. For example, research on the effects of pornography consumption on youth attitudes and behaviours will be explored in Chapter 5. In Chapter 6, we will see how the perceived effects of advertising on youth underlies, in part, social control efforts regarding tobacco use.

The Media Constructs Deviance and Normality

The critical approach to media studies, which was also presented earlier in this chapter, draws our attention to the second relationship that exists between media and deviance. Critical research rests on the assumption that the media influences the culture as a whole (rather than specific individuals) through its power to define boundaries, identify social problems, and shape public debates. For example, the way the media frames ethnicity and gender is intertwined with the locations of different social groups in the structure of power, perpetuates those locations, and can be integrated into people's identities. Thus, the media socially constructs deviance and normality, shaping the dominant moral codes that govern what is perceived as acceptable and unacceptable behaviour, characteristics, and people.

The view that the media plays an important role in socially constructing deviance and normality will be put forth throughout the remaining chapters in the book. The role of the sex industry, as well as sexuality within mainstream media (e.g., television), in constructing perceptions of deviant and normal sexuality will be addressed in Chapter 5. In Chapter 6, the way that media portrayals of youth crime and gangs contribute to moral panics is explored. When it comes to aspects of physical appearance, as will be discussed in Chapter 7, the media is central, both in terms of the incorporation of body modification in mainstream media (even children's media) and in creating the social standards that define particular bodies as "too fat," "too thin," or "ideal." In Chapter 8, we will see that the ongoing stigmatization of mental illness is reflected in television and movies, and those reflections help to perpetuate that stigmatization. Finally, Chapter 9 will explore how the media plays an important role in popular perceptions and stigmatization of particular religious groups as "cults."

Ask Yourself

Have you or anyone you know ever engaged in any of the following acts: visited a pornography website; submitted a term paper that was purchased online; downloaded music or software without paying for it; accessed someone's computer files, email, or social networking profile without their permission; harassed someone via email or social networking sites; used someone else's wireless signal; created/transmitted a computer virus or malware; hacked an organization's computer system; stolen someone's identity with information found online?

When we think of the relationship between the media and deviance in the twenty-first century, the many ways that the media can be *used* for acts of deviance may first come to mind. The *Ask Yourself* exercise lists some forms of **cyberdeviance** (deviant acts that are committed using a computer). Some cyberdeviance is unique to the cyberworld (e.g., creating/spreading viruses and malware or using someone else's wireless signal), while other forms of deviance that occur in the online world can also occur in the offline world (e.g., bullying, watching pornography). Like deviant acts in general, there are high-consensus forms and low-consensus forms of cyberdeviance (see Chapter 1).

Cybercrime

The Internet can be used as a tool for a variety of different criminal activities, including credit card fraud, identity theft, and computer hacking. In the summer of 2012, a two-year undercover investigation known as "Operation Card Shop" resulted in dozens of arrests in 13 countries, including Canada (Canadian Press, 2012; US Attorney's Office, 2012). This particular organized crime ring used the Internet to buy and sell stolen identities, exploit people's credit cards, create and exchange counterfeit documents, sell hacking tools (including software that enables "cybervoyeurs" to hijack an unsuspecting individual's personal computer camera), and create and spread a number of computer viruses and malware. More than 400 000 individuals and dozens of businesses were victimized by this cybercrime ring.

One American survey (Holt & Turner, 2012) found that 10 percent of people surveyed reported being victims of identity theft in the previous 12 months. The more time people spent online, the greater the risk of having their identities stolen. Ironically, those at greatest risk were individuals who engaged in various forms of cyberdeviance themselves, such as illegally downloading software or music, cyberbullying, using someone else's wireless signal, accessing someone's computer files without permission, or accessing someone's computer files by guessing their password.

People who access computer systems without authorization and sometimes use that access for malicious purposes are known as **hackers**. Activities can range from hacking celebrity Twitter accounts to plant humorous outgoing messages (Complex Magazine, 2011) to placing viruses in a government's computer system. Computer hacking can have significant economic consequences for society. In the United States alone, American businesses lost more than $30 million in 2005 because of hacking (CSI/FBI Computer Security Survey, cited in Holt & Turner, 2012), and a single computer virus (the Melissa virus) caused $80 million in damages worldwide (Taylor et al., cited in Holt & Turner, 2012).

Hackers use computers in two ways: first, as their means of attack, and second, as a way of communicating with other hackers. Holt and Turner (2012) found that a complex hacker subculture exists both online and offline. By analyzing hacker Web forums, interviewing several active hackers, and conducting observations at the annual hacker convention in Las Vegas (DEFCON), the researchers identified five "normative orders" (p. 179) that characterize the hacker subculture: technology, knowledge, commitment, categorization, and law.

- Hackers express a deep overriding interest in understanding and manipulating *technology*, which they report emerging from an early age (sometimes as young as seven). Hackers use Web forums as an important resource for obtaining technical skills, while offline most of the sessions at DEFCON provide a wide range of technical information.

- The continuous quest for *knowledge* is the foundation for hacker identities. Hackers define themselves as people in pursuit of knowledge, and different labels are applied to individuals with varying levels of knowledge. Those with an extensive body of knowledge are considered "hackers," and having a particularly impressive body of knowledge makes one an "elite hacker," also known as "1337" or "'leet" (p. 184). People with little or no knowledge have derogatory labels applied to them and are deviantized. Those who have limited knowledge and whose hacking activities are perceived as simplistic are known as "script kiddies" or "noobs" (p. 184). People who have no hacking knowledge at all and yet still attend the DEFCON convention are labelled "scene whores" (p. 184).

- Pursuing knowledge and using it to master technology requires deep *commitment*. An individual must be dedicated and willing to persist despite the many obstacles and failures they will inevitably encounter.

- Learning is a process, and as such there are questions about *categorization*. The subculture is characterized by debates over the point at which an individual can be considered an authentic hacker, and there are variations in the point at which individuals integrate "hacker" into their own identities.

- Subcultural debates also revolve around the *law*. These debates revolve around questions about the legality of specific behaviours, as well as what forms of hacking are considered acceptable or unacceptable. Some hackers consider all forms of hacking to be acceptable; others make distinctions between the "normal" hacking community and malicious hackers, who are perceived as "the scum of the earth" (p. 192).

The most malicious hacking, such as using computer viruses and malware to attack societal infrastructure, is frequently referred to as **cyberterrorism**. Although cyberterrorism takes place within a unique online environment, it has many of the same characteristics as offline forms of terrorism. Matusitz (2008) explores these characteristics in a comparison of two terrorist groups. The first group was known as the Zealots, a Jewish extremist group that existed within the Roman Empire. They refused to pay taxes and sought to overthrow the government through the use of weapons and violence. Members of this group committed suicide in 73 AD. The second group is Titan Rain, a cyberterrorist group accused of working for the Chinese government. This group attempted to hack the computer systems of US military bases as well as defence contractors and aerospace companies to steal American government and military secrets.

Despite existing almost 2000 years apart, these two terrorist groups show three similarities in their activities. First, they have similar patterns of communication in that they each had to manage networks of criminals through long-range communication. Likewise, both groups sent deceptive signals to fool authorities; Zealots used handshakes and gestures, while cyberterrorists send deceptive online messages to trick people and computer systems into providing access to information. Second, the two types of terrorist groups have similar connections and kinship webs. Both are built via **chaining**—an individual can only join the network after being introduced and recommended by an existing member. Furthermore, both are structured by relatively independent nodes within a network, rather than by a cohesive, hierarchical body. Finally, both types of terrorist groups face similar obstacles, particularly the *protection of property* on the part of their victims. In the Roman Empire, individuals and governmental bodies physically protected their property from theft or destruction by the Zealots (such as through armed guards). Cyberterrorists encounter many forms of virtual protection of property, such as firewalls and software that protects against viruses and malware.

Digital Piracy

Various forms of cybercrime, such as identity theft, credit card exploitation, malware, and hacking government or military computer systems, can be considered high-consensus forms of deviance—large numbers of people (albeit not everyone) would agree that these behaviours are unacceptable and should face measures of social control. However, there are other types of online activities that while technically "illegal," could be considered low-consensus forms of deviance—relatively fewer people would agree that those activities are unacceptable and in need of social control. In fact, many people might not even attach the label of "cybercrime" to some of these activities. Digital piracy is one of those activities.

Digital piracy refers to the illegal downloading of music, software, and video. Although some creators make this content available online at no charge, a great deal of digital content is protected by copyright or licensing; to download it without having paid for it is illegal. Although illegal, this activity is widespread. As one active digital pirate states, "it's like jaywalking—everybody does it and no one cares" (Holt & Copes, 2010, p. 637).

Piracy is not unique to the Internet environment. VCRs enabled people to make illegal recordings from television to videocassettes; other pieces of equipment allowed material contained on one videocassette to be transferred to another. The same was true of music cassette tapes. With an inexpensive tape recorder, people could record music from a vinyl record onto a cassette tape, or transfer music from one tape to another. In fact, in the Soviet Union (where music from the West was banned), individuals would smuggle a single copy of a popular album into the country, where it was "pirated" using equipment that imprinted grooves onto discarded X-ray films then sold on the black market.

Although pirating is not new, the Internet facilitates piracy through its anonymity, speed of transmission, and "a shift in mindset about ownership given the perception that anything available online is free for others to download with impunity" (Hinduja & Higgins, 2011). The financial impact of digital pirating on creators and artists, companies within the associated industries (e.g., movie studios), and distributors (e.g., retail stores) is of considerable magnitude. It is estimated that in the United States alone, the financial costs in 2005 were almost $55 billion and accounted for more than 370 000 jobs lost (Hinduja & Higgins, 2011).

The nature of digital pirating has changed since the late 1990s. At that time, piracy was technologically complex, so only individuals who had a relatively high level of expertise in computer technology were able to engage in piracy. However, now the dominant mode of piracy is via peer-to-peer torrent file sharing. With this process, an individual who wants to download a particular movie or song is able to "grab" bits and pieces from multiple random computers that are linked into the process, while at the same time allowing other users access to the bits and pieces of digital content on his or her own computer. This process is fast and easy to use, which means that most pirates no longer need to have any significant expertise in computer technology. Torrent file sharing is also much less vulnerable to detection by authorities, as one instance of sharing may be traced to 10 000 (or even more) nodes in the file-sharing network (Holt & Copes, 2010).

A number of sociological theories have been used to explain digital piracy (Holt & Copes, 2010; Hinduja & Higgins, 2011). Using differential association theory (see Chapter 2), researchers analyze the techniques and motives of piracy that are learned in online environments, such as how to recognize files that may contain viruses or malware. Several different techniques of neutralization (Chapter 2) are used by active digital pirates to rationalize their actions. They *deny injury* by stating that corporations in the related industries have more than enough money already; a little bit of downloading won't hurt them. They *condemn the condemners* by claiming that those industries also exploit consumers with high prices. And they *appeal to higher loyalties* by arguing that online material should be free to all so that one's socioeconomic status is not the sole determinant of the media content they are able to access. Interpretive theories (see Chapter 3) explore processes of identity formation and labelling in digital pirates. For example, Holt and Copes (2010) found that even active digital pirates (people who have downloaded an average of five files per week for the past six months) may identify themselves as "pirates" as a personal identity but do not identify themselves with the online pirating subculture. From this perspective, these researchers also found that there is labelling and stigmatization within the pirating community. Those who sell pirated materials (rather than freely share them) are considered "lowlife shit(s)" (p. 642), and people who download significantly more files than they *seed* (i.e., share) are labelled "leeches" (p. 642).

Although digital piracy is an activity that is subjected to formal measures of social control (through legislation and persecution), it is a common activity in contemporary society and is considered by many to be normal and acceptable. In contrast, another form of cyberdeviance has been increasingly perceived as deviant in recent years and subjected to numerous formal and informal measures of social control—cyberbullying.

Cyberbullying

As with terrorism and piracy, bullying is an activity that can occur both online or offline. However, the Internet (and other forms of computer-mediated communication) provides a level of anonymity that does not exist in offline bullying (Hinduja & Patchin, 2008). Although a number of instances of cyberbullying have been covered in the news media, the 2012 suicide of BC teenager Amanda Todd captured the public mind, perhaps largely because prior to committing suicide she posted a heart-wrenching video on YouTube that described her experiences of being bullied—a video that was played repeatedly in the media following her death. **Cyberbullying** refers to "the use of information and communication technologies . . . to support deliberate, repeated, and hostile behavior by an individual or group that is intended to harm others" (Li, 2010, p. 373). It can consist of numerous specific behaviours, ranging from excluding someone from an online group to harassing individuals with threats of harm to posting embarrassing information about someone (see Figure 4.4).

More than 40 percent of undergraduate students say that they have been cyberbullied at some point in their lives; visible minorities, women, and those who are homosexual or bisexual are especially at risk. Most cyberbullying occurs at the hands of strangers (44 percent) and friends or acquaintances (39 percent) (Reyns, Henson, & Fisher, 2012). As with being victimized by cybercrime (e.g., identity theft), those who spend more time online (especially in chatrooms and on social networking sites) are more likely to be cyberbullied, especially if they share a great deal of personal information on those sites (Marcum, Higgins, & Ricketts, 2010). Problems in school and substance use are also associated with being cyberbullied (Hinduja & Patchin, 2008).

In an analysis of 15 classes of students in Grades 7 through 12 from across Western Canada, Li (2010) analyzed responses to being cyberbullied. Almost 40 percent said that they hadn't told anyone about it, and less than 12 percent had told an adult; the vast majority of students said they either tried to get away from the bully or did nothing.

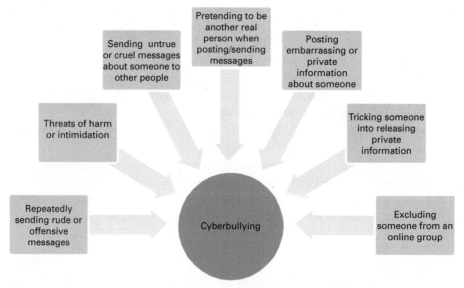

Figure 4.4 Forms of Cyberbullying

Unfortunately, it seems that telling someone does not necessarily improve the situation; only 15 percent of students reported that telling someone made the situation any better.

An online survey of more than 1000 adolescents found that 18 percent of boys and 16 percent of girls admit to participating in cyberbullying. Acts of cyberbullying and traditional bullying are related, in that individuals who participate in one are likely to participate in the other as well. The gender differences in perpetrating acts of cyberbullying are not statistically significant; this differs from traditional bullying, where boys predominate as perpetrators (Hinduja & Patchin, 2008).

The impact that cyberbullying has on victim's lives has resulted in widespread social control efforts, both online and offline. In June 2012, the Standing Senate Committee on Human Rights held a series of meetings on cyberbullying and prepared reports and resource materials not only for the Senate, but also for school boards, teachers, parents, and children.

TIME TO REVIEW

Learning Objective 5

- What five relationships exist between the media and deviance?

- In what ways is the media seen as a cause of deviance?

- In what ways does the media socially construct deviance?

- What are the different ways that the media can be used as a tool for deviance?

- What is *cybercrime* and what are some of the forms it takes?

- What are the characteristics of the hacker subculture?

- How has piracy changed over time and what theories have been used to analyze digital piracy?

- What proportion of youth say they have either been cyberbullied or participated in such bullying?

The Media and the Deviance Dance

The media serves as a social typer of deviance. Through its framing of issues, events, and identities, it shows us who should be considered deviant, why they should be considered deviant, and what should be done about it. Even though particular frames predominate in the mainstream media, differing points of view, debates, and resistance can also be found. Some parts of the media may socially type a specific person, behaviour, or characteristic as deviant, while other parts of the media contradict or resist that deviant label. One set of media voices may declare a certain solution to a form of deviance, but other media voices may put forth a very different solution. The media may support dominant ideologies and the status quo, yet it may also promote alternative ideologies and provide the means by which to dismantle the status quo.

The multifaceted nature of the media means that the deviance dance is an inherent part. Smoking is pervasive on fictional television programs and in movies, yet during commercials it is common to see public service announcements about the dangers of smoking. Some music lyrics may promote acts of violence while others extol the virtues of peace. Media images frequently present a narrow vision of the "ideal" body, while at the same time magazine articles and television talk shows may discuss how unrealistic those images are (see Chapter 7).

One of the clearest ways we can see the deviance dance within the media is in the fact that although the media can be used as a tool to commit various deviant acts (cybercrime, digital piracy, cyberbullying), it is also used as a tool to exert measures of social control on deviant acts. For example, Facebook has a technology that scans postings and chats for evidence of criminal activity, such as cyberterrorism and the distribution of child pornography (Menn, 2012). Authorities scan torrent file-sharing sites for the IP addresses of the heaviest digital pirates, resulting in a number of prosecutions in the United States (Holt & Copes, 2010).

Cyberbullying is socially controlled within cyberspace itself, with anti-bullying campaigns on YouTube and anti-bullying websites. For example, a website dedicated to Amanda Todd (**www.amandatoddlegacy.org**) provides information and resources not only about bullying, but also about suicide, depression, and substance abuse. While looking at a memorial page on Facebook for Amanda Todd, an Alberta woman came across a post that actually spoke in favour of Amanda Todd's death. Tracing the message back to the poster's own Facebook page, the woman found his employer's name listed; she contacted his employer, showed them the messages, and the employer subsequently fired him for his actions. Although many people applauded the woman's actions, she found herself subjected to measures of social control as well, with others claiming she herself was now a "bully" for having cost the man his job (CBC News, 2012b).

The media is used as a tool for the social control of offline deviant behaviour as well, ranging from human rights abuses to crime to obesity. For example, human rights groups train people in closed countries (e.g., Libya, Syria) how to take high-quality video on their smartphones and upload them to websites so that human rights abuses can be documented and brought to the world's attention. Following the 2011 Stanley Cup riot in Vancouver, the Vancouver Police Department created a website containing images and video footage of rioters they were hoping visitors to the site might be able to identify (**riot2011.vpd.ca**); as of December 2012, reports to the website had resulted in 1040 charges laid against 315 rioters (Vancouver Police Department, 2012). The Internet also contains a plethora of resources for people with substance abuse problems, those who are trying to lose weight or get fit, people with mental disorders or who care about someone with a mental disorder, those wondering if a new religious group they are a part of might be "destructive," and more.

The media is a tool for resistance to the social typing process as well. Social groups that are stigmatized offline—such as people with disabilities or illnesses, transgendered persons, and members of various lifestyle groups (e.g., rave, straightedge)—are able to find online communities of support. In addition to providing individuals with support, the presence of these online communities also serves as a way to attempt to change society's dominant moral codes.

The nodal network known as "Anonymous" uses the Internet to resist social typing and change moral codes as well. Even though these people are computer hackers and are committing cybercrimes, they do not perceive themselves as criminals. Instead, they consider themselves to be "hacktavists"—social activists who hack computers to improve society. "Anonymous" hacks computers to expose pedophilia online and to reveal corruption by religious organizations, but it is perhaps most well known for its relationship with WikiLeaks. They hack government computer systems to obtain information that they believe the government is hiding and the public has the right to know. After obtaining this information, they post it online for all to see, such as on the WikiLeaks website.

Deviantizing the Media

At times, media products themselves are socially typed as deviant and are subject to measures of social control. When the media is deviantized, it might be subjected to formal social control (e.g., censorship or regulation through policy). For instance, in the 1980s a group of wives of American politicians who were concerned about sexually explicit music lyrics formed the Parents Music Resource Center (PMRC). Initially calling for specific songs to be banned, eventually their efforts resulted in the labelling of albums containing explicit lyrics. Given their location in the structure of power, their concerns elicited formal Senate hearings over the issue. Not only did members of the PMRC and various scientific "experts" testify, so did several musicians who were opposed to the PMRC's efforts, such as Frank Zappa and Dee Snider; the full PMRC Senate hearing is available on YouTube.

Informal social controls can be exerted as well, whether through parental restrictions on media use or audience boycotts. For instance, the website of the Parents Television Council provides weekly lists of the "worst" television shows for families based on characteristics such as references to sexuality (especially homosexuality) and substance use.

Springhall (1999) suggests that youth forms of media are especially likely to be deviantized. In fact, he claims that youth media are perennially deviantized because of their presumed negative effects on youth (and thereby on society). Penny theatres and dime novels in the nineteenth century, gangster films of the 1930s and 1940s, American horror comics of the 1950s (which were banned in Great Britain), gangsta rap in the 1990s, and various video games more recently have all stimulated public criticism and attempts at regulation.

At times, youth media is deviantized because of its presumed effects on youth. We see this in contemporary debates over violent video games, but we can see it historically as well. For example, in the 1920s it was argued that the rhythms and instrumentation of jazz stimulated the sexual energies of youth and contributed to the "outrageous" style of dancing (e.g., the Charleston), the physical appearance of young women (with short skirts, short hair, and makeup), and behaviours like smoking and drinking (especially in females). Some politicians, along with popular women's magazines, called for an outright ban on jazz music (Fass, 1979).

At other times, youth media may be deviantized because of its association with a group of youth who are considered troublesome. Under the Nazi regime in Germany, youth who were part of the swing music subculture were subjected to surveillance by the Gestapo, arrest, expulsion from high school or university, assignment to the front lines during the war, and even imprisonment in concentration camps. These social controls were not imparted because of swing music's perceived effects on youth, but rather because everything about the swing subculture contradicted the social order the Nazis were trying to create. The Nazi government wanted a clean-cut, militaristic, uniform youth culture that supported their social and military goals. In contrast, the "swing kids'" style was English in nature, and the British were Germany's enemy. The boys wore baggy trousers with an English newspaper in the back pocket, trench coats, and hung a closed umbrella over one arm. They did not listen to German folk music, but rather English and American music. Their slouching walk was anything but militaristic, and instead of greeting each other with "Heil, Hitler," their greeting was, "Swing, heil"—expressing an allegiance to the music rather than to the nation's leader (Wallace & Alt, 2001).

Springhall (1999) states that although the deviantization of youth media is frequently rationalized in terms of its effects on audiences, if we look at all of the various forms of youth media that have been deviantized in the past and present, similar motivations are apparent. The process of deviantization is not really about the youth themselves, but rather it is indicative of the fear of technological change, the future, and challenges to dominant moral codes in some parts of the adult world.

TIME TO REVIEW

Learning Objective 5

- What are some of the ways that the deviance dance is evident in the media?

- What are some examples of the media being used to socially control online and offline deviance?

- What are some examples of the media being used to resist a deviant label and change society's dominant moral codes?

- What are some forms of youth media that have been deviantized?

- Why was jazz music deviantized in the 1920s?

- Why was the swing music subculture deviantized in Nazi Germany?

- What forms of youth media are frequently deviantized?

As one of the central pedagogical forces in the twenty-first century, the media and deviance are intimately intertwined. The media can be analyzed as a cause of deviance, as a site where deviance and normality are socially constructed, as a tool to be used for acts of deviance, as a site for the deviance dance, or in terms of its own deviantization. Although only a limited number of illustrations of the media–deviance relationship have been addressed in this chapter, in the remainder of the book you will continue to see that studying deviance necessarily means studying the media as well.

CHAPTER SUMMARY

- It is important for sociologists to study the media because of the amount of time we spend engaged with it and the impact that it has (both on individuals and on society). (2)

- Most time online is spent on social networking sites, although the amount of time spent watching videos online is rapidly increasing. The media has an impact on individuals and society in that it serves as one of the primary definers of boundaries between groups and the communities within, identifies social problems, and shapes public debates. (3)

- *Administrative* approaches to media studies focus on the effect of media messages on individuals. Findings from this type of research can be of value to media itself, such as in creating more effective advertisements. Findings can also be of value to groups who are concerned about the potential role played by the media in creating social problems, such as violence. (4)

- *Critical* approaches to media studies analyze processes of social control, structures of power, and the relationship between the media and "domination, contradiction, and struggle" (Hamilton, 2010, p. 12). (4)

- Through *framing*, the media constructs a reality for us to see. The way it frames issues, events, and identities has an impact on individuals, interpersonal interactions, institutions, and larger cultural norms, values, and beliefs. (4)

- Critical scholars claim that framing is influenced, in part, by the structure of media ownership, which is increasingly characterized by convergence and concentration. (4)

- The media–deviance nexus is characterized by five different types of relationships: The media is a potential cause of certain types of deviance (e.g. violence), serves as a site for the social construction of deviance, is a tool used for the commission of acts of deviance (e.g., cybercrime or cyberbullying), is a site of the deviance dance (e.g., social control and resistance), and is sometimes deviantized itself (e.g., jazz). (5)

MySearchLab®

⊙–Watch Go to MySearchLab to watch the video called "Everything's Cool".

Apply What You Know: Consider the narrator's comments about the strategy of the energy industry to counteract concerns over global warming. What does this strategy tell us about the importance of framing and its relationship to what is considered to be problematic for society?

MySearchLab with eText offers you access to an online interactive version of the text, extensive help with your writing and research projects, and provides round-the-clock access to credible and reliable source material.

Chapter 5
"Deviant" and "Normal" Sexuality

© albund/Shutterstock

Learning Objectives

After reading this chapter, you should be able to

1 Identify the two theoretical perspectives that dominate sociological studies of sexuality.

2 Contrast the sexual cultures of traditional Aboriginal societies with that of the colonizing Europeans, and explain how colonization affected Aboriginal sexual cultures.

3 Describe how deviant sexuality was defined and regulated from the seventeenth century through the twentieth century, explaining how the changing sexual cultures reinforced class, gender, and racial hierarchies of the times.

4 Explain how consent, nature of the partner, nature of the act, frequency, and setting serve as criteria by which we judge deviant and normal sexuality.

5 Outline the nature of the deviance dance surrounding the issues of exotic dancing, pornography, and prostitution.

What Is Deviant Sexuality?

Renowned sexuality researcher Alfred Kinsey (2006) claims, "the only unnatural sexual act is that which you cannot perform." In contrast, author W. Somerset Maugham (1998) suggests that "there is hardly anyone whose sexual life, if it were broadcast, would not fill the world at large with surprise and horror."

Ask Yourself

In your opinion, what is "normal" sexuality? What is "deviant" sexuality? In your response, you might refer to fantasies, behaviours, identities, or more abstract ideals. Now answer a slightly different question: In Canadian society, what do you think is considered to be "normal" and "deviant" sexuality? How similar is this list to the one you made of your own opinions?

These two quotations demonstrate the complexity of sexuality in human societies and point to the different ways sexuality can be perceived—biologically and sociologically. Kinsey's view of sexuality draws on biology as the foundation upon which normal and deviant sexuality is defined, and says that normal sexuality is simply that which is physically possible. However, Maugham suggests that we all judge people's sexuality, and that most people's sexual lives, if known, would be judged negatively. Evidently, something more than biology plays a role in how sexuality is perceived and in the aspects of sexuality that are defined as deviant or normal. There appears to be a substantial difference between what is biologically possible and what is considered socially acceptable.

The *Ask Yourself* exercise asks you to think about your own perceptions of "normal" and "deviant" sexuality. If you compared the list you made to the list that someone else made you would probably see some differences. You might be shocked by something that someone else is not shocked by and vice versa. In other words, what is considered acceptable varies between individuals. However, as pointed out in the first chapter of this book, a deviant label is not a product of individual perceptions but rather of social processes, processes that you were referring to in the *Ask Yourself* exercise.

Social processes determine what is considered deviant and normal sexuality in society. More objective deviance specialists refer to cultural and historical variations in the norms that are used as the standard against which deviance is judged, and more subjective deviance specialists refer to processes of social construction. Social processes determine who is socially typed as deviant through the processes of *description* (placed in a category because of their sexuality), *evaluation* (judged on the basis of the category into which they have been placed), and *prescription* (made subject to particular measures of regulation or social control). Thus, although similar sexual activities and characteristics may be found throughout the world, there is variation across cultures and time as to where those characteristics fit within the social hierarchy, the roles assigned to people who exhibit those characteristics, and the meanings attached to those characteristics.

In the contemporary sociology of sexuality, the constructionist perspective predominates. Consequently, the interactionist and critical theoretical perspectives presented in Chapter 3 are the lenses through which sexuality is most often studied.

Interactionist perspectives address the processes by which people come to understand and attribute meaning to their own sexuality and the sexuality of others. For instance,

Seidman (2002) interviews gays and lesbians to determine what "the closet" means to them. Similarly, Shirpak, Maticka-Tyndale, and Chinichian (2007) explore how Iranian immigrants understand Canadian sexuality, and find that they perceive Canadian society to be too sexually permissive, which they consider a potential threat to their own family lives. Later in this chapter you will see how exotic dancers understand and attribute meaning to their interactions with customers, the organizational rules they work under, and their sense of self.

Critical perspectives analyze the ways that power influences people's understandings and attributions of meaning. From this perspective, the power-reflexive work of Foucault is emphasized in that it is considered by many to be at the core of contemporary sociological studies of sexuality (Moon, 2008). Foucault (1978) and the many sociologists of sexuality who have followed in his footsteps emphasize the role of *elite discourse*—that is, the knowledge about sexuality that is conveyed by those in authority and that subsequently comes to be perceived as truth. For example, Foucault draws attention to the distinction between sexual behaviour and sexual identity, pointing out that the two do not necessarily correspond; one can engage in a particular behaviour and yet not perceive that behaviour to be an essential component of one's self. He claims that although homosexual activities have always existed, it was only when the science of psychology began to propose the existence of the "self" in the late nineteenth century that homosexual *identities* (and indeed, identities of any type) became possible.

In the present day, Foucauldian sociologists who study sexuality analyze the ways that scientific, political, legal, religious, and media discourses of sexuality "shape the ways audience members can imagine organizing their lives" (Moon, 2008, p. 193). Elite discourses place limits on "what kinds of persons it is acceptable or even possible to be" (p. 194) at a particular sociohistorical moment, such that individuals cannot even imagine possibilities that lie outside of those limits.

As you progress through the remainder of this chapter, which addresses the social construction of sexuality cross-culturally, historically, and in contemporary Canadian society, you will see that even when interactionist and critical theories are not being explicitly addressed in research on sexuality, their core assumptions still serve as the implicit framework for such research.

The Cultural and Historical Construction of Sexuality

Even a brief look at cultural and historical variations in sexuality reveals how the perceptions, meanings, and control of sexuality in contemporary Canada represent only a small portion of that which is found throughout the world. Your own perceptions and meanings of sexuality, as revealed in the list you made near the beginning of this chapter, are an even smaller segment of what people in the world think and feel about sexuality.

Cross-cultural variations in sexuality have been studied for a century, particularly by anthropologists. For instance, Herdt's classic (1984) research on the Sambia of New

Guinea found ritualized same-sex sexual activities among males during a certain period of life. These activities, required of all males without exception, were intended to reproduce the distinct roles of men and women, the patriarchal structure of society, and the ability of men to be fierce and powerful warriors should the need arise.

Historians and classicists have also drawn attention to cultural and historical variations in sexuality. For example, Arkins (1994) has shown that in Athens during the fifth century BC, "normal" and "deviant" sexuality were defined on the basis of power. They focused on the needs and desires of aristocratic males (the only "citizens" of Athens) and reproduced the existing social structure. Aristocratic males were permitted marital sex for the purpose of producing male heirs, as well as sexual relationships with other women, slaves, foreigners, and aristocratic adolescent boys for the purposes of pleasure. However, sexual activity was only acceptable between two persons occupying higher and lower positions on the hierarchy of power in society; sexual activity between two aristocratic men (i.e., two "equals") was considered unacceptable and subjected to measures of social control.

Looking at the sexual cultures of Sambian society, ancient Athens, or any other number of cultures around the world shows us the power of elite discourses of sexuality. Elite discourses place boundaries around what individuals in those cultures perceive as being acceptable, normal, or even possible. At the same time, the elite discourses of sexuality that govern Canadian society in the twenty-first century influence our reactions to the sexual cultures of other societies as well as our own sexual choices. The elite discourses of sexuality in our society today have undergone a long evolution. That evolution begins with traditional Aboriginal cultures prior to and after being impacted by colonization, and continues through considerable social changes from the seventeenth through the twentieth centuries.

Traditional Aboriginal Cultures: From Holism to Oppression

The arrival of Europeans in what is now the Americas and their subsequent colonization of that land and its indigenous peoples had a massive impact on all aspects of Aboriginal societies. For hundreds of years, various facets of Aboriginal cultures were suppressed, facing potential and actual eradication at the hands of political and religious authorities.

Historical knowledge about sexuality in traditional Aboriginal cultures is somewhat limited. However, the available evidence clearly points to a dramatic contrast between the perceptions of sexuality in Aboriginal and European cultures (Windecker, 1997; Barman 1997/1998). The different constructions of sexuality were so distinct that sexuality became a nexus of conflict and subsequent social control as colonization progressed (Mandell & Momirov, 2000).

There was considerable variability across Aboriginal cultures in the dominant moral codes governing sexuality. In some cultures, premarital and extramarital sexual activity among women were considered unacceptable and subjected to measures of social control, while in others, premarital and extramarital sex were accepted practices and might involve gifts being given to the woman's family (Windecker, 1997). However, amidst these differences a commonality was that sexuality was considered to be inextricably interwoven with all other aspects of social life (Newhouse, 1998). Life was viewed as consisting of four components: physical, intellectual, emotional, and spiritual. Because life was seen as consisting of these components, so was sexuality; the physical, intellectual, emotional, and spiritual were perceived as existing in sexuality, and sexuality was thought to enhance these four components in the rest of a person's life. Sexuality was not stigmatized. Sexual terms were integrated into some place names, and sexuality was incorporated into myths and stories. For instance, one Anishinabe story describes how the Creator made sex an act of pleasure so that men and women would come to live together and thereby increase the population (Newhouse, 1998).

In some Aboriginal cultures, this pleasure was acceptable between members of the same sex as well. Recognizing more than two sexes and more than two genders, many cultures perceived a wider range of sexualities (and genders) as "normal" (Nelson, 2006). Sexuality/gender variants in biological males have been recognized in 110 to 150 Aboriginal cultures, and variants in biological females in 55 to 75 cultures (Nanda, 2000). For instance, the Navajo used the term **nadleeh** to refer to both masculine female-bodied and feminine male-bodied members of the community. European explorers used the derogatory term **berdache** ("male prostitute") to refer to biological males who assumed female roles, including sexual relationships with men. In some Aboriginal cultures, sexual relationships between two biological males were acceptable as long as they were of different "genders."

But not only were people who were attracted to members of the same sex accepted in these cultures and given specific roles in the social structure, they were perceived as "normal" and even "necessary." As Newhouse (1998, para. 16) points out, "Mojaves believed that 'from the beginning of the world, it was meant that there should be homosexuals.'" At times, the moral codes of Aboriginal cultures regulated particular sexual *behaviours*, but in other cases social control was instead directed at proper types of *relationships* between people—ones that, within the spiritual belief systems, were considered necessary to maintain harmony and balance in social life and in the larger society (Newhouse, 1998).

For the colonizing European cultures of the time, sexuality had a very different meaning. Sex was for the purpose of reproduction, and even then notions of pleasure were frowned upon; sexuality was sinful, requiring careful and stringent control. Sexuality was not integrated into social life, but rather isolated from it, almost as a necessary evil, and infused with guilt (Newhouse, 1998; D'Emilio & Freedman, 1997). The only nondeviant sexuality was that which occurred between husband and wife, and even then only if their sole sexual behaviour was intercourse, if it took place in the "missionary" position, and if they did not enjoy it too much or do it too often. The sexuality of women in particular had to be strictly controlled to maintain the purity and sanctity of the home—and to assure paternity (Barman, 1997/1998). Same-sex activities were unacceptable and subject to both informal sanction (e.g., by the community) and formal sanction (e.g., excommunication from the church) (D'Emilio & Freedman, 1997).

Of course, with these considerably divergent sexual cultures, conflict between European and Aboriginal peoples became inevitable. The gifts that were given within some sexual relationships in Aboriginal cultures were labelled by Europeans as indicative of "prostitution" (Barman, 1997/1998). The sheer variability in sexuality across Aboriginal cultures was, in itself, perceived as problematic. However, during the early years of colonization in Canada, sexual unions between white men and Aboriginal women were common because of the relative scarcity of white women as well as the usefulness of Aboriginal women's skills in trapping, languages, diplomacy, and other areas (Mandell & Momirov, 2000; Das Gupta, 2000; Razack, 2002). The Aboriginal women with whom early European settlers formed relationships were called *les femmes du pays*, or "country wives" (Mandell & Momirov, 2000, p. 22). Such pragmatic concerns led the Hudson's Bay Company to not only allow but encourage these interracial relationships among employees for a period of time. Even missionaries during the early years did not actively discourage the unions (Razack, 2002). However, as colonization progressed, Aboriginal sexuality became one of the things that the emerging authorities felt the need to regulate: "missionaries attempted to eradicate 'devilish' practices such as polygamy and cross-dressing, and condemned the 'heathen friskiness' of the natives" (D'Emilio & Freedman, 1997, p. 6).

Changes in the social perceptions of sexual relationships between Aboriginals and Euro-Canadians occurred as settlement progressed and as the fur trade was slowly replaced by agriculture as Canada's primary economic activity. Relationships between Euro-Canadian men and Aboriginal women were discouraged as the population of mixed-race women, such as Métis, grew. Being of mixed ancestry, these women were perceived as more acceptable partners (Das Gupta, 2000; Mandell & Momirov, 2000). Even in Western Canada (which was settled considerably later), by the mid-nineteenth century "colonial officials and religious authorities began to fear the consequences of this widespread 'race-mixing'" (Razack, 2002, p. 52). Laws were instituted at various times in various parts of Canada as well as the rest of the Americas prohibiting white–Aboriginal relationships.

However, such relationships continued in various forms. For example, during the gold rush of the mid-nineteenth century, men could form sexual relationships with Aboriginal women in the many "dance halls" that were found along the west coast; outside of the dance halls, it is estimated that one in ten Aboriginal women in British Columbia were cohabiting with a non-Aboriginal man during this time. Although many of these relationships were consensual, some were not. Some cases of Aboriginal fathers trading their daughters for gold or other resources have been documented (Barman, 1997/1998). In other cases, it is suggested that the "wild west" environment of the gold rush, where women were outnumbered by men by as much as 200:1, placed all women (and especially Aboriginal women) at risk of sexual victimization; in these instances, the "choice" to cohabit with a man was less an illustration of free will and more a desire for safety (Windecker, 1997; Barman, 1997/1998).

Thus, over time, we can see Aboriginal sexuality being socially typed—it was described as "heathen friskiness," judged as being "devilish," and made subject to a wide range of prescriptions, including Aboriginals being taught by church fathers the "right" way to have sexual intercourse (hence the phrase "missionary position"). With such overt attempts to regulate and control Aboriginal sexuality, substantial changes occurred in the sexual cultures of Aboriginal societies as they adopted and integrated many aspects of European sexual culture (Newhouse, 1998).

Sexual cultures are composed of dynamic and ever-changing processes, whether we are speaking of Aboriginal cultures or other cultures of the world. As cultures continuously evolve and transform, so does sexuality, as we can see by looking at how the meanings and place of sexuality in the social structure have changed in the dominant culture of North America over the last few centuries. It is by looking at trans-historical changes—changes over time in a single society—that the powerful role of social processes in the creation of sexual cultures and sexual identities becomes acutely evident.

North America: The Evolution of Meanings of Sexuality

The past few hundred years have been a time of immense social change in North America. And as economic, religious, familial, scientific, and other cultural changes have occurred, sexuality has changed as well. Looking at social changes in Canadian and American history reveals that the meaning of sexuality, its place in the social order, how it is judged, and the agents of its regulation have all fluctuated over time and been intertwined with racial, class, and gender hierarchies of the broader society (D'Emilio & Freedman, 1997; Valverde, 1991). Since the seventeenth century, the meaning of sexuality has transformed from being primarily associated with reproduction within a powerful structure of kinship to being primarily associated with emotional intimacy in marriage, and then to being associated with personal fulfillment for individuals (see Figure 5.1).

The seventeenth century in Canada was a time of early exploration and settlement, and economic activities revolved around the fur trade. As described previously, sexual relationships between Aboriginal women and white men were common and

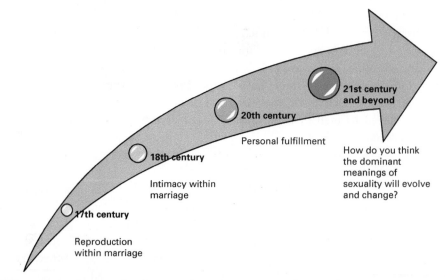

FIGURE 5.1 Changes in the Dominant Meaning of Sexuality

accepted during this time, despite broad differences between Aboriginal and European sexual cultures. Meanwhile, among the small number of European families who had settled in Eastern Canada, ownership of black slaves also sprang up during this era and continued until the early nineteenth century (Das Gupta, 2000). The practice of slavery was closely intertwined with the control of sexuality. Slave owners frequently determined who was permitted to mate with whom for the purposes of reproduction (and when). Female slaves were valued in part for their reproductive capacities, and certain male slaves were selected as "studs" to impregnate these females (Das Gupta, 2000). Female slaves were also expected to be continually sexually available for male members of the owner's family. Even the sexuality of free blacks came to be socially controlled, as laws were instituted prohibiting black individuals from marrying outside their race (Das Gupta, 2000).

In the more urbanized United States, sexuality during this era was channelled into marriage for the purpose of reproduction, although some sexual activity was tolerated in courtship. Sexuality outside of the arenas of courtship and marriage was considered unacceptable, and sexuality was formally and informally controlled by the local Christian church, the courts, family, and the community. Premarital pregnancy would usually result in marriage being enforced, often at the insistence of the young woman's father. The young couple would respect the father's directive because the kinship system was considered a legitimate regulator of sexuality and reproduction.

The community was also seen as a legitimate regulator of deviance, and it was not uncommon for neighbours to report sexual improprieties to relevant family members or community and church leaders. Individuals could be excommunicated from the local church for deviant sexuality, and in some regions certain forms of sexual deviance were considered criminal and even punishable by death. However, during this era in the United States, deviating individuals were more often seen as having made an error in judgment— it was the behaviour that was viewed as deviant rather than the person. Thus, some form of punishment for the unacceptable behaviour was dispensed so individuals could learn the error of their ways (e.g., via public whipping or sitting in the stocks) and thereby be accepted back into the family, the community, and the church.

The specific nature of the punishment dispensed depended on the social characteristics of the person involved. The higher the socioeconomic status of the sexual transgressors, the less severe their punishments. In the case of rape, upper-class men were less likely to go to trial and usually received milder penalties if they did, while more severe penalties were dispensed to lower-class men. Women and men also regularly received different types of punishment. Men, who often owned property, were more likely to be fined, while women, who did not own property, were more likely to be physically punished. Women were also more likely than men to be punished for sexual deviance such as adultery.

Racial hierarchies embedded in the social structure of the time were also reflected in colonial society's sexual culture and its definition and regulation of deviant sexuality. In many American colonies, black men convicted of raping white women (but not black women) were castrated. In contrast, white men convicted of raping either white or black women were not castrated; in fact, in most regions, it was unlikely that a white man could be considered as having "raped" a black woman.

The various ways that deviant sexuality was controlled and defined revolved around dominant meanings of sexuality during the seventeenth century, meanings which incorporated both pragmatic considerations as well as cultural ideals. In the growing Euro-Canadian and Euro-American cultures, the nature of the definition and control of sexual deviance "served the larger function of reminding the community at large that sexuality belonged in marriage [or in Canada, marriage-like relationships between European men and Aboriginal women] for the purpose of producing legitimate children" (D'Emilio & Freedman, 1997, p. 28). The definition and control of sexual deviance also reinforced socioeconomic class, gender, and racial hierarchies through which society was constructed.

Near the end of the eighteenth century and throughout the nineteenth century, Canadian and American society underwent significant changes that affected the way sexuality was perceived (Valverde, 1991; D'Emilio & Freedman, 1997). Urbanization and wage labour outside of the kinship system took hold and progressed at a rapid pace, creating more anonymous lives distanced from extended family members and community surveillance. Religious shifts transferred the responsibility for salvation onto the individual, reducing the role of the church and subsequently the state as regulators of morality. Economically based and arranged marriages declined, people were more likely to be marrying for "love," and more open expression of affection emerged.

Enlightenment ideology within philosophy and science identified nature (including sexuality) as inherently good. These changes permeated the sexual culture of the time, such that the language of sexuality was no longer reproductive but based on *emotional intimacy* in marriage. The role of the church in regulating sexuality declined, as did the role of the state. The family was becoming more of an isolated unit in society, recognized as a *private* realm outside of the surveying gaze of many others. However, the role of other social control agents grew: women, the medical profession, social reformers, and culture industries (D'Emilio & Freedman, 1997; Valverde, 1991).

Women played a larger role in regulating sexuality through their efforts at reducing pregnancy rates. Previously, high infant mortality rates meant that women would have many babies to ensure that a sufficient number of them survived into childhood to contribute to the maintenance of the family. During the nineteenth century, infant mortality rates declined, but perinatal and postnatal mortality rates of women did not. With the tremendous health risks associated with pregnancy and childbirth, and less need for large numbers of children, middle- and upper-class women acted to reduce pregnancy by abstaining from sex with their husbands for extended periods of time and by using contraception.

The use of contraception was aided by the medical profession, which was growing in size, knowledge, and legitimized power. The medical profession came to have a more encompassing role in the regulation of sexuality by "scientifically" defining sexual deviance (such as the "disease" of sodomy) and by conveying medical knowledge to the broader community. For example, medical knowledge at the time described the body as a closed energy system, wherein overindulgence in any activity (including sexual) could be dangerous to physical health—*self-control* became a dominant theme in the contributions of science to the sexual culture of the time.

Self-control as a means to avoid illness and energy depletion was perceived as particularly important during this era because of its relevance to commercial expansion. The "self-made man" was idealized in politics, religion, and popular culture; to achieve such success in this new industrial and capitalist economy, he had to ensure that he did not waste too much of his bodily energy elsewhere. Controlling his sexual passions would enable him to focus his energies on economic success.

The economic changes that were occurring in society at this time included the emergence of a powerful culture industry—newspapers, magazines, mass-produced books, and more. On one hand, the culture industry contributed to the sexual culture of the era in terms of the spread of the sex industry, such as in pornography (in the form of stories, books, drawings, burlesque shows, and early photography). But other facets of the culture industry regulated sexual deviance. For example, young women were viewed as being extremely vulnerable to the sexual appetites of unsavoury young men in growing cities. In response to this problem, poems and stories in popular publications warned young women of these dangers, and these stories frequently ended with the untimely death of the young woman who had been led astray.

The **social purity** or **sex hygiene movements** emerged, which equated social purity with sexual purity; sexuality was seen as the heart of morality, which was defined as the

Nellie McClung was a suffragette, and also a member of the Woman's Christian Temperance Union.

cornerstone of society. Social purity activism was well established by the late 1800s in Canada, the northeast United States, and Britain and included a number of alcohol temperance groups, such as the Woman's Christian Temperance Union as well as female suffragettes (Valverde, 1991). The concerns of these groups included "prostitution, divorce, illegitimacy, 'Indian and Chinese [male immigrants],' public education, suppression of obscene literature, prevention (of prostitution) and rescue of fallen women, and shelters for women and children" (Valverde, 1991, p. 17). Social purity efforts were directed particularly at the lower classes, which by virtue of simply being lower class were presumed to be sexually depraved as well.

The specific ways in which sexual deviance was defined and regulated depended on social characteristics, just as it had in earlier eras. Racial ideologies continued to infuse sexual culture. In the media, black men's sexuality was portrayed as dangerous and uncontrollable, making them liable to rape white women. Chinese men, brought to Canada as labourers to build the railway, were also perceived as a threat to young white women, who might be easily lured by what was perceived as the men's more innocent countenance and by the opium they might supply. It was thought that opium had strong sexual qualities, which would result in "the amazing phenomenon of an educated gentlewoman, reared in a refined atmosphere, consorting with the lowest classes of yellow and black men" (Emily Murphy, cited in Valverde, 1991, p. 184). In the early twentieth century such attitudes would serve as a rationale for Emily Murphy's efforts to regulate immigration (Valverde, 1991).

The nineteenth century, then, brought considerable transformation to Western sexual culture. The meaning of sexuality changed, and responsibility for controlling sexual deviance shifted to individuals and their own self-control. The role of the state in regulating sexual deviance declined somewhat in the early part of the nineteenth century. However, as moral entrepreneurs identified and drew attention to sexual "diseases" (e.g., sodomy, homosexuality), the sex industry, and female sexual exploitation, the state's role in controlling sexual deviance and regulating morality grew once again.

With the dawn of the twentieth century, the sexual culture of North American society continued to transform. The dominant meaning of sexuality eventually shifted from a focus on emotional intimacy in marriage to a focus on *personal fulfillment* regardless of marriage (D'Emilio & Freedman, 1997). In other words, sexual activity came to be accepted not only in marriage but also in courtship, casual dating, and even much briefer relationships. Sexuality continues to be controlled in many arenas, including the criminal justice system and the culture industry. In the realm of criminal justice, criminal codes regulate sexual deviance by criminalizing particular aspects of sexuality, such as sexual assault and public indecency.

Ask Yourself

Reflecting on what you have learned about the way sexuality was socially constructed in Canadian and American culture during the nineteenth century and into the early twentieth century, consider the following questions: Who was doing the social typing of deviant sexuality? What was the foundation for their arguments—that is, did they type certain sexual behaviours as deviant because they thought those behaviours violated norms, engendered a negative societal reaction, or were statistically rare or harmful? How did the social typers and the larger society benefit?

The culture industry grew rapidly during the twentieth century to become the dominant force it is today. Today, the culture industry, through the sex industry and integration of sexuality into mainstream media (television, movies, music, advertising, etc.), is perhaps the predominant contributor to sexual culture. At the same time, moral entrepreneurs and special interest groups also use the media as a tool for communicating their positions in the deviance dance. For example, public service campaigns promote "safer sex" in magazines, the pharmaceutical industry creates television commercials for the drug Viagra, and gay rights organizations send out press releases about their organizations' activities.

Exercise Your Mind

For this exercise, watch television, go to the movie theatre, or rent a movie. And yes, you can tell everyone that you are doing this as an exercise for your deviance class. Spending a night watching television or movies is a good way to see the role played by the culture industry in the way sexuality is socially constructed in modern society. As you watch these television shows or movies, think about the broader sexual culture involved. What are these shows or movies saying about sexuality? What meanings of sexuality are they communicating to the audience? What is "acceptable" and "deviant" sexuality according to whatever shows or movies you are watching? Are there conflicting or opposing messages about sexuality being conveyed?

You may want to rent some movies or watch reruns from different time periods to see the ways in which the sexual culture has changed or stayed the same. Movies you might want to choose from include *Gone with the Wind* (1939), *The Philadelphia Story* (1940), *The Graduate* (1967), *Animal House* (1978), *Porky's* (1982), *American Pie* (1999), and *Bridesmaids* (2011). Easily found television shows from different eras include *I Love Lucy*, *M*A*S*H*, *Seinfeld*, *Two and a Half Men*, and *Californication*.

If you have engaged in the *Exercise Your Mind* activity, you now have some additional insight into the media as one facet of sexual culture and into how, even when focusing solely on mass media, there have been considerable changes in the way sexuality has been socially constructed over the past several decades. The way that sexuality is constructed has a tremendous impact on how we, as people living in a given society at a precise moment in history, think and act, and how we are treated by others in terms of sexuality. The last few centuries have been characterized by changes in the dominant meanings of sexuality, and as broader social and cultural forces continue to change, our dominant meanings of sexuality will continue to evolve as well. This realization brings us to the present moment and the sexual culture of *our* time. In the following sections of the chapter, we will more closely examine the sexual culture of contemporary Canadian society.

Learning Objective 1

- Which theoretical perspectives underlie contemporary sociological research about sexuality?

Learning Objective 2

- How was sexuality embedded in the holistic Aboriginal view of life, and how did that contrast with the Euro-Canadian view of sexuality?

- How did the prevalence of sexual relationships between Aboriginal women and Euro-Canadian men change over time, and why?

Learning Objective 3

- How have the dominant meanings of sexuality changed in North America since the seventeenth century, and how has sexual regulation change during that time?

- How were the meanings of sexuality and its regulation integrated with hierarchies of race, class, and gender from the seventeenth century onward?

Sexual Culture Today

If you participated in the *Exercise Your Mind* activity, you spent some time watching television or movies to learn something about sexuality in contemporary society. In watching television or movies, you have been able to observe the construction of deviance and normality in those arenas—what is considered acceptable, what is considered deviant, and what happens to those who are deviant. These are precisely the issues we will direct our attention to in this section of the chapter. We will explore some of the criteria by which sexual deviance and normality are determined in the sexual culture of our time, and some of the contrasting viewpoints in this deviance dance.

Ask Yourself

How can you determine whether someone's sexuality is "deviant" or "normal"? Make a list of the criteria that you use when you make judgments about other people's sexuality or your own.

Criteria for Determining Deviance

A closer look at our contemporary sexual culture reveals a number of criteria that are used to evaluate sexuality as either "deviant" or "normal." Dimensions that have been explored by other deviance specialists include the degree of consent, nature of the sexual partner, nature of the sexual act, setting, frequency, time, age, and number of partners (Wheeler, 1960; Goode, 1997). We will explore consent, nature of the partner, and nature of the act as core criteria by which we determine "deviant" sexuality, and setting and frequency as two of the more peripheral criteria.

Consent

One of the criteria we use to determine sexual deviance is that of **consent** (Wheeler, 1960; Goode, 1997), and some researchers (e.g., Mackay, 2000) use the concept of consent as the defining characteristic of "normal" sex. Although the notion of consent is commonly used within legal and social discourses, conceptually there is some disagreement regarding how consent can be defined (Beres, 2007). Is "consent" an attitude (based on the intention to engage in certain sexual activities)? If that is the case, then determining whether consent is present in a particular situation requires access to a person's thoughts and state of mind. Or is it a behaviour (based on particular actions)? If that is the case, then determining whether consent is present in a certain situation requires comparing actions that have (or have not) occurred to some type of agreed-upon list of precise behaviours that constitute "consent."

Despite different conceptions of how consent is defined, there is some consensus that at its broadest level, "consent represents some form of agreement to engage in sexual activity" (Beres, 2007, p. 97). Is consent involved in the sexual act in question? Is it even possible for consent to be involved in this act? The most obvious use of this criterion is by the criminal justice system in cases of sexual assault; if there is no consent involved, then the act is a criminal one, making it necessarily deviant.

In fact, the complete lack of consent leads many people to interpret sexual assault as an act of violence rather than a sexual act. In court cases involving "date rape"—that is, a victim sexually assaulted by a date—the issue of consent is usually central to the case. The defence attorney will argue that the victim did consent, or at least that the defendant reasonably thought that consent had been given, and the prosecutor will argue that the victim did not consent. In the courtroom, the way date rape cases are argued elicits the question of whose story is more believable—the defendant's or the victim's.

The question of whether it is possible for consent to be involved is another aspect of this criterion for judging sexual deviance. Beginning in the late 1990s, the use of **date rape drugs** escalated. These drugs, such as Rohypnol (also known as "roofies" or "roopies") and GHB (also known as "G" or "Liquid X"), are odourless and tasteless, and when mixed with alcohol cause intense drowsiness and memory impairment. If one of these drugs is slipped into someone's drink, that person will not know it is there and may not be able to remember anything that happens in the ensuing hours. These drugs are referred to as "date rape drugs" because they have been used to have sex with someone without having to get consent.

Because of the effects of these drugs, they have been labelled as dangerous, and formal and informal regulation has emerged. It is likely that the student services organization at your university has had campaigns to raise people's awareness of these drugs and the way they are used. For example, you may have seen posters displayed on your campus that provide information about how to avoid being a victim. When you and friends go to bars or nightclubs, perhaps you do not accept drinks being brought to you by anyone other than the bar server. The legal system has determined that having sex with someone after giving them these drugs constitutes sexual assault, arguing that in these situations the person is not in a state of mind where giving consent is possible.

Courts have also argued that consent is not possible in situations involving sexual acts between children and adults. Due to the level of cognitive development as well as significant power differentials, a child is not considered capable of giving consent, especially to an adult. Thus, sexual acts between children and adults are defined as crimes on the part of the adult. You can see a description of Canada's age-of-consent laws—and their complexities—in Box 5.1.

Although sexual interaction between adults and children is necessarily deviant because it is forbidden by the Criminal Code, social characteristics of the child and the adult may

Canada's Age-of-Consent Laws

What is the age of consent for sexual activity in Canada? The answer to that question is not as straightforward as one might initially think. Canada's age-of-consent laws are multifaceted and complex. Under current legislation, the laws governing sexual behaviour, in which age of consent is an issue, are as follows:

Sexual Assault: A common defence in sexual assault trials is that the accused believed there was consent involved in the sexual activity. However, if the complainant is under the age of 16, the accused cannot make the claim of consent; consent is perceived as not being possible in that instance.

Sexual Interference: This is a crime defined by the sexual touching of a body of someone under the age of 16. The lack of the possibility of consent is what defines this crime.

Invitation to Sexual Touching: This is a crime defined by requesting someone under the age of 16 to sexually touch the accused. Again, the lack of the possibility of consent is what defines this crime.

The above age-of-consent laws are further complicated by the question of the age of the accused. That is, consent *is*

considered possible in regard to the above behaviours if the complainant is 12 or 13, if the accused is no more than two years older than the complainant, *and* if the accused is not in a position of trust and authority over the complainant. Consent is also considered possible if the complainant is 14 or 15 and if the accused is less than five years older and is not in a position of trust or authority over the complainant. In these instances, legislation prevents the criminalization of sexual activity between youth of similar ages who are in a dating relationship.

Bestiality in the Presence of a Child: Bestiality (sexual activity with an animal) is itself a crime. However, committing an act of bestiality in front of a child under the age of 16, or inciting a child under the age of 16 to commit an act of bestiality, is a specific subsection of that same law.

Sexual Exploitation: Although the age of 16 is highlighted in the age-of-consent laws described above, sexual exploitation involves sexually touching (or inviting sexual touching from) someone under the age of 18 if the accused is in a position of trust or authority over the complainant.

play a role in public perceptions of deviance or normality. The age of the child and the age of the adult may influence public perceptions of whether consent is possible. For example, an 8-year-old may be perceived as much less capable of giving consent than a 13-year-old. And if a 13-year-old is having sex with her 16-year-old boyfriend, in contrast to her 37-year-old boyfriend, the public may view it as a consensual relationship (even if they disapprove of 13-year-olds being sexually active in general). The interaction of gender with age may affect public perceptions of deviance or normality as well. That is, teenage boys are often seen as being more capable of giving consent to adults than teenage girls are.

Issues of consent are perceived differently across place and time. Although "no means no" even within marriage in Canadian society, in many countries consent is not considered necessary between husband and wife; sexual relations are prescribed as required in the marital relationship. In fact, it was only in 1983 that the Canadian legal system defined sexual assault as being possible in marriage. Similarly, it was only in 1987 that our legal system made sexual assault laws gender-neutral, recognizing that it is possible for a man to be raped by either another man or a woman (Nelson & Robinson, 2002); many societies today continue to define the crime of sexual assault only in terms of a male perpetrator and a female victim.

In the historical section of this chapter, we saw that from the seventeenth century through most of the nineteenth century, black women were expected to be sexually available to white men (Das Gupta, 2000; Mandell & Momirov, 2000; D'Emilio & Freedman, 1997). Because of this expectation, white men were unlikely to be charged with raping black women if there was no consent. In fact, if the black woman was a slave and the white man a member of the slave-owner's family, then consent was a nonissue because she was considered a piece of the family's property, to do with as they pleased.

Today, divergent points of view exist even on the issue of the age at which consent is possible, not only across cultures but within North America itself. The North America Man/Boy Love Association (NAMBLA) argues that teenagers are capable of giving consent in sexual relationships with adults, and some members of NAMBLA suggest that even younger children are capable of giving consent (NAMBLA, n.d.). Of course, as you may have expected, tremendous opposition exists to NAMBLA's message and to the organization itself. Afraid of being associated with this organization, gay rights organizations have been especially vocal in their opposition, "deploring NAMBLA and everything it advocates which basically amounts to a push to legitimize child molestation," and arguing that the organization "has no legitimate place in society, Queer or Straight" (NAMBLA Controversy, n.d.). Obviously, the debate over age-of-consent laws is a highly contentious one. By challenging one of society's most firmly held beliefs, members of organizations like NAMBLA have been socially typed as deviant—they are described as "pedophiles," evaluated in an extremely negative light, and face intense public opposition.

Nature of the Sexual Partner

The historical and cross-cultural variations that were presented earlier in this chapter pointed to the role that the **nature of the sexual partner** plays in determining sexual deviance. In Athens during the fifth century BC, acceptable sexual partners for aristocratic men included wives, prostitutes, slaves, foreigners, and adolescent males, while men of equal social status were defined as inappropriate sexual partners. In the dominant Europeanized culture of North America from the seventeenth century onward, marriage gradually lost its monopoly as the only legitimate outlet for sexual behaviour, and a wider range of sexual partners came to be deemed appropriate. However, despite this transition to more freedom in the selection of a sexual partner, there still is not *complete* freedom in the choice of a sexual partner in contemporary North America.

Beginning with the law, we can see particular people being defined as unacceptable sexual partners. We already addressed the issue of age-of-consent laws, making individuals who are under the age of consent inappropriate sexual partners. The Criminal Code also prohibits sexual relationships between close family members—parents, children, grandparents, grandchildren, siblings, and half-siblings. Violating this prohibition between close family members constitutes the crime of *incest*. Bestiality is a crime in Canada, making animals unacceptable sexual partners. Finally, several sexual laws in the Criminal Code (such as "sexual exploitation") define anyone over whom the individual is in a position of trust or authority as an inappropriate sexual partner, or anyone who is in a relationship of dependency with the individual.

The nature of the sexual partner is also controlled outside the legal system. The choice of sexual partners is formally regulated in some places of business, where company policies may prohibit intimate relationships between bosses and employees or between co-workers. Some universities prohibit sexual relationships between professors and students. Within the psychiatric and psychological communities, professional organizations define sexual relationships between therapists and clients as a violation of the professional code of ethics. Additionally, if the sexual partner in question is not a person but an object that is necessary for sexual stimulation to occur, the psychiatric community labels the sexual activity a *fetish*, for which treatment can be obtained.

At an informal level, particular sexual partners may be perceived as socially unacceptable. For example, although the law does not prohibit sexual relations between first cousins, such relations would still push the boundaries of social acceptability (although, in other cultures, it is quite common for marriages to be arranged between first cousins). And even though many universities do not have policies prohibiting intimate relationships between students and professors, within the cultural climates of those institutions professors who engage in such relationships may still be stigmatized.

At both formal and informal levels, members of the same sex continue to be defined as inappropriate sexual partners to some extent. We have come a long way since Everett Klippert was sent to prison as a dangerous sex offender in 1967 for having admitted that he was gay. There have been significant changes in social attitudes regarding homosexuality over the past several decades as a result of social activism and education, and these changes have increased individual freedom to choose a member of the same sex as a sexual partner.

©Philip Scalia/Alamy

The Stonewall Inn, in Greenwich Village, New York City.

In large part, these changes stem from the Stonewall riots in New York's Greenwich Village in 1969. In the early morning hours of June 28, police conducted yet another raid of a gay bar, this one located in the Stonewall Inn. But this time, instead of quietly accepting it, the patrons fought back. This event was followed by several days of riots and protests in the streets of Greenwich Village, which heralded the beginning of the modern gay rights movement. The Stonewall Inn was declared a National Historic Landmark in 2000.

During the same year as the Stonewall riots, the Canadian government decriminalized same-sex sexual activities between consenting adults. Then Justice Minister Pierre Trudeau (who would later become prime minister) stated that "There's no place for the state in the bedrooms of the nation" (CBC News, 2012a). Three years later, homosexuality was removed from the *Diagnostic and Statistical Manual of Mental Disorders*.

Despite the changes that were occurring at that time, the Canadian federal government was still trying to purge homosexuals from the public service, based on the belief that homosexuals had psychological characteristics that made them more vulnerable to communist influence (Kinsman & Gentile, 2009). Over a period of 30 years (and extending into the 1980s), suspected homosexuals in the public service underwent interrogation, surveillance, and illegal searches by the RCMP. They were tested using a machine that tracked heart rate, eye movements, and sweat reactions while they were shown a series of sexually explicit photos of someone of the same sex. Confessing their sexual orientation was not sufficient; they were also expected to provide a list of names of other homosexuals with whom they associated. Groups that were a part of the gay rights movement were also subjected to RCMP surveillance and later raids throughout the early 1980s.

The continued efforts of the **LGBT** (Lesbian, Gay, Bisexual, and Transgendered) movement have created some significant changes since that time. In 1996, Parliament voted to add sexual orientation to the *Canadian Human Rights Act*. Same-sex common-law couples began to receive the same benefits as opposite-sex common-law couples in 2000, and same-sex couples gained the right to legally marry across Canada in 2005 (CBC News, 2007). However, despite some changes in prevailing social attitudes, gays and lesbians continue to be deviantized in many ways because of the nature of their sexual partners. Of course, the stigmatization experienced by gays and lesbians in North America may not be as formal and as overt as in some other cultures around the world, where homosexuality is a crime punishable by the death penalty—such as Iran, Mauritania, Pakistan, Saudi Arabia, Sudan, United Arab Emirates, and Yemen (Mackay, 2000). But even in the United States, the fight continues for the right to legally marry.

In the informal realm of everyday interaction, the stigmatization of gays and lesbians is evident as well. LGBT individuals are at greater risk of criminal victimization than the general population and may be subjected to hate crimes in particular. In Canada, approximately 10 percent of all police-reported hate crimes are committed on the basis of sexual orientation, placing it in the top three motivations for hate crimes, following race/ethnicity and religion. Hate crimes based on sexual orientation are far more likely to be violent in nature compared to hate crimes based on other characteristics (Walsh & Dauvergne, 2009).

The consequences of stigmatization can be especially severe for LGBT youth. LGBT students report that they hear anti-gay comments or experience name-calling an average of 26 times a day. More than one-quarter are told by their parents to leave home, and as a result LGBT youth are at greater risk of becoming homeless (PFLAG Canada, 2009). They are more likely to be bullied, and in the Internet age bullying is not limited to school but follows them home as well, on their smartphones, in their emails, and on their Facebook pages. Stigmatization by strangers, family members, and peers can take its toll. According to PFLAG Canada (2009), 43 percent of transgendered youth attempt suicide and almost one-third of youth suicides are among those who are LGBT. The problem of suicide among LGBT youth has resulted in multifaceted efforts to intervene (see Box 5.2).

Overall, Western cultures are characterized by considerably more freedom in the choice of sexual partners today than in the past. However, freedom is not unlimited. The choice of sexual partners is still regulated by the law and other formal processes, as well as informal means like social stigmatization. The nature of the sexual partner is an important criterion in our evaluations of people's sexuality as either deviant or normal (Goode, 1997; Wheeler, 1960). However, even if the sexual partner is considered acceptable and "normal," other criteria become involved in our evaluations as well, such as the nature of the sexual act.

Nature of the Sexual Act

Even if your choice of sexual partner is defined as normal and acceptable, is what you are doing with that partner considered "kinky" (Goode, 1997, p. 208)? That is, are you engaging

Box 5.2

Providing Support Online

New media provide expanded opportunities for stigmatizing LGBT youth, such as through cyberbullying (which was discussed in detail in Chapter 4). But new media also provide opportunities to resist stigmatization and its potential consequences. Online communities of similar others provide an interactive support network. Formal and informal YouTube campaigns provide emotional support as well. The international "It Gets Better" campaign features videos from people from all walks of life (from a young man living in Toronto to well-known celebrities), telling LGBT youth that life can get better for them, and suggesting ways to make their own lives better. The European "Stand Up!" campaign deviantizes homophobia

and urges youth to stand up against the homophobic bullying of their peers. A number of organizations provide a variety of resources online as well. In the United States, "The Trevor Project" was established specifically to provide crisis intervention for suicidal LGBT youth. Its website offers resources and a special suicide hotline. PFLAG Canada's website provides information for LGBT youth, family members, friends, and educators. It includes a series of video clips featuring LGBT individuals of all ages and ethnicities, parents of LGBT children, and children being raised by same-sex parents; there is a link for visitors of the site who would like to be considered for telling their own story in a video clip.

in "normal" or "deviant" sexual acts? The answer to that question is both culturally and historically specific and at times can also be tied in with the nature of the partner. For example, following European colonization of the Americas, sexual intercourse between husbands and wives was the only acceptable sexual act and only if in the "missionary" position.

Even over the last century there have been significant changes in the way that sexual acts are perceived as being "deviant" or "normal." For example, in Chapter 1 there was a discussion of the extreme measures taken in the early twentieth century to prevent masturbation in children based on medical discourses of the time, which claimed there were a wide range of physical, mental, and social harms as consequences of masturbation. Now, in the early twenty-first century, the same stigma is no longer attached to masturbation. The growing sexual freedom of the last century has allowed a range of sexual acts to be seen as more acceptable. Walk into any bookstore or public library and you will find books that present information on various sexual positions to try and techniques to use. Retail stores (both online and offline) that sell a variety of "sex toys" to incorporate into sexual acts abound, and some sex toys can even be found in your local drug store.

Due to the rapid growth in sexual freedom over the last century, greater subjectivity has emerged in precisely which sexual acts are perceived as "kinky." In other words, what is considered a sexually deviant act is now more in the eye of the beholder than was true in the past. Our sexual culture has come to be infused with an ideology of privacy; as long as a particular sexual activity is performed by consenting adults outside the view of others, we define it as being nobody else's business. And although each of us individually might perceive particular sexual acts as "kinky," the ideology of privacy limits contemporary social controls on sexual behaviours, particularly at a formal level. Just as Pierre Trudeau suggested that the government had no place in the bedrooms of adult Canadians, today we also think that none of us as individuals has a place in the bedrooms of others.

The issue of consent, the nature of the sexual partner, and the **nature of the sexual act** are three of the core criteria by which we evaluate sexuality and subsequently judge it as either deviant or normal. In addition to these three core criteria, there are also a number of more peripheral criteria that are used for judgment in contemporary sexual culture (Goode, 1997). For example, sexual activities in certain locations are considered deviant.

An episode of the popular TV show *Seinfeld* highlights the issue of location in determining deviance. In this episode, George Costanza has a sexual encounter with the cleaning lady in his office cubicle. The next day he is called into his boss's office and fired for that encounter, despite his protests that he had never been warned that the company frowned upon having sex in the office. This *Seinfeld* episode points out that the workplace is seen as an inappropriate setting for sexual activity in North American society. In Canada, the law defines certain locations (i.e., public places) as unacceptable for sexual activities. People who enjoy having sex in places where others might see them are labelled **exhibitionists**.

The frequency of sex is another one of the more peripheral criteria used to evaluate sexuality. Is someone having sex too often, not often enough, or just the right amount? This is a common question asked of advice columnists, sex therapists, and marriage counsellors. One issue of the women's magazine *First for Women* (August 6, 2001) devoted an entire article to what constitutes "normal" sex, including a table that readers can use to determine the "normal" frequency of sex based on age at marriage and number of years married. In fact, this table is titled "How Much Sex Is Normal?"—implying that frequency outside of the numbers listed is "abnormal." This magazine article also addresses the previous criterion mentioned, that of the nature of the sexual act, explaining to the hundreds of thousands of monthly readers which particular acts are "normal."

Those who have sex too frequently may be labelled "nymphomaniacs" or may even be diagnosed with a sexual "addiction." In the recent past, people who had sex too infrequently were often perceived as "frigid" (Goode, 1997). However, in the twenty-first century infrequent sexual activity may be considered a sexual dysfunction.

Contemporary society is one in which sexuality has become highly medicalized (and commercialized). Drugs like Viagra, which were initially marketed to aging men with erectile dysfunction, are now used by increasingly younger men as part of a demonstration of sexual prowess and masculinity (Marshall, 2006; Tiefer, 2006); on the popular television sitcom *Two and a Half Men*, even Charlie and Alan (two characters in their early 40s) have each used "the little blue pill" during nighttime marathons. Low sexual desire in women is now being similarly medicalized, and its solution is found not in changing relationships and gendered responsibilities, but rather in the search to develop the "Pink Viagra" (Marshall, 2006, p. 287). And in the world of email spam, pills, lotions, and gels designed for improved sexual performance are common. In our current "Viagra culture" (Potts & Tiefer, 2006, p. 267), where sexual desire (for women) and sexual prowess (for men) are essential components of the discourses of sexuality, masculinity, and femininity, frequency has assumed a whole new level of importance.

Discussions of frequency, location, nature of the act, nature of the partner, and the issue of consent point to both the increasing freedom that has come to characterize our sexual culture and the formal and informal limitations that continue to be placed on that freedom. As a society, we perceive a narrower range of behaviours as sexually deviant than we did in the past, but through the use of various criteria sexual deviance continues to be defined, identified, and controlled. However, the processes of defining, identifying, and controlling sexual deviance are not uniform; they are part of the "deviance dance."

TIME TO REVIEW

Learning Objective 4

■ What roles do *consent, nature of the partner, nature of the act, location,* and *frequency* play in our perceptions of deviant and normal sexuality?

■ How do perceptions of *consent* vary based on marital status, gender, race, and age?

■ How was the gay rights movement affected by the Stonewall riots?

■ How were homosexuals treated by the federal government from the 1950s through the 1980s?

■ In what ways have individuals of the same sex come to be seen as more acceptable sexual partners? In what ways do they continue to be perceived as unacceptable sexual partners?

■ What role do new media play in stigmatizing LGBT youth but also in helping them resist stigmatization?

Sexuality and the "Deviance Dance"

In any given culture at any particular time in history, certain trends or characteristics can be identified in sexual culture. However, a multiplicity of perceptions, reactions, and social controls are also intertwined with those broader trends. Sexual relationships between aristocratic adult and adolescent males, although common in fifth-century BC Athens, were not uniformly accepted. Segments of Athenian society were critical of such relationships, and often sought to initiate levels of control for the purposes of protecting these "exploited" adolescent males (Bloch, 2001). The discussion of Canadian and American history presented earlier in this chapter captured some of the diversity entwined within sexual culture, wherein class, race, and gender variations were central to the ways that sexuality was constructed and controlled. During the Victorian era, considerable restrictions on sexual behaviour were countered with the expansion of the sex industry—photographs, books, and sexually oriented live performances (D'Emilio & Freedman, 1997; Ullman, 1997).

In contemporary North America, considerable debate exists over many aspects of sexual culture. The large numbers of shops selling sexual "toys" coexist with organizations that condemn TV programs that include explicit sexual references, such as to masturbation, oral sex, and partial nudity (Parents Television Council, 2012). Gay, lesbian, and bisexual activist groups and changing human rights legislation coexist with segments of society that continue to stigmatize and condemn homosexual practices. Widespread efforts to eliminate the sexual abuse and exploitation of children even coexist with organizations trying to place limits on those controls, like NAMBLA. Many of the debates surrounding sexuality revolve around issues related to the sex trade, such as exotic dancing, pornography, and prostitution.

Exotic Dancing

Exotic dancing has a long history in North America, with burlesque shows and other forms of "stripping" going back centuries. However, after a period of stagnancy, exotic dancing has gained in popularity over the last decade. This trend has contributed to a rapidly growing body of research, which explores the meanings that dancers attribute to their experiences and the structure of power that underlies those experiences.

There are ongoing debates between radical feminist and sex-radical feminist perspectives: "The former views all sex work as being exploitative of women within the patriarchal structure in which we operate as a society, often taking a view of the sex worker as a *victim*; the latter views sex work as subversive of this structure and maintains that the decision to participate in sex work is a choice that women make, and that they further exercise their agency through the individual negotiations that occur within that context" (Morrow, 2012, pp. 359–360). Some research does find support for the victimization hypothesis: substance abuse, life histories of physical/sexual/emotional abuse, low self-esteem, and backgrounds characterized by risky sexual behaviours are common among exotic dancers (Mestemacher & Roberti, 2004). Furthermore, many women enter the occupation because of financial desperation (Sloan & Wahab, 2004; Wesely, 2003).

However, other researchers go beyond the victimization debate and instead explore the everyday experiences of women involved in the industry. Sloan and Wahab (2004) find that a "continuum of work and life experience" (p. 19) is characteristic of the exotic dancing subculture. They describe four different types of female exotic dancers. First, there are **survivors**, who have extensive histories of childhood abuse and who felt forced into the industry because of few available alternatives. Second, there are **nonconformists**, rebels who come from privileged, educated backgrounds and who have the freedom to enter and leave the industry as they wish. When dancing is no longer "fun," they change careers (by going to medical school, for example). Third, there are **dancers** who have considerable training in dance and who enjoy the artistic and creative expression of the industry. Finally, there are **workers**, women primarily from working-class backgrounds who become exotic dancers because of the money they can earn.

Regardless of the type of exotic dancer, all dancers must negotiate relationships with customers, as well as their own identities, within a structure of power inside the industry. That structure of power is multifaceted, existing at the individual, organizational, and institutional levels (Deshotels, Tinney, & Forsyth, 2012). At the individual level, power manifests itself in the interactions between dancers and customers. The dancers are objects of the customers' desire and must embody the fantasy that brought the customers into the club. That is, the dancers must be whatever or whomever the customers want them to be because their job is to make the customers stay in the club and spend money on drinks. As one dancer says, there are times when she really wants to say to the customer, "'shit I don't wear these heels at home! I am a regular girl. I wear flannel pajamas and you are ugly!'" (Egan, 2003, p. 113).

Even though in some ways the dancers appear to be subjected to the power of customers, they are also active agents of their own power. They perceive their male customers as "'lonely and . . . want[ing] somebody to make them feel better'" (Egan, 2003, p. 114). The women use their bodies to manipulate customers and earn more money, creating a fantasy relationship based on "counterfeit intimacy" (Mestemacher & Roberti, 2004, p. 49). For example, in the fantasy relationship they create, they may secretly "confess" to a customer what their "real" names and life stories are—however, it is all a lie designed to "'hook a regular customer'" and "'keep him coming back'" (Egan, 2003, p. 112). Part of the image that dancers create is that of the customer being in control of the interaction (Morrow, 2012).

As each dancer negotiates a relationship with customers, she must make decisions about personal boundaries—what she will and will not do for money (Wesely, 2003; Kaufman, 2009). Give a lap dance? Go to a private room? Leave the club with a customer if he offers enough money? Dancers' boundaries frequently change over time as they become more embedded in the industry (Wesely, 2003). As the boundaries change and become more flexible, many dancers end up feeling violated, not by customers but by themselves; the gap grows between their *ideal selves* (who they want to be) and their *perceived selves* (who they see themselves as being currently) (Wesely, 2003). As a result, some dancers talk about loosening boundaries in both their work lives and personal lives through exhibitionism and promiscuity: "'You've given yourself up to so many situations, it really doesn't matter anymore'" (p. 498). One dancer says, "'About a year and a half into it, it was hard to separate the stage Julie from the real-life Julie'" (p. 499). Others speak of becoming numb and losing their sense of self over time: "'There is no real identity there'" (p. 500).

The interactions between dancers and customers within the individual level of the power structure take place within a larger context of the organizational level of the power structure. The organizational level comprises the rules governing customer and dancer behaviour, such as customers being prohibited from touching dancers and dancers having to share tips with servers, bouncers, and bartenders. At first glance, it appears that the clubs' rules exert control over the dancers' actions. However, Deshotels and Forsyth (2008) have found that dancers use the rules to their advantage to make more money and protect themselves. By giving extra tips to the bartender, the dancer receives information about which customers are the big spenders based on how many (and what kind) of drinks they have ordered. The bartender will then also make stronger drinks for those customers, loosening their inhibitions and their wallets. Separate rooms provide a venue for possible rule breaking, and an extra tip to the bouncer in the room makes him look the other way. The stricter the rules governing dancer–customer interactions, the more the dancer can charge a customer for prohibited behaviours. By using counterfeit intimacy, the dancer convinces the customer that although she is already in trouble with her boss, she is willing to break this rule for him, because he is special. At the same time, dancers can enforce the rules when they wish, if they have made a choice to not give private dances as part of their job, if they don't like a certain customer, or if he is not spending enough money. Thus, the "rules of exotic dancing establishments, although regulating behaviour at the meso/organizational level, also allow individual women to control customers, as well as raise their income by supplying forbidden behaviour" (Deshotels & Forsyth, 2008, p. 485).

Individual power relations take place within the context of organizational power. Yet both exist within the larger context of institutional power. The exotic dancing industry is affected by the structure of contemporary capitalism and by cultural ideals of female beauty. Sociologist Max Weber (1946) claimed that in the twentieth century, capitalism was increasingly characterized by rationalization. Ritzer (2006) suggests that this is particularly evident in the routinization of activities. He refers to this as the **McDonaldization of society**, which consists of four components: efficiency, predictability, control, and calculability. These four characteristics govern all industries, including the exotic dancing industry (Deshotels, Tinney, & Forsyth, 2012). Dancers make efficient use of their time, trying to interact with as many customers as possible during a shift. As one dancer notes, "I realized early on to watch for the cues to see when I had maxed out his wallet" (p. 143). Predictability is reflected in "product specification" (p. 143), where a specific standard of beauty is applied in hiring dancers. The more elite the club, the higher the standard of beauty, with the ideal being "what you would see in *Playboy* magazine" (p. 143). That standard of beauty is enhanced (and enforced) through control by the club owner or manager and the dancer herself—wearing extremely high heels to make the legs look longer, shaving all body hair, and using camouflaging body makeup to hide imperfections. Plastic surgery (e.g., breast implants, buttock implants) is encouraged and sometimes even financially supported by club owners. Control is also evident in the standard set of "characters" that dancers dress as (e.g., schoolgirl), their dance moves, and the lines they use with customers to get more money. Finally, calculability emerges in the dancers' song selection and timing. When on the main stage, dancers select songs of a particular length, just long enough to tease the customers and make them want more (and thereby be willing to pay for a private dance).

Female exotic dancers are active agents of power at the individual and organizational levels. However, their power at those levels is dependent on the extent to which they reproduce dominant ideals of female beauty for the pleasure of male customers within the context of contemporary capitalism—what Deshotels and colleagues (2012) call "McSexy" (p. 140). At the institutional level, dancers' power is also influenced by the nature of ownership within the industry (see Box 5.3).

Box 5.3

Organized Crime and Human Trafficking

The structure of ownership of exotic dancing clubs is an additional dimension of the institutional level of power. Many (if not most) exotic dancing clubs in Canada are not owned by individual entrepreneurs, but rather by units of organized crime. Historically, the clubs were typically owned by motorcycle gangs, such as the Hells Angels or the Outlaws. Although this continues to be the case in some regions of Canada, a growing proportion of exotic dancing clubs are now controlled by the Russian mafia, various organized crime syndicates originating in countries that used to be part of the Soviet Union. The Russian mafia is known to be involved in **human trafficking** (illegal trade in human beings for the purposes of sexual exploitation, forced labour, or slavery), among other criminal activities. Consequently, a concern arose that some temporary foreign workers employed as exotic dancers may actually be victims of human trafficking by organized crime syndicates.

As a result, the federal government enacted a National Action Plan to Combat Human Trafficking. As part of this plan, employers in the sex trade (e.g., exotic dancing clubs, escort services, massage parlours) were immediately prohibited from hiring temporary foreign workers, and those currently employed in the sex trade would not have their visas renewed (Human Resources and Skills Development Canada, 2012).

The Adult Entertainment Association argued that the plan would cause their industry undue economic hardship, just as prohibiting temporary foreign workers in Alberta's oil industry would cause that industry a hardship. It would immediately affect approximately 800 (out of an estimated 38 000) exotic dancers in Canada and would cause a labour shortage. The association's efforts to halt the plan were not successful, and it was implemented in July 2012. In response, club owners would now have to attract more Canadian women into the industry. To do this, Godfrey (2012) reports that the Adult Entertainment Association was preparing to recruit high school students in the Toronto area. They were creating brochures to hand out outside of high schools, which assured potential applicants that sexual activity was not a part of the job and claimed "working as a dancer pays well, offers flexible hours, and makes a great part-time job to raise college tuition."

Are exotic dancers exploited through a patriarchal structure, as radical feminists suggest? In some ways, it appears they are. Are they agents of choice and power within their everyday lives as workers? In other ways, it appears they are. The deviance dance surrounding the issue of exotic dancing is extremely complex.

Although the "deviance dance" is evident in many issues related to sexuality, including exotic dancing, it is particularly evident when considering the issue of pornography. Anti-pornography activism exists alongside anti-censorship groups seeking to control the influences of such activism, and the question of whether pornography is "harmful" continues to be a nexus of passionate debate. Even the question of what pornography *is* remains subject to debate.

TIME TO REVIEW

Learning Objective 5

- How is sexuality involved in the "deviance dance"? Give cross-cultural, historical, or contemporary examples.

- What are the four types of exotic dancers?

- In what ways does power manifest itself at the individual level in exotic dancing?

- How do exotic dancers use organizational rules to their advantage?

- In what ways is the "McDonaldization of society" evident in exotic dancing?

- How has the federal government recently intervened in the exotic dancing industry in terms of hiring dancers?

Pornography

What is **pornography**? Is it harmful? Should it be controlled, and if so, how? These questions represent continuing discrepancies of opinion when the topic of pornography arises. Many definitions of pornography incorporate some notion of *explicit sex*, which at the surface seems a common sense assumption. However, even this common sense assumption is more ambiguous than it may initially appear (Childress, 1991).

A certain level of subjectivity is involved when trying to determine precisely what constitutes "explicit" sex—whether it can be found in mainstream media like *Sex and the City* or solely in those videos and magazines that only adults may purchase. The often-cited words of US Supreme Court Justice Potter Stewart (see Childress, 1991) suggest that despite the difficulties in defining pornography, we all know it when we see it. However, as Childress (1991, p. 178) points out, "Although everyone knows hard-core pornography when they see it, they see it in strikingly different places, and so no one really knows it at all."

Academics, politicians, and social activists have tried to define pornography, resulting in several different types of definitions. Some are **functional definitions** that suggest pornography is anything used by an individual for the purposes of sexual arousal (Goode, 1997)—pornography is "in the groin of the beholder" (McKeen, 2002, p. D6). The broad nature of this definition means that the women's undergarment section of the Eaton's catalogue of the early twentieth century (which boys would sneak peeks at), the Victoria's Secret catalogue today (which many boys and men sneak peeks at), and women's romance novels (e.g., Silhouette Desire) could all be considered "pornography" if they are used by people to become aroused.

Other definitions are **genre definitions** (Goode, 1997), which propose that products created for the purposes of arousing the consumer constitute "pornography." Even the definition of pornography offered in the Merriam-Webster dictionary (2013) adheres to this principle: Pornography is "the depiction of erotic behavior (as in pictures and writing) intended to cause sexual excitement." Of course, this type of definition leads us to try to infer what the producer's intentions were, in some cases. Are Harlequin romance novels trying to cause sexual excitement? How about the publishers of *Maxim* magazine or the *Sports Illustrated* swimsuit issue?

Labelling definitions of pornography focus on community standards—anything that community members deem obscene (Goode, 1997). The notions of obscenity and community standards are central to Canadian law. Section 163 of the Criminal Code defines an obscene publication as "any publication a dominant characteristic of which is the undue exploitation of sex, or of sex and any one or more of the following subjects, namely, crime, horror, [or] cruelty and violence." Exceptions to this definition include publications that have artistic or literary merit or that are for educational or medical purposes. The "community standards test" has traditionally been one way of determining whether a publication can be considered obscene. The question here is what a majority of Canadians would not tolerate other people seeing (rather than what they might find personally distasteful).

The legal definition of **child pornography** is considerably clearer. Section 163 of the Criminal Code defines child pornography as any representation of someone under the age of 18 engaged in explicit sexual activity or any representation of someone under the age of 18, "the dominant characteristic of which is the depiction, for a sexual purpose, of a sexual organ or the anal region." Again, materials having artistic or literary merit or those that are for educational or medical purposes are excluded from this definition, as are personal writings that are kept private (such as a diary or short story) and self-photographs that are kept private. However, even though the legal definition of child pornography has greater clarity than the legal definition of obscenity (not involving children), both have been subject to social and legal debate.

Ask Yourself

In 2012, discussion of the *Fifty Shades of Grey* book trilogy filled the media. A story of a woman's sexual life, the books contain extremely explicit descriptions of bondage and sado-masochistic sexual activities. Both celebrated and vilified in the media as "mommy porn," many female readers credited it with saving their marriages. The first book in the trilogy became the fastest selling paperback book in history, and the trilogy sold more than 25 million copies in the United States alone in only four months. In your opinion, is *Fifty Shades of Grey* "pornography?"

One of the current social and legal debates about child pornography is whether adolescents who text or email nude or partially nude photos of themselves (such as to a boyfriend or girlfriend) should be charged with child pornography. Dozens of youth in the United States have been charged with child pornography for doing so. In one particularly well-known case in Florida, a 16-year-old girl shared a nude photo of herself with her 18-year-old boyfriend. He then shared that photo with a friend, was subsequently convicted of distributing child pornography, and was forced to register as a sex offender. In Canada, fewer cases have been reported, and early social control efforts have leaned toward diversion programs to educate girls about the consequences of **sexting** in lieu of criminal charges. For example, the Essex County Diversion Program in Windsor offers the M.E.S.S.A.G.E Program to girls between the ages of 12 and 17 who are in this situation (Essex County Diversion Program, 2012).

Social and legal debates over obscenity were highlighted in 1992 when the Supreme Court of Canada reviewed the Butler case (*R. v. Butler*, 1992). In this case, a store owner had been convicted of selling obscene materials portraying homosexual acts. The defence claimed that prohibiting the possession of or selling obscene materials was a violation of the freedom of expression guaranteed in the Charter of Rights and Freedoms. The Supreme Court agreed but stated that the violation was reasonable in pursuit of the protection and greater good of society.

Debate over this issue extended beyond the criminal justice system as well. In the ensuing years, some Canadian feminist groups protested that the Butler decision had resulted in the biased suppression of the sexual expression of minorities, such as materials portraying gay and lesbian sexuality. They argued that because homophobia pervades society, those "community standards" that are used as a test for obscenity integrate homophobia and result in discrimination based on sexual orientation within the criminal justice system (Bell, Cossman, Ross, Gottell, & Janovicek, 1998).

More recently, the Supreme Court has moved away from the concept of "community standards" of tolerance in favour of the concept of "harm" when determining whether obscenity laws have been violated. Even the prohibition against possessing child pornography has been challenged. In 2001, the Supreme Court of Canada once again agreed that the law does violate freedom of expression, but that it is a reasonable violation of that freedom in the name of the protection of children's rights (*R. v. Sharpe*, 2001). They ruled that although scientific research could not definitively prove that people who possess child pornography will subsequently sexually harm particular children, the possessors of child pornography create a demand that results in the production of child pornography, which does harm the children represented in that pornography.

The question of whether pornography that includes only adults is harmful has been a matter of considerable debate as well, both inside and outside the legal realm (Childress, 1991; Greco, 1995; Stark, 1997; Davies, 1997). Some participants in this debate focus on the question of physical harm—whether male consumers of pornography will be driven to sexually victimize women. Other participants in this debate focus on the question of a broader harm to the functioning of society—that is, whether pornography affects attitudes toward and perceptions of women in society. Still other participants direct their attention at questions of ontological harm. Such questions may address religious issues or concerns about the moral fibre of society.

The foundation for the public debates over harm stem from academic research that looks at the effects of media on consumers (see Chapter 4). Just as the Internet has increased the availability of various forms of media content, such as magazines, movies, music, and books, it has also increased the availability of pornography. Now a world of pornography is immediately available, in massive amounts, and frequently free of charge. Given the extent to which youth use the Internet, recent research has focused on the effects of pornography on youth in particular. A recent review of the research (Owens, Behun, Manning, & Reid, 2012) analyzed the relationship between adolescent consumption of pornography and sexual attitudes, sexual behaviours, and self-concept. They found that much of the research is contradictory. Some research finds an association between the consumption of pornography and more permissive sexual attitudes, unrealistic ideas about sex, and a preoccupation with sexual thoughts, but other research does not find this association. Some research finds that greater consumption of pornography is associated with earlier sexual experimentation and riskier sexual behaviours, but other research does not. There are two areas in which research is more consistent. First, there is a correlation between the consumption of violent pornography and sexually aggressive behaviours. Second, pornography appears to affect adolescents' self-concepts. Girls worry about not looking like the women in pornography, while boys worry about not being able to perform sexually like the men in pornography.

More recently, research on pornography has undergone a paradigm shift (Attwood, 2011). A growing number of scholars are stepping outside of the effects-based research and debates over harm that have dominated the discourse. Instead, they provide a more complex analysis of pornography, looking at the consumption and significance of pornography for specific groups and communities. For example, research with undergraduate students finds that pornography use has become normalized, compared to just a decade ago (Beaver & Paul, 2011). The Internet has facilitated normalization. Between 1998 and 2007, the number of sexually explicit websites increased from only 8000 to more than 4 million, many of them "altporn" sites to which people can upload their own personal photos or videos. In addition, one-quarter of search engine requests are pornography related.

Beaver and Paul (2011) found that Internet pornography use among undergraduates cuts across social groups—it does not vary on the basis of family structure, parental supervision during adolescence, parental use of Internet filters, family income, academic achievement, depression, residential status, or religiosity. There is widespread acceptance of Internet pornography, although there are some gender differences. Males are more likely than females to access Internet pornography (although approximately one-third of visitors to pornography sites are women). Two-thirds of males consider pornography use to be completely or somewhat normal, while women are relatively equally divided on whether it is normal or deviant. Males also express more positive attitudes toward pornography: 94 percent of males, compared to 65 percent of females, enjoy it or feel neutral about it.

Pornography use has become more normalized, but at the same time there remains an ambivalence about it. A study of Swedish youth found Internet pornography use to be common (Löfgren-Mårtenson & Månsson, 2010). They access it in groups of peers to laugh at it, joke about it, and critique it. They use it as a source of information about sexuality, sexual activity, and physical appearance. They also use it as a stimulus for sexual arousal. The extent of Internet pornography use among youth shows the pornographic script to be "a frame of reference for young people in relation to physical ideals and sexual performance" (p. 576). And yet the youth recognize that males and females are portrayed unequally in pornography. They realize that "love" is missing from the pornographic equation, and that real relationships are better. Many girls express being disgusted by pornography, even though they are physically aroused by it. And some male users say they are simply tired of it. Pornography use may be considered normal in many ways, and it may serve a variety of functions in youths' lives, but there continues to be some mixed feelings about it. The specter of "deviance" is still there (Löfgren-Mårtenson & Månsson, 2010).

TIME TO REVIEW

Learning Objective 5

- How do functional, genre, and labelling definitions of pornography differ?
- What is child pornography?
- What are some of the social and legal debates surrounding child pornography and "obscenity"?

- What are the effects of pornography on adolescents?
- In what ways is Internet pornography use among youth characterized by both normalization and ambivalence?

Prostitution

When it comes to the issue of prostitution, the cornerstone for differing views and debates is social policy—what should be done *with* prostitution, what should be done *to* sex workers, and why. However, in debates about prostitution, "it [is] not really prostitution but 'something else' that [is] being discussed" (Ball, 2012, p. 36). Precisely what that "something else" is varies over time.

Ball (2012) has found that over the course of the nineteenth century, Canadian debates over prostitution were really about "relationships between women and men in general and between middle-class and upper-class women and men in particular" (p. 27). As the ideals governing relationships between women and men changed during the course of the century, so did perceptions of prostitutes and the social policies targeting them. In the early part of the century, the prostitute was considered a fallen angel, in contrast to the saintly nature of the ideal woman. Discourses of morality first labelled the prostitute herself with moral weakness, but later on assigned that weakness to deceitful males who seduced unsuspecting young women. Through this interpretive lens, the solution to prostitution was religious intervention to strengthen morals. As the century progressed, political, medical, and commercial voices guided discussions of prostitution. These discussions integrated public health and commercialism. Prostitution became state regulated to reduce the spread of contagious diseases and to protect male consumers of the trade from "'faulty goods'" (p. 31).

Suffragettes voiced a contrasting view of prostitution: They claimed women and men should be equals. Victimization dominated this view. Prostitutes were victims, not of deceitful men who seduced them, but rather of bullies who forced them into prostitution. Politicians, who regulated prostitution but did not criminalize it, were considered "male allies of male bullies" (Ball, 2012, p. 31). Soon, discourses of victimization became more pronounced, and prostitutes were seen as white slaves to highly organized groups. Through this lens, prostitutes needed protection for their own good and against their wills if necessary. Prostitution was finally criminalized in An Act Respecting Vagrants in 1869, where punishments were directed at the prostitute herself. Nearing the close of the nineteenth century, legislation continued to criminalize prostitutes but was also extended to male customers who seduced young women between the ages of 12 and 16.

More than a century later, discourses of morality and victimization continue to underlie debates over prostitution. The "oppression paradigm" (Weitzer, 2010, p. 15) has dominated media reports and public policy, equating prostitution with the epitome of male violence against women in a patriarchal society—for example, as "rape that's paid for" (Raymond, cited in Weitzer, 2010, p. 17). From this perspective, sex workers are considered incapable of being agents of choice or power. However, Weitzer (2010) is critical of this view, suggesting that it is not based on reliable research evidence but rather on moral rhetoric. First, he is critical of research that is based in the oppression paradigm for discounting "inconvenient findings" (p. 21). When sex workers being interviewed for the research disagree with some aspect of the oppression paradigm, their voices are discounted by the researcher as indicative of their inability to notice their own oppression. Second, research within the oppression paradigm tends to make sweeping generalizations. Individual stories of horrific abuse within the industry are presumed to be representative of the industry as a whole. All types of sex workers are considered the same, when other research shows significant differences between the working conditions and experiences of sex workers on the street and sex workers in indoor establishments (e.g., brothels or bawdy houses) (Seib, Fischer, & Najman, 2009; Weitzer, 2010). Weitzer argues that the oppression paradigm should be replaced by a "polymorphous paradigm" (p. 26) that recognizes the varied working conditions and experiences of different groups of sex workers in varying arenas.

Similarly, van der Meulen (2011) calls for discourses of morality and victimization to be replaced by discourses of human/worker rights in policies governing prostitution. Prostitution itself is not illegal; it is various activities surrounding prostitution that are criminalized in the Criminal Code, such as seeing clients at a fixed address, sharing a work location, and driving a sex worker to a location used for prostitution. The result is that sex workers are placed in unsafe working conditions, prevented from taking measures that would improve worker safety in a job that is, in itself, legal. After many years of effort by a number of sex workers and the organization Sex Professionals of Canada, in 2011 the Court of Appeal for Ontario agreed, saying that some of these laws "place unconstitutional restrictions on prostitutes' ability to protect themselves" (Humphreys, 2012). In this ruling, soliciting customers on the street remains illegal, as does living off the avails of prostitution in circumstances of exploitation (i.e., by pimps). The law criminalizing brothels or bawdy houses was overturned, and sex workers would be able to hire body guards, drivers, and support staff.

However, some former sex workers are opposed to any such legal changes. They argue that moving sex workers indoors makes it more difficult for social workers and police officers to offer assistance to underage workers or those needing help to leave the job, and sends a message to children that prostitution is acceptable. Thus, at the present time we see discourses of morality, victimization, and worker rights comingling within the deviance dance surrounding the issue of prostitution.

Sexual culture is of considerable complexity, integrating sexual, scientific, religious, political, family, and popular discourses. What is considered sexually deviant varies among cultures on the basis of these varying discourses. However, all cultures do differentiate between deviant and normal sexuality, and all cultures formally and informally regulate sexuality.

TIME TO REVIEW

Learning Objective 5

- In what way did discourses underlying the issue of prostitution change during the nineteenth century, and how did these changes affect social policy?

- In what ways are nineteenth-century discourses underlying the issue of prostitution still evident today?

- How do the oppression paradigm and polymorphous paradigm differ?

- In what ways are discourses of human/worker rights reflected in recent rulings on prostitution laws?

CHAPTER SUMMARY

■ Perceptions of "deviant" and "normal" sexuality vary cross-culturally and historically, but also vary among different social groups in a particular culture at a particular time in history. (1)

■ Traditional Aboriginal societies had very different sexual cultures than those of the colonizing Europeans. With European colonization, the sexual cultures of Aboriginal societies were subjected to significant measures of social control. (2)

■ In North America from the seventeenth century to the twentieth century, meanings of sexuality shifted from focusing on *reproductive ideals*, to *intimacy in marriage*, to *personal fulfillment*; agents of social control changed during this time as well. During all eras, hierarchies of race, class, and gender influenced the complexities of sexual culture. (3)

■ In North America today, although sexual freedom has increased considerably since previous eras, judgments of "deviant" and "normal" sexuality continue to be made. Criteria we use to make these judgments include *consent, nature of the sexual partner, nature of the sexual act, location,* and *frequency.* (4)

■ In any given culture at any given time, there is a multiplicity of perceptions, reactions, and social control measures surrounding sexuality. (5)

■ In contemporary society, the deviance dance is particularly evident when considering issues related to sex work, such as exotic dancing, pornography, and prostitution. (5)

MySearchLab®

⊙—Watch Go to MySearchLab to watch the video called "Alternative Sexual Orientation".

Apply What You Know: Consider the question posed by Dr. Elia in the video regarding why we are so often driven to seek the cause behind lesbian, gay, or bisexual behaviour. Why is this question problematic? How might a concern with the desire to seek out causes of sexual behaviour relate to other "deviant" sexual practices?

MySearchLab with eText offers you access to an online interactive version of the text, extensive help with your writing and research projects, and provides round-the-clock access to credible and reliable source material.

Chapter 6

The Troubling and Troubled World of Youth

© Nejron Photo/Fotolia

Learning Objectives

After reading this chapter, you should be able to

1   Compare popular images of youth crime with statistics on the nature and prevalence of youth crime, and explain why a gap exists between the perceptions and realities.

2   Describe theoretical and empirical research on youth crime and gang involvement.

3   Explain how gangs and youth crime are socially controlled.

4   Describe the extent and patterns of use of tobacco, drugs, and alcohol among youth, as well as how their usage is socially controlled.

5   Explain what the concept of "at-risk youth" means and what the "science of risk" does.

6   Describe how *all* teenagers are perceived as deviant in society, and explain the nature of the generation gap in the past, present, and future.

Ask Yourself

When you think of "youth crime," what images and information come to mind? Is youth crime a problem in Canadian society? How big a problem is it? Where do those images and pieces of information come from?

"Youth" and "deviance" frequently go hand in hand in the public mind, whether reading newspaper headlines about youth crime being out of control or expressing concerns about the music, movies, or video games youth are consuming (Tanner, 2001). More than any other age group, it is youth who are perceived as having lifestyles built around deviance. They are seen as being both "troubling" and "troubled"—and "troubling *because* they are troubled" (Tanner, 2001, p. 2). **Troubling youth**, such as young offenders, gang members, and street youth, are seen as threats to society. **Troubled youth** are perceived first and foremost as threats to themselves (for example, through substance abuse); they are also seen as potential threats to society, likely to become "troubling" if their problems are not solved early enough. However, at some level *all* youth are viewed as potential threats to both themselves and the larger society. It is not just *some* youth who are seen as being deviant; rather, youth culture, and indeed this period in the life cycle itself, is deemed to be deviant and in need of social control.

But precisely what time in life is captured by the term "youth"? **Youth** generally refers to a transitional time in life between childhood and maturity; one is no longer a "child," but is not yet an "adult." However, what this actually means varies across cultures, over time, and even across contexts within a particular culture at a specific point in time; in other words, the concept of "youth" is socially constructed (Tyyskä, 2001). Some constructions define it on the basis of age. For instance, the Youth Criminal Justice Act (YCJA) defines youth on the basis of age (12–17), as does the United Nations (15–25). Others define youth on the basis of social status rather than age; for them, youth refers to anyone who has not achieved full economic and social independence. In everyday conversation, the meaning of the term can be much more diverse, referring to adolescents or teenagers, university-age adults, and even individuals in their mid-twenties (Tyyskä, 2001). As you progress through the chapter, you will see that this diversity in definition is reflected in research on various subjects—crime, substance use, and those perceived as responsible for the "generation gap."

Deviant Youth: "Troubling" Youth
Youth Crime

Before continuing, take a moment to look at the *Ask Yourself* exercise. When we think of deviant youth, those who are criminals are likely to come to mind first. Indeed, when the search terms "youth and deviance" are inserted into numerous academic and popular databases, the majority of articles retrieved are about youth crime. Comparing these articles brings forward a central theme: There are significant differences between the *perceptions* of youth crime and *patterns* of youth crime (Tanner, 2010). Your responses to the *Ask Yourself* questions may reflect images and information contained in popular discourse that illustrate "the singular collective perception that kids are out of control, are more dangerous now than ever, and that youth crime is expanding at an alarming rate" (Schissel, 2001, p. 86). Calls for a "crackdown" on youth crime can be heard on the news, in politicians' comments to the press, and from victims of youth crime. But to what extent is this perception of youth crime accurate? Are kids out of control? Is youth crime expanding at an alarming rate?

Schissel (2001) points out that there is a vast "gulf between reality and perception" (p. 86). The extent and nature of youth crime is far from approximating the frightening picture painted in the popular mind by media images and recent changes in government legislation. Official statistics gathered through the Uniform Crime Reporting Survey reveal that both adult (ages 18 and over) and youth (ages 12–17) crime rates increased between 1962 and 1990 (Statistics Canada, 1992). However, analysts point out that some of this increase in youth crime rates is due to factors *other than* actual increases in youth crime, such as changing policing and administrative practices, changes in legislation, and greater public pressure to control youth crime, all of which may have resulted in more youth being brought into the criminal justice system over that period of time (Schissel, 1997).

Since 1992, there has been a steady downward trend in adult and youth crime rates. In 2011, the overall crime rate was at its lowest point since 1972 (Brennan, 2012). Since 2001, youth crime rates have shown slight increases or decreases from year to year (see Figure 6.1), but within an overall downward trend since a peak in 1991 (Taylor-Butts & Bressan, 2008). Although 12- to 17-year-olds are overrepresented in the criminal justice system, 18- to 24-year-olds are the most over-represented age group in the criminal justice system, and adults are responsible for the majority of crimes in every criminal offence category, including almost 85 percent of violent crimes (Statistics Canada, n.d.). In fact, if we look at the most violent of crimes, homicide, the largest proportion of male offenders is in the 18–24 age group (37 percent) and the largest proportion of female offenders is in

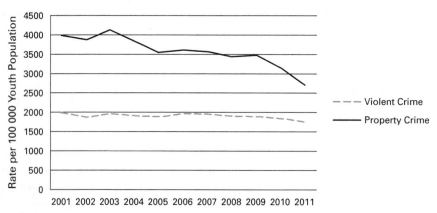

Figure 6.1 Youth Accused of Police-Reported Crime, Canada, 2001–2011

Adapted from: Brennan, S. (2012). Police-reported crime statistics in Canada, 2011. Table 7a (Youth accused of police-reported crime in Canada, 2001–2011), p. 35. *Juristat*, July 26, 2012. Statistics Canada Catalogue No. 85-002-X. Reproduced and distributed on an "as is" basis with the permission of Statistics Canada.

the 30–39 age group (32 percent). Only 14 percent of male homicide offenders and 15 percent of female homicide offenders are ages 12–17 (Statistics Canada, 2008). There is no criminal offence category for which youth constitute the majority of offenders.

Looking at this data, you may find the answer to the question of whether youth crime is a problem for society to be somewhat different from the answer you gave to that question earlier. Of course, any level of crime is a problem for society and for those victimized by such crimes. But youth crime is no more of a problem—and indeed may be less of a problem—than adult crime. One area where issues of youth and crime are certainly more problematic than issues of adults and crime is that of victimization. Children and youth are far more likely to be the *victims* of crime than adults are. For example, those aged 18 and under comprise 61 percent of sexual assault victims, and although 14- to 17-year-olds constitute only 5 percent of the population, they comprise 17 percent of robbery victims (AuCoin, 2005). These are likely surprising statistics for those who rely primarily on popular or media images as their source of information about crime in Canada.

Where does this gap between the perceptions and patterns of youth crime come from? Many criminologists attribute the gap in part to **moral panics**. This concept was popularized by Cohen (1973) based on his analysis of the aftermath of a minor altercation between two groups of youth ("Mods" and "Rockers") at a British seaside resort in 1964. Although the incident itself was relatively minor, in the following days (and in fact for the next three years) the media exaggerated and distorted the magnitude of the events with headlines such as "Day of Terror by Scooter Groups" and "Seaside Resorts Prepare for Hooligans' Invasion." Public fear grew, and pressure was placed on law enforcement and politicians to crack down on the youth-inspired terror that was gripping the nation.

The concept of moral panic refers to exaggerated and sensationalized concerns of a particular phenomenon. Goode and Ben-Yehuda (1994) list five elements of a moral panic: heightened concern, hostility toward the offending group, a certain level of consensus that there is a real threat, disproportionality (the attention given to the phenomenon is far greater than the level of objective threat that the phenomenon presents), and volatility (it erupts suddenly and then may just as suddenly disappear, although some may become institutionalized and therefore reappear time and again). This concept has since been applied to the analysis of diverse youth cultural phenomenon (e.g., concerns over youth-oriented media) and has been used to explain the gap between the perceptions and patterns of youth crime.

Moral panics are constructed within the media, wherein youth crime is overrepresented, portrayed as a new problem for society, and consistently linked to particular ethnic groups and classes (Tanner, 2001, 2010; Bortner, 1988; Pearson, 1983). But as Pearson's (1983) analysis of British media illustrates, this portrait of youth crime has been repeatedly painted since the early twentieth century—public concerns about youth crime today are quite similar to public concerns about youth crime 100 years ago. Even a century ago, there were gaps between the perceptions and realities of youth crime, and moral panics about youth crime were conveyed in popular discourse, creating a distorted view of youth crime in the eyes of the public. Moral panics about youth crime are not limited to contemporary North American society; they have also been found in Austria, Germany, and other European societies as far back as the late nineteenth and early twentieth centuries (Wegs, 1999).

Even though the nature and extent of youth crime diverges considerably from public perceptions and media portrayals, concerns about those youth who *are* involved in criminal activity have stimulated a significant body of research over the past several decades. Thus, research on the causes of youth crime abound. Many of the theories of deviance that lean toward the more objective end of the objective–subjective continuum (which were addressed in Chapter 2) are used to explain youth crime. Its existence (or its absence) has been variously explained as resulting from the following: learning deviant techniques and motives from peers (differential association theory); bonds with others that restrain most of us from crime (social bonds theory); the level of self-control developed early in life (self-control theory); structural inequalities in access to legitimate opportunities (Merton's strain theory) and to illegitimate opportunities (differential opportunity theory); and the system of rewards, punishments, and role models we have been exposed to in life (social learning theory).

Empirical research has also tried to establish the causes of youth crime and has investigated the roles of intelligence (Liska & Reid, 1985); family structure and processes (Baumrind, 1991; Thornberry, Lizotte, Krohm, Farnworth, & Jang, 1991); school performance (Davies, 1994); and peer influences (Regioli & Hewitt, 1994). Parent and peer influences have been the particular subject of many analyses of the causes of youth crime. Early research suggested a link between single motherhood and delinquent behaviour in children, but that link has subsequently been shown to be relatively weak; the quality and effectiveness of parenting rather than the structure of the household itself is more important in determining delinquent behaviour (Milan, 2000; Wells & Rankin, 1991).

Parenting style incorporates several characteristics, including supervision, parental control, and emotional ties between parent and child. Although different researchers label parenting styles in various ways, their conclusions about parenting characteristics that improve child outcomes are quite similar. Moderate control of the child's behaviour combined with moderate levels of supervision and strong, positive, emotional ties between parent and child are effective means of influencing child behaviour in both the short and long term, as the children develop their own internal moral standards and higher levels of self-control. This parenting style involves having high expectations for children, knowledge of and interest in who the children are socializing with and what they are doing, as well as clearly explained rules and consequences for breaking those rules.

In addition to high expectations, there is also some flexibility (e.g., parents are willing to listen to the children's point of view) and substantial levels of warmth and affection. This kind of parenting reduces the risk of negative outcomes in children, including criminal activity, substance use, poor school performance, low self-esteem, and susceptibility to negative peer influence. In contrast, both lax and extremely strict parental controls, as well as weak or nonexistent emotional ties, are associated with negative child outcomes (Baumrind, 1991; Thornberry et al., 1991; Jang & Smith, 1997; Brook, Brook, De La Rosa, Whiteman, & Montoya, 1999).

Parenting styles combining control, supervision, and high levels of affection are associated with a wide range of positive child outcomes, including a lower risk of criminal behaviour.

Not only do family variables influence child outcomes themselves, they also affect peer influence. Effective parenting styles are associated with children who select higher quality peers as friends; have stronger, more emotionally intimate and trusting relationships with those friends; and are less susceptible to negative peer influences. These relationships have been found in a number of societies in the world, including Colombia, where, despite extremely high societal levels of drug use and violence, parenting variables improve child outcomes and mediate negative peer influences such as criminal behaviour and marijuana use (Milan, 2000; Brook et al., 1999).

The single most effective predictor of criminal activity among youth is criminal activity among friends (Zeman & Bressan, 2008); consequently, the role that parenting plays in peer selection and influence is significant. Parenting is central in reducing the likelihood of the initial association with criminally involved peers and the likelihood of adopting criminal behaviour if a relationship with a criminally involved peer does form. However, neither parenting styles nor peer influence exist in a vacuum. The International Youth Survey (administered in more than 30 countries, and in Toronto for the Canadian version) finds that a complex set of factors is associated with criminal behavior among youth (Zeman & Bressan, 2008) (see Box 6.1).

Although the crime problem, and in particular the youth crime problem, is nowhere near the level that public images convey, crime is a social issue in need of control. In recent years, a particular form of youth criminal behaviour has come to predominate in the public mind: gangs (Schissel, 2001).

Box 6.1

Factors Influencing Youth Crime

Property Crime

- single-parent or blended family
- no university aspirations
- skipping school
- perceiving school environment as unsafe
- having been stolen from
- going out at night without adult supervision
- spending time alone rather than with family
- spending time with friends rather than with family
- peer acceptance of illegal acts

Violent Crime

- male
- no university aspirations
- skipping school
- having been discriminated against on the basis of race, language, or religion
- having been stolen from
- having been threatened
- perceiving school as unsafe
- negative relationship with father or mother
- going out at night without adult supervision
- spending time with friends rather than with family
- peer acceptance of illegal acts

Exercise Your Mind

In order to further explore the linkages between theory and empirical research, identify which of the risk factors in Box 6.1 might fit within (a) Merton's strain theory; (b) Cloward and Ohlin's differential opportunity theory; (c) Sutherland's differential association theory; (d) social learning theory; (e) Hirschi's social bonds theory; and (f) Gottfredson and Hirschi's self-control theory (i.e., general theory of crime).

Youth Gangs

Youth street gangs are a popular topic for newspaper articles, politicians' speeches, movies, and both fictional and nonfictional television. Youth gangs can be found throughout much of the world; however, the prevalence of youth gangs in the United States, combined with the emphasis placed on youth gangs in the American media, means that much of the research done on gangs is American. In fact, Canadian research on youth gangs continues to be comparatively sparse, and American research has dominated Canadian academic, public, and governmental policy discussions (Tanner, 2010; Grekul & LaBoucane-Benson, 2007; Chatterjee, 2006; Gordon, 2001). The American-centric nature of gang research is problematic when one considers Canadian–American differences in gun control legislation, drug laws, government policies, ethnic and cultural composition, and social supports (Grekul & LaBoucane-Benson, 2007). Research on the prevalence of gangs in Canada is virtually nonexistent. One 2002 survey of police officers reported a total of more than 6000 youth gang members in Canada in almost 500 gangs (cited in Chettelburgh, 2007).

Two broad streams of research on youth gangs can be identified. One of those streams focuses on causation or motivation: why gangs form, why youth join gangs, and why gangs engage in particular behaviours. The second stream of research focuses on various aspects of the social construction of the "gang problem," such as how and why moral panics about gangs emerge and even the problems involved in the very definition of "gang" itself.

The "How" and "Why" of Gangs

What has been labelled "traditional criminology" has dominated theorizing about gang emergence and gang membership (Hagedorn, 2007), bringing us back to a number of the theories reviewed in Chapter 2. For instance, the underlying proposition of strain theories is that gangs will emerge in socially and economically disadvantaged communities. In such communities, where legitimate opportunities to achieve social status and economic success are limited, gangs form as an alternative way of achieving status, social acceptance, and economic success (e.g., Merton's strain theory).

The status and economic success to be gained via gang activity is not to be underestimated, given the amount of money that can be made in the drug trade. However, the pursuit of economic success is not central to the activities of all youth gangs. Other theorists have asserted that different types of gangs have different types of activities as their foundation. Status frustration theory suggests that lower-class boys, if unable to live up to the middle-class measuring rod that pervades the education system, would join with other similar boys in forming gangs that engage in expressive, destructive, non-utilitarian behaviours (e.g., vandalism, violence) rather than economically driven activities (Cohen, 1955).

Differential opportunity theory proposes that the nature of the illegitimate opportunities present in the community determines the nature of gang behaviour; particular illegitimate opportunities result in the formation of gangs that may be economically enterprising, violent, or drug using and retreatist (Cloward & Ohlin, 1960). Although the pursuit of economic success is not a component of all youth gangs, the pursuit of status is—but the type of status that can be achieved through gang membership depends on the gang in question.

Although positivist theories dominate the area, research on gangs does also come from more subjective theoretical orientations. For instance, drawing on the critical Marxist perspective of the Birmingham Centre for Contemporary Cultural Studies, Bourgois (1995) analyzes youth gangs as sources of identity and expressions of resistance among youth who are structurally marginalized. Pointing to the interactionist perspective, Venkatesh (2003) discusses the fact that individual members within a gang have different interests, motivations for gang membership, and understandings of what it means to be in a gang member.

Ethnographic research, emerging from the interactionist perspective, involves researchers embedding themselves in gangs for extended periods of time, interviewing gang members, and observing their daily activities. For example, Jankowski (1991) conducted an ethnographic study that is one of the few pieces of research to explore the relationships between gangs, other people, and other organizations within the community (Venkatesh, 2003). Jankowski concluded that individuals join gangs for a variety of different reasons rather than for any one reason (such as blocked opportunities).

The various reasons for joining a gang are based on a rational calculation of what is in the best interests of the individual at a particular time. First, Jankowski (1991) suggests that one reason for gang membership is **material incentives**. Some people join gangs based on the belief that the gang will provide an environment that increases the chances of making money—more regular money and with less individual effort than if pursuing economic success individually. Jankowski found that material incentives also include financial security for gang members and their families during difficult times, as well as networking for future economic endeavours.

Recreation serves as another reason for gang membership. That is, gangs provide entertainment and a social life, and in some communities may serve as the primary social institution in the neighbourhood, promoting social events and supplying drugs and alcohol. The comments of one gang member illustrate the recreational aspect of gang membership: "'Man, it [the gang] was a great source of dope and women. Hell, they were the kings of the community so I wanted to get in on some of the action'" (Jankowski, 1991, p. 283). Gangs may serve as a **place of refuge and camouflage**, motivating some individuals to seek gang membership. Being just "one of the gang" provides a level of anonymity, removing a sense of personal responsibility for illegal activities—"'the gang is going to provide me with some cover'" (p. 283).

Other people are drawn to gangs for the **physical protection** they provide from known dangers in the neighbourhood. As gang member Cory points out, "'Now that I got some business things going I can concentrate on them and not worry so much. I don't always have to be looking over my shoulder'" (Jankowski, 1991, p. 284). For some people, joining a gang may serve as a **time to resist** living the kinds of lives their parents lived. In this vein, becoming a gang member is a statement of rejection to society, a rejection of the type of lives being offered. At the same time, the economic prospects of gang membership may be a way of avoiding just that type of life: "'Hey, I just might make some money from our dealings. . . . If I don't [make it, at least] I told those fuckers in Beverly Hills what I think of the jobs they left for us'" (p. 284).

In some neighbourhoods, certain gangs have existed for generations, so that individuals whose fathers, uncles, and grandfathers have been members of the gang at some point in their lives feel a **commitment to the community** and join the gang to continue a tradition. As Pepe states, "'A lot of people from the community have been in [the gang]. . . . I felt it's kind of my duty to join 'cause everybody expects it'" (Jankowski, 1991, p. 285). Feeling a commitment to the community, along with the other possible motivations for gang membership, leads individuals to conclude that joining a gang is currently in their best interests.

Grekul and LaBoucane-Benson (2007) combine positivist (social bonds), critical (conflict), and interactionist (labelling) theories in their analysis of Aboriginal gangs in Canada. Interviews with former gang members, police officers, and corrections workers reveal that weak bonds of attachment, commitment to conventional society, involvement in conventional society, and beliefs that support conventional society play a significant role in gang membership. The legacy of colonization and residential schooling (which will be discussed further in Chapter 9) has had a lasting effect on Aboriginal families, contributing to family instability and violence. For example, Grekul and LaBoucane-Benson (2007) report that in the Edmonton area Aboriginal children are six times more likely to be involved with child protection services, and it is these children who are prime targets for gang recruitment efforts in that region.

Although there have been considerable increases in high school completion and post-secondary education, dropout rates continue to be considerably higher among Aboriginal youth, with higher unemployment rates as a consequence. Ongoing discrimination continues to be a problem as well: "One of our respondents recalled being called a 'dumb little Indian who would never amount to anything' by one of his school teachers" (Grekul & LaBoucane-Benson, 2007, p. 33). The negative effects of being labelled have an impact; one respondent states, "'police called them a gang so they began to act that way and identify themselves that way'" (p. 42). All of these factors have an interactive effect, and gangs are able to step in and "fill the gap for disenfranchised and marginalized" (p. 2) Aboriginal youth.

A number of different variables, including personal, family, community, and educational factors, increase the likelihood of gang involvement (e.g., Gordon, 1995; Flannery, Huff, & Manos, 2001; Edmonton Police Service, 2009). In Box 6.2 you will find a summary of these factors, illustrating that gang involvement emerges in part from unhealthy personalities, unhealthy relationships, unhealthy families, and unhealthy communities. Interviews with 125 Toronto youth (ages 16–24) who identify themselves as gang members found that a combination of push and pull factors are associated with gang affiliation. Unstable home environments drove many of these youth to hang out on the streets, while negative school experiences (e.g., bullying, histories of school discipline) propelled youth to turn to similar others for support. Gang affiliation offered a number of benefits, including companionship and social support (which was typically lacking in their home lives), money, and respect. As one gang member stated, "It was the image. It was the money. It was the power" (Tanner, 2010, p. 186).

The Construction of the "Gang Problem"

While the first stream of gang research explores the causes of or motivations for gang emergence, membership, and behaviour, the second stream concentrates on a different set of issues related to social construction. Within the latter stream, some researchers emphasize the social construction of "gangs" themselves. For instance, Sanday (cited in Venkatesh, 2003) asks why fraternities are not considered to be gangs. One of the more commonly used definitions of "**gang**" (albeit far from being agreed upon) is "any denotable . . . group [of adolescents or young adults] who (a) are generally perceived as a distinct aggregation by

Box 6.2

Factors Influencing Gang Involvement

Family Indicators

- excessive parental controls
- lax parental controls
- low parental nurturance
- abuse/neglect
- low parental educational level
- criminality among other family members

Personal Indicators

- low self-control
- low motivation
- truancy
- failing grades
- low aspirations or goals in life
- substance abuse

Community Indicators

- community disorganization
- high crime rate
- high population turnover
- lack of cultural resources
- lack of recreational resources
- gang presence

School Indicators

- negative school environment
- violence in the school
- low expectations for students
- inadequate funding for school resources (e.g., library books, extracurricular activities)
- lax control over students

others in the neighbourhood, (b) recognize themselves as a denotable group (almost invariably with a group name), and (c) have been involved in a sufficient number of [illegal] incidents" (cited in Chatterjee, 2006). Fraternities are most certainly perceived as a distinct group, both by others and themselves, and Sanday points out that "theft, vandalism, sexual conquest (read: harassment), and the imbibing of alcohol (read: underage drinking)" (Venkatesh, 2003, p. 5) are common and are even explicitly included in some fraternity charters or manifestos.

Others who are embedded within the latter stream of research focus more on the social construction of the **"gang problem."** Discussions of media representations of gangs have been central to research from this perspective. The way youth gangs are represented in the media and other forms of public discourse is similar to the portrayal of youth crime more generally. Gangs are portrayed as a new and growing problem for society, one that is out of control (Fasiolo & Leckie, 1993; Tanner, 2001; Gordon, 1993, 2001).

Just as with images of youth crime more generally, public images of gangs surpass their actual existence. Not only are stories about gangs found on television news and in newspapers, they can also be easily found in the fictional media—on television shows such as *Criminal Minds* and *CSI: Crime Scene Investigation*, in movies, and in the glamourized images of gangs within some rap and hip hop music lyrics and videos (Delaney, 2005). The involvement of particular ethnic and age groups is a significant component of public images of gangs.

Canadian newspapers **racialize** the "gang problem" (Bell, 2002). In other words, stories about gangs frequently include references to specific racial or ethnic groups (Grekul & LaBoucane-Benson, 2007; Gordon, 2001). This is problematic on two fronts. First, a distorted picture of Canadian gangs is presented to the audience, when the reality is that gangs are ethnically diverse (Tanner, 2010; Gordon, 2001; Chatterjee, 2006). Second, race and ethnicity are only overtly linked in the media to gang activity when it is nonwhites that are involved. "We read and hear of the 'Asian' gang problem, the problem of Jamaican Blacks in the east, and 'Aboriginal gangs.' We don't often hear of 'Caucasian' or 'White' gangs. Racial and ethnic stereotyping leads to processes such as racial profiling and creates misunderstanding, labelling, mistrust, and hostility between groups" (Grekul & LaBoucane-Benson, 2007, p. 25).

Media representations of the gang problem vary in different parts of Canada, particularly in Quebec as compared with the other provinces and territories. In Quebec, the racialization of gangs is less common. Instead, age is one of the areas of focus in the media: gangs are most commonly referred to as "youth gangs" (Fasiolo & Leckie, 1993). Just as with race and ethnicity, the linking of "youth" and "gangs" is inaccurate in that most Canadian gangs have considerable age diversity. The 2002 Canadian Police Survey found that the age range in gangs is from 8 to over 50, and that fewer than half of street gang members are under the age of 18 (Chatterjee, 2006). Thus, although calls from politicians and the general public to strengthen young offender legislation often follow publicized gang incidents, it is adults who predominate in Canada's gang landscape. When combined, the media's overrepresentation of gangs, its racialization of gangs, and its distortion of the age composition of gangs all contribute to a view of Canada's gangs that is quite different from the reality—showing that a "moral panic" has been created.

Certain groups may benefit from the creation of a moral panic about street gangs. Drawing on the conflict and critical theoretical perspectives addressed in Chapter 3, a number of researchers suggest that not only does the media benefit from the creation of moral panics, so do some politicians, interest groups, and law enforcement agencies (Bell, 2002; Tanner, 2001; Gordon, 2001; Schissel, 2001; Cohen, 1973). By presenting sensationalistic and fear-provoking stories, the media draws an audience and thereby increases profit. Some politicians may similarly engage in fear mongering and then vow to toughen legislation and enforcement if elected. By contributing to moral panic and then promising to reduce the social problem, they are able to obtain more votes. Interest groups and community agencies who want legislation strengthened or who provide social programs may receive more funding by exaggerating the nature of the problem. Law enforcement agencies may also benefit in some communities by receiving more funding to hire more officers or create specialized gang units if they are able to convince municipal, provincial, and federal politicians that the "gang problem" is out of control. Some researchers suggest that even gangs themselves may benefit from this moral panic, which provides them with free publicity and may thereby increase their membership and power in the community. Youth who are currently not involved in gangs may form new gangs to protect themselves from the perceived threat (Tanner, 2001).

However, although the gang research done in this second stream suggests that the moral panic surrounding youth gangs surpasses what is actually going on and that various groups benefit from this moral panic, it does not claim that gangs are a figment of the social imagination or that gangs are nothing to worry about. Indeed, the gangs that do exist must be socially controlled.

Controlling Youth Gangs and Youth Crime

"How do you deal with youth crime? 'Toughen up' the Youth Criminal Justice Act, send 'bad guys' (and girls) to jail for a very long time . . . and keep the problem away from our homes and families. Easy, simple, quick fix" (Grekul & LaBoucane-Benson, 2007). In fact, as Grekul and LaBoucane-Benson go on to point out, the effective control of gangs and of youth crime more generally is far from an easy, quick fix. Throughout North America, street gangs are socially controlled at multiple levels—formal and informal, retroactive and preventative. These social control efforts occur in families, communities (schools, community agencies, community organizations, businesses, and religious institutions), and the criminal justice system (government, courts, and law enforcement).

At a formal level of regulation, many schools have integrated gang awareness programs to teach children about the dangers of gangs and the consequences of gang membership. These programs are intended to prevent children from joining gangs. Community agencies, particularly those operating in gang-ridden neighbourhoods, frequently have both retroactive and preventative programs. Retroactive programs are designed to try to persuade existing gang members to leave that lifestyle. They may offer educational upgrading, job training, assistance in finding employment, free tattoo removal, and various types of counselling.

Preventative programs in communities may operate in conjunction with schools, teaching young children basic life skills (e.g., nutrition, grooming) and social skills (e.g., problem solving, anger management), or providing organized community activities. Many police departments in North America have specialized gang units who become familiar with and closely monitor known gang members, as well as deal with gang issues and events that arise. Governments provide gang-related legislation and social programs (e.g., job-training programs).

The Community Solution to Gang Violence (CSGV) in Edmonton is a large-scale formal effort that integrates all of the groups listed above. Administered through Native Counselling Services of Alberta, this program combines intervention and prevention, bringing together 40 community organizations, the Edmonton Police Service, and all levels of government (municipal, provincial, and federal). Informal social controls occur at the level of everyday social interaction, typically focusing on preventative efforts. This includes parenting efforts (e.g., parenting style, talking to your children about gangs) and community involvement with neighbourhood children (e.g., becoming a soccer coach, helping the neighbourhood children organize a food drive).

Coordinated efforts at gang control at multiple levels are the most effective means of prevention and response to the gang problem. However, the regulation of gangs is even more complex in that different types of specific controls may be required in cities with varying levels of gang activity. A community that currently has no signs of gang presence requires a basic foundation of control, which can be provided by community parenting programs, teaching children multicultural sensitivity, and reinforcing codes of conduct. In contrast, a community with the highest level of gang activity—that is, one where gangs dominate the neigbourhood—will require the assistance of anti-gang professionals and intense efforts to reclaim the neighbourhood (Edmonton Police Service, 2003).

Measures to control youth gangs are intertwined with the regulation of youth crime in general. Many of the formal and informal social controls that were discussed in the context of gangs are also used in relation to youth crime—it is presumed that the prevention of gang involvement is also the prevention of crime at a broader level. For instance, effective parenting, community involvement in children's lives, and effective classrooms will reduce not only the likelihood of gang involvement, but also the likelihood of all types of criminal activity.

Over the past century, there have been considerable changes in the way youth crime has been formally controlled or regulated. Public concerns about youth crime gained force during the late nineteenth century. This was a period of tremendous social and economic change in Canadian society. The process of industrialization was well underway, cities were growing, and an identifiable working class was present. Because of the long hours that working-class parents had to spend at work simply to ensure the survival of their family, their children were left unsupervised more than the children of middle-class parents. Social reformers during that era were concerned with the lack of supervision these children faced as well as the subsequent danger they presented to middle-class personhood and property (Leon, 1977; Sutherland, 1976).

Various small pieces of legislation encompassed the control of youth crime, neglected children, and abandoned children. Children under the age of 7 were presumed not to know the difference between right and wrong, and so could not be charged with criminal offences. If it was proven that a child between the ages of 7 and 14 knew the difference between right and wrong, the child could be subject to the same sentence as an adult; thus, it was possible for a 7-year-old child who had committed a crime to be sentenced to life in prison or even death. Youth over the age of 14 were considered equal to adults in criminal law.

In 1908, the Canadian juvenile justice system was created with the implementation of the Juvenile Delinquents Act. Its foundation was the principle of *parens patriae* ("parent of the country"), meaning that the state would act in the best interests of children under the age of 16 if it became clear that their own parents were unwilling or unable to—and both neglected and delinquent children were presumed to need such legislative attention. Although it controlled youth criminals, the Juvenile Delinquents Act was more a *child welfare* piece of legislation since it was believed that with the right assistance and correct teaching, young criminals could be set on the right path in life. Separate detention facilities and jail facilities were created for youth based on the belief that integrating juvenile delinquents with adult criminals would simply further juvenile delinquency (Reitsma-Street, 1989–1990).

The Juvenile Delinquents Act was amended several times over the ensuing decades, and in 1984 it was replaced by the Young Offenders Act. This new piece of legislation was based on *justice* principles rather than child welfare principles. It extended the legal rights of adult offenders (e.g., due process, the right to an attorney) to youth as well, who were not guaranteed such protections under the Juvenile Delinquents Act. Youth who committed crimes were no longer perceived as juvenile delinquents but as **young offenders**; an offending youth was now seen as a *criminal* rather than a child gone astray (West, 1984; West, 1991). After a number of amendments throughout the 1990s, the Youth Criminal Justice Act replaced the Young Offenders Act on April 1, 2003.

Under this most recent legislation, chronic or violent young offenders are treated more stringently, while first-time and nonviolent young offenders are more likely to be treated via community and alternative measures. The Youth Criminal Justice Act is one component of the federal government's Youth Justice Renewal Initiative, a multifaceted initiative involving the criminal justice system, schools, community agencies, and more. Its underlying principles are prevention, meaningful consequences for youth crime, and intensified rehabilitation and reintegration.

The social control of youth crime has been modified in substantial ways over the past century, and more recently has included efforts to control gangs. Although legislation, criminal justice programs, and social programs are continually changing, the desire to control "troubling" youth is as old as civilization itself. However, youth who are perceived as threats to society because of their criminal activities are not the only ones considered deviant and in need of social control—"troubled" youth are a focus of concern as well.

TIME TO REVIEW

Learning Objective 1

- In what ways are youth perceived as both "troubling" and "troubled"?

- What are the broader patterns of youth crime, and how do these compare with common perceptions of youth crime? Is the "moral panic" over youth crime unique to the twenty-first century?

Learning Objective 2

- Which theories have been used to explain youth crime, and what has empirical research found about the roles of family structure, parenting style, and peers?

- In what way do positivist, interpretive, and critical theories contribute to our understanding of gang emergence, membership, and behaviour?

- How does the media represent the "gang problem," and who potentially benefits from the moral panic about gangs?

Learning Objective 3

- In what way is the social control of gangs intertwined with the control of youth crime more generally, and how are gangs controlled within families, schools, community agencies, and the criminal justice system?

- How has legislation governing youth crime changed over the past century?

Deviant Youth: "Troubled" Youth

Some youth are considered deviant and are made subject to measures of social control not because they are "troubling," and therefore currently a danger to society, but because they are "troubled." "Troubled" youth are first and foremost a danger to themselves; their behaviour threatens their own well-being, physical or mental health, and future. But "troubled" youth are also perceived as potentially "troubling"—if they are uncontrolled or if their problems are not effectively dealt with they may become not only a danger to themselves but a danger to society as well.

Youth who abuse drugs or alcohol, engage in premature sexual activity, or become teenage parents are just some of those youth who are considered "troubled." When considering "troubled" youth, one of the areas of greatest public concern is substance abuse because of its potential effects on the substance abusers themselves, others, and the larger community.

Substance Use among Youth

Ask Yourself

Estimate how many youth use the following substances: alcohol, tobacco, marijuana, and other illegal drugs. What did you base your estimates on—youth whom you know personally, your own observations, media portrayals, public information campaigns, or your own usage patterns?

We live in a culture where substance use, in some form, is widely evident. Step outside the doorway of office buildings, shopping malls, and even hospitals and you will see groups of people gathered, a haze of cigarette smoke hovering over their heads. Attend a wedding, retirement party, or dinner party and alcohol will likely be served. Prior to New Year's Eve, liquor stores sell out of bottles of champagne. Some single people who are searching for Mr./Ms. Right (or Mr./Ms. Right Now) carry out those searches in bars—bars that likely have a happy hour (when drinks are less expensive) or even a ladies' night, where schoolgirl attire buys five drinks for five dollars. Attend certain concerts (e.g., Kid Rock, Wiz Khalifa), and although cameras may be confiscated, marijuana will not, and even those members of the audience who are not drug users will find themselves getting a secondhand high. On television and in movies, characters may be smoking, drinking, or using drugs. For example, on an episode of *Friends*, when "Fun Bobby" became sober, he was no longer fun, and despite everyone's best efforts to support his sobriety, they eventually found themselves trying to convince him to start drinking again.

The related social controls we see around us are further evidence of substance use. Walk into your university's student resource centre and you will find pamphlets about alcohol abuse, smoking, and "club drugs." Prior to reading week (or spring break), abuse prevention campaigns might be displayed throughout your campus. If you tell someone you are going to a club, they may warn you about the dangers of "date rape" drugs. In school, you may have been exposed to educational programs about smoking, alcohol use, and drug use, often beginning in early elementary school. Rarely does a day go by when each of us does not see someone using such a substance (whether in person or in the media) or see some type of substance control efforts.

The most commonly used substances among Canadian adolescents and young adults have traditionally been, in order of use, alcohol, tobacco, cannabis (marijuana and hashish), and hallucinogens (e.g., LSD). A recent survey of students in Grades 7 through 12 found that the three most commonly used substances (excluding tobacco) are alcohol (52.6 percent use in the past year), cannabis (26.9 percent use in the past year), and ecstasy (5.8 percent use in the past year) (Canadian Centre on Substance Abuse, 2011).

Substance use among youth peaked in 1979 and then steadily declined until the early 1990s. Usage increased throughout the 1990s (Roberts et al., 2001) but has since declined, such that drug use overall is lower today than it was in 1979 (although the use of some specific drugs, such as hallucinogens, is higher) (Adlaf & Paglia-Boak, 2007). More than one-quarter of students in Grades 7 through 12 are substance free, a lower proportion than in the early 1990s, but still a higher proportion than in the 1970s (Canadian Centre on Substance Abuse, 2011)

Tobacco

The health risks associated with smoking and secondhand smoke exposure have now been well established by medical research. When those risks were first publicized during the 1970s, smoking rates among youth began a steady decline that lasted until 1990. But beginning in 1990, youth smoking increased once again and continued to grow throughout the decade (Health Canada, 1999). Another shift has occurred since that time, such that from 2001 through 2011 smoking among 12- to 17-year-olds declined (see Figure 6.2) (Janz, 2012). Because most adult smokers indicate they started smoking prior to the age of 18 (Janz, 2012), declines in youth smoking are most likely indicative of further declines in adult smoking in the coming years.

Youth say that the primary motivation for smoking comes from friends or peer pressure (Health Canada, 2005a). Research also shows that the likelihood of smoking is

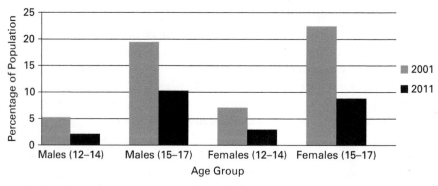

Figure 6.2 Proportion of Male and Female Smokers, Ages 12–14 and 15–17, 2001 and 2011

Data from Janz, T. (2012). "Current Smoking Trends". *Health at a Glance, July 2012.* Statistics Canada Catalogue No. 82-624-X.

associated with family income, highest level of education in the household, and parental smoking behaviour (Janz, 2012; Shields, 2005).

Youth smoking is socially controlled in a variety of ways. The federal Tobacco Act prohibits the sale of cigarettes to those under the age of 18, although provincial legislation can increase the minimum age requirement to 19. This kind of legislation has existed for many years, but enforcement has been lax for much of that time. In the 1970s, it was not uncommon for children as young as six or seven to be sent to the corner store to buy cigarettes for a parent or an older sibling. More recently, enforcement has become more stringent and penalties for selling cigarettes to minors have become more severe. For example, Alberta retailers risk a $3000 fine for a first offence and up to a $50 000 fine for a second offence (Gregoire, 2003).

And most retailers in Canada are complying. Health Canada conducts regular investigations of retail outlets in 30 cities across Canada. A research team of one youth and one adult go into a retail outlet (although not as an identifiable pair), and the youth requests a package of cigarettes. The youth lies about his or her age, if asked, but does not carry any identification. Using this methodology, Health Canada (2005b) found that 80 percent of retailers complied with legislation, refusing to sell cigarettes to the youth. Alberta has taken an additional step and is the first province to create legislation targeting underage smokers themselves, wherein anyone under the age of 18 who is caught smoking in "public" is subject to a $100 fine (Gregoire, 2003). However, the enforcement of this legislation is another issue; as one police officer states, "'It's not something we're going to devote a lot of time to . . . arresting kids [for smoking]'" (para. 6). The Alberta legislation does not operate in isolation, but rather is just one piece of a larger $11.7 million strategy that also involves school education packages, websites, and seminars.

Social control efforts specifically aimed at curtailing youth smoking are part of broader forms of regulation for smoking. We have come a long way from the days when cigarette commercials appeared on television, people smoked anywhere they wished (including university classrooms and hospitals), and doctors prescribed smoking as a weight-loss tool. Today, cigarette commercials cannot be shown on television, and cigarette advertising is in fact widely restricted. The media is now a central source for public service campaigns to reduce smoking.

In many communities, recent laws have banned smoking in many workplaces, shopping malls, hospitals, and restaurants. Other communities have taken this legislation a step further, prohibiting smoking in all public buildings, including bars. And, of course, instead of prescribing smoking as a weight-loss tool, contemporary doctors try to convince their patients to stop smoking and provide resources to help them quit (e.g., nicotine patches, access to support groups). A growing proportion of households are smoke-free. The Canadian Community Health Survey (Statistics Canada, 2006) found that smoking is banned in 64 percent of households, an increase from 57 percent in 2003. This relatively simple act has a significant impact on youth, who are less likely to smoke if they live in households where smoking is prohibited. This is the case even if parents are smokers themselves (Shields, 2005).

The use of this animated character in cigarette advertising was highly criticized for its apparent attempts to attract the attention of children.

The health dangers of smoking are well known and have led to comprehensive anti-smoking efforts for people of all ages. However, smoking among youth is a public concern not only because of the health dangers, but also because of its association with other forms of substance use. Youth who smoke are more likely to use other drugs, particularly marijuana (US Department of Health and Human Services, 2000); half of 12- to 17-year-olds who smoke have used marijuana, compared to only 4 percent of those who do not smoke (Health Canada, 2005a).

Drug Use

Cannabis is the most widely used psychoactive drug among Canadian youth (excluding alcohol) (Adlaf & Paglia-Boak, 2007). The *Cross-Canada Report on Student Alcohol and Drug Use* has found that between 4.2 and 6.5 percent (depending on the province) of youth in Grade 7 have tried cannabis; by Grade 12, between 39.8 and 62.6 percent of youth have used cannibis (Canadian Centre on Substance Abuse, 2011) (see Figure 6.3). However, although a considerable proportion of youth have tried marijuana, they do not use it regularly. For example, only 17.1 to 26.8 percent of youth in Grade 12 have used cannabis in the past month (Canadian Centre on Substance Abuse, 2011).

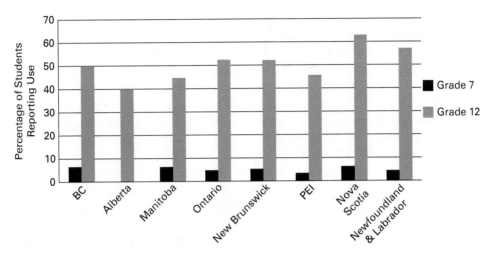

Figure 6.3 Self-reported Cannabis Use, Grade 7 and Grade 12, by Province

Data from Canadian Centre for Substance Use (2011). *Cross Canada Report on Student Alcohol and Drug Use*. Table 24, p. 18.

Other psychoactive drugs have lower rates of usage than cannabis, although rates did increase during the 1990s (Health Canada, 1999). University-age youth have higher rates of illicit drug usage than adolescents, but even among university students less than 10 percent have used an illicit drug (other than marijuana) within the previous year, and only 2 percent have used one within the past month (Adlaf, Demers, & Gliksman, 2005). Canadian youth are more likely to use psychoactive drugs (including marijuana) than are European youth, even those European youth who live in nations with more lenient marijuana laws (Harkin, Anderson, & Goos, 1997; Health Canada, 1999).

Although the regular use of psychoactive drugs is fairly uncommon among Canadian youth, those who do regularly use psychoactive drugs tend to do so problematically, increasing their risk of negative life consequences. In Quebec, of those adolescents who have used an illegal substance more than five times, more than half have gone to school stoned or used an illegal substance in the morning or while participating in a competitive sport (Roberts et al., 2001).

The reasons for drug use vary among different groups of Canadian youth. Some may use drugs for reasons similar to adult drug users—to relieve stress, as a form of escapism, or as a social activity. However, youth may also have distinctive motivations for drug use, such as to satisfy their curiosity, show their independence, or become part of a peer group (Roberts et al., 2001). The relationship between an individual's drug use and drug use among peers is especially strong. Among youth who report having friends who use drugs, 80 percent also use drugs themselves; in comparison, only 7 percent of youth whose friends are drug free use drugs themselves (Hotton & Haans, 2004).

Whether drug use becomes problematic depends on individual, community, family, and school factors (Roberts et al., 2001)—all factors that also influence youth crime or gang membership. *Individual* factors that influence whether substance use becomes problematic include the following: genetic and environmental predispositions, degree of personal competence (e.g., extent to which the individual feels in control of his or her life and optimistic about the future), connection with violent behaviour, and gang involvement. *Community* factors include norms about substance use, prevalence of crime, price and availability of substances, economic conditions, and nature of peers. At the level of the *family*, parenting style, degree of parent–child emotional attachment, and family history in relation to substance use play significant roles. Finally, within the *school*, academic success, reading skills, problem-solving abilities, participation in extracurricular activities, and feelings of belonging influence the nature and extent of drug use (Brounstein & Zweig, 1999; Benard, 1991).

Due to the multiple factors operating at different levels that influence youth drug use, effective programs are comprehensive, targeting factors at all levels and thus involving families, communities, schools, and youth themselves (Roberts et al., 2001; Health Canada, 1999). Programs must be age-appropriate and occur *prior to* the child's likely exposure to particular types of drugs. Effective programs integrate youth's own perceptions of drugs and drug use and realistically take their lifestyles into consideration. For example, the "Just Say No" campaign is seen by many adolescents as being unrealistic, not providing them with the tools they really need to deal with the situations they will encounter in their lives.

The problematic nature of drug use among regular users makes the reduction of drug use an important goal for these comprehensive programs. However, it is important to keep in mind that only a small percentage of youth use drugs and an even smaller percentage use them regularly. In contrast, the use of alcohol is far more prevalent among Canadian youth.

Alcohol Use

Alcohol use is a normative behaviour for youth in Canadian society. By Grade 7, between 8.4 and 28.1 percent (depending on the province) of youth have used alcohol within the past year; that proportion increases to between 75.1 and 83.0 percent by Grade 12 (Canadian Centre on Substance Abuse, 2011). The average age of first drunkenness is 14 (Adlaf & Paglia-Boak, 2007). The problem of youth alcohol use is not just Canadian or North American—in Europe, the frequency of adolescent drunkenness increased by the turn of the twenty-first century (Hagmann, 2001).

The alcohol industry has been widely criticized for its role in facilitating or even promoting this phenomenon by targeting adolescents with the creation of "alcopops" (low-alcohol beverages intended to taste like soda) and other fruit-flavoured alcoholic beverages (Mosher & Johnsson, 2005). These types of drinks are frequently promoted in conjunction with music that is particularly popular with adolescents (e.g., providing a free music download with purchase) and in venues frequented by adolescents (e.g., youth-

Ask Yourself

How do you define "binge drinking"? What proportion of students at your university do you think engage in binge drinking?

oriented websites) (Center on Alcohol Marketing and Youth, 2004). As a result of these commercial efforts, research in the United Kingdom has found that 13- to 16-year-olds are the largest group of consumers of this kind of beverage (Health Education Authority, cited in Jernigan, 2001).

Although drinking is common in youth of all ages, more recently one particular aspect of problematic alcohol use has garnered public attention: binge drinking among university students.

Binge Drinking among University Students. Research on **binge drinking** (five drinks in one sitting for males and four drinks in one sitting for females) among university students has found it to be a rather unique pattern of behaviour, different from alcohol use in younger youth or even among youth the same age who are not university students. The unique nature and pattern of university binge drinking necessitates distinct social control measures.

In many people's minds, "university" and "parties" go hand in hand. In fact, the 2004 Canadian Campus Survey found that 86 percent of undergraduates have used alcohol within the past year, and 77 percent within the past month (Adlaf, Demers, & Gliksman, 2005). Popular university rating guides often rate universities not only on academic factors but also on social factors, such as the best "party universities." Picture yourself at a university party such as a fraternity party. The images that come to mind likely contain large numbers of people present and loud music playing. Some of you might picture a few party attendees smoking marijuana or using other types of drugs, but in all likelihood it is images of alcohol that prevail—kegs of beer, drinking contests, and large punch bowls of brightly coloured and highly potent beverages. You might imagine people at these parties consuming five, six, or even more drinks in one evening, perhaps even passing out. These kinds of images reflect the "binge-drinking problem" on university campuses.

Most of our knowledge about university binge drinking comes from the United States, where research shows that approximately 40 percent of university students are binge drinkers (i.e., have engaged in binge drinking within the past two weeks), a proportion that has remained consistent since 1993 (Wechsler & Nelson, 2008; Wechsler, Seibring, Liu, & Ahl, 2004; Weitzman & Nelson, 2004; Adlaf, Demers, & Gliksman, 2005). However, the prevalence of binge drinking varies across various subgroups of students. The "traditional" university student (aged 18 to 23 and living away from parents) is much more likely to binge drink. Among this group of students, 51 percent report having engaged in binge drinking within the past two weeks. In this specific student population, we can look at further subgroups as well. For example, binge drinking is more common among members of fraternities, sororities, and university athletic groups (Wechsler et al., 2002).

Although the proportion of binge drinkers has remained consistent since the early 1990s, some important changes in binge-drinking patterns have emerged. Alcohol use

Binge drinking and the university lifestyle go hand in hand in the popular imagination.

among university students has become more polarized: the proportion of abstainers (people who do not drink alcohol) has grown to 20 percent of university students, but the proportion of "frequent" binge drinkers (three or more binge-drinking episodes within the past two weeks) has grown to 23 percent of university students (Wechsler et al., 2002). Another change in binge drinking is that it has increasingly moved off campus (Keeling, 2000, 2002).

It has been suggested that more stringent university alcohol policies that emerged during the 1990s may have created a more supportive environment for abstainers, contributing to the increase in the proportion of nondrinkers. However, for heavier drinkers and for student subcultures in which drinking is more common, the more stringent policies may have facilitated resistance and rebellion. As these subcultures isolate themselves within their more accepting social networks and move their drinking activities to less-supervised off-campus areas, bingers' social contact with nondrinkers declines. Bingers are increasingly surrounded by heavier drinkers, subsequently raising the proportion of university students who are "frequent" binge drinkers (Keeling, 2000, 2002).

Individual binge drinking is correlated with the rate of binge drinking among peers, particularly close friends; that is, binge drinkers associate with other binge drinkers, and non–binge drinkers associate with other non–binge drinkers (Weschler & Kuo, 2000). Patterns of binge drinking change during the academic year. There is a significant amount of binge drinking at the beginning of the year, but as class demands increase during the middle portion of the academic year and students become entrenched in their study routines, binge drinking declines. However, it increases once again following exams. It is especially prevalent during students' first year at university and then declines during subsequent years (Brower, 2002).

When university binge drinking first came to widespread public awareness, a common concern was that the current cohort of binge drinkers would turn into the alcoholics of the future. However, research conducted over the past decade finds no evidence that binge drinking in university is associated with alcohol abuse or alcoholism in later life; in fact, binge drinking usually ceases following graduation (Brower, 2002).

But even though university binge drinking is not associated with problem drinking in later life, there is no doubt that it does create problems. Of students who are binge drinkers, approximately 30 percent have experienced one or more of the following consequences: missed classes, regretted actions while drunk, driving while drunk, or forgotten where they had been or what they had done the night before (Wechsler et al., 2002).

People who are exposed to binge drinkers experience negative consequences as well—study or sleep interruptions, having to "babysit" a drunken peer, and being insulted are a few examples (Wechsler et al., 2002). At a community level, binge-drinking rates among this age group are associated with rates of automobile accidents, deaths in automobile accidents, drownings, falls, suicides, and homicides. This association has been found not only in Canada and the United States, but in numerous other countries as well (Jernigan, 2001). Thus, a wide range of preventative and retroactive social control measures have been implemented on campuses throughout North America to curb the problematic consequences of binge drinking.

The majority of students in the Harvard College Alcohol Study report that they have been exposed to the following preventative controls: being informed of the university's alcohol rules and penalties for violating those rules, being targeted by educational campaigns about the dangers of consuming too much alcohol, and being informed of where they can seek help for alcohol problems (Wechsler et al., 2002). For students who have violated university alcohol policies or who have been otherwise identified as problem drinkers, a wide range of retroactive controls are used—written reprimands, fines, mandatory attendance at alcohol education programs, community service, and referral to alcohol treatment programs (Wechsler et al., 2002).

Preventative and retroactive social controls that target the individual and attempt to motivate them to refrain from problematic drinking are the most common social controls found at universities. In other words, the most prevalent university controls are efforts at stimulating self-control or self-regulation. However, the effectiveness of these efforts is questionable, as illustrated by the fact that despite increasing control efforts, the prevalence of binge drinking has remained unchanged for the past 20 years. And although there are more abstainers than in the past, there are also more "frequent" binge drinkers.

Brower (2002) proposes that the shortcoming of many traditional social control efforts is that they mirror approaches for controlling alcohol abuse in society at large, which is based on the presumption that university binge drinking is the same as any other type of "problem drinking." However, the fact that binge drinking usually stops following graduation suggests that it is a product of the university environment rather than being associated with alcoholism or other types of "problem drinking." Treating alcoholism (or other types of problem drinking) effectively typically means using individual treatments that are based on complete abstinence from alcohol. But if binge drinking is a product of the university environment, then control efforts must modify the role that alcohol plays in that environment.

A growing body of evidence from countries around the world suggests that the only effective means of control may be changes to regulatory environments, that is, changes in the university environment and the larger societal environment. At a societal level, a considerable amount of research, including research done by the World Health Organization, has found that the harmful consequences associated with binge drinking are significantly lower in communities that have higher alcohol taxes, a higher minimum drinking age, and stricter legislation or policies regarding alcohol accessibility and availability and driving while intoxicated (Wechsler & Nelson, 2008; Jernigan, 2001).

In the university environment, there is a **prevention paradox** (Weitzman & Nelson, 2004); the growing efforts to help "problem" drinkers on campus have not reduced the extent of harm caused by alcohol consumption because, in fact, most of the harm comes from the larger number of low- to moderate-risk drinkers rather than the smaller number of high-risk drinkers (Weitzman & Nelson, 2004).

Thus, a *population prevention* approach has been found to be most effective in reducing harm (Wechsler & Nelson, 2008). This type of approach targets the university environment as a whole, rather than trying to change the behaviour of particular individuals. It includes regulating the prices of alcohol in university venues (e.g., policies governing drink specials, promotions, and alcohol advertising on campus), mandatory responsible beverage service (e.g., policies requiring employees at university venues to refuse further service to intoxicated people), limitations on the number of campus outlets that sell alcohol, and policies governing the overall accessibility and availability of alcohol (Weitzman & Nelson, 2004).

However, it is also the case that taking extreme measures in which students are not consulted (e.g., "dry" campuses) is ineffective as well, because "students—like most of us—will react defensively and angrily to actions taken 'against' them" (Keeling, 2002, para. 29). What controls *do* students approve of? Wechsler and colleagues (2002) found that students approve of the following measures: making the rules clear, providing more alcohol-free recreational and cultural activities, offering more alcohol-free residences, prohibiting kegs on campus, and banning alcohol advertising on campus.

> ### Ask Yourself
> What is your university doing to curb binge drinking? Your student resource centre may have information on the various aspects of your university's social control efforts—education programs, peer support, services for students with serious drinking problems, and university policies.

Binge drinking among university students, teenage alcohol use, drug use, and teen smoking are harmful to the individual consuming those substances but are also perceived as potentially dangerous to society. Youth who engage in these behaviours are therefore seen as both "troubled" and potentially "troubling." Young offenders, youth gang members, and young people who engage in substance use are just some of those youth who are considered deviant in our society and made subject to various measures of social control. However, other youth are also considered "troubled" or "troubling," such as street kids, runaways, and those who are prematurely sexually active. More recently, the concept of "at-risk youth" has emerged, which is able to encompass all of these groups of deviant youth—and even more.

Youth "At Risk"

The concept of "**at-risk youth**" has come to permeate many sectors, including health, social services, education, policing, and even industry (Bessant, 2001; Ericson & Haggerty, 2001). This concept emerges from the broader notion of a **risk society**, which Beck (1992, 1999) suggests has emerged over the past several decades—a society in which knowledge experts warn us that risks are everywhere around us. It is the job of professionals to then identify those populations that are "at risk" of various negative outcomes and implement programming that will manage those risks. The precise nature of those risks and their potential negative consequences depend on the particular social group in question. For youth, the risks and consequences are seen as many: "It has become part of the contemporary common sense that leaving school 'early,' living in certain family arrangements and having a particular socio-economic or ethnic background put a young person 'at risk' of various other social ills like unemployment, crime, suicide, homelessness, substance abuse and pregnancy" (Bessant, 2001, p. 31).

Particular groups of youth are labelled "at risk" because of numerous personal, family, community, and educational factors, similar to those we addressed in looking at youth crime, gang involvement, and substance use. Those particular outcomes are just some of the possible consequences when risks remain unmanaged; thus, "at-risk youth" has become a label that replaces "troubling," "troubled," "delinquent," and "maladjusted." It is an encompassing category into which those youth who are threats to the social order or threats to themselves can be placed and then subsequently controlled through the **science of risk** (Bessant, 2001; Ericson & Haggerty, 2001). The science of risk, constructed by those experts and professionals who are presumed to have the necessary knowledge in that area, enables management of young criminals, gang members, substance abusers, street kids, teenagers who are prematurely sexually active, runaways, and even those youth whom the science of risk identifies as having a higher probability of any of those outcomes *in the future*.

Via the social typing process, "at-risk" youth are identified in schools, community agencies, or by the police, and they are then subjected to particular risk management strategies. For example, schools in "high-risk" neighbourhoods may have their own police officers to provide drug education, interact with students to create more favourable perceptions of the police, help resolve conflicts so that they do not escalate, and liaise with other individuals or agencies that can help individual youth whom the police have identified as facing more "risks" than others (Ericson & Haggerty, 2001). High-risk youth will find themselves on the receiving end of an array of risk management strategies. They may be entered into special educational programs in their school to increase their commitment to education and grades, they may be provided with necessary types of counselling or personal programs (e.g., anger management), or their families may be provided with needed resources or counselling.

In practice, professionals in the numerous sectors permeated by the science of risk frequently implement risk management strategies with *all* youth, rather than distinguishing between those who are and are not "at risk"; the implication is that all youth are "at risk" (Bessant, 2001; Ericson & Haggerty, 2001). Bessant (2001) suggests that although the label "at risk" has replaced older categories of troubled and troubling youth, "the youth-at-risk categories are different from the older categories in terms of their capacity to incorporate the entire population of young people" (p. 32). All youth are perceived as being potential threats to the social order, or threats to themselves and their own futures. The very nature of youth itself is seen as being deviant and in need of social control. "The wider culture constitutes youth as a symbolic threat. Disorderly youth are an expression of 'respectable fears' . . . about disorder and decline in general" (Ericson & Haggerty, 2001, p. 107).

Aren't All Youth Deviant?

One magazine writer speaks of her own experiences with parenthood: "It was about the fourth time my daughter Katie had made cookies on her own. She was 12, which is precariously close to 13, which in humans is not an age but a serious mental disorder" (Beck, 2001, p. 69). Although intended to be humorous, her statement reflects the perception that youth are problematic—not just *some* youth, but *all* youth. The popular image of the teenager is imbued with both "troubled" and "troubling" facets. Most of us have heard (or even participated in) conversations about the problems of adolescents. Themes in these conversations typically include phrases like the following: "They have no respect for authority anymore!" "When I was young, things were different!" As a university professor, I even hear my own students, in their early twenties, making these statements. These kinds of laments portray adolescents as a distinct and separate group, a group that is at the very least an annoyance and that may even pose a danger to themselves, to society, and to the future of civilization. As the title of Patricia Hersch's (1998) book suggests, they are considered "a tribe apart."

As we look around, it does appear that teenagers might be "a tribe apart." We often see a separation of the world of adults and the world of adolescents, suggesting that there may be a separate youth subculture, one that many members of the adult world perceive as breaking all of the rules—a subculture that is deviant and in need of intense control. We see youths congregating in groups that are all roughly the same age; 12- and 13-year-olds are usually with others of the same age, not with 20-year-olds and not with 9-year-olds.

We see teenagers attending concerts that fewer adults are attending (e.g., Justin Bieber) and listening to music their parents often describe as "noise." In the family room, those watching certain television shows (e.g., *The Secret Life of the American Teenager*, *Pretty Little Liars*, *90210*) are predominantly junior high and high school students. Particular subgroups of teenagers are often seen wearing similar clothes, a teenage "uniform" that will most certainly be different at the time you are reading this than at the time it was written. If we go into a shopping mall, teenagers are shopping at particular clothing stores that carry the "uniform" and that have certain types of music playing in the background. In these stores, parents and their teenage children can be heard arguing over the clothes being too revealing, too expensive, or too sloppy. Continuing a journey through the mall, if we enter a bookstore we can see that family conflicts are becoming too much for some parents, who are in the "Parenting" section of the bookstore perusing titles like *How to Talk so Your Teen Will Listen*, or *How to Survive Your Child's Adolescence*.

The problematic nature of adolescence began receiving widespread public attention not long after the "teenager" was labelled in the 1950s. At that time, articles about how to parent teenagers could be found in women's magazines such as *Ladies' Home Journal* and *Good Housekeeping*, and parenting manuals were written that focused specifically on teenagers. However, since the 1950s the problem of teenagers has been seen not only as a problem for the parents raising them, but also a problem for society as a whole. That is, those problems that result in conflicts between parents and teenage children in individual families are perceived as indicative of problems between the adult and adolescent generations in the broader society.

A euphemism that many of us are familiar with—the **generation gap**—captures this perception. Why does a generation gap exist between adults and teenagers? According to this widespread perception, the generation gap is certainly not because of the adults—it is because of the teenagers, who are the problem that needs to be controlled. Adolescence itself has come to be defined as a time in the life cycle that is inherently deviant. We can see this perception reflected in the media; for instance, in an article titled "Your Teenager: An Owner's Manual (For the Bewildered Parent)," a popular Canadian women's magazine refers to adolescence as a time that is characterized by four "technical glitches" (*Canadian Living*, 2006, p. 162), implying that there is something inherently wrong with teenagers. Surveys reveal that more than 70 percent of adults describe youth as rude, wild, and irresponsible; they state that compared to youth 20 years ago, young people today are more selfish, materialistic, and reckless (Bostrom, 2001). Because perceptions of adolescents are based on these types of characteristics, considerable social control or regulation is seen as necessary.

We can see the formal regulation of adolescents in debates over the value of school uniforms in high schools, community curfews for those under the age of 18, special laws for teenagers (e.g., in Canada, the Youth Criminal Justice Act), special risk management programs in many junior high and high schools, and more. In all of these instances, the intent is to regulate, monitor, and control what is perceived as the inherently problematic nature of adolescence. We can see informal regulation in the changed approaches to parenting once adolescence arrives, the greater monitoring of teenagers in retail stores, the desire to sit as far away from a group of teenagers on the subway as possible, and the informal conversations we hear about "those kids today." Such forms of formal and informal social control are intended to manage the deviant nature of adolescence and the subsequent "generation gap."

The Generation Gap: The Past

The perception of youth as a problem in need of control is nothing new, extending back thousands of years. Socrates complained that youth "contradict their parents" and "tyrannize their teachers" (cited in Arnett, 1999, p. 317). Aristotle (384–322 BC) described youth as having an absence of self-control (especially sexual self-control), being prone to angry emotional outbursts, spending too much time with friends, and thinking they know everything (*Rhetoric, Book II*). At the turn of the twentieth century, psychologist G. Stanley Hall (1904) spoke of the *sturm und drang* (storm and stress) of adolescence, suggesting that individual development mirrors the evolution of the human species. According to Hall, the process of growing up is a transition from "beast-like" to "human-like" where the period of adolescence mirrors the evolutionary stage of primitive man. The problems of adolescence could not be avoided, but with the appropriate controls to deal with that stage of psychological development and to minimize the damage adolescents might do, adolescents would eventually "grow out of it" as they reached the civilized stage of adulthood.

The "original" teenagers of the 1950s (Doherty, 1988, p. 45) were born during and immediately after World War II. They differed from previous generations in terms of their sheer number, economic prosperity, and generational cohesion in that they had an "awareness of themselves as teenagers" (Doherty, 1988, p. 45). Society accorded them a particular social status—"teenager"—and this group became part of a recognized youth culture. There was some dismay at the arrival of the teenager and its associated youth culture, which "cultural guardians . . . likened to *barbaric hordes descending upon a city under siege* [italics added]" (Doherty, 1988, p. 51).

Research in the mid-twentieth century frequently concluded that teenagers were a distinct and oppositional subculture and that the future of society was at risk. For example, research found that for teenage boys, being a star athlete was of ultimate importance, and for teenage girls, being popular was most important. These kinds of empirical results reinforced the perception that teenagers were as different from adults as possible and that all adolescents were "troubling," a threat to the social order (Tanner, 1992). Other researchers (e.g., Berger, cited in Tanner, 1992), who suggested otherwise, were largely ignored in popular discourse. They claimed that the generations are far more similar than they are different, that most parents and their teenage children get along fairly well, and that there are many issues on which they agree. Berger suggested that it is parents who bring the emphasis on sports to their sons' lives and the emphasis on popularity to their daughters' lives. Furthermore, interests in sports and peer acceptance are not limited just to the lives of teenagers, but pertain to adult lives as well (Tanner, 1992). Moving to the present day, we can still see the reality of Berger's claims.

The Generation Gap: The Present

Why do children get involved in organized sports? They play sports because their parents get them involved, and this occurs at increasingly younger ages. How many 4-year-olds are actually the ones insisting that they want to join the community T-ball league? Parents enroll these young children in sports because they are quite adorable to watch. Where do children learn that sports are important? Again, they learn this from the adults in their lives—parents, teachers, coaches, and the media. Children's sporting leagues have had to institute regulations governing parental behaviour, simply because of the preponderance of cursing at the officials, name calling of children on other teams, and even physical violence (including assault and even murder).

The extreme behaviour of parents at children's sporting events demonstrates to children from an early age how important sports are. The importance of sports is also emphasized by the fact that some of the most highly paid people in North America are professional athletes, who make millions of dollars every single season. Dozens of televisions channels are devoted solely to sports, as are entire sections in the daily newspaper. If sports are important to teenagers, it is only because their parents and other adults put so much stress on them. Berger (1963) made this basic claim 40 years ago, but in contemporary society this pattern is even more evident than it was then.

Why is popularity important to teenagers? Again, it is because adults have made it so. Parents, teachers, and other adults encourage children to "make friends" and express concern if their children have too few friends. At a very young age, how many of us have heard adults say, "You must share your toys *or the other kids won't like you*," or "You have to be nice, *or the other kids won't want to play with you anymore*"? The importance of having the other kids like you and want to play with you is made clear before a child even enters Grade 1.

Popularity is also important in the adult world, although we are unlikely to use the word "popularity" to describe it. The phrase "keeping up with the Joneses" refers to adults who want the same status of car, house, boat, or vacation as their neighbours or co-workers. An acquaintance of mine once told me of having to buy a new car upon starting a new job because hers was the only "clunker" in a parking lot filled with brand new, expensive sedans. In my own neighbourhood, once two or three families had garages built, everyone else immediately began building garages as well (although oddly enough, few people seem to actually park their cars in them).

This begs the question of whether these examples are really any different than teenagers who want the same kind of clothes or shoes as their peers. Many of us have felt obligated to go along with a group of co-workers for drinks or coffee after work, even when we would rather have gone straight home. As adults, when we move to a new city or some traumatic life change occurs (e.g., divorce), the advice we are given is to join clubs or community organizations so we can make new friends—as if finding more friends is the solution to our problems. And recent research being widely reported in the media points out the link between physical health and the extent of one's social network; these popular magazine articles are telling us we have to "make friends" because our lives really do depend on it!

Adults and youth are more similar than early research claimed. Most teenagers conform to the larger society, get good grades in school, go on to post-secondary education, and never get into trouble with the law, use drugs, or get pregnant (or get someone else pregnant). In fact, by taking a closer look at families, we see that parent–teen conflict is not as large a problem as popular images suggest. Disagreements are quite common, with 39 percent of teenagers saying they have disagreements with parents at least once per week (Bibby, 2009). However, conflicts are usually over smaller daily issues rather than large life-altering issues (Smetana, 1988). When conflicts do occur, they frequently relate to social life, peer groups, social customs, and household responsibilities, rather than educational plans, career goals, or moral issues (Laursen, 1995).

A survey of teenagers in 2000 (Bibby, 2001) finds the single most common source of parent–teen conflict to be household tasks, but even then only slightly more than half of teens say they argue about this issue "fairly often" or "very often." Even though conflicts do increase during adolescence (Arnett, 1999), 67 percent of teenagers say family life is "very important" to them (the highest proportion in the more than 30 years that sociologist Reginald Bibby has been conducting regular surveys of Canadian adolescents), 80 percent say they get a "high level" of enjoyment from interactions with their mothers, and

89 percent say that their mothers have a high level of influence in their lives (82 percent say the same about their fathers) (Bibby, 2009). In the end, the vast majority of teenagers turn out all right. In fact, Bibby finds that in many ways, today's Canadian adolescents are doing better than ever.

Thus, some scholars say that the concept of the "generation gap" is an exaggeration facilitated by stereotypes of teenagers, sensationalistic media portrayals that will attract an audience, and moral panics stimulated by interest groups who want to advance a political or economic agenda. Even research itself tends to focus on problems with teenagers rather than on the rather mundane everyday lives of most teenagers. Although Bibby's research finds that contemporary teens are doing remarkably well compared to other cohorts over the past 30 years, concerns about adolescents are more prevalent than ever. For instance, Bibby says, "I've sometimes been appalled at the negative reaction of people involved in the drug field when I bring some good news about drug use being down—or the wincing of teachers when I suggest students are feeling more positive about school than they did in the past. I am treated like the bearer of bad news" (Bibby, 2009, pp. 67–68). Our cultural focus on problems leads us to lose sight of the fact that most families and most teenagers are doing just fine.

The Generation Gap: The Question of the Future

Although a considerable amount of research has claimed that the concept of the "generation gap" and the notion that adolescence is an inherently deviant time in the life cycle are exaggerations, the teenage years are accompanied by increases in "storm and stress," such as conflicts with parents (Laursen, Coy, & Collins, 1998), extremes of emotion (Larson & Richards, 1994), and risk-taking behaviour (Arnett, 1992). Some social analysts are now expressing the concern that, given contemporary social patterns and family trends in particular, the possibility of a significant generation gap may arise in the near future.

Some scholars suggest that beginning in the late 1990s contemporary family life became more characterized by a culture of busy-ness, where scattered work, education, and extracurricular schedules of family members often mean that they spend little time with each other. The lives of teenagers may be especially impacted by these changes, in that they are perceived as needing less direct supervision than younger children, making it easier for parents to leave them on their own in the midst of complex family schedules. To some people, contemporary teenagers have become "a vague mass of kids growing up in a world that rushes past them until one of them steps out of the shadows and demands attention by doing something extraordinarily wonderful or troublesome, outrageous or awful. The rest of the time, especially for the average, everyday kid who goes along not making any waves, the grown-up world doesn't pay much attention" (Hersch, 1998, p. 11).

It is in this aloneness that the potential for a new and significant generation gap emerges. In living, to some extent, separate lives, the possibility of similar values, similar interests, and an enjoyment of time spent together declines. Furthermore, considering the central roles that parenting factors (like the quality of parent–teen relationships) and community structures (that support and integrate youth) play in the emergence of youth crime, gang involvement, and substance use, adolescents' aloneness may set the stage for such "troubling" and "troubled" behaviours to emerge in the future.

The exaggerated generation gap of the past may become a reality in the future, although Bibby's research suggests that this may not be the case. But even if a growing generation gap does emerge, will it be because of the inherently deviant and problematic nature of adolescence itself? It may be that just as in the past, today's teenagers are simply living the lives that adults are creating for them. Youth who end up being "troubled" or "troubling" and those who are identified as being "at risk" then require social control. But even more significant is that the perceived "deviant" nature of adolescence and youth culture may be reinforced by the resulting realities of their lives.

TIME TO REVIEW

Learning Objective 5

■ What leads groups of youth to be considered "at risk," and how has the science of risk expanded in recent years?

Learning Objective 6

■ What does the "generation gap" refer to, and what has traditionally been considered the cause of the generation gap?

■ How are teenagers perceived and socially controlled in society?

■ How were youth perceived in ancient Greece, at the turn of the twentieth century, and in the 1950s?

■ What led some mid-twentieth-century researchers to conclude that teenagers formed a distinct and oppositional subculture?

■ Why do some people claim that youth are *not* an oppositional subculture?

■ Why might a new and significant generation gap emerge in the future?

CHAPTER SUMMARY

■ Youth and deviance seem to go hand in hand in Canadian culture. Of particular concern are "troubling" youth, "troubled" youth, and "at-risk" youth; however, to some extent, all youth are perceived as deviant. (1)

■ The "troubling" youth who receive the greatest attention are those involved in crime and those who are members of gangs. However, a gap exists between popular images of youth crime and gangs and their actual prevalence and nature. The media particularly contributes to a moral panic, from which various groups potentially benefit. (1)

■ Concerns over those youth who *are* involved in crime and gangs have stimulated a wealth of research. Research has highlighted the role of family factors in explaining youth crime and a complex set of individual, family, educational, and community factors in explaining the emergence of and involvement with gangs. The social control of gangs is intertwined with the control of youth crime more generally, which has shown considerable variation over the past century. (2, 3)

- "Troubled" youth, who are of particular concern in contemporary society, include those who use various substances. Although almost all youth have used alcohol by the time they graduate from high school, fewer youth regularly use tobacco, marijuana, or other drugs. Over the past decade, binge drinking on university campuses has drawn widespread attention, resulting in a wide range of social control efforts. (4)

- The concept of "at-risk youth" is a recent formulation that integrates various types of "troubling" and "troubled" youth. The science of risk attempts to identify those youth who are at greater risk of negative outcomes in their lives and then target risk management efforts at those youth. (5)

- To some degree, *all* youth are perceived as being deviant and in need of social control. Adolescence is seen as an inherently deviant time in the life cycle, creating a "generation gap" between teenage and adult generations. Although the generation gap may be more of an exaggeration than a reality, some researchers suggest that current social patterns open the door for a real generation gap to emerge. (6)

MySearchLab®

👁 Watch Go to MySearchLab to watch the video called "MS13 Gang-Life".

Apply What You Know: In what ways do you think this video about the MS13 gang represents the difficult reality of youth crime, and in what ways does it simply contribute to the ongoing moral panic surrounding gangs?

MySearchLab with eText offers you access to an online interactive version of the text, extensive help with your writing and research projects, and provides round-the-clock access to credible and reliable source material.

Chapter 7
Looking Deviant: Physical Appearance

© Kathleen Finlay/Masterfile

Learning Objectives

After reading this chapter, you should be able to

1   Explain the role of "body projects" in people's lives and what the appearance of people's bodies tells us.

2   Describe the different kinds of information that are obtained about body modification when studied from various locations along the objective–subjective continuum.

3   Define the "ideal" body weight according to scientific standards and social standards, and describe how many people are "too fat" and "too thin" according to these standards.

4   Explain how people who are overweight are perceived and treated, and describe the range of social control measures targeted at "too fat."

5   Explain how people who are underweight are perceived and treated, and describe the range of social control measures targeted at "too thin."

6   Describe the various ways that the social typing of "too fat" and "too thin" as deviant characteristics is resisted.

An old Chinese proverb claims that "talent counts thirty percent; appearance counts seventy" (Columbia World of Quotations, 1996). Half a world away and several centuries later, that statement still rings true in many ways. We do live in a culture where physical appearance is important. Think of your own physical appearance and how you maintain it. You have chosen a particular hairstyle and perhaps even hair colour. Every morning you might blow dry, straighten, curl, gel, or spray your hair in order to achieve a specific look. Perhaps you put on makeup. Then you choose certain clothes, depending on what your plans are for the day. Are you going to work, school, a job interview, a date, dinner with your grandparents, a club, or to write a final exam? For all but the last item on that list, you probably choose your clothes carefully. Maybe you have a tattoo, piercings, or some other type of body art. Perhaps you are dieting to lose weight, working out to become more sculpted, or taking supplements to increase muscle mass. As one of a select few, you may be gulping milkshakes to gain weight. You may even be contemplating plastic surgery to fix your nose, lift your eyes, suck the fat out of your love handles, or increase the size of your breasts. The time, effort, and money we spend on our physical appearance illustrate how important it is to us.

Our appearance is important to us in part because we wish to express ourselves and paint a picture of who we are. But our appearance is also important because we know people judge us by how we look. The way we look can affect whether we get hired for a job, what our grandparents think of us, who will and will not want to start a conversation with us, whether we are asked on a date by the person we are interested in, and whether people stare at us as we walk down the street.

Physical appearance is the stimulus for the social typing we do every day and to which we are subject every day. But social typing based on physical appearance goes beyond our own individual likes and dislikes. Regardless of our own personal preferences for appearance, there are larger patterns of social typing that occur in our society. For instance, we all know that our chances of being hired are small if we appear at a job interview wearing sweatpants. Similarly, we know that someone wearing dress pants and a button-down shirt is far less likely to be stared at or teased than is a person dressed in a goth style—and yet, that person chooses to dress in a goth style anyway, despite (or perhaps because of) that social reaction.

Voluntary and Involuntary Physical Appearance

Some forms of physical appearance are voluntarily adopted—hairstyles, clothing, makeup, and body art. Precisely which forms of voluntary physical appearance are considered deviant depends on the sociohistorical context. Slicked-back hair, "dungarees" (jeans), and leather jackets were perceived so negatively in the 1950s that they were prohibited in many high schools. Men with long hair who wore beads were considered deviant in the 1960s and 1970s. Some store windows contained signs saying "No Hippies Allowed."

During most of the twentieth century, people with tattoos were viewed negatively and were presumed to have other negative characteristics as well (Sanders, 1989). However, by the end of the twentieth century tattoos and other forms of body art (e.g., body piercing) were less stigmatized, and in many other cultures body art has been commonplace for centuries.

Voluntary aspects of physical appearance that may be deviantized also include those associated with certain lifestyle groups, such as goths (Tait, 1999), ravers (Wilson, 2002; Weber, 1999), and punk rockers (Baron, 1989; Davies, 1996; Mattson, 2001). In these cases, appearance is only one aspect of an overall lifestyle based on political, philosophical, or social foundations.

Other forms of physical appearance are involuntary in nature, such as height, the size of one's nose or shape of one's eyes, or visible disabilities. Although individuals have little or no choice regarding these aspects of their physical appearance, they may still be stigmatized in our society—stared at, laughed at, teased, or excluded from opportunities, activities, and relationships (Westbrook, Legge, & Pennay, 1993; Gardner, 1991). In Nazi Germany, people with visible disabilities were even targets of genocidal efforts (Mostert, 2002).

However, the boundary between voluntary and involuntary forms of physical appearance is somewhat blurred. Some forms of physical appearance combine voluntary and involuntary aspects. A good example of this is body weight. People choose how much to eat and how much physical activity to participate in (voluntary); however, psychological factors, social factors, and biological factors may influence those outcomes (involuntary). Furthermore, what is considered to be "voluntary" varies across cultures and over time, and may even vary across subgroups within a single culture. For instance, in Canada today, members of particular ethnocultural or religious groups may adhere to dictates of clothing or hairstyle. In contemporary Canadian society, forms of body modification such as tattooing, piercing, and branding are voluntary; however, historically, slaves since at least the time of ancient Greece have been forcibly branded as a sign of ownership. Similarly, criminals were tattooed in many cultures around the world, as were concentration camp prisoners during the Nazi era.

Shilling (1993) uses the term **body projects** to refer to the ways that each of us adapts, changes, or controls characteristics of our bodies and whether those characteristics are voluntary or involuntary. If you have poor eyesight, you may get glasses; if you do not like the look of glasses, you might get contact lenses. If you think you are too short, you may

Ask Yourself

We all engage in various types of body projects. What types of body projects do you engage in and why? What makes your body projects similar to or different from those of people you see around you? What does your body say about you? What does it say about your social relationships? What does it say about Canadian society?

wear shoes with higher heels; if you think you are too tall, you may slouch as you walk. If you consider yourself too fat, you may start working out or go on a diet; if you consider yourself too thin, you may begin taking supplements to build muscle mass.

There are four different categories of body projects. First are **camouflaging** projects—"normative . . . techniques of body manipulation, learned in socialization processes" (Atkinson, 2003a, p. 25). Examples include makeup, clothing, and hairstyle. Second are **extending** projects that attempt to overcome one's physical limitations, such as in the case of using contact lenses or a cane. Next are **adapting** projects, where "parts of the body are removed or repaired for a host of aesthetic . . . or medical . . . reasons" (p. 26). These include weight loss, muscle building, and laser hair removal. Finally, there are **redesigning** projects that "reconstruct the body in lasting ways" (p. 26), such as plastic surgery, tattoos, and body piercing. Various body projects may change the functioning of our bodies (e.g., contact lenses) or modify the appearance of our bodies (e.g., weight loss). This chapter emphasizes the latter, not only because physical appearance is important in our culture, but also because the appearance of people's bodies tells us something.

What is it that people's bodies tell us? The answer depends on one's location along the objective–subjective continuum. When looking at the issue from the more objective end of the continuum, bodies tell us about the characteristics of individuals involved in particular body projects, such as their age, sex, socioeconomic status, family structure and functioning, academic performance, personality, and psychopathology. Moving toward the more subjective end of the continuum, bodies tell us about the self, identity formation, and how people come to understand themselves and attribute meaning to their physical appearance. In other words, body projects "are integral in constructing and representing identity over the life course" (Lévi-Strauss, cited in Atkinson, 2002, p. 219).

From this more subjective vantage point, bodies also tell us about the characteristics of the broader society and culture. They are "text[s] upon which social reality is described" (Foucault, cited in Schildkrout, 2004, p. 319). For example, Lévi-Strauss explained the purpose of tattooing in the Maori culture of New Zealand as "not only to imprint a drawing onto the flesh but also to stamp onto the mind all the traditions and philosophy of the group" (cited in Schildkrout, 2004, p. 321).

Among the endless variety of body projects that can affect physical appearance, two types are noteworthy. First, there are redesigning projects commonly known as body modification or body art—activities such as tattooing, piercing, branding, and scarification. These activities have become increasingly common over the past few decades, as well as increasingly accepted. They are an interesting illustration of how perceptions of what is deviant and normal change over time. Second, there are adapting projects related to body size or body weight. The social typing of body weight saturates all of us living in Canadian society today, permeating the fields of medicine, media, commercial industry, education, and even our daily interactions. Because the social typing of body size is so pervasive and affects so many lives, it is an interesting illustration of how the social construction of deviance and normality is an ongoing part of all of our lives.

With all forms of physical appearance that may be socially typed as deviant, it is not necessarily appearance itself that generates a negative reaction but rather the meanings, stereotypes, and interpretations that are attached to that appearance. Physical appearance constitutes what Howard Becker (discussed in Chapter 3) called a **master status**, a category we immediately place people in upon first seeing them, which subsequently defines who the person is. The auxiliary traits we attach to master statuses are what make them significant. Thus, people with disabilities were systematically killed by the Nazis not simply because of their appearance, but because they were perceived as a drain on society. Similarly, people who are obese are not stigmatized because of their appearance per se, but because that appearance is presumed to be indicative of laziness, a lack of self-control, and psychological problems. Some forms of body modification are socially typed as deviant in part because they are perceived as being associated with other risk-taking behaviours and with a broader opposition to the social order.

Body Modification

The history of tattooing, piercing, branding, and scarification is a long one, perhaps as long as the history of humanity itself. Whether forms of body modification have been stigmatized or considered acceptable has varied across cultures and over time. Body modification has been "variously used to mark outlaw status and nobility, insiders and outsiders, soldiers and slaves" (Schildkrout, 2004, p. 325). The remains of a 5000-year-old "Iceman" discovered in the Alps had several visible tattoos (Spindler, cited in Schildkrout, 2004), and throughout the world archaeologists have found evidence of tattooing and piercing on bodies and represented on artifacts (Schildkrout, 2004).

In the early Christian and medieval eras, some Europeans had tattoos representing their religious affiliations and dedication, although that practice was largely abandoned over time (Atkinson, 2003a; Schildkrout, 2004). The processes of European colonization brought such practices to broader public awareness. As European explorers found new lands and new peoples, and European governments colonized those lands, innumerable body modification practices were discovered (Atkinson, 2003a; Schildkrout, 2004). In diverse cultures, tattooing, branding, piercing, scarification, and implanting served as rites of passage, ritual initiations, or symbols of sexuality (Stirn, 2003).

However, European discourses that supported colonization emphasized the "civilized" nature of European societies in contrast to the "primitive" nature of other cultures. From this perspective, body modification was equated with savagery, primitiveness, and heathenness (Atkinson, 2003a). Colonization also meant Christianization, and the Old Testament dictates that "Ye shall not make any cuttings in your flesh for the dead nor print any marks upon you" (Leviticus 19:28, cited in Cronin, 2001, p. 380). Although body modification was socially typed as deviant in Euro-dominant societies, the public's fascination with "primitive" cultures meant a growing interest in it. During the late eighteenth and early nineteenth centuries, people with extensive body modifications were featured in carnival side shows, partially nude and frequently dressed as savages (Atkinson, 2003a; Schildkrout, 2004).

Over time, body modification left the carnival community and entered society at large (Atkinson, 2003a). This transition is especially evident with changes in attitudes toward tattooing. By the 1950s, tattoos had become an established means of symbolizing masculinity and brotherhood in working-class communities and the military (Sanders, 1989). In the 1960s, criminal communities also increasingly adopted tattooing, with male convicts, motorcycle gangs, and street gangs using tattoos to indicate their memberships and allegiances. The countercultural era of the 1960s and 1970s brought the emergence of a number of youth subcultures who used tattooing and other types of body modification as "collective representation" (Atkinson, 2003a, p. 41) of their subcultures and political/social ideologies.

Since that time, both tattooing and piercing have increasingly entered female and middle-class communities (DeMello, 2000). By 1997, body modification was in the top six fastest growing industries in the United States (Stirn, 2003). In the twenty-first century, body modification is pervasive within popular culture, from tattooed celebrities to television series (e.g., *LA Ink*). The commodification of body modification, particularly tattoos, is also evident when one sees the range of tattoo-related products targeted at children, "such as Tattoo Barbie, The Sesame Street Talent Show: Tattoo Tales, Around the World in Tweety Time: Tattoo Storybook, and the Power Puff girls' Ruff n' Stuff Tattoo Book, that include tattooed figures, colour-in tattoo kits, and temporary tattoos" (Kosut, 2006). Now you can even obtain a tattoo or body piercing in a chain outlet at your local shopping mall, between your shampoo purchase and a new pair of shoes.

left: © Thinkstock Images/Getty Images [small tattoo picture]; right: © Andrey Kiselev/Fotolia [tattoo collector]

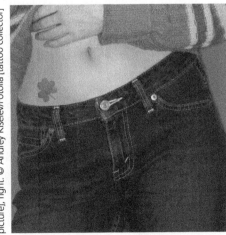

The practice of tattooing spans a wide range of people, from individuals who obtain one small tattoo to elite tattoo collectors who display "artwork" across their bodies.

In this marketplace, body modification has become more prevalent (Atkinson, 2003a; Burger & Finkel, 2002). Most research has focused on tattooing and piercing and has found both to be particularly common among adolescents and young adults. Mayers and Chiffriller (2008) found that 22 percent of university undergraduates have tattoos, and 51 percent have piercings (other than earlobes). Among youth, females are more likely to have tattoos and piercings. In one sample of 12- to 18-year-olds in Quebec, 10 percent of females had tattoos (compared to 6 percent of males) and 44 percent had piercings (compared to 11 percent of males) (Deschesnes, Demers, & Finès, 2006). The increasing prevalence of body modification, especially among youth, has caused an upsurge in research on its participants. There is consensus that body modification conveys important information, but there are different points of view on precisely what that message is.

What Do Modified Bodies Tell Us?

Characteristics of Body Modifiers: Risk and Motivation

As we move from one end of the objective–subjective continuum to the other, we learn that bodies with tattoos, piercings, and other forms of body modification can potentially provide us with a great deal of information. Beginning at the far objective end, we hold the individual under the microscope—tattooed and pierced bodies tell us about the characteristics of that individual. From this viewpoint two central issues are emphasized: risk and motivation. Here, the presence of tattoos and piercings (above all, among youth) is associated with a broader range of risk, such that youth who have forms of body modification are perceived as being "at risk" more generally. For example, in an analysis of more than 4000 members of an online body modification site, Liu and Lester (2012) find extensive histories of physical, sexual, and mental abuse as well as emotional abandonment, particularly for females (and especially for those with body piercings). Similarly, Roberts and Ryan (2002) suggest that youth with tattoos and piercings are more likely to come from single-parent homes, belong to the lowest income quartile, have parents with high school diplomas or less, and have peers who use various substances. However, the growing prevalence of body modification in university and university populations (e.g., Armstrong, Roberts, Owen, & Koch, 2004) increasingly calls these conclusions into question.

Much of the risk-oriented research highlights psychological and behavioural risk, analyzing the association between body modification and other problematic characteristics such as risky sexual behaviour, substance use, violence, eating disorders, educational difficulties, and suicide (Hicinbothem, Gonsalves, & Lester, 2006; Carroll, Riffenburgh, Roberts, & Myhre, 2002; Burger & Finkel, 2002). Dukes and Stein (2011) found that in a sample of adolescents in Grades 9 through 12, body modification was associated with poorer attitudes toward school, lower educational aspirations, weapons possession, substance use, delinquency, and poor self-esteem.

However, research that explores the relationship between body modification and other types of risk is inconsistent. Although some research finds a relationship between body modification, low self-esteem, and subclinical psychopathy (Nathanson, Paulhus, & Williams,

2005), other research does not. Frederick and Bradley (2000) compared people ages 16 to 30 with and without tattoos or piercings on several psychological measures such as depression, anxiety, vitality, psychopathy, and self-esteem. When comparing individuals with and without piercings, no significant differences emerged, although age of first piercing was associated with greater psychopathy (those who had obtained a piercing in early adolescence scored higher). When comparing individuals with and without tattoos, the only significant difference to emerge was that those with tattoos actually had higher self-esteem.

From this more objectivist vantage point, tattooed and pierced bodies tell us about the psychology and the behaviours of individuals who have them, although there is debate about precisely what characteristics such individuals have. The proposed association between body modification and other risks is directly linked to social control efforts. Many publications about youth and body modification are found in journals directed at pediatric professionals, and they contain explicit directives for clinical practitioners to consider the presence of tattoos or piercings as an indicator of potential psychological and behavioural problems and to conduct assessments for other high-risk behaviours (e.g., Carroll, Riffenburgh, Roberts, & Myhre, 2002; Burger & Finkel, 2002).

Researchers with a more objectivist orientation also draw attention to the potential harms of body modification, although Mayers and Chiffriller (2008) found that only 19 percent of individuals in their sample who had piercings (and no individuals who had tattoos) experienced any medical complications. Numerous health risks are associated with tattooing and piercing, such as bacterial infections, hepatitis B and C, cracked teeth (related to facial piercings), and problems with X-rays (Jafari, Copes, Baharlou, Etminan, & Buxton, 2010; Vanston & Scott, 2008). Given the potential risks of harm inherent in body modification, the question then becomes one of motivation or causation. Why would an individual engage in a behaviour that carries these risks?

For some people, aesthetic motivations predominate; they acquire tattoos or piercings to improve their appearance or because they think body modification is attractive to the opposite sex, referring to their modifications as beauty, fashion, or art (Deschesnes, Demers, & Finès, 2006; Wohlrab, Stahl, & Kappeler, 2006; Claes, Vandereycken, & Vertommen, 2005; Stirn, 2003).

Others are motivated by the pursuit of an identity. One type of identity is social identity, the portion of the person's identity that is based on the groups to which the person belongs. Body modification may symbolize our affiliations with particular groups and thus contribute to the development of our social identities (Carroll & Anderson, 2002; Claes, Vandereycken, & Vertommen, 2005). Specific forms of body modification have been found to serve as indicators of group affiliation in prison and motorcycle and street gangs (Atkinson, 2003a), among elite collectors of tattoos (Irwin, 2003), the straightedge youth subculture (Atkinson, 2003b), modern primitives (Atkinson, 2001), and cyberpunks (Millanvoye, 2001).

A second type of identity is individual in nature, and many studies of adolescents and young adults have found individual identity formation and development to be the primary motivation for body modification; that is, they wish to express themselves or feel unique

(Wohlrab, Stahl, & Kappeler, 2006; Caliendo, Armstrong, & Roberts, 2005; Claes, Vandereycken, & Vertommen, 2005). Because identity formation is particularly important among youth, some researchers recommend that youth practitioners develop an understanding of the role body art plays in identity development (e.g., Armstrong, Roberts, Owen, & Koch, 2004), even though others advise pediatric practitioners to associate body modification with risk.

Individual and social identities are also explored as we begin to move toward the subjective end of the objective–subjective continuum. However, subjective researchers treat identity differently. In a more subjectively oriented analysis of body modification, bodies are not perceived as telling us about the characteristics of individuals who have tattoos and piercings, but rather telling us about the development of understanding and meaning, processes of social interaction, and structures of power. Subsequently, in contrast to the more objectively oriented analysis of identity as a "cause" of body modification, a more subjectively oriented analysis examines identity in terms of understanding the self. In this context, researchers investigate the role of body modification in understanding and developing meanings of the self in relation to others and within a broader societal and cultural framework.

The Self and Society: Understanding, Meaning, and Resistance

Body projects are "integral in constructing and representing identity over the life course" (Atkinson, 2002, p. 219). That is, the physical body reflects the individual's understandings of self and society. The body becomes a story of the individual's interests, desires, friendships, and love relationships (Ferreira, 2009). As one person with body art states, his tattoos "mark moments in my life, sort of a story of myself and my beliefs" (Orend & Gagne, 2009, p. 501). However, according to interpretive approaches, the self is not purely individual in nature, but emerges via processes of social interaction. As we interact with those with whom we are close (significant others) and with society in general (the generalized other), we try to see society from their points of view. Their points of view, and their views of us in particular, influence how we understand ourselves and our places in the world.

Thus, through our interactions with others we come to understand what role body modification will play in our lives. From a dramaturgical perspective, the decisions about whether to engage in body modification and the precise nature of any body art are all part of constructing our "front-stage" selves and "back-stage" selves (see Chapter 3). We decide on the image that we intentionally project to others and whether we want body art to be a part of that image. People with body art engage in impression management surrounding that art, deciding how large it will be, where it will be located, and to whom it will be displayed (Armstrong, Roberts, Owen, & Koch, 2004). Will the tattoos, piercings, or brandings be visible to the general public, co-workers, and parents on the front stage? Or will the modifications be visible only to intimate partners on the back stage? Will it be part of the costume on all front stages, or only on certain ones (e.g., at a concert, but not at work)?

Interactions with family members and peers are particularly significant. In general, the disapproval of one's family and friends makes body modification less likely (Koch,

Roberts, Cannon, Armstrong, & Owen, 2005), although interactions with different people play varied roles. Within families, interactions with parents have an influence on the individual's decisions about whether to obtain body art, its design, and its location (Atkinson, 2003a). If people perceive their parents as disapproving of body art, they may select a design their parents are less likely to disapprove of (e.g., a small tattoo of a flower) or a location that can be easily hidden from their parents (e.g., a nipple or genital piercing). But at the same time, among adolescents body modification is often an expression of protest against parents or the parents' generation (Wohlrab, Stahl, & Kappeler, 2006).

However, having body art that they know their parents disapprove of or having to continually hide it from their parents can have an impact on people's perceptions of self (Atkinson, 2003a). Peers play somewhat different roles. Individuals are more likely to actively seek the opinions of their peers when deciding whether to engage in body modification. But once the decision to obtain some form of body art has been made, individuals intentionally seek out more interactions with peers that also have body art. Interviews reveal that these interactions make individuals feel better about their decisions and provide a validation of self (Atkinson, 2003a). The attitudes of co-workers or employers have much less of an effect on feelings about oneself; however, they play a considerable role in decisions regarding body art display and the distinction between front-stage and back-stage selves. For many people with body modifications, the workplace is a context within which body art is hidden from view, either because it is formally sanctioned or because people are concerned about threats to their professional image (Atkinson, 2003a).

Indeed, when an individual is on the front stage playing a professional role, the audience may react negatively to the presence of tattoos or piercings. For example, one study examined patients' perceptions of facial piercings in physicians (Newman, Wright, Wrenn, & Bernard, 2005). Approximately half of patients surveyed indicated that facial piercings are "inappropriate" for physicians, and more than half said it would personally bother them to have a physician with a facial piercing.

Patients who had engaged in body modification themselves had more positive attitudes, but even then 33 percent considered a facial piercing to be inappropriate for a physician. Patients' attitudes are not solely based on physical appearance; they are also affected by meanings or auxiliary traits attached to that appearance. For example, survey participants perceived doctors with facial piercings as less competent and less trustworthy. Thus, although body art is central to self and "symbolically represent[s] and physically chronicle[s] changes in one's identity, relationships, thoughts, or emotions over time" (Atkinson, 2001, p. 118), the expectations associated with one's professional role may place constraints on the nature and extent of self-expression. In the case of physicians, their desire for self-expression must be balanced with their obligation to make patients feel comfortable, to put them at ease, and to reduce their anxiety (Newman, Wright, Wrenn, & Bernard, 2005).

In addition to our professional or occupational roles, each of us holds numerous other roles as well. The nature of each different role we play influences people's perceptions of and reactions to any body art we may have. That is, people's attitudes toward body modification may vary depending on whether the modified body is that of a physician or rock star, university student or professor, financial adviser or landscaper, neighbourhood teen-ager or their children's babysitter. But at an even more fundamental level, whether one is male or female influences perceptions of body art.

Women and Tattoos.   Tattooing has a long-standing association with male communi-ties and masculinity. Even though there has been a significant increase in the prevalence of tattooing among females, females with tattoos remain stigmatized, being perceived as more promiscuous, less attractive, and heavier drinkers (Swami & Furnham, 2007). Hawkes, Senn, and Thorn (2004) presented Canadian undergraduate students with vari-ous written scenarios about a female university student. The scenarios varied in terms of the presence of a tattoo, its size, and its visibility. Researchers found that, overall, tattooed females were perceived more negatively than non-tattooed females. Females with large or highly visible tattoos were perceived more negatively than those with small or nonvisible tattoos. It appears that tattoos continue to be perceived as violating some of the standards of feminine appearance. The gender of the observer plays a role as well, in that men had more negative perceptions of tattooed females than women did. Whether the observer also had tattoos influenced their perceptions as well, however highly visible tattoos were perceived negatively by both male and female observers with and without tattoos.

The fact that gender role attitudes influence people's perceptions of women with tat-toos points to the importance of discourses of gender in the larger society, which affect people's attitudes toward others' body projects. But in addition to influencing attitudes toward the body projects of others, discourses of gender also play a significant part in people's own body projects and the relationship between those projects and the develop-ment of a gendered self. For instance, Atkinson (2002) has found that tattooing is used by women in the development of their gendered identities, which emerge from and have an impact on structures of power in society.

Some women use tattooing in the development of an established femininity, while others use it in the development of a resistant femininity. **Established femininity** embod-ies the dominant cultural constructions of what a female body should look like. Thus, some women interviewed by Atkinson used tattooing to enhance their femininity. Their thoughts about how men would perceive their bodies played a role in their initial decision to get a tattoo. One woman said, "I think it looks sexy, and so do all my male friends" (p. 224). They spoke of their tattoos as making them more attractive to their boyfriends or to men in clubs, and perceived too many tattoos or too-large tattoos as unattractive and unfeminine. Their choice of images reflected the desire to enhance their femininity—for example, small flowers, celestial motifs, and insects such as ladybugs—as did their chosen tattoo locations, such as sexualized parts of the female body like the back of the shoulder. Thus, just as with breast implants and extreme dieting, some women's use of tattooing reinforces traditional gender ideals where the female body is an object for men's desires (Bordo, cited in Atkinson, 2002). Atkinson's discussion of tattooing and established fem-ininity emphasizes constructions of female physical attractiveness. However, established femininity can also refer to other traditional female roles, such as motherhood; this is illustrated in a growing trend of women getting tattoos of their children's names or portraits (Withey, 2012).

Resistant femininity opposes dominant gender ideals, and thereby serves as a form of resistance to existing structures of power in society. For some women, tattooing is part of this resistance. They get tattoos precisely because of the association with male communities. These women select larger designs, more "masculine" images (e.g., daggers), and more visible locations to actively express the self and resistance to patriarchal power relations. One woman stated, "My temple [body] is worked with symbols that read—a strong and independent woman lives here . . . forever" (Atkinson, 2002, p. 228). For other women, their statement of resistance is private rather than public, a negotiation between established and resistant femininity. Their tattoos are a form of personal liberation from traditional discourses of gender, yet their concern about possible stigmatization leads them to get their tattoos in concealable locations.

But whether women's tattoos are an expression of negotiation, resistance, or conformity, they are telling us about discourses of gender and structures of power in society. We can learn more about the larger society by examining other groups of body modifiers as well, such as the straightedge subculture.

Straightedge Tattoos.   You were first introduced to the straightedge subculture in Chapter 3. Although it consists of various divergent subgroups, its core ideology is one of resistance to the perceived hedonism and self-indulgence of the modern world (Irwin, 1999; Wood, 1999, 2001). In response, straightedgers build lives around physical purity and control of one's body—no drinking or drugs, no casual sex, and for some, no caffeine, no prescription drugs, and no over-the-counter drugs.

However, their ideology is about more than just lifestyle and individual identity—it is about actively trying to change the society within which hedonism and self-indulgence have emerged. In addition to their punk-style clothing and hairstyles, tattoos are a reflection of their ideology (Atkinson, 2003b). The most common type of design is composed of "symbols of lifestyle declaration" (p. 210), a clear signal of their group membership (e.g., "Straightedge," "sXe," and "XXX"). The next most common are "symbols of pacification" (p. 212), signifying having control of one's body (e.g., "poison-free," "100% pure"). Finally, there are "symbols of indictment" (p. 213), declarations of what is wrong with society (e.g., "nation of zombies"). Their tattoo designs spread specific messages; thus, though the design may vary, the process of tattooing is itself intertwined with straightedge ideology.

Because tattooing has been associated with various groups of rebels and protestors, tattooing is intentionally used by straightedgers to draw attention to their message. In addition, enduring the physical pain of tattooing demonstrates that they have control over their bodies rather than their bodies having control over them (Atkinson, 2003b). So not only are messages about the larger society (its hedonistic nature) and straightedge subculture (its ideology of purity and control) visible on straightedge bodies in a passive manner, straightedgers actively and intentionally use their bodies as a medium for conveying those messages and for living out their ideals.

Tattoos, piercings, and other forms of body modification convey many different messages to us, depending on the point along the objective–subjective continuum from which one is examining modified bodies. Body modification may tell us something about the individuals who have body art, such as their likelihood of substance use or violence, their desire to look attractive, or their need for self-expression. They may tell us about the role of body art in developing an understanding of the self and how interactions with various others have an influence. They may tell us something about the broader society, such as the expectations associated with different social roles, discourses of gender, the structure of power, and how body modification can be used as a form of resistance. Furthermore, they tell us something about the "dance" that surrounds what are considered "deviant" and "normal" bodies.

Whether or not we have body art and the nature of any body art we do have influences others' perceptions of and reactions to us. However, most of us still do not have tattoos, piercings, or other types of body modification. Although the proportion of the population with body modification is growing, these are simply not body projects that the majority of Canadians have undertaken. But in our society today there is one aspect of the social construction of deviant and normal physical appearance that is part of every one of our lives on a daily basis—body size or weight.

TIME TO REVIEW

Learning Objective 1

- What are the differences between voluntary and involuntary physical appearance?
- What are the different types of body projects?

Learning Objective 2

- In what ways does one's location along the objective–subjective continuum determine one's perception of what people's bodies can tell us?
- How have body modification practices changed over time?
- Based on the more objective end of the continuum, what risks are associated with body modification and what motivations are involved in modification practices?
- How can the dramaturgical perspective be applied to an understanding of body modification, and what role do social interactions play in the development of "front-stage" and "back-stage" selves?
- How are physicians with facial piercings and women with tattoos perceived?
- Considering both women and the straightedge subculture, what do tattoos tell us about the larger society and how can tattoos be used as a form of resistance?

"Too Fat," "Too Thin," and "Ideal"

Try to picture the ideal body. Notice the details. What does the ideal body look like? Is it a female body? If so, who does that body type most closely approximate—a model like Gisele Bündchen, an actress like Scarlett Johansson, a "plus-size" model like Mia Tyler, a competitive athlete like a member of the Canadian women's hockey team, or the average woman you see on the street? If it is a male body, who does that body most closely approx- imate—a competitive bodybuilder, heartthrob actor Channing Tatum, a male figure skater, or the average man you see on the street?

Early twentieth-century socialite Wallis Simpson claimed that "you can never be too rich or too thin" (Klauer, 2005). In the twenty-first century, does that phrase still hold true? Is thinner better? Is it possible to be too thin? In any culture at any specific time in history, only a certain range of body sizes are perceived as normal, conforming, or ideal. A body outside of that ideal is considered unacceptable, deviant, and requiring modification—overweight or underweight or, using more popular terminology, "too fat" or "too thin."

Take a moment to look at the *Ask Yourself* exercise. Once you have done so, consider the image that first emerged in your mind. If the ideal body you initially pictured was a female body, you should not be surprised. Body size and weight is more likely to be used as an evaluative criterion for women than for men. For the latter, a wider range of body types are perceived as acceptable (Rabak-Wagener, Eickhoff-Shemek, & Kelly-Vance, 1998). But even though men tend to have more freedom in what is considered an acceptable body, at some point they are also subject to the judgments of others based on their weight or the size of their bodies.

What is the ideal body according to our current cultural standards? To some extent, the answer to that question depends on whose criteria we are using—the criteria used by physicians in their evaluations of health, or the criteria used by average people in their judgments of people's physical appearance.

The Ideal Body According to Science

In the field of medicine, acceptable and deviant body weights are determined on the basis of "risks" for negative health consequences. Relative risk can be measured in a number of ways, such as waist-to-hip ratio and simple height–weight tables. However, the most common measurement tool used by physicians and scientists today is the **body mass index (BMI)**. An individual's BMI is determined through a comparison of height and weight according to the following formula:

$$[\text{weight in pounds} \div (\text{height in inches} \times \text{height in inches})] \times 703$$

The standards of the World Health Organization (2002a) categorize a BMI between 18.5 and 24.9 as in the "normal" range, because it is associated with the lowest health risks. A BMI between 25.0 and 29.9 is considered **overweight** because of increased risks of high cholesterol, type 2 diabetes, heart disease, high blood pressure, arthritis, and more. A BMI of 30.0 and higher is categorized as **obese**, with considerable risks for these illnesses. A BMI of 18.4 and lower is considered **underweight** because of greater risks of heart prob- lems, lowered immunity, anemia, depression, and death.

According to these standards, being overweight is a significant problem throughout much of the world. Approximately 1.4 billion adults aged 20 and older are overweight; of these, 200 million men and 300 million women are obese. Almost 3 million adults die every year because they are overweight or obese. Worldwide, 65 percent of the world's population lives in countries where more people die of complications from being overweight than of complications from being underweight (World Health Organization, 2012). In Canada, 67 percent of men and 54 percent of women are overweight or obese (Statistics Canada, 2012a). Even among children, obesity has been defined as a serious problem. In Canada, almost 20 percent of children ages 5 through 17 are overweight, and another 12 percent are obese (Statistics Canada, 2012b). Throughout much of the world, children are developing diseases related to being overweight (e.g., type 2 diabetes, high cholesterol, cardiovascular disease), diseases that used to be limited to adults (World Health Organization, 2012).

Far fewer people worldwide are underweight than overweight, and they tend to be concentrated in developing nations where being underweight is often associated with malnutrition. For example, by 2015 it is projected that 19 percent of children in developing countries will be underweight, compared to less 1 percent in developed nations (World Health Organization, 2004a). In Canada, approximately 2 percent of adults and children are considered underweight based on BMI standards (Statistics Canada, 2012a, 2012b). In the developed world, extreme thinness may signal the presence of anorexia (see Box 7.1).

Box 7.1

What is Anorexia?

Anorexia Nervosa is one of several different eating disorders, all of which are considered to be mental disorders. As such, there are formal diagnostic criteria defined by various health organizations, such as the American Psychiatric Association (in the *Diagnostic and Statistical Manual of Mental Disorders*) and the World Health Organization (in the *International Classification of Diseases*); both of these documents can be found, in their entirety, online. Formal diagnostic criteria can vary across defining bodies, as well as over time (see Chapter 7), however the broader characteristics of anorexia are well recognized (National Eating Disorder Information Centre, 2012; Canadian Mental Health Association, 2013; National Institutes of Mental Health, 2011). Anorexia is characterized by a combination of physical and psychological symptoms that are dependent on the progression of the illness, including (but not limited to) the following: extreme weight loss to the point of emaciation, which is achieved through severe calorie restriction and/or obsessive exercise; distorted body image, where the individual denies any problem and continues to see themselves as overweight; loss of female menstruation; growth of fine white hair over the body (in the body's attempt to keep warm); yellowing of skin; anemia; heart problems; brain damage; and multi-organ failure. Anorexia nervosa has the highest mortality rate of any mental illness.

Based on the diagnostic criteria, 0.9 percent of females and 0.3 percent of males in Canada will develop anorexia at some point in their lives (Hudson, Hiripi, Pope, & Kessler, 2007). Anorexia appears to peak in the transition from adolescence to young adulthood (Hoek, 2007), such that its prevalence in women ages 15 to 24 is 1.5 percent (Government of Canada, 2006). It is estimated that approximately 10 percent of individuals with anorexia will die within 10 years as a result of the physical complications that arise. Among males, **muscle dysmorphia** is more common than anorexia and is sometimes called "bigorexia" (Leone, Sedory, & Gray, 2005, p. 352). This refers to a preoccupation with being too thin or small and results in an obsession with weightlifting accompanied by anxiety or mood disorders, extreme body dissatisfaction, distorted eating attitudes, and anabolic steroid use.

The negative health and social consequences of anorexia, being overweight, or being obese have stimulated an abundance of research on how people come to have these experiences. Genetic, psychological, family, and larger sociocultural factors have all been areas of focus for those researchers who take a more objective approach to these conditions by searching for causes (e.g., Sandbek, 1993; Gordon, 2000; Caldwell, 2001; Levy, 2000). Research on being overweight consistently identifies consuming more calories than are being expended as the direct cause, but the factors underlying that cause are multifaceted—for example, the inability to deal with negative emotions effectively or the way that unhealthy food saturates our culture.

Research on being underweight, and in particular anorexic, identifies four general categories of causal theories (McLorg & Taub, 1987). First are **ego-psychological theories**, which emphasize impaired psychological functioning emerging from the child–mother relationship. Second are **family systems theories**. These theories suggest that anorexia is facilitated by emotionally enmeshed, rigid, overly controlling families. The third type of explanation are **endocrinological theories**, which explore various hormonal defects. The last category of explanations is **sociocultural theories**, looking at social norms emphasizing thinness, media images, and social learning or modelling. The causes of muscle dysmorphia are just beginning to be explored. Some explanations emphasize psychological factors while others focus on media images (Leone, Sedory, & Gray, 2005).

The research on causation and prevalence that emerges from scientific definitions of the ideal body is positioned on the more objective end of the objective–subjective continuum. Deviance specialists working from the more subjective end shift their attention elsewhere—to social definitions of the ideal body, the social control of body weight, and the implications of those social messages. While scientific definitions are based on medical implications, social definitions have a very different foundation. Social judgments of body weight more typically emerge from tacit definitions of the ideal body rather than scientific definitions; that is, when we react to our own weight or the weight of people we see, health risks are rarely the stimulus for our responses.

The Ideal Body According to Social Standards

As we judge the physical appearance of others or as our own physical appearance is judged, medical standards such as BMI or the diagnostic criteria for eating disorders rarely come into the picture. Instead, social standards determine the nature of the social typing process. These standards vary across cultures and over time, but at any given cultural moment we can identify what standards constitute the ideal body (see Figures 7.1 and 7.2).

Looking at our current cultural standards, a small range of bodies is considered "ideal." Note that the ideal body for both men and women leans toward the "thin" side of the continuum; our current cultural standards define a greater degree of "thinness" than "fatness" as being acceptable. You will also note that the ideal range is thinner for females than for males. While the ideal female is thin with large breasts, the male ideal is tall, lean, and muscular (Tylka & Calogero, 2011).

A body outside of this ideal range is judged as in need of fixing—popular discourse labels it as either "too thin" or "too fat." At the extreme ends of the continuum are "anorexic" and "obese"; however, the popular usage of these terms does not necessarily correspond to the medical criteria for those conditions. In fact, there is a considerable discrepancy between what people consider to be a "normal" body weight and what they consider to be an "attractive" body weight. In one study, participants ages 4 through 26 were shown a series of photos that varied in terms of the body sizes represented. They were asked to rate the photos in terms of body normality and body attractiveness. In all age groups, the bodies rated high in attractiveness were considerably thinner than those rated high in normality (Brown & Slaughter, 2011).

The ideals of physical attractiveness stem, in large part, from media portrayals. A study of male and female university students found strong support for the statements "adult models in advertisements have an ideal body size and shape," and women or men "would look more attractive if their body size or shape looked like most of the models in advertising." They consider that media images represent the ideal, even though they acknowledge that looking like those images would not necessarily be good for one's health (Rabak-Wagener, Eickhoff-Shemek, & Kelly-Vance, 1998). Research suggests that the greater an individual's exposure to media images of idealized bodies, the more likely he or she is to internalize those images and personally come to perceive them as being "ideal" (Sands & Wardle, 2003).

In other cultures, ideal body weight can be substantially different than the North American ideal. The slender ideal for women is characteristic of industrialized countries where food is plentiful. In contrast, in developing countries where food availability is less consistent, larger bodies are idealized. Once those cultures that have traditionally valued plumpness become more permeated with American media influences, the standards for the ideal body weight (especially for women) become considerably thinner (*The Futurist*, 2004; Shuriquie, 1999).

Figure 7.1 The "Ideal" Female Body: Current Cultural Standards

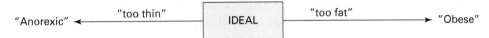

"Anorexic" ◄—— "too thin" —— IDEAL —— "too fat" ——► "Obese"

Figure 7.2 The "Ideal" Male Body: Current Cultural Standards

"Too Fat": Commercialization, Societal Reaction, and Social Control

Perceptions of People Who Are Overweight

Although more than half of Canadian and American adults are either overweight or obese, people who are overweight face considerable stigmatization. They are stereotyped as emotionally and socially handicapped, lazy, sad, and lacking in self-control (Taylor, 2011; Schwartz, Vartanian, Nosek, & Brownell, 2006; Roehling, 1999). Approximately one-quarter of schoolteachers say that "the worst thing that can happen to a person" is obesity, and a similar proportion of nurses say they are "repulsed" by obese people (Puhl & Brownell, 2001). Even health professionals who specialize in treating obesity stereotype obese individuals as lazy, unattractive, ugly, and bad (Puhl & Heuer, 2009).

Among the general population, 46 percent of adults say they would rather die one year earlier than be obese, and 30 percent would prefer divorce over obesity (Schwartz et. al., 2006). The stigma we attach to people who are overweight is overwhelmingly clear when looking at the perceptions of children. Latner & Stunkard (2003) presented children in Grades 5 and 6 with photographs of various types of disabled children (on crutches, in a wheelchair, with an amputated hand, and with a facial disfigurement) and overweight

left: © stryjek/Fotolia; right: © Megapress/Alamy

The "ideal" body weight according to current North American standards is very different than in many other parts of the world.

children. The overweight children were rated as the least desirable as friends. Anti-fat bias is pervasive in children as young as Grade 3 (Bissell & Hays, 2011).

The negative way that "too fat" is perceived in our society is also widely evident with media portrayals of body weight. The average female fashion model is 20 percent thinner than is healthy and is significantly thinner than in the mid-twentieth century (International Size Acceptance Association, 2003). Since the 1950s, *Playboy* centrefolds became increasingly thinner (Owen & Laurel-Seller, 2000), such that by the turn of the twenty-first century they were at their thinnest point ever. Almost all centrefolds are underweight according to health standards, and approximately 30 percent meet the weight criteria for anorexia (Spitzer, Henderson, & Zivian, 1999). More recently, a survey of British fashion models found that half considered anorexia to be a problem in the modelling industry, and 70 percent claimed that over the previous five years, the trend had been for models to be increasingly thinner (British Fashion Council, 2007).

The gap between the body size of women in the media versus the average woman in society is considerable. An analysis of the 10 most popular television series during the 1999–2000 season found that only 10 percent of female characters were overweight and 3 percent were obese (Greenberg, Eastin, Hofschire, Lachlan, & Brownell, 2003), compared to more than 25 percent of real-life American women who are overweight and 33 percent who are obese (Tjepkema, 2005). Approximately one-third were underweight (Greenberg et al., 2003), compared to less than 5 percent of real women (Tjepkema, 2005). Among male characters, 17 percent were overweight and 7 percent were obese (Greenberg et al., 2003), compared to 41 percent and 27 percent of real American men (Tjepkema, 2005) (see Figure 7.3). In fact, a recent analysis of children's television shows and characters on

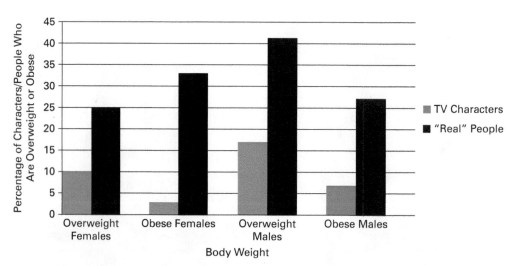

Figure 7.3 Body Weight of TV Characters Compared to "Real" People (1999–2000)

Data from Greenberg, B. S, Eastin, M, Hofschire, L, Lachlan, K, & Brownell, D. (2003). Portrayals of overweight and obese individuals on commercial television. *American Journal of Public Health, 93*(8), 1342–1348.

Discovery Kids, Nickelodeon, and The Disney Channel found that overweight characters are more likely to be portrayed in negative ways, such as lonely, lacking in friends, and unattractive (Robinson, Callister, & Jankoski, 2008).

The analysis of media portrayals of male bodies is complicated by the fact that the media focuses on a combination of weight and muscularity. In various forms of media, images of men became larger and more muscular during the latter half of the twentieth century (Wroblewska, 1997). An analysis of male images in GQ, *Rolling Stone*, and *Sports Illustrated* between 1967 and 1997 illustrates the emergence of the muscular ideal (Law & Labre, 2002). The proportion of "very muscular" images increased over that period of time from 9 to 35 percent, while the proportion of "not muscular" images declined from 42 to 16 percent. The proportion of "somewhat muscular" images remained relatively stable at 49 percent (see Figure 7.4).

The popular perceptions of people who are overweight and the media's portrayal of ideal body size constitute the evaluation component of the social typing process. Of course, this leads to our discussion of the third component of the process: prescription. Various social control measures, both informal and formal, are directed at people who are deemed to be "too fat."

Controlling "Too Fat"

Negative perceptions of people who are overweight are accompanied by particular behaviours or forms of social control. Children and adolescents who are "too fat" most frequently experience direct and intentional teasing or name-calling by classmates. They are verbally teased, physically bullied, and face social exclusion by peers (Warschburger, 2005; Puhl &

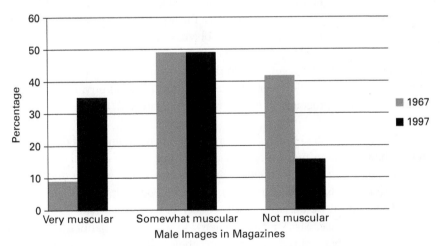

Figure 7.4 Male Images in Magazines, 1967 and 1997

Data from Law, C, & Labre, M. P. (2002). Cultural standards of attractiveness: A thirty-year look at changes in male images in magazines. *Journalism & Mass Communication Quarterly, 79*(3), 697–711.

Latner, 2007); obese children are twice as likely to be victimized in these ways than non-obese children (Hayden-Wade, Stein, Ghaderi, Saelens, Zabinski, & Wilfley, 2005). In fact, Puhl and Brownell (2001) found that overweight youth receive less financial support for university from their parents than normal-weight youth do (controlling for grades and family income). Critical comments and name-calling have a significant impact on adolescents' own perceptions of weight and their feelings about their own bodies. Youth say that media messages, comments from peers, and comments from family members (respectively) have the greatest impact (Wertheim, Paxton, Schutz, & Muir, 1997). In adulthood, teasing and name-calling may become less frequent, replaced by subtler messages from peers and strangers such as staring and whispering.

Behaviours extend beyond the casual comments of peers, family members, and even strangers. Research has consistently found that people who are overweight face discrimination in the institutions of society—education, health care, and employment (Puhl & Heuer, 2009; Puhl & Brownell, 2001). In lab settings, several studies have asked participants to pretend to be employers making hiring decisions. They were provided with hypothetical resumés and photographs of job applicants. The results of these studies conclude that people who are overweight are significantly less likely to be hired for jobs, even given equivalent qualifications as normal-weight applicants. As a result of discrimination in hiring and promotion, wages are affected (Puhl & Heuer, 2009). Mildly obese women have an average wage that is 6 percent lower than that of normal-weight women, and significantly obese women have an average wage that is 24 percent lower (Roehling, 1999). The implications for men's wages are not as significant. Obesity lowers men's wages only at extreme levels; in fact, the average wage of mildly obese men is actually higher than that of normal-weight men.

A number of social control measures are directed specifically at trying to "fix" people who are "too fat." Some measures aim to reduce the health risks associated with the scientifically defined categories of overweight and obese, while others are based on reinforcing the overly thin social standards that define the ideal body. All of these control efforts ultimately are related to self-regulation; in the end, we are supposed to monitor and control our own body weight. However, the media, commercial industry, medicine, government, and community programs all make efforts to "fix fatness."

Media. Media permeates our lives. Not only does it contain images of the ideal body, it also tells us how to control our bodies. Magazines are one of the principal media sources of social control efforts. In any given month at a magazine stand, you can find at least one magazine cover that shares the secret of how to get a body just like that of a particular celebrity. There are entire magazines for both men and women devoted to creating the perfect body (e.g., *Shape*, *Men's Fitness*, *Fitness*). In women's magazines, morality is frequently linked to body weight, fitness, and food choices (Pongonis & Snyder, 1998). The "right" body, fitness level, and eating habits are represented as indicators of strong morality, while the "wrong" physical characteristics are indicative of a lack of morality in the individual. For example, ads for a certain type of low-fat breakfast bar have a photograph of a woman with a giant pastry around her waist or cinnamon buns protruding from her hips. The tag line reads, "Respect yourself in the morning," suggesting that only by eating this low-fat breakfast bar can a women respect herself—and conversely, eating a pastry means a woman is undeserving of respect.

Exercise Your Mind

Take a trip to the nearest magazine stand and look at the covers of the women's and men's magazines. First, take note of the women and men featured on the covers and what they look like. Then look at the headlines for the main stories in each magazine. How many headlines regarding body size and shape do you see? What messages do these magazines send?

Media are also a tool used by other agents of social control. For example, a recent public health campaign by the organization Children's Healthcare of Atlanta features billboards, online videos, and local television commercials to educate parents on the emotional and physical harms that can accompany being overweight. However, the campaign itself was immediately criticized for contributing to the stigmatization of children who are overweight, such as by featuring an image of an overweight, unhappy girl accompanied by the text, "Warning: It's hard to be a little girl if you're not" (Youngblut, 2012).

An additional aspect of the media's control of body size lies in its integration of advertisements and commercials for weight-loss and fitness products. The commercialization of weight loss exists not only in the media, but also outside of the media.

Commercialization.   Commercial industry provides a massive range of products for controlling body size—books, videos and DVDs, packaged foods, weight-loss programs, gym memberships, fitness equipment, pills, powders, patches, and more. In the United States alone, it is estimated that in 2010 the diet industry made more than $60 billion in revenues, an increase of $2 billion from two years earlier (PRweb, 2011). Just as weight loss is highly commercialized, especially for females, so is muscle growth—especially for males. Gym memberships, protein shakes, anabolic steroids, and pills that purport to increase muscle mass are all aspects of controlling the muscular aspect of body size. It is in the best interests of commercial industry to attract as many consumers as possible; thus, the more of us who can be convinced that our bodies are lacking in some way, the more money the diet and fitness industry makes.

The role of commercial industry in regulating "too fat" extends to children as well. In 2012, Disney World created its new "Habit Heroes" attraction, intended to educate children about healthy habits in a fun way. Shortly after opening the attraction, Disney chose to close it in the face of intense criticism. Part of the attraction involved children fighting overweight villains, such as "Snacker," "Glutton," and "Lead-Bottom." Critics argued that these portrayals would not improve health habits in children, but rather stigmatize over-weight children even more (Anderssen, 2012). Freedhoff (2012) asked, "what kid doesn't want to be made to feel like a personal failure while on a Disney family vacation?"

Medicalization.   Despite the profit-driven motives of the diet and fitness industries, which may distort facts through their efforts to convince people they are overweight, there is no doubt that being overweight is a health risk. The World Health Organization and many national governments emphasize these health risks. Heart disease is the number-one cause of death in adults in North America, and being overweight is one of the central risk factors for heart disease. Consequently, the medical community is heavily involved in the social control of people who are "too fat." The most common forms of social con-trol directed at overweight patients by doctors are instructions to decrease calories (92 percent), suggestions to join a commercial weight-loss program (84 percent), referrals to a dietician or nutritionist (76 percent), and suggestions to engage in regular aerobic exer-cise (75 percent) (Price, Desmond, Krol, Snyder, & O'Connell, 1987). Most of these forms of medicalization are based on the goal of reducing the health risks associated with being overweight.

However, the medical control of people who are "too fat" sometimes steps outside the realm of health and into the realm of physical appearance—in the past, for example, doc-tors told women who wanted to lose weight to take up smoking! From the 1950s through the 1970s, amphetamines were prescribed for weight loss. Beginning in the 1980s, other medications that decrease appetite were developed. In the 1990s, some of these medica-tions were taken off the market because of health complications (and deaths), but were replaced by new drugs. A recent commercial for one of these weight-loss drugs lists its pos-sible side effects as nausea, vomiting, headaches, and uncontrollable bowel movements. The complications from weight-loss surgery are even more frightening. Even the normal consequences of gastric bypass surgery sound unappealing. Only a few tablespoons of food can be eaten at one time: "one bite of the wrong thing or even a morsel too much of the right thing can cause vomiting, explosive diarrhea, or a frightening attack of cramping and faintness known as dumping" (Dunleavey, 2001, p. 174). Liposuction, which is surgery that uses a vacuum-like instrument to suck fat cells out of specific parts of the body, has nothing to do with health and is based solely on physical appearance. In fact, medical criteria for the procedure say that liposuction should not be done on someone who is medically overweight.

Governments.   The health risks associated with being overweight have a significant impact on the health of the world's population. By negatively impacting the health of large numbers of people, nations experience economic drains from consequences like health care costs, absenteeism from work because of illness, and lost tax revenue. Katzmarzyk and Janssen (2004) calculated the annual costs of overweight and obese populations in Canada to be $4.3 billion, and the annual costs of physical inactivity (which is associated with being overweight, but is frequently found among normal-weight individuals as well) to be $5.3 billion. As a result, several governments have recently initiated considerable efforts to reduce the proportion of overweight people in their countries.

In 2011, Denmark became the first country to implement a "fat tax," that is, an additional tax levied on foods containing high levels of saturated fat. One year later the tax was repealed. Insufficient time had passed to determine whether the tax was effective in changing people's eating behaviours, but sufficient time had passed for opponents to draw attention to the negative economic consequences. They argued that lower-income households were unduly affected by the tax, that retailers had increased prices beyond the fat tax, and that the Danish economy was losing money because of increased cross-border shopping into Germany and Sweden. Despite Denmark's repeal of the fat tax, other countries are moving in a similar direction. France has implemented a tax on products containing palm oil, and Hungary is in the process of implementing a tax on foods that are high in fat, salt, and sugar. In Canada, the Ontario Medical Association has begun lobbying for the taxation and labelling of unhealthy foods (Ha, 2012).

In Canada, the federal government's Integrated Pan-Canadian Healthy Living Strategy has set 2015 as a target date for increasing by 20 percent the proportion of Canadians with a "normal" body mass index, who engage in daily physical activity, and who make healthy food choices (Health Canada, 2005c). Some provinces have a mandatory amount of daily physical activity in schools, and parents can receive tax deductions for their children's sports activities. But federal, provincial, and territorial governments are not the only bodies developing effective programs and policies for weight loss: so are individual communities.

Communities. Individual communities have developed a wide range of measures to reduce the proportion of people who are overweight. In the Aboriginal communities of the Interlake region of Manitoba, an integrated program run by the Anishinabe Mino-Ayaawin has been implemented. The Aboriginal people of these communities are at a higher-than-average risk of weight-related health complications such as heart disease and diabetes. As a result, a comprehensive program was initiated to (1) educate children and adults in a variety of settings about nutrition and physical fitness, (2) provide healthy breakfast and lunch programs in schools, and (3) build new recreational facilities for people of all ages (DeMont, 2002).

Efforts to reduce the proportion of overweight children have also been integrated into a number of school programs elsewhere in Canada. For example, at Evangeline Middle School in New Minas, Nova Scotia, all children are required to play intramural sports; however, this school program goes one step further by having intramural games played during regular classroom hours rather than at lunchtime or after school. The gymnasium remains open every evening, every weekend, and throughout the summer for those students and parents who want to use the facilities (DeMont, 2002).

Informal interactions, community programs, government programs and policies, members of the medical community, commercial industry, and the media all interact to create a complex web of social control for body size and shape. Some of these control measures emerge from concerns over the health consequences of being overweight. However, the regulation of body size extends beyond health to concerns over physical appearance for those who are perceived as "too fat" (by others or by themselves), regardless of whether they are overweight.

Consequences of Social Control

We are surrounded by a multitude of measures to control body size, with consequences for people's perceptions of their own bodies, psychological and physical health, and dieting patterns. Once again, we find that the media is particularly influential. Some research finds that girls and women feel worse about their own bodies, experience declines in their self-esteem, and show increases in depression and sadness after seeing images of models (Stice & Shaw, 1994; Crouch & Degelman, 1998) or even the female characters on the television show *Friends* (Want, Vilkers, & Amos, 2009). However, other research suggests that this effect only occurs in those who identify with media images and personally aspire to them (Bell & Dittmar, 2011). Recent research also finds that men experience greater body dissatisfaction and higher levels of depression after seeing advertisements or television commercials featuring the images of the muscular-yet-lean male ideal (Baird & Grieve, 2006; Agliata & Tantleff-Dunn, 2004).

The official position of the Canadian Paediatric Society (2004) is that the media has an unhealthy influence on adolescents, providing them with "information [that is] dubious and unreliable, motivated less by scientific evidence than by fad trends and financial incentives. The net result is that many teenagers feel the cultural pressure to be thinner than is required for good health, and may try to achieve this goal through poor and sometimes dangerous nutritional choices" (p. 287).

A significant proportion of people are currently dieting, in either healthy or unhealthy ways. The National Eating Disorder Information Centre in Toronto (2008) reports that at any given time, 70 percent of women and 35 percent of men are dieting. Furthermore, between 41 and 66 percent of adolescent girls and between 20 and 31 percent of adolescent boys have dieted at some point in their lives (Daee et al., cited in Canadian Paediatric Society, 2004, p. 487). Many of these children are not in need of losing weight for health reasons. One study found that among Grade 10 boys and girls who were of a normal weight (based on medical standards), 19 percent considered themselves to be "too fat" and 12 percent had tried to lose weight (Boyce, King, & Roche, 2008). Among adolescent boys, the use of steroids is increasing in their efforts to attain the ideal body—among boys in Grades 9 and 10, 4 percent report having used anabolic steroids to increase size or muscle mass (Boyce, 2004). The long-term health consequences as these boys grow into adulthood remain to be seen.

The pressure placed on youth by the media is particularly intense and influences body image and dieting practices (Bell & Dittmar, 2011). However, comments by or pressure from peers and family members have consequences as well. Overweight youth report that comments made by family members can be hurtful (Neumark-Sztainer, Story, & Faibisch, 1998). Girls who are teased by family members about their weight are significantly more likely to engage in binge eating and unhealthy weight-loss behaviours in the future (Neumark-Sztainer, Wall, Haines, Story, Sherwood, & van den Berg, 2007).

Comments made by others trigger the adoption of a "fat" identity in individuals. Even people who may have been overweight since early childhood do not come to see themselves as "fat" until external cues give them that indication (Degher & Hughes, 2003). External cues may be of an active type (e.g., comments from others) or a passive type (e.g., seeing one's own reflection in a store window), but it is the active type of cues that have the greatest influence. Comments from others lead to the personal recognition that one does not have a "normal" body but a "fat" body. A deviant definition of the self is subsequently internalized and a "fat" identity emerges. Being subjected to the social typing process by others thus leads people to socially type themselves, changing an individual's understanding of self.

The social controls placed on body size, especially the controls exerted by the media, peers, and family members, have considerable influence on the way people feel about themselves, their self-esteem, and their self-regulation practices (like dieting or using anabolic steroids). However, as public control measures for body size have burst onto the scene in a magnitude never before seen over the past two decades, the proportion of both adults and children who are overweight or obese has actually grown rather than declined.

Resisting a Label of "Too Fat"

The fact that being overweight has become so stigmatized in society and that the social definition of what constitutes "too fat" has reached absurd standards has done more than simply raise a few eyebrows. Many individuals and various organizations are taking active steps to curb this social typing process. A number of "fat acceptance" groups have formed in Canada, the United States, and Western Europe (e.g., the National Association to Advance Fat Acceptance). They provide information on current obesity research, facts about weight-loss drugs and surgeries and the dangers of them, and litigation updates. They also facilitate advocacy by, for example, providing instructions on writing effective complaint letters and leading activism efforts. Other organizations have created beauty magazines, websites, and clothing lines for people who are overweight.

Although the media is one of the primary social control agents for "too fat" and the central reproducer of overly thin body images, at times it also integrates aspects of resistance to the social typing process. Some women's magazines have profiled women who have suffered weight-loss surgery disasters (Dunleavey, 2001), and provided information on "wacky weight-loss products" and their ineffectiveness (Seligson, 2001). However, these types of articles constitute the minority in women's magazines and are contradicted by the preponderance of thin images.

Fat acceptance organizations, websites, television personalities, and magazine articles are all participants in resisting the social typing process. The areas of emphasis for these resistance activities are twofold: first, to promote sound nutrition and physical fitness in pursuit of good health; and second, to remove the social stigma from people who are overweight, thus broadening the standards of physical attractiveness in our culture. Views of health and physical appearance are the two foundations (albeit sometimes contradictory ones) in the stigmatization and social control of "too fat," just as they are key elements in the resistance to these processes. Health and physical appearance are also foundations to discussions of the other deviant body size in our society—"too thin."

"Too Thin": Commercialization, Societal Reaction, and Social Control

Perceptions of People Who Are Underweight

The ideal body size in a particular society is one that is perceived as normal or conforming. In many Western industrialized societies today, widespread cultural perceptions support an extremely thin ideal. Consequently, considerable thinness is necessary before a "too thin" label is attached and the social typing process is triggered. This is especially true when considering social definitions rather than scientific ones.

Based on scientific definitions, approximately 2 percent of adults and children in Canada are underweight (Statistics Canada, 2012a, 2012b). Social definitions likely put those numbers even lower, considering the value placed on underweight females as images of beauty and the frequency of dieting among females who are at a healthy weight or even underweight. However, at some point a "too thin" label does emerge. In a classic analysis, McLorg and Taub (1987) found that among people belonging to an eating disorders support group, family members and friends did not perceive them as "too thin" or "anorexic" until they had reached the point of being emaciated. Prior to that point, family members and friends actually encouraged them in their pursuit of weight loss and congratulated them on their successes. Once that label was finally attached, social control measures kicked in.

Controlling "Too Thin"

Medicalization, Education, and Formal Intervention. "Too thin" is socially controlled at various formal levels. The medical community, frequently in conjunction with social agencies and programs, makes people who are at the most extreme end of thinness (anorexic) subject to social control efforts. When an individual is in immediate danger of sudden death, the medical community pursues intervention. The difficulty in preventing and treating anorexia and other eating disorders has resulted in a range of approaches that are employed at different points in the progression of this condition (National Eating Disorder Information Centre, 2008; Lock, 2001; Matthews, 2001; Levenkron, 2000; Levine & Maine, 2005).

Physicians, psychiatrists, psychologists, and nurses carry out some of the formal social control measures described in Box 7.2, while social agencies and programs carry out others. For example, at Eastwood Collegiate Institute in Kitchener, Ontario, guest speakers

Box 7.2

Preventing and Treating Anorexia

1. Prevention

You know the old saying: "An ounce of prevention is worth a pound of cure." Preventing eating disorders is emphasized by many different social organizations (National Eating Disorder Information Centre, 2008; Costin, 1999; Levine & Maine, 2005).

Primary prevention involves efforts to prevent eating disorders from occurring in the first place. It entails school and community programs that raise awareness of eating disorders and their associated dangers as well as the unrealistic body ideals portrayed in popular culture (National Eating Disorders Information Centre, 2008; British Columbia Eating Disorders Association, 2003; Matthews, 2001). However, primary prevention must also go much further than this. At a societal level, the culture's obsession with thinness must be chipped away at, the gendered norms that constrain both men and women must be changed, and institutions (e.g., schools) must adopt processes that facilitate the development of self-esteem and efficacy in a wide range of areas (Levine & Maine, 2003; Lock, 2001; Levenkron, 2000).

Secondary prevention involves identifying those young men and women who may be in the very early stages of an eating disorder. This kind of prevention entails educating parents, teachers, and coaches about the warning signs of eating disorders and effective means of intervention (e.g., National Eating Disorders Association, 2003).

2. Treatment

An extensive range of treatments are available for eating disorders, though which treatments are most effective depends entirely on the individual. People with eating disorders may choose from diverse forms of therapy and counselling—psychotherapy, group therapy, family counselling, and cognitive behavioural therapy (Lock, 2001; Levenkron, 2000; Costin, 1999; Levine & Maine, 2005; British Columbia Eating Disorders Association, 2003). For therapy to be effective, it must deal not only with the eating disorder itself but also with the psychological, familial, and cultural factors that contributed to the eating disorder in the first place (Levine & Maine, 2005). There are medications that can help some individuals with eating disorders, such as anti-anxiety drugs or anti-depressants. Support groups are useful tools. The nature of support groups is quite varied, with some following a program pattern similar to Alcoholics Anonymous (e.g., Anorexia and Bulimics Anonymous). When severe health dangers are imminent, hospitalization or residential programs may be necessary so that medical monitoring and health supports are available around the clock (British Columbia Eating Disorders Association, 2003; Levine & Maine, 2005; Levenkron, 2000).

are brought into the school to talk to girls about eating disorders and body image. Eating disorder associations frequently sponsor group meetings and peer support for people who have eating disorders like anorexia. People who work with adolescents in a variety of arenas—schoolteachers, coaches, school counsellors, and youth care workers—are educated about the signs of anorexia and other eating disorders.

Even governments and the fashion industry are becoming involved in the control of extreme thinness by banning underweight models from various types of work. In 2006, runway model Luisel Ramos died of complications from anorexia during a runway show; six months later, her sister Eliana (also a model) died for the same reason (Beckford, 2007). Following those events, the fashion industry in some countries (e.g., India and Italy) banned underweight models in runway shows. In 2012, the government of Israel went a step further, passing legislation that prohibits models who have BMIs under 18.5, or who even *appear* to be underweight, from all types of modelling work in Israel (Reuters, 2012).

Media.   The social control of "too thin" is evident in the media as well, although to nowhere near the extent of the social control of "too fat." For example, magazine cover stories often ask questions about the health of shrinking celebrities such as Keira Knightley. Kim Kardashian's ample bottom, initially the subject of media jokes, is now described as a "sexy" alternative to the waif-like look of many other female celebrities. Extremely thin celebrities are now having negative labels attached to them—"Rwandan chic" (in reference to the appearance of people living through the famine in the African country of Rwanda), and "lollipop heads" or "lollipop girls" (referring to stick-like bodies topped by comparatively large-looking heads).

Changing Ideals, Interactions with Family and Friends, and Informal Controls.
Although common media representations of thin ideal bodies influence the stigma and stereotyping of the overweight in society, there are indications that some people's perceptions of the ideal body may be changing. In a popular survey of adult men and women, participants were shown four different female body types: curvy and fit (e.g., an actress from *Baywatch*, a 1990s TV series about lifeguards), a toned athlete (e.g., professional volleyball players), "skinny" (e.g., a runway model), and muscular (e.g., Ms. Fitness America). Participants were asked which of those body types they found the most and least attractive. The most attractive body type, according to more than half of the men and women, is curvy and fit, and the toned athlete was ranked second. The least attractive body type is the muscular woman, according to approximately half of female and male participants. The attractiveness of the "skinny" runway model was ranked between the toned athlete and the muscular woman, although more men than women considered that body type to be attractive (Fleming, 1999).

Although the "skinny" body type was not considered the most attractive in this survey, the fact that this body type was considered more attractive than the muscular body type illustrates that, to some degree, the value placed on a thin female body continues to be high. More recently, interviews with female aerobic exercisers and instructors similarly found the perceived ideal body type to be lean, toned, and curvy—"like the supermodels in the Victoria's Secret catalogue—but not too muscular" (Greenleaf, McGreer, & Parham, 2006, p. 192). However, in making those statements, interviewees failed to realize that most Victoria's Secret models are, in fact, underweight.

Women who are hyper-muscular (i.e., competitive female bodybuilders) are perceived as having a variety of negative attributes when compared to the "average woman": having fewer feminine interests and a more masculine gender identity, less intelligent, less educated, less popular, less sexually attractive, less romantically attractive, and less likely to be a good mother (Forbes, Adams-Curtis, Holmgren, & White, 2004). Because female bodybuilders oppose the socially ideal female body, and in what is perceived as a masculinized way, some researchers interpret these body projects as expressions of resistance against traditional norms of femininity (e.g., Shea, 2001)—just as with women who have larger or more masculine images as tattoos. Regardless of whether muscular women are actively resisting traditional gender norms that oppress women, research on people's perceptions of female body types shows us that it is better for a woman to be extremely thin than to be extremely muscular.

When individuals are finally socially typed as "too thin," everyday interactions with family members and friends exert measures of control (McLorg & Taub, 1987). Individuals' eating habits are closely watched and then openly identified as the cause of everything bad that happens in their lives, such as falling grades and the loss of friendships. People with more moderate degrees of "too thin" may have food pushed on them, as family members and friends try to get them to eat more. Once others identify them as "anorexic," on the other hand, people may not offer them anything to eat or drink, even at social gatherings. Friends and family members withdraw from interactions with them, making them feel increasingly isolated and stigmatized. Even so, many people who have anorexia nevertheless feel that the stigma attached to their emaciated appearances and strange eating patterns is preferable to the stigma of being overweight. It is through these everyday social interactions, however, that people with anorexia eventually develop an "anorexic" identity. McLorg and Taub (1987) apply labelling theory (discussed in Chapter 3) to this process. Identifying friends or family members as "anorexic" leads to the distinct types of treatment described above. People labelled in this way are isolated from "normal" relationships in their lives, and even say that others come to expect them to act anorexic. An "anorexic" identity forms and a lifestyle becomes entrenched—processes that are the hallmarks of the transition from primary to secondary deviance.

Resisting a Label of "Too Thin"

Although "too thin" is considered deviant and made subject to measures of social control largely because of severe and immediate health dangers, there is still resistance to this process of social typing. While resistance to the social typing of overweight people includes efforts to increase "fat acceptance" (change societal norms governing body ideals), measures that are intended to increase extreme thinness (and even anorexia) constitute the bulk of resistance to the social typing of "too thin."

The idea that you can never be too rich or too thin, for example, illustrates resistance to the idea that thinness is deviant and in need of social control. The extent to which weight-loss products and messages permeate our media and commercial industry reinforces this notion. And although most of us would agree that the extreme thinness of anorexia is in need of both preventative and retroactive measures of control, resistance to the social typing and social control of anorexia is evident in some arenas, including the Internet.

Over the last decade, popular discourse has come to include "Ana." Dozens of websites are devoted to "Ana," which refers to anorexia. These websites do not provide help with and support for ending anorexia; rather, they help maintain anorexia. They include photographs of models and actresses as motivation for continuing the pursuit of weight loss. There are tips for losing weight faster, charts listing the calorie count of different foods and the calories burned by different activities, and advice for maintaining motivation. Additional advice tells people how to dress so that others will not detect their extreme weight loss and how to fool others into thinking they are eating normally. Avoiding a deviant label is important because detection results in social control measures, which interfere with weight loss. There are even tips on how to resist active control efforts, such as how to avoid weight gain while hospitalized for treatment. Chatrooms and discussion groups provide an arena for support in resisting the deviantization of anorexia. "Ana" websites themselves have now been identified as dangerous, and efforts are underway to control them. Several Internet providers remove pro-anorexia sites once they are discovered.

Ask Yourself

How is the appearance of your body affected or socially controlled by other people in your life, groups you belong to, and cultural norms? What influence does the appearance of your body have on other people, groups you belong to, and the larger society?

Look in the mirror. Is your body "too fat," "too thin," or "just right"? Answering that question rests on the foundation of our cultural standards of the ideal body. The bodies we see in the media and elsewhere around us, as well as people's responses to those bodies, tell us what "too fat," "too thin," and "just right" mean. The medical community, commercial industry, social agencies and organizations, and individual people we encounter in our lives let us know the status of our own bodies and exert means of control if our bodies need to be "fixed" in some way. In the end, we are expected to self-regulate our bodies—realize when we are "too fat" and take steps to lose weight, or notice when we are "too thin" and take steps to gain weight.

Body weight is only one of many aspects of physical appearance that can potentially be socially typed as deviant and made subject to measures of social control. Additional aspects include tattoos, piercings, and other forms of body modification. The appearance of our bodies is an expression of other characteristics we may have (e.g., personality traits), our selves and identities, our culture's (or subculture's) norms and ideologies, and structures of power in society. Our bodies say a great deal—what does your body say?

TIME TO REVIEW

Learning Objective 3

■ How is the ideal body defined according to scientific standards and social standards? How prevalent are "deviant" bodies according to each of these standards?

■ What are the causes of overweight/obesity and anorexia?

■ In what way are ideal male and female bodies reflected in the media and how has that changed over time?

Learning Objective 4

■ How are overweight people perceived and how are they socially controlled by the media, commercial industry, medicine, government, and communities?

Learning Objective 5

■ How is "too thin" socially controlled at a formal level, by the media, and by family and friends?

Learning Objective 6

■ How are the labels of "too fat" and "too thin" each resisted?

CHAPTER SUMMARY

■ Physical appearance is extremely important. All of us engage in body projects that change our bodies' functioning or appearance. Social scientists propose that the appearance of people's bodies can convey many important messages. (1)

■ A growing proportion of people alter their appearance through body modification. Body modification may tell us about the characteristics of individuals, the processes involved in coming to understand the self, and the discourses and structures of power in the larger society. (2)

■ Other body projects are based on body weight and size. Body size and weight is a nexus for social typing that occurs everywhere around us on a daily basis. The "ideal" body weight can be defined scientifically on the basis of health risks or socially on the basis of social standards. (3)

■ People who are considered "too fat" are perceived negatively in our society and subjected to a wide range of informal and formal social controls. Informal social interactions, discriminatory practices, the media, commercial products, medical services, government programs, and community services all target "too fat." (4)

■ A label of "too thin" is usually not attached to people until they reach an extreme level of thinness. Once that label is attached, social control efforts are initiated through formal prevention and intervention measures, the media, and personal interactions. (5)

- Labels of "too fat" and "too thin" are resisted in numerous ways. The former is resisted through fat acceptance organizations and some elements of the media. The latter is resisted through the "Rwandan chic" that permeates Hollywood, which suggests that there is no such thing as "too thin." Pro-anorexia websites have even emerged on the Internet, providing support for people to maintain anorexia and avoid detection by others. (6)

MySearchLab®

Watch Go to MySearchLab to watch all four parts of the video series called "Flesh Wounds: Marked Bodies in the Civilising Process".

Apply What You Know: Consider Dr. Atkinson's comments about tattooing being related to both the crisis of masculinity and to the individualism of contemporary culture. To what extent do you think that body modification projects like tattooing are an expression of an individual's uniqueness or a reflection of his or her conformity?

MySearchLab with eText offers you access to an online interactive version of the text, extensive help with your writing and research projects, and provides round-the-clock access to credible and reliable source material.

Chapter 8
Mental Disorders

© paradox/Fotolia

Learning Objectives

After reading this chapter, you should be able to

1 Describe the prevalence of mental disorders in Canada and worldwide, as well as patterns of mental disorders across various social groups.

2 Describe the costs of mental illness for individuals, their families, and the larger society.

3 Explain how mental disorders are subject to social control through (1) the stigmatization of mental illness and (2) the medicalization of mental disorder.

4 Describe the efforts to reduce the stigmatization of mental illness and to improve the resources that are available to people with mental disorders.

5 Explain why the diagnostic handbook used by mental health professionals is criticized.

6 Describe Rosenhan's classic study on mental illness and explain the consequences of his research.

What images come to mind when you think of mental disorder? Caplan (1995) suggests that "usually, images of difference and alienation" first come to mind, "suggesting that 'they' are not as competent, human, or safe to be around as the rest of 'us'" (p. 11). The concept of mental disorder consists of two different dimensions. First, it entails the experience of the disorder itself—the ways that the illness affects people's thoughts, feelings, or behaviours. But, as Caplan points out, mental disorder also has a social dimension, that is, the ways that others perceive and treat those with mental illnesses. Via both dimensions, mental disorder enters the realm of deviance.

Research on mental disorder reflects both of these dimensions as well and emerges from various points along the objective–subjective continuum. It includes research on the prevalence and patterns of mental disorder, the costs of inadequately treated mental illness, stigmatization, and medicalization. Contemporary sociological research on mental disorder tends to lean toward the more subjective end of the continuum, focusing on stigmatization, experiences of self, and the social construction of mental illness, with a strong interactionist theoretical foundation.

Mental disorder, by definition, is a psychological, biological, or behavioural dysfunction that interferes with daily life—"alterations in thinking, mood or behaviour … associated with significant distress and impaired functioning" (Health Canada, 2002, p. 7), such as "impaired judgment, behaviour, capacity to recognize reality, or ability to meet the ordinary demands of life" (Alberta Mental Health Act, n. d., p. 7). The "bad day" (or "bad week") that all of us have at times is not sufficient to be considered mental illness; the distorted thoughts, moods, and behaviours must be of a magnitude and duration substantial enough to interfere with our daily functioning. The *Diagnostic and Statistical Manual of Mental Disorders* (DSM), the diagnostic handbook created by the American Psychiatric Association, clearly outlines precisely what types of thoughts, moods, and behaviours constitute mental illness and under what circumstances. Mental health professionals use the *DSM*'s checklist of symptoms to determine which (if any) mental disorder a given individual may have (e.g., schizophrenia, generalized anxiety disorder, gender identity dysphoria, major depressive disorder).

Exercise Your Mind

You can find a copy of the *DSM-V* in the DSM Library at www.psychiatryonline.org. Browse through the diagnostic categories to see what types of thoughts, moods, or behaviours are defined as constituting mental illness. Select three different diagnostic categories—a psychotic disorder, a mood disorder, and an anxiety disorder—and look at their descriptions and lists of symptoms. How do these three different disorders encapsulate the "distress" and "impaired functioning" that definitions of mental illness focus on? How do you think the daily lives of people with these symptoms would compare to your own daily life in terms of differences and similarities?

Who Has Mental Disorders?

Mental disorders can strike anyone and affect the majority of Canadians either directly (through experiencing a mental disorder themselves) or indirectly (by having a friend, family member, or co-worker with a mental disorder). Health Canada (2002) has found that approximately 20 percent of adult Canadians have a mental illness and 80 percent of Canadians know someone with a mental illness.

Although most national data on mental illness is drawn from medical treatment records (e.g., hospitalization records), some smaller scale general population surveys have also addressed the topic of mental disorders, enabling researchers to identify the proportion of the population that has not sought professional assistance for their psychological problems. For example, one survey found that more than one-third of Canadians say they have experienced depression or anxiety (Health Canada, 2002).

Worldwide, the extent of the problem of mental illness is staggering. The World Health Organization (2001) has found that mental disorders affect 25 percent of the world's population at some point in their lives; at any given point in time, more than 450 million people are experiencing a mental disorder (World Health Organization, 2010). The most common mental disorders—depressive disorders, anxiety disorders, and somatic complaints—strike one in three individuals. In 2001, more than 120 million people around the world experienced depression, and 24 million were living with schizophrenia. In total, mental disorders constitute more than one-third of all disabilities in the world (World Health Organization, 2001).

Although mental illness can strike anyone, some social groups are more susceptible than others. Early research done in the United States and Britain claimed that more women than men experienced mental disorders. However, later research found that the surveys underlying these conclusions were methodologically flawed. By focusing their questions on the types of psychological distress that are more common in women and excluding questions on the types of distress that are more common in men, these surveys overestimated women's mental health problems and underestimated men's (Simon, 2002). Today, researchers agree that the overall rates of mental disorder are virtually identical in men and women, but recognize that there are distinct differences in the patterns and types of mental illness (Simon, 2002; World Health Organization, 2001).

Anti-social personality disorder, substance abuse dependency disorders, and conduct disorders are much more common in men. For example, anti-social personality disorder is three times more common in men than in women (Simon, 2002; Health Canada, 2002; World Health Organization, 2001). Those disorders that are classified as the "common mental disorders" (or CMDs)—depression and anxiety—are much more common in women (Piccinelli & Homen, 1997; Health Canada, 2002). The reasons why women in countries throughout the world are more likely to experience depression and anxiety are largely sociocultural in nature. Although there are strong arguments for biological predeterminants of many if not most mental illnesses, including depression and anxiety, CMDs have been consistently linked to particular life stressors and negative life events—ones that, on average, are more prevalent in women's lives than men's—including low income or income inequality, low or subordinate social status, extensive responsibility for the daily care of others (spouses, children, elderly parents), and victimization by violence (World Health Organization, 2001, 2010; Roberts, Lawrence, Williams, & Raphael, 1998; Patel, Araya, deLima, Ludermir, & Todd, 1999).

Although socioeconomic status interacts with gender, both women and men of low socioeconomic status have higher rates of most types of mental illness, especially depression and anxiety (World Health Organization, 2010; Dohrenwend, Levav, Shrout, & Schwartz, 1992; Miech, Caspi, Moffitt, Wright, & Silva, 1999; Patel et al., 1999; Williams & Takeuchi, 1992). A longstanding question about the relationship between socioeconomic status and mental illness has been about the direction of causation. The **social causation hypothesis** suggests that more life stresses and fewer resources characterize the lives of the lower class, contributing to the emergence of mental disorders.

This was, in fact, mentioned in Robert Merton's strain theory (discussed in Chapter 2). Although his theory and its later applications largely focus on crime, he did suggest that mental illness can emerge in response to the gap between institutionalized goals and the legitimate means for attaining those goals. The mode of adaptation that he labelled **retreatism**, wherein people give up on pursuing the goals as well as the legitimate means of attaining those goals, can include alcoholism, drug use, or mental illness. In contrast, the **social selection hypothesis** proposes the reverse—that people with mental disorders can fall into lower economic strata because of their difficulties in daily functioning (Eaton, 2001).

Although some debate continues among mental health experts, recent research finds that the direction of causation depends on the specific mental disorder in question. Individuals with schizophrenia, conduct disorders, and attention deficit disorder are more likely to fall into the lower socioeconomic strata and are less likely to be able to rise out of the lower strata, supporting the social selection hypothesis. Conversely, social causation appears to underlie depression, anxiety, substance use disorders, and anti-social personality disorder. The life stresses associated with economic difficulties contribute to the emergence of these disorders (Kessler et al., 1994; Dohrenwend et al., 1992; Turner, Wheaton, & Lloyd, 1995). In fact, the World Health Organization (2010) states that a variety of social conditions are associated with poor mental health, including poverty, low levels of education, human rights violations, gender discrimination, rapid social change (which reflects Durkheim's notion of **anomie**, discussed in Chapter 2), and stressful work conditions.

Independent of socioeconomic status and gender, age is also correlated with mental illness. Mental illness is more prevalent among adolescents and young adults, and most mental disorders first emerge during this time in life (Health Canada, 2002). Biological factors play a role in this pattern, as do psychological and social factors such as the struggles involved in identity formation during this time, the dramatic nature of the transitions that occur after graduating from high school, and the stresses associated with developing an "adult" role (e.g., deciding what type of education and career to pursue, becoming financially independent, and participating in the mate-selection process). The demands of university are particularly stressful, resulting in a higher prevalence of psychological distress among university students; for example, a survey of almost 8000 Canadian university students found that more than 30 percent reported significant levels of psychological distress (Adlaf, Gliksman, Demers, & Newton-Taylor, 2001).

Age, socioeconomic status, and gender are significant factors related to the prevalence and patterns of mental illness. But although certain types of mental illness are more prevalent in particular social groups, mental disorders can affect anyone. Some American research claims that half of the people in the United States will experience a psychological disorder at some point in their lives (Kessler et al., 1994). The resulting costs of mental illness are substantial.

The Costs of Mental Illness

Mental disorders have a considerable impact on both people's lives and the larger society. Research that emerges from the more objective end of the objective–subjective continuum shows us that having a mental disorder can contribute to a wide range of negative life outcomes. For example, having a mental disorder is associated with higher rates of teen pregnancy and early marriage and a greater risk of marital instability, all of which contribute to difficulties for the children being raised in those environments (Kessler, cited in Ettner, Frank, & Kessler, 1997). Children being raised by parents with mental illnesses are more likely to have problems in cognitive development as well (World Health Organization, 2001). Mental illness is also associated with lower levels of educational attainment, lower employment rates, and lower incomes. For example, each year individuals with mental disorders earn thousands of dollars less than those without mental disorders (Ettner, Frank, & Kessler, 1997). In addition, individuals with mental illnesses, along with their families, must bear direct and indirect financial costs (e.g., the costs of health care or the costs associated with unemployment) (World Health Organization, 2001).

Some mental illnesses are correlated with other physical ailments; for example, depression is related to a higher risk of heart disease. Furthermore, people with mental disorders are less likely to comply with medical instructions for other physical ailments, such as high blood pressure, diabetes, or cancer, resulting in poorer health overall and a greater likelihood of complications (World Health Organization, 2001). Finally, the emotional burden of living with a mental disorder creates a considerable challenge to all aspects of daily living and influences the quality of life overall.

Beyond the level of individuals and their families, insufficiently treated mental disorders also have a considerable impact on society. Five of the ten leading causes of disabilities in Canada are mental illnesses (Alberta Alliance on Mental Illness & Mental Health, 2003). Depression alone is the fourth leading global disease burden, and by 2020 it is projected to be the second leading global disease burden, behind only heart disease (Murray & Lopez, 1996; World Health Organization, 2001). National economies experience costs from mental illness because of premature deaths from suicide, absenteeism from work, lost productivity while at work, family members' absence from work to provide care, and more (Mental Health Commission of Canada, 2012a). Conservative estimates are that the economic costs of mental illness in Canada total $50 billion every year, which is 2.8 percent of the GDP. Almost one-third of short- and long-term disability claims among employed Canadians are the result of mental illness, and lost productivity and absenteeism from work alone results in economic losses of $6.3 billion per year (Mental Health Commission of Canada, 2012a).

The magnitude of these various impacts means that effective treatment of mental illness would benefit the individuals who have mental illnesses, their families, and society as a whole. The Mental Health Commission of Canada (2012a) reports that by reducing the incidence of mental illness by a mere 10 percent, within 10 years the Canadian economy would save $1.7 billion every year, and after 30 years those savings would be almost $5 billion per year; reducing remission rates by 10 percent would increase savings even further. However, in North America estimates are that only half, or even fewer, of those with mental disorders ever see health professionals (Sareen, Cox, Afifi, Yu, & Stein, 2005; Mosher, 2002; Health Canada, 2002). Worldwide, two-thirds of people who have mental disorders are never treated (World Health Organization, 2001) for a variety of reasons including lack of services (e.g., long waiting times), perceptions of treatment as inadequate, discomfort with the level of self-disclosure that accompanies diagnosis and treatment, perceptions of stigmatization, or neglect within their own families and communities (Sareen et al., 2005; Mosher, 2002; World Health Organization, 2001).

Coming from a more subjectivist perspective, Wolff (2007) suggests that cost-of-illness estimates should be viewed with some level of caution. First, she points out that these estimates "are not just a product of biochemistry; biochemistry interacts with economics and social norms" (p. 73). For example, if drug costs were lower, then the costs of mental disorder would be lower as well. Second, she points out that these estimates fail to take into account the many ways that individuals with mental disorders contribute to society as parents, neighbours, and volunteers. That is, cost-of-illness estimates themselves are, in part, reflective of the negative attitudes that surround mental illness. Overall, she argues that cost-of-illness estimates only take on social meaning when we look at "the ways in which we collectively view and treat people with mental illness" (p. 75).

Controlling Mental Disorder: Perceptions, Stigmatization, and Treatment

The reactions of other people are an integral part of the experience of having a mental disorder. As we have already seen, one of the main reasons that people with mental disorders do not seek assistance from health professionals is because of the presumed reactions of other people, as well as the general stigma that is associated with mental illness in our society. The *stigmatization of mental illness* constitutes one of the major dimensions of social control, and this will be the first aspect of social control that we will explore. The second major dimension of control, which we will explore later in the chapter, is embodied by the *medicalization of mental disorder*.

Stigmatization and Perceptions of Mental Illness

From the perspective of one individual with a mental disorder, having a mental illness is "sort of like having 'crazy bitch' stamped across my forehead and everybody treats you differently" (cited in Bassett, Lampe, & Lloyd, 1999). A half century ago researchers began identifying the prejudice and discrimination that people with mental disorders face (Scheff, 1966). Since that time attitudes have not significantly improved, and some researchers suggest they have even worsened (Bourget & Chenier, 2007; Sayce, 2000).

We have only to look at the media to see the way mental illness continues to be stigmatized. When mental illness is addressed in the media, it is portrayed in an exceedingly negative light and is typically associated with violent behaviour (Hannigan, 1999; Wahl, 1992; March, 1999). For example, one study found that 72 percent of those dramatic characters on prime-time television who were portrayed as having a mental illness were associated with violence or evil (Signorielli, cited in March, 1999). More recently, the 2012 movie *Silver Linings Playbook*, starring Bradley Cooper and Jennifer Lawrence, was criticized for its portrayal of mental illness (Fekete, 2012). In the movie, the male protagonist has bipolar disorder. Although the movie goes on to be a romantic comedy, the movie opens with the character being hospitalized in a forensic institution for having committed a violent crime—that is the audience's first view of mental illness. Negative portrayals of mental illness are pervasive even in children's media, including children's animated television programs, G and PG rated films, and popular movies such as the Harry Potter franchise. In children's media, people with mental disorders are portrayed as unattractive, aggressive, violent, criminal, and failures in life (Wahl, 2003).

This type of media imagery has a notable impact on people's own perceptions of mental illness. Granello, Pauley, and Carmichael (cited in March, 1999) found that one-third of undergraduate students they surveyed said the media is their primary source of information about mental illness and the number one influence on their own attitudes toward people with mental disorders. Given the biased portrayals of mental illness in the media and their impact, it is not surprising that public attitudes toward mental illness are negative as well.

Studies conducted in countries around the world have consistently found extreme prejudice against people with mental disorders. This prejudice manifests itself in social rejection and discrimination (Sayce, 2000; Wahl, 1999; Read & Harre, 2001). A Health Canada (2002) survey found that more than one-third of adult Canadians believe that others would think less of them if they had a mental disorder, such as depression or anxiety—and unfortunately they are right! People with mental disorders are perceived as being unpredictable, violent, dangerous, and uncontrollable (Dobson, 1996; Stip, Caron, &

Lane, 2001). As a consequence of these stereotypes, more than two-thirds of people surveyed express reservations about dating someone with a mental disorder or even living next door (Read & Harre, 2001). In Great Britain, 34 percent of people with mental illnesses say they have been fired or forced to resign. Almost half have been abused or harassed by strangers in public, and 14 percent have been physically attacked (Dobson, 1996).

These attitudes are not limited to uneducated or uninformed laypersons, but are also found within the medical community itself (Lawrie et al., 1998; Monahan, 1992). Approximately half of people with mental disorders say health professionals have treated them unfairly, particularly in dealing with the individual's physical complaints. When their own doctors fail to lend credence to their physical complaints—instead blaming those symptoms on the mental disorder—actual physical illnesses remain untreated, only to worsen and potentially threaten patients' lives.

Mental illness can even be stigmatized by some mental health professionals, who frequently admit that they try to avoid having to treat patients with more severe mental illnesses (Overton & Medina, 2008; Mental Health Commission of Canada, 2009; Read & Harre, 2001). Corrigan (cited in Overton & Medina, 2008) goes as far as to say that "most well-trained professionals subscribe to the same stereotypes about mental illness as the general public" (p. 146) and fall into an "us" versus "them" mindset that is conducive toward stigmatization (Martin & Johnston, 2007). Covarrubias and Han (2011) found that among students pursuing a master's degree in social work, stereotypes of people with serious mental illnesses are common, except among those who have had more personal social contacts in the form of friends with serious mental disorders. Mental health professionals may subscribe to even more stereotypes than others because they typically see their clients when symptoms are at their worst.

At a personal level, stigmatization has a negative impact on the quality of life of people with mental disorders. The sense of loneliness and isolation that accompanies social rejection can amplify psychological symptoms, actually making mental illnesses worse. Kroska and Harkness (2006) found that stigmatizing personal experiences are not even necessary for these types of negative consequences to occur. Simply being aware of negative social perceptions of mental illness lowers self-esteem and increases feelings of demoralization among those with mental disorders. This can contribute to **self-stigma** and consequences similar to those described by labelling theories (see Chapter 3); individuals internalize the label of "mentally ill" as well as its evaluative components (e.g., uncontrollable), becoming less likely to conform to treatment regimens or even to seek treatment. However, Markowitz, Angell, and Greenberg (2011) found that among people with schizophrenia, self-appraisals had a greater impact on symptoms, self-efficacy, and life satisfaction than did their mothers' appraisals of them. Whether through stigmatization by others or self-stigmatization, the effectiveness of treatments is hindered and recovery impeded (Overton & Medina, 2008; World Psychiatric Association, 2003; World Health Organization, 2002b).

These exceedingly negative perceptions of mental disorder contribute to discrimination in employment, health care, and housing (World Health Organization, 2001; Overton & Medina, 2008; Sayce, 2000). For those individuals residing in psychiatric institutions,

Despite the fact that mental illness is a leading cause of disability in the world, and hundreds of billions of dollars are lost each year as a result, mental health policies and programs are not perceived as priorities.

- 40% of countries have no mental health policy.
- 30% of countries have no mental health program.

- More than 33% of countries allocate less than 1% of their budgets to mental health.
- Another 33% of countries allocate 1% of their budgets to mental health.
- More than half of the countries in the world have only one psychiatrist for every 100 000 people.
- 40% of countries have less than one hospital bed reserved for mental health issues for every 10 000 people.

their experience in many countries includes poor living conditions, inadequate care, and harmful treatment. The stigmatization of mental illness in this way affects program and policy development as well; societies that are characterized by extremely negative attitudes toward mental disorder also tend not to rate mental illness as a policy or programming priority (World Health Organization, 2001, 2002b; March, 1999). Unfortunately, this is characteristic of most countries in the world (World Health Organization, 2002b) (see Box 8.1).

TIME TO REVIEW

Learning Objective 1

- What is "mental illness" and how many people have mental disorders?

- How do the prevalence and patterns of mental illness vary on the basis of gender, socioeconomic status, and age? What are the explanations for these variations?

Learning Objective 2

- What costs are associated with mental illness for individuals, their families, and society?

- How many people with mental disorders seek professional help and what prevents some people from doing so?

Learning Objective 3

- How is mental illness portrayed in the media and what perceptions of mental illness are found in the general population and among medical professionals?

- How does the stigmatization of mental disorders influence quality of life, discrimination, and mental health policies and programming?

The Medicalization of Mental Disorder

The medicalization of deviance has been addressed in previous chapters. For example, in the chapter on physical appearance (Chapter 7) we saw how medical science defines what deviant body sizes are, explains why those body sizes are deviant, and then provides social control measures to ameliorate those problems (e.g., prescriptions for diet pills, references to a nutritionist, or information about physical fitness). Similarly, mental disorders are also medicalized. Psychiatrists determine which thoughts or behaviours constitute mental illness and then incorporate that into the *DSM*. They explain that these particular thoughts and behaviours are deviant because they cause significant distress and impairments in daily functioning. Finally, they provide measures of social control—that is, treatments for mental disorders to improve quality of life and level of functioning. However, a historical analysis reveals that medical treatment to improve functioning has not always been the focus of social control measures.

The History of the Social Control of Mental Illness

Through much of Western history, the thoughts and behaviours that we now define as mental illness were instead seen as demonic possession, and the "treatment" was physical torture to drive out the demons. During the Middle Ages and early Renaissance, a refusal to conform to society's norms (even by those people who would now be considered to have mental disorders) was considered a sign of allegiance with the devil. As a result, people

© xunantunich/Fotolia

During the Middle Ages, people with mental illnesses were some of those convicted of witchcraft and burned at the stake.

were labelled "witch" or "heretic," put on trial, virtually always convicted, and put to death (e.g., by burning at the stake).

As religious explanations were replaced by scientific explanations, authorities no longer saw these non-normative behaviours as signs of possession or allegiance with the devil. Families and communities took care of those individuals who exhibited "strange" thoughts and behaviours. As the size of communities grew, prisons were built to house not only criminals but also the poor and people with mental illnesses (Grob, 1994). In the eighteenth century, "madhouses" were created specifically for those with mental illnesses. The purpose of these madhouses was not treatment or rehabilitation, but simply warehousing the disordered so that society's "normal" citizens could feel safe and secure (Rothman, 1971; McGovern, 1985). In the late nineteenth century, madhouses were replaced by "asylums" as some doctors proposed that, with appropriate treatment, people with mental illnesses could be trained to conform to society's norms. This is the era when the medicalization of mental illness came to predominate in Western cultures (Grob, 1994). These "asylums," later to be known as "mental hospitals" or "psychiatric institutions," continued to grow well into the 1950s.

The treatments for people with mental illnesses provided in psychiatric institutions included practices that many people now see as almost barbaric—lobotomies and fever therapies, for example (McGovern, 1985). The failure of these types of therapies to "cure" mental illness combined with social concerns about their harshness eventually led many of them to be abandoned. Broader concerns about the effectiveness of hospitalization itself began to take hold in the late 1950s as well. People began to wonder how removing individuals from their homes, from the support of their families, and from the semblance of normality that existed within their communities and instead placing them in institutions where they were dehumanized and isolated could possibly help in recovery from mental illness. These questions, along with new drug therapies that effectively controlled many forms of mental disorder, eventually led to **deinstitutionalization**—the social control of people with mental illnesses in community-based programs rather than in institutions.

Treating Mental Illness Today

The medicalization of mental disorders in contemporary society involves an extensive range of treatment options—psychotherapy, cognitive-behavioural therapy, medication, occupational therapy, and social supports. Treatment options today have become quite effective in improving functioning and the quality of life for individuals with mental disorders. Effective treatment helps 60 percent of people with depression fully recover and prevents relapses in 80 percent of people with schizophrenia (World Health Organization, 2001).

The combination of medical support (e.g., medications) and psychosocial support (e.g., therapy, community resources) is particularly effective for even the most severe mental illnesses (World Health Organization, 2002b). For example, without any treatment 55 percent of people whose schizophrenia goes into remission will have a relapse within one year. Among those who receive psychopharmaceutical treatment alone, 20 to 25 percent will relapse within one year. Of those who receive both psychopharmaceutical treatment and psychosocial supports for the family, only 2 to 23 percent will relapse within one year (World Health Organization, 2002b).

As a result of the deinstitutionalization movement, hospitalization is reserved for only the most severe cases of mental illness, and even then it is perceived as a short-term intervention that will form only one small part of the overall program of treatment. Hospitalization today is primarily voluntary in nature, with individuals themselves formally consenting to be hospitalized. Involuntary admissions to hospitals for psychiatric reasons are governed by the **"least restrictive alternative"**—legislation stating that involuntary admission can occur only if there are no reasonable noninstitutional alternatives (Krieg, 2001).

The Legacy of Deinstitutionalization. When the deinstitutionalization movement began in the early 1960s, it was perceived as an evolution in treatment that would bring nothing but benefits—to the individuals who would receive treatment in their own homes and communities, to society in terms of the higher rate of recovery, and to the government and taxpayers in terms of cost savings. Indeed, many of these benefits have been realized to some extent. Treatment in the community is generally more effective in the long term than treatment in institutions, and it is considerably less expensive (World Health Organization, 2002b). There is also no doubt that many people consider it to be more respectful, more humane, and less emotionally disturbing. In fact, most people with mental illnesses want to live in the community while receiving treatment, keeping their daily lives as "normal" as possible (Tanzman, 1993). However, deinstitutionalization has had its drawbacks as well. The *Ask Yourself* exercise begins to explore some of these drawbacks.

In the *Ask Yourself* exercise, perhaps you mentioned close families or friendship networks that can help provide necessary support or care. Deinstitutionalization did, in fact, emerge during an era when the image of the "ideal" family was everywhere. Popular television series such as *Leave It to Beaver*, *Father Knows Best*, and *Ozzie and Harriet* portrayed family life in a way that few people in reality ever experienced (Coontz, 1992). This type of popular imagery helped create the assumption that families were always caring, supportive, united, and happily willing to work together to overcome any difficulties. This was one of the key underlying assumptions of deinstitutionalization; that is, shifting the care of people with mental illnesses into the community was perceived as nonproblematic because it was assumed that they would have loving families to help them (Accordino, Porter, & Morse, 2001).

> ## Ask Yourself
> In order for people with mental illnesses to be successfully treated in the community rather than in institutions, what kinds of resources are necessary? That is, what might people with mental illnesses need if they are to successfully recover in their own homes and neighbourhoods?

Of course, many of us do not have that type of network of family relationships. Some of us are closer to our families than others are; some of us are able to depend on our families more than others are; some of us may have close marital relationships that are a source of support while others do not; furthermore, the experience of any type of serious illness contributes to the dissolution of many marriages. With all of these variations in family form and quality of family relationships, the assumption that there exists a social support network within the family for people with mental illnesses is a precarious one. Those people who have close support networks may do very well with community-based treatment, but those who are lacking such networks may not.

In your response to the last *Ask Yourself* question, you may have said that an accepting community that is free from stigmatization is necessary for successful community-based treatment. The prejudice and negative attitudes that pervade public perceptions of people with mental disorders have been addressed earlier in this chapter; stigmatization is a central obstacle to successful recovery and integration into the community (Accordino, Porter, & Morse, 2001). Although institutionalization was perceived as degrading to people with mental disorders, living in communities permeated with negative perceptions of mental illness and the resulting discrimination may be just as degrading to some individuals (Krieg, 2001).

Perhaps you listed adequately funded community resources as necessary for successful noninstitutional treatment for people with mental disorders. In fact, this is one of the biggest problems worldwide that has plagued the deinstitutionalization movement (World Health Organization, 2002b). Although the intent was quite different, the reduction in hospital-based service was accompanied by insufficient increases in community-based resources. This was because of the negative social perceptions of mental illness (that make related programs and policies difficult for politicians to "sell" to voters), a lack of adequate health care funding overall, and the prioritizing of other areas of government spending (World Health Organization, 2002b; Krieg, 2001). The nature of available resources is also dependent on community size. Individuals living in large urban centres have more community mental health resources available to them than do those living in rural areas. People with mental disorders who live in rural areas have a particularly difficult time with recovery and are more likely to experience negative outcomes, including participation in and victimization by criminal behaviour (Sullivan, Jackson, & Spritzer, 1996).

You may have mentioned that in order for people to have a successful recovery in their own homes, they actually need their own homes— that is, somewhere to live. Simply having a place to live can be a considerable challenge for some people with mental disorders, especially when we consider insufficient community resources and the stigmatization that inhibits integration within communities. As a result of discrimination or the symptoms of their disorders, some are unable to find employment or housing and may become dependent on family or friendship support networks. If those networks are lacking, and the resulting stresses exacerbate the illness, possible outcomes include alcohol or drug abuse (Davidson, Hoge, Godleski, Rakfeldt, & Griffith, 1996) and a failure to take medication prescribed for the illness. The end result can be homelessness. It is estimated that in North America, between 25 and 50 percent of the homeless population are mentally ill (Mental Health Commission of Canada, 2008; Krieg, 2001). Research done by various organizations in Toronto finds that between 11 and 30 percent of the homeless there have serious psychotic disorders like schizophrenia (Valpy, 1998).

The deinstitutionalization movement has benefited many people, but others have fallen through the cracks of the mental health care system.

Homelessness adds one more dimension to the social typing process that individuals must experience: not only do they face the consequences of being socially typed as mentally ill, they also must face the consequences of being socially typed as homeless. Homeless people with mental disorders who also have substance abuse problems face the additional predicament that some community resources are designed to deal with either substance abuse or mental illness, but not both. That is, some organizations help only the homeless mentally ill (and do not address substance abuse problems), while other organizations are able to help homeless people with substance abuse problems (but are not equipped to deal with those with mental illnesses). Recently, a growing number of communities have piloted new projects based on the principle of "housing first"—placing individuals in safe and comfortable housing to begin with, and then building specific treatment programs to address mental illness and addiction. One of the first of these programs, a five-year $110 million project known as "At Home," housed almost 1000 people with mental illnesses in several cities across Canada and provided them with mental health support (McIlroy, 2012).

The costs of community-based treatment are usually described as being lower than the costs of hospital-based treatment. However, when a significant number of people fall through the cracks of the community mental health system, other costs accompany deinstitutionalization. The costs associated with reducing homelessness are compounded by the social and economic losses emerging from higher suicide rates among individuals with untreated mental illnesses, more accidents, and a greater number of untreated physical illnesses (Krieg, 2001). The symptoms of some mental disorders, difficulties in finding employment or housing, and the emotional consequences of stigmatization lead some individuals into crime (Krieg, 2001; Sullivan, Jackson, & Spritzer, 1996; Accordino, Porter, & Morse, 2001), adding another layer of costs to society.

The rate of criminal activity among people with major mental disorders is considerably higher than among those without mental disorders (Hodgins, 1993). A study at Toronto's Don Jail found that during an 18-month period, 469 of the admissions (1 in 12) involved individuals with major mental disorders, and approximately 70 percent of criminals with major mental illnesses had multiple jail admissions (Valpy, 1998). American estimates suggest that 16 percent of the prison population has a mental disorder (Wolff, 2007). In the five mental health treatment facilities operated within the criminal justice system in Canada, 700 beds are available; this stands in stark contrast to the 1500 inmates across Canada who require daily care for serious mental disorders (Bailey & Bronskill, 2007).

As with homelessness, criminality adds a second dimension to the social typing process for some individuals with mental disorders. They face the consequences of not only being socially typed as mentally ill, but also of being socially typed as criminals. Problems with mental health programming emerge in some communities, in that community resources that help people with mental illnesses may not help those with criminal records, and resources that help former criminals may not be equipped to deal with the mentally ill. Consequently, "the streets and prisons [have become] the asylums of the 21st century" (Bailey & Bronskill, 2007).

More than a half century ago, Penrose (1939) proposed that a *hydraulic* relationship exists between the mental health care system and the criminal justice system: when one contracts the other expands. Wolff (2007) argues that this is precisely what occurred when deinstitutionalization was not accompanied by sufficient community resources—the mental health care system contracted and the prison population expanded. Conversely, expanding the extent and nature of resources within the mental health care system should reduce the prison population.

The emphasis placed on deinstitutionalization by governments in North America and Western Europe over the past few decades has resulted in another problem—the reduction in hospital services for those people who may benefit from such services. For example, in the 1950s Ontario had 40 beds for the mentally ill for every 10 000 people; by 1995 that number had been reduced to five beds for every 10 000 people. In comparison, in 1995 Britain had 7.4 beds for the mentally ill for every 10 000 people, Spain had 1.7, and the Middle East had 1.4 (Valpy, 1998). The World Health Organization (2002b) reports that 40 percent of countries in the world have less than one hospital bed for the mentally ill for every 10 000 people. Despite the best of intentions on the part of its exponents and the positive outcomes for millions of people with mental disorders, deinstitutionalization has also had unintended negative consequences for millions of people worldwide.

More recently, research looking at changes in the number of service spots (e.g., treatment beds) in several European countries suggests that a "new era of reinstitutionalization" (Priebe et al., 2005, p. 124) has begun. Just as the emergence of a *risk society* has had consequences for the social control of youth (risk management strategies are addressed in Chapter 6), reinstitutionalization stems from a concern with *risk containment*—reducing the risks for individuals who may have fallen through the cracks with deinstitutionalization, but also reducing the *perceived* risks for a society characterized by negative perceptions of the mentally ill.

The Deviance Dance: Resisting Stigmatization, Inadequate Care, and Psychiatry Itself

Mental disorders are socially typed as deviant at many different levels. Seen as "crazy" and "dangerous" by the general public, people with mental illnesses face stigmatization in everyday interactions and discrimination in employment, housing, and medical care. To add to this burden, sometimes the treatments offered for these conditions fail to give the mentally ill control over their own lives.

It is true that once diagnosed with particular mental disorders according to the *DSM*, individuals have a wide range of treatments available to them. The nature of these treatments has changed and expanded over time, making possible the deinstitutionalization movement that began in the 1960s. The move toward community-based treatment has benefited many and is the preferred form of treatment among people with mental disorders. However, it has also had a number of unintended negative consequences for people who happen to fall through the cracks of the community mental health system. Such consequences include homelessness, criminality, suicide, substance abuse, and a lower quality of life. Individuals and groups in society are, therefore, engaging in resistance against both stigmatization and inadequate treatment, trying to change the nature of the social typing process.

The policies and programs addressing treatment and support available to people with mental disorders arise from the **disease paradigm** of mental illness, which emphasizes ameliorating symptoms that distress and impair individuals' functioning. Other policies and programs emerge out of the **discrimination paradigm** of mental illness, which emphasizes the role that stigmatization plays in the daily experiences of people with mental illnesses. These programs and policies constitute part of the "deviance dance"—that is, people resisting and fighting back against the inadequate treatment of mental illness and the social rejection or discrimination faced by individuals with mental disorders.

Resisting Stigmatization

People with mental illnesses may use a number of stigma management techniques to deal with their spoiled identities (see Chapter 3). Some may **try to pass** by hiding their disorders. Some may **divide their social worlds**, carefully managing who is and is not permitted to know about their illnesses. However, others more actively resist the imposition of stereotypes about mental illness. Two such techniques are **deflecting** and **challenging** (Thoits, 2011).

Efforts at deflecting block the stigmatizing external force. Through a variety of means, individuals are able to distance themselves from the label of mentally ill. Individuals may draw upon the public, mass-mediated images of people with mental illnesses as dangerous and overtly "crazy," emphasizing how they personally bear no resemblance to those images. They may emphasize that their disorder is only one small part of their lives, so that their identities are not based solely on the disorder. Some individuals reframe the label, stating that they do not have a "mental illness," but rather are just tired, or need to work things out, or had a temporary breakdown.

In contrast to deflecting, efforts at challenging more actively fight back against the external stigmatizing force. Sometimes this involves directly confronting people who stigmatize them or who express a stigmatization of mental illness more generally. At other times, challenging is less about confrontation, and more about educating others when those situations arise. Challenging can also take on a more personal form, where the individual overcompensates for stigmatization, trying to show themselves as being extra competent compared to the average person (Thoits, 2011).

Under what conditions will people with mental disorders actively resist stigmatization rather than try to pass or divide their social worlds? Thoits (2011) finds that five factors are associated with active resistance: past experience with stigma resistance (such as in response to racial or gender discrimination); past familiarity with mental illness in a friend or family member; greater coping resources, such as high self-esteem and a strong support network; holding and identifying with multiple roles in daily life; and less severe, more time-limited mental illnesses.

At the government level, many nations have instituted legislation and policies prohibiting discrimination against people with mental disorders in housing, employment, health care, and more. Some policies target persons with mental illnesses specifically. In other cases, people with mental illnesses are included under broader human rights legislation. For example, the Canadian Charter of Rights and Freedoms guarantees equality and prohibits discrimination on (among other things) the basis of mental and physical disability. At an international level, the Universal Declaration of Human Rights has a similar declaration. Provincial human rights codes also integrate similar policies.

The medical community is also involved in trying to reduce negative attitudes toward mental illness. For example, Alberta's "My Mental Health" campaign was created to eliminate misconceptions about mental illness to reduce stigmatization and increase people's attention to their own mental health (including their willingness to seek out services). The World Psychiatric Association coordinates an international program ("Open the Doors") to reduce the stigma of schizophrenia in many countries, including China, Egypt, Greece, and India. The World Health Organization (WHO) devoted 2001's World Health Day to mental health, emphasizing issues of prejudice and discrimination. Reducing the stigma associated with mental illness is one of the dimensions of their Mental Health

Global Action Programme (mhGAP), whereby they will coordinate advocacy efforts in member states to educate the public about mental illness and protect or promote patient rights (World Health Organization, 2002b).

Self-help groups for people with mental illnesses can be found in many countries as well. One of their mandates is acting to reduce the stigmatization of mental disorders through education, communication, and media information. For example, the Canadian Mental Health Association sponsors an annual Mental Health Week that is intended to dispel myths and reduce stereotypes. These types of groups also provide information about legislation, updates of mental health-related court cases, and materials to assist persons with mental illnesses in employment, housing, parenting, and more.

Not only do governments, the medical community, and self-help or advocacy groups act to reduce the stigma associated with mental illness, they are also involved in the resistance to inadequate care for individuals with mental illnesses.

Resisting Inadequate and Insufficient Care

In addition to providing public awareness to reduce stigmatization, self-help groups are also involved in lobbying governments for better funding and improved services for people with mental disorders, as well as providing information to mental health consumers about the nature and appropriateness of the resources that are available to them. Support groups for specific mental disorders (e.g., depression and schizophrenia) provide detailed information about new medications that are available, the effectiveness of specific types of treatments, and research about potential negative side effects of different medications and treatments.

The medical community, of course, is continually engaged in research on new and improved treatments for different disorders. They also monitor the professional behaviours of their members and negatively sanction those who do not provide appropriate care to patients. For example, professional associations of psychiatrists or psychologists provide ethical guidelines to their members, governing appropriate and inappropriate behaviours when counselling clients. On an international level, groups like the World Health Organization integrate their anti-stigmatization efforts with efforts to increase government funding for mental health and improve the training of mental health professionals. Their Mental Health Global Action Programme's mission is to "support Member States to enhance their capacity to reduce risk, stigma, and burden of mental disorders and to promote the mental health of the population" (2002b, p. 11). To this end, their approach includes four core strategies (see Figure 8.1).

As one of the WHO's member states, within Canada the Standing Senate Committee on Social Affairs, Science, and Technology subsequently analyzed the status of mental health services, releasing its final report (*Out of the Shadows at Last*) in 2006. One of its recommendations was that a Mental Health Commission of Canada (MHCC) be created (and funded) by the federal government to move forward on the fact that Canada was the only G8 nation to lack a national mental health policy. The foci of the MHCC are

Figure 8.1 Strategies of the World Health Organization's Mental Health Global Action Programme

Based on World Health Organization (2002b). *Mental Health Global Action Programme.* Geneva, Switzerland.

(1) an anti-stigma campaign, (2) a program to reduce homelessness, (3) a knowledge exchange centre, and (4) a mental health strategy. Extensive consultation with researchers, service providers, individuals affected by mental illness, and the general public serves as the foundation for the MHCC's work. A series of open consultations was held across Canada to inform the creation of a national mental health strategy, based on a foundation of eight goals. Arising from those consultations, Canada's Mental Health Strategy was developed and shared with the public in 2012; that strategy will now inform the development of policies, programs, and research initiatives throughout the country. The strategy is composed of six strategic directions (see Box 8.2) (Mental Health Commission of Canada, 2012b).

Individuals and groups who are involved in reducing the stigmatization of mental illness and ameliorating the problems of insufficient and inadequate care are trying to change aspects of the social typing process. Groups involved in the former efforts are working toward removing the label of "crazy," the evaluation of persons with mental illnesses as "dangerous" and "unlikable," and reducing the social rejection and discrimination that result. Groups involved in the latter efforts are trying to improve the ways that persons

Canada's Mental Health Strategy

The Mental Health Strategy for Canada is the country's first. Released by the Mental Health Commission of Canada in 2012, it has six strategic directions:

■ Promote mental health across the lifespan in homes, schools, and workplaces, and prevent mental illness and suicide wherever possible.

■ Foster recovery and well-being for people of all ages living with mental health problems and illnesses, and uphold their rights.

■ Provide access to the right combination of services, treatments, and supports when and where people need them.

■ Reduce disparities in risk factors and access to mental health services, and strengthen the response to the needs of diverse communities and Northerners.

■ Work with First Nations, Inuit, and Métis to address their mental health needs, acknowledging their distinct circumstances, rights, and cultures.

■ Mobilize leadership, improve knowledge, and foster collaboration at all levels.

Source: Mental Health Commission of Canada (2012). *Changing Directions, Changing Lives: The Mental Health Strategy for Canada: Executive Summary.* Calgary, AB: Author.

with mental disorders are treated in the mental health system—ensuring that enough of a priority is placed on mental health, that there are sufficient resources available, that harmful or ineffective treatments are stopped, and that more effective treatments are instituted.

However, resistance to stigmatization and to inadequate treatment is not the only way the "deviance dance" is evident in the realm of mental illness. Some people resist the medicalization of mental disorders overall, and even question the very notion of mental illness.

Resisting Medicalization

Resistance to the medicalization of mental disorders can occur at a number of levels, from criticisms of the *DSM* to criticisms of the daily practices of mental health professionals to questions about whether "mental illness" even exists.

Criticizing the *DSM*

Since its first edition, the *DSM* has been subject to some criticism. Much of the criticism has been based on the inclusion of particular disorders in the *DSM*. For example, homosexuality was included in the *DSM* from 1952 until its removal in 1973—it was first classified as a "sociopathic personality disorder" and then as a form of "non-psychotic sexual deviance." Factors contributing to its removal from the *DSM* included research demonstrating that homosexuality was not pathological and was not related to pathological outcomes, as well as the activism of gay and lesbian rights' groups (see Chapter 5).

More recently, controversy has emerged over the diagnostic category of attention deficit hyperactivity disorder (ADHD). Most experts agree that this is a disorder that affects people's lives by interfering with their abilities to concentrate on tasks, follow instructions, and sit still in situations that require it. However, critics argue that in North America, far too many children are being diagnosed. In Britain, where different diagnostic criteria are used and different attitudes prevail, a significantly smaller proportion of children are diagnosed with this disorder (McConnell, 1997). One concern is that normal childhood restlessness and inattention is being diagnosed as a mental disorder.

Another concern is that behavioural or attention problems that are actually being caused by social forces (e.g., family conflicts) are being diagnosed as mental disorders, while the true cause of the problems remain untreated (McConnell, 1997; Shute, 2000). Furthermore, some social analysts suggest that the inability to focus or pay attention is a logical outcome for children growing up in a society in which the adults pride themselves on "busy-ness" and multitasking, and where being "stressed out" is seen by many as a sign of how important you are. All of these concerns reached a climax in 2000, when a class action lawsuit was launched against the American Psychiatric Association and the pharmaceutical company that manufactured the first drug for ADHD (Ritalin) for constructing a nonexistent mental illness. The lawsuit was later dismissed (Shute, 2000; Peck, 2001).

While some critics of the medicalization of mental disorder focus their disapproval on the inclusion of specific categories of disorder within the DSM, other critics express concerns over the DSM itself and the power it holds. Caplan (1995) points out that when some research claims half of Americans experience a mental disorder at least once in their lives, it suggests that what is considered to be a "mental disorder" has escalated to ridiculous proportions. Critics of the DSM not only point to methodological shortcomings in its creation, but also to the role played by power (and economics) in determining what is and is not included in the list of mental disorders. This has led some critics to suggest that the DSM is just as much a political document as a medical document (e.g., Armstrong, 1993).

Despite its shortcomings, there is considerable agreement that the DSM does capture many diagnostically useful sets of symptoms that *are* distressful to the people that experience them and that *do* impair effective daily functioning. Furthermore, there is a sizable overlap in the psychiatric diagnostic categories contained in the DSM and in the *International Classification of Diseases* (ICD) used by the World Health Organization. However, even those social analysts and health professionals who acknowledge the validity of the DSM recognize that problematic patterns in its usage and in other practices of mental health professionals can occur. Research finds that variables other than medical ones may influence the diagnoses and treatments for mental disorders.

Being Sane in Insane Places: Criticizing Mental Health Professionals

Rosenhan (1973) was one of the early mental health professionals who documented the influence of social factors and other biases on psychiatric diagnoses. His influential study stirred tremendous controversy in the mental health community, but also motivated considerable changes in the mental health system. Rosenhan began with the question, "If sanity and insanity exist, how shall we know them?" That is, his fundamental question was whether the sane can be distinguished from the insane—whether the salient characteristics leading to diagnosis lie within the individual or in the environment. The medical view is that people present themselves with symptoms, which are then recognized by professionals as constituting a diagnosis, leading to treatment. As a parallel, people who present themselves with certain other characteristics may also be told by professionals that those are not symptoms of any mental disorder.

Rosenhan had eight research associates (including students, homemakers, and a psychiatrist) attempt to have themselves admitted to psychiatric hospitals. These "pseudo-patients" presented themselves to mental health admissions people at 12 different hospitals, claiming that they had been hearing voices for the past few weeks that were saying "empty," "hollow," and "thud." Rosenhan's underlying assumption was that if their sanity was not detected, it would indicate that the salient characteristics involved in psychiatric diagnosis reside more in the environment than within the individual. All of these research associates were admitted to hospitals with diagnoses of schizophrenia.

Once they were admitted, they were to begin acting normally, report that the voices had stopped, and try to get discharged. In interactions with the mental health professionals, they were to be truthful about the characteristics of their lives (with the exception that those in mental health professions would allege another occupation to avoid special treatment)—their relationships with family members, their life histories, their frustrations and joys in life. As patients, they were completely cooperative with staff, doing everything they were told to do (although they did surreptitiously flush their medication down the toilets). In the end, the pseudo-patients spent between 7 and 52 days hospitalized prior to being discharged, with the average stay being 19 days. The psychiatrists at the hospitals never detected the pseudo-patients' sanity; they were discharged with diagnoses of "schizophrenia in remission," suggesting that their mental illness was still there, but simply dormant for the present moment.

The lack of detection was not because they were not acting "sane" enough. They received daily visitors, who were to look for any potential abnormal behavioural consequences resulting from hospitalization, but the visitors detected no abnormal behaviours. Furthermore, in many cases *other patients* detected the sanity of the pseudo-patients, saying things like, "You're not crazy" or "You must be a journalist or professor checking up on the hospital." Inside the hospitals, the mentally ill label that they had received affected the nature of all of their interactions with staff.

Normal behaviours were overlooked or misinterpreted through the lens of the diagnosis of mental illness. For example, although the pseudo-patients initially tried to hide their note-taking (for fear of being detected), it quickly became apparent that note-taking was seen as a *sign* of their mental disorder. As boredom set in and mealtime became a highlight of the day, waiting in the hallway for the cafeteria doors to be opened was described as indicative of the "oral-acquisitive nature" of schizophrenia. In a session with a psychiatrist, one male pseudo-patient spoke of how, as a little boy, he was closer to his mother, but as he progressed through adolescence he became closer to his father and more distant from his mother; psychiatric notes described this as "considerable ambivalence in relationships." When he described his marriage as generally positive with just occasional arguments, the case notes identified those occasional conflicts as "angry outbursts."

Of course, one factor that might contribute to misdiagnosis is the desire of mental health professionals to err on the side of caution. It may be safer to mistakenly label a healthy person as ill than to mistakenly label an ill person as healthy and not provide them with the treatment they need. Rosenhan suggested that this desire to err on the side of caution can explain misdiagnosis at the initial time of admission, but is less able to account for continued misdiagnosis after a lengthy period of observation and analysis.

So, why *did* the misdiagnosis continue all the way until the time of discharge? One reason could be the lack of interaction between the mental health professionals and the patients. Nursing attendants, nurses, and even the psychiatrists actively avoided contact with the pseudo-patients. When the pseudo-patients intercepted staff members to ask them simple questions, the psychiatrists averted their eyes and walked away 71 percent of the time, as did 88 percent of the nurses and nursing attendants. Another reason, one emphasized by Rosenhan, is the power that a diagnosis of mental illness carries. He concluded that the initial "schizophrenic" label given upon admission to the hospitals provided staff with a **schema**, or mental framework, that affected their interpretations of the pseudo-patients' behaviours—*all* behaviours then came to be interpreted as indicative of pathology. In contrast, those very same behaviours exhibited by someone who had not been diagnosed as mentally ill would not be perceived as indicative of pathology. What was Rosenhan's conclusion? The salient characteristics in the diagnosis of mental illness lie more within the social context, or the environment, than within the individual.

As you can imagine, the results of this research project caused quite a stir in the psychiatric community. An outcry from psychiatric hospitals throughout the United States claimed that something like that could certainly never happen at their hospitals, suggesting that the hospitals used in Rosenhan's study must have been poorly run. Rosenhan therefore created a follow-up study to look into this possibility.

Rosenhan selected a well-known and very well-respected teaching hospital. He told administrators that within the next three months, at least one pseudo-patient would attempt to be admitted as a psychiatric patient. Hospital staff, including the psychiatrists, were asked to rate each person admitted during that time as to the likelihood that this was one of the pseudo-patients. During that period of time, a total of 191 psychiatric patients were admitted to this hospital. Of these patients, the hospital staff identified 41 as having a high likelihood of being pseudo-patients. At least one psychiatrist identified as many as 23 patients, and both a psychiatrist and at least one additional staff member identified 19 patients as being likely pseudo-patients.

How many pseudo-patients had Rosenhan actually sent in? None. Rosenhan concluded that even mental health professionals have difficulties distinguishing the sane from the insane.

Rosenhan's research seemed to present a resounding critique of the efficacy of mental health professions. First, by illustrating that people without mental disorders could be kept in hospitals and not have their "sanity" detected, it raised significant concerns about those patients who had been committed to psychiatric hospitals involuntarily. It was possible that some of these patients, being kept against their wills, did not have any mental disorder. These types of concerns stimulated governments throughout the Western world to create or intensify legislation governing involuntary psychiatric admissions. In Canada, all provinces have mental health legislation that outlines the conditions under which individuals can and cannot be admitted for psychiatric care against their wills and sets procedural safeguards in place for reviewing such cases at regular periods following admission. Within the government, many provinces have a Mental Health/Psychiatric Patient Advocate Office whose role is to advise involuntarily committed patients and their families of their rights in such situations.

Second, Rosenhan's research described the dehumanizing treatment that patients in psychiatric hospitals frequently faced, such as being ignored by staff when asking a question, being prescribed large numbers of pills (altogether, the eight pseudo-patients in the first study were given a total of 2100 pills during their hospital stays), and being mistreated in many other ways. For example, in one instance a nurse unbuttoned her shirt to adjust her bra right in front of a group of male patients. It was not a teasing or sexual demonstration, but rather reflected her view that it was no big deal because these were "mental patients" rather than "real" men. These observations reinforced Goffman's (1961) argument that psychiatric hospitals were *total institutions*, similar to prisons and concentration camps, wherein "inmates" had no choice but to accept restriction and dehumanization; their identities were dismantled and new "inmate" identities created, identities that would be carried into the community following release from the institution. Although Goffman's sociological work of more than a decade earlier had pointed to some of the negative implications of treatment within an institutional setting, Rosenhan's empirical documentation of dehumanization raised greater awareness, contributing to changes in the practices in psychiatric hospitals and the growth of mental health advocacy groups.

Third, Rosenhan's research had, and continues to have, broader theoretical implications. Rosenhan's first study illustrates important aspects of labelling theories, which emphasize the influence that labels have on the way people are subsequently treated. In particular, it reflects the assumption that labels have negative consequences by closing the doors of acceptance within the "normal" world. However, even though Rosenhan's research is reflective of the negative consequences of labels, stigmatization can have potentially positive consequences as well (see Chapter 3). Several decades later, debates over whether stigmatization on the basis of mental health has positive or negative effects continue. One perspective points to the harmful effects that stigmatization has on the self-concept, which has implications for treatment outcomes and the magnitude of symptoms.

Opponents in this deviance dance bring attention to the fact that stigmatization can improve self-concept, in that being labelled is the key factor in opportunities for effective treatment, which improves well-being. It may be that receiving a formal label of mental illness enables the individual to be assigned a **sick role**. Parsons (1951) claimed that although illness was dysfunctional for society in general, under certain conditions people with illnesses could be assigned a role that would accord them certain rights; but along with those rights came certain responsibilities. A person who has been assigned a sick role is given a temporary reprieve from some of life's responsibilities and is not blamed for their condition, but is rather given sympathy. However, that person must clearly be trying to get well, must seek professional help, and must adhere to the physician's treatment plan. Consequently, having received a formal label can be considered indicative of seeking professional help and attempting to get well.

Perry (2011) found that being labelled as mentally ill has a positive impact on people with more severe, rather than less severe, mental disorders. For these individuals, being formally labelled results in larger, more functional support networks for the individual. Why might labelling have a more positive impact on people with more severe mental illnesses? More severe psychiatric symptoms may be more overt, resulting in others placing less blame on them for their behaviours; milder symptoms may be more subtle to outside observers, such that others may wonder why the individual cannot simply "snap out of it." In fact, De Maio (2010) suggests that not everyone who is ill will be assigned a sick role. The process is dependent, in part, on the severity of the illness.

Finally, Rosenhan's research pointed to the unintentional influence of social factors on diagnostic processes. Considering the awareness stimulated by Rosenhan's research, one might think that, since that time, the influence of social factors in diagnosis has declined. Is this the case?

The Role of Social Factors in Diagnosis and Treatment

Given the way that social factors permeate every aspect of our daily lives and the subsequent influence they have over our thoughts, feelings, and behaviours, it should not be too surprising that social factors continue to have the potential to influence diagnosis and treatment. Loring and Powell (1988) presented psychiatrists with case summaries after manipulating the sex (male or female) and race (black or white) in the cases. They found that sex and race both influenced the diagnoses and other aspects of the psychiatrists' perceptions of the individuals contained in the case summaries. For example, black individuals in the case summaries were more likely to be described as "dangerous" and "suspicious" than were white individuals, even when everything in the case summary (other than the race of the individual) was identical.

Ask Yourself
Why do you think race and sex might influence the diagnosis and treatment of mental disorders?

Other research has found that women are more likely to be diagnosed with depression than men are, even when they present the same symptoms (Stoppe, Sandholzer, & Huppertz, 1999). However, there is some debate over the influence of sex on diagnosis, as some other studies have not detected this pattern (Gater, Tnasella, Korten, Mavreas, & Olatawura, 1998). Despite the continued debate about whether there are sex differences in diagnosis, the evidence is quite clear that there are sex differences in treatment—women are far more likely to be prescribed psychotropic drugs (Simoni-Wastila, 2000).

When you thought about your answer to the *Ask Yourself* exercise, you may have referred to something like stereotypes—assumptions about what people of different races and genders are like or should be like. Because of prejudicial attitudes that continue to pervade society, blacks and whites are perceived in different ways. So are men and women. Indeed, researchers working in the various critical theories that were explored in Chapter 3 (e.g., feminist theories) explain these research results in precisely those terms (Loring & Powell, 1988; Simoni-Wastila, 2000).

Thus far, we have looked at resistance to the medicalization of mental disorder in three different ways. One form of resistance emphasizes the ways that some normal social behaviours have been deviantized within the *DSM*. A second form of resistance launches broader critiques against the *DSM*, showing us the political dimension of the document. The third form of resistance focuses on some of the inaccuracies and biases that occur in the daily practices of mental health professionals, revealing the power of the labelling process and the influence of social factors on diagnosis and treatment.

There is one last form of resistance to the medicalization of mental illness that moves to a much broader, more abstract level, criticizing the concept of "mental illness" itself as being a false label that denies free will (Szasz, 1994). Thomas Szasz (a psychiatrist himself) acknowledges that there are physical diseases of the brain, but argues that virtually none of the disorders listed in the *DSM* have been proven to be physical diseases of the brain. Instead, people use the diagnostic categories of the *DSM* to involuntarily treat people who do not want treatment and to enable others to avoid responsibility for criminal acts. Szasz's arguments have stimulated controversy since the 1950s and continue to stimulate controversy today.

However, most people agree that mental disorders *do* exist, and that some people with mental disorders do not have everything they need to successfully recover or achieve a high quality of functioning in daily life. The continued stigmatization of mental illness is one of the central obstacles to recovery and high functioning, and even influences the extent and quality of policies and programs available. Governments, the medical community, and self-help/advocacy groups continue to work toward improving the lives of people with mental disorders—reducing the stigma and increasing the available resources. At another level, people are bringing to the forefront the political nature of the process by which diagnostic categories are created and the social factors that can influence or bias diagnosis and treatment.

Learning Objective 3

■ How has the social control of mental illness changed throughout Western history?

■ What are the necessary prerequisites for deinstitutionalization to be successful, and why has reinsitutionalization emerged?

■ What role does mental illness play in homelessness and in crime?

Learning Objective 4

■ What types of policies and programs emerge from the *discrimination* and *disease paradigms*?

Learning Objective 5

■ What criticisms have been directed at the *DSM*?

Learning Objective 6

■ What happened in Rosenhan's two studies and what were his conclusions?

■ What were the implications of Rosenhan's research?

■ What influence do sex and race have on the diagnosis and treatment of mental disorders and why?

■ What are Thomas Szasz's criticisms of the medicalization of mental illness?

CHAPTER SUMMARY

■ *Mental illness* refers to thoughts, moods, and behaviours that cause significant distress or impaired functioning for individuals. The nature of these impairments is further delineated in the diagnostic categories listed in the American Psychiatric Association's *Diagnostic and Statistical Manual of Mental Disorders* (DSM). (1)

■ The estimates of the proportion of people who experience mental illness at some point in their lifetime range from 20 to 50 percent. Some social groups face higher risks for mental illness than others. Women and men show equivalent overall rates—but different patterns—of mental disorder. People in low socioeconomic status groups show higher rates of mental illness, as do adolescents and young adults. (1)

■ Considerable costs are associated with mental illness for the individuals experiencing the illness, their families, and society as a whole. (2)

■ Negative perceptions of people with mental disorders are found in media representations, attitudes of the general public, and even attitudes of health professionals. These negative attitudes hinder recovery of people with mental disorders, contribute to discrimination in many areas, and result in mental health programs and policies not being seen as priorities. (3)

- Although mental illness has been treated in various ways throughout history, in the late nineteenth century it became *medicalized*. Over the last several decades, the *deinstitutionalization* movement has helped millions of individuals with mental disorders; however, there have also been unintended negative consequences. More recently, *reinstitutionalization* has emerged. (3)

- Mental health policies and programs are embedded within two different paradigms: the *disease paradigm* and the *discrimination paradigm*. The first paradigm emphasizes the role of symptoms of the disorders themselves in people's experience of mental illness. The second paradigm emphasizes the role of stigmatization and prejudice in people's experience of mental illness. (4)

- The medicalization of mental disorder is being resisted and changed in a number of different ways. Critics express concerns about the diagnostic handbook, the *DSM*, for (1) the inclusion of some normal behaviours as "disorders," such as homosexuality and ADHD, and (2) the political nature of the process by which disorders are included in the *DSM* and the subsequent power the handbook has. (5)

- Other people have raised questions about mental health professionals themselves. Rosenhan's classic study concluded that the salient characteristics in diagnosis lie more within the social context than in the individual. Decades later, researchers continue to find that social factors have an impact on psychiatric diagnosis and treatment. Thomas Szasz (1994) takes his criticisms of psychiatry the furthest, suggesting that mental illness is a "myth." (6)

MySearchLab®

👁‍[Watch] Go to MySearchLab to listen to the audio clip called "Rift from Father's Sex Change Healed".

Apply What You Know: Consider the fact that transgendered individuals have commonly had to cope with being labelled mentally ill. What does this story tell us about the importance of treating those labelled mentally ill with respect? What do you think is the best way to show respect for those labelled mentally ill?

MySearchLab with eText offers you access to an online interactive version of the text, extensive help with your writing and research projects, and provides round-the-clock access to credible and reliable source material.

Chapter 9

What Do You Believe? Religion, Science, and Deviance

© bbbar/Fotolia

Learning Objectives

After reading this chapter, you should be able to

1   Identify the two types of relationships that exist between belief systems and deviance.

2   Describe the traditional typology that helps determine which religions are "deviant," and explain why sects and cults are considered "deviant."

3   Describe the different levels of social control that are directed at "deviant" religions and the ways that deviant labels are resisted.

4   Explain how religion served as a social typer of deviance in the cases of the witch persecutions, residential schooling, and the child-savers movement.

5   Describe the origins, causes, and control of scientific misconduct.

6   Explain why a science's location on the deviant science–real science continuum may change over time.

7   Describe why science is a powerful social typer of deviance and how that power has manifested itself through history.

Scientist J. B. S. Haldane (1927) suggested that "the wise man regulates his conduct by the theories of both religion and science. But he regards these theories not as stringent statements of ultimate fact but as art forms." This quotation indicates that both religious and scientific belief systems are vital parts of our daily lives. It also suggests that these belief systems can serve social control functions, and if we are wise we will act on the basis of religion and science. In the quote, Haldane also points to the subjectivity of religious and scientific belief systems. Although these belief systems proclaim truths, they emerge through processes of social construction or creation, just as art does.

Anything that you personally think is true represents one of your **beliefs**, regardless of whether it is actually true or not. Some of your beliefs might be entirely unique to you, while in other cases a group of people might accept the same truths that you do. And frequently, single beliefs are combined with other interrelated beliefs into organized sets of **belief systems** (Stebbins, 1996). Religious doctrines (e.g., Christian, Islamic), the knowledge contained in particular disciplines of science (e.g., astronomy, zoology), and the ideologies of specific political parties (e.g., Liberals, New Democrats) are all belief systems that are shared among large groups of people.

There are two different types of relationships between belief systems and deviance. First, we can look at belief systems *as* deviance, when acts of deviance occur within groups of people who adhere to particular belief systems, or when an entire belief system itself is socially typed as deviant. Second, we can explore belief systems as social typers of deviance, wherein the truths proclaimed by belief systems dictate to us who should be considered deviant and what the consequences should or will be. Both religion and science have these two types of relationships with deviance.

Religion

Sociological analyses of religion explore the social embeddedness of religious belief systems—the processes by which religious belief systems emerge, the role that religion plays in people's lives, and the relationships between religion and other social structures or processes.

The *Ask Yourself* questions on the following page lead you to make the transition from thinking about religion as a belief system to thinking about religion as a social organization that holds a particular place in the community and in the larger society. If you are like

81 percent of Canadians, you have religious beliefs (Clark & Schellenberg, 2006) but you do not necessarily attend a church, temple, mosque, or synagogue on a weekly basis. In fact, attendance at organized religious services declined from 78 to 66 percent between 1985 and 2005 (Lindsay, 2008). If you do regularly attend a place of worship, you will be aware that it holds a particular role in the community in terms of the way it is perceived by other members of the community and the activities it may engage in within the community. Your religious belief system may be disparaged by others, that is, considered to be "deviant." Conversely, your religious belief system may provide you with a moral code that defines certain others as being "deviant."

Religion as Deviance: "Deviant" Religions

When considering religion and deviance, many of you may initially think of abuses carried out by representatives of different religions, such as instances of child sexual abuse by religious leaders and allegations that churches tried to cover up those incidents. In addition to deviant acts carried out by religious institutions or representatives of those institutions, talking about **religion as deviance** also brings to mind those religious groups that are thought of as deviant in their entirety.

Which religions are considered deviant and which are considered normal? Traditionally, religious belief systems were categorized using various typologies based on characteristics of the particular group in question. A religious group's location in the typology determined whether it was considered deviant. More recently, these traditional typologies have been questioned and even abandoned by some researchers, resulting in quite a different view of "deviant religions."

Deviant Religions According to Traditional Typologies

Different scholars have proposed various typologies of religious groups (McGuire, 1997; Stark & Bainbridge, 1996), but a review of these frameworks reveals that four categories of religious groups are common. Deviance is determined by which category a religious group is assigned to.

Ecclesia refers to state religions: a specific religious belief system is adopted at a governmental level and becomes a nation's "official" religion. Islam is an ecclesia in Iran, as is the Anglican denomination of Christianity in England and the Lutheran denomination of Christianity in Sweden. The extent to which other religions are practised in these countries depends on the nation in question. Some nations identify an ecclesia and yet declare freedom of religion for their citizens (e.g., England); in other cases, noneccleseiastic religions are banned (e.g., Europe during the Middle Ages).

Churches are not "official" religions of an entire society, but they are large and powerful religious groups. The religious groups commonly perceived as being the world's major religions—Islam, Judaism, Hinduism, Buddhism, Sikhism, and Christianity—are categorized as *churches*. They are well established in society, highly bureaucratized (having complex hierarchies of leadership and administration, as well as formalized rituals and practices), and have millions of members around the world. The largest religious groups in the world are Christianity (33 percent of the world's population), Islam (21 percent) and Hinduism (14 percent); by 2025 it is estimated that Christianity and Islam will reverse their rankings (Adherents.com, 2007; Ontario Consultants on Religious Tolerance, 2003). Churches are further subdivided into **denominations**, such that there are different types of Christianity (e.g., Catholicism), Islam (e.g., Sunni), and Judaism (e.g., Orthodox). The same can be said of all of the other churches of the world. In Canada, the predominant religious denomination is Roman Catholicism, practised by 43 percent of Canadians who have a religious affiliation (Clark & Schellenberg, 2006).

Sects are smaller religious groups that have usually broken away from larger churches at some point in their history. They are less established in society than churches, have fewer members, more rigid doctrine formed in reaction to the doctrine of the larger church, and require higher levels of commitment from their members (e.g., clothing, behaviour, and food). The Amish and the Hutterites are examples of sects that are offshoots of the larger Christian church, while the Taliban is a sect that has broken away from mainstream Islam.

Cults are usually smaller than sects, frequently having only a handful of members. Their doctrine is even more reactionary and oppositional, and intense levels of commitment are required of members. A single, charismatic leader serves as a source of inspiration,

© Somatuscani/Fotolia

The Amish are a Christian-based sect who reject modern technology and live in communal settings.

convincing followers that the secret to salvation can be found in that group. Examples are the Branch Davidians, Heaven's Gate, and The Family of Love.

This framework has traditionally been used as the foundation for decisions about whether a particular religious group is deviant. Ecclesia, which declare an entire nation's citizens as members (at least on a theoretical level), are not considered deviant in those societies. Of course, there may be some groups in those societies that do attempt to deviantize that religion as part of the "deviance dance." Churches, with millions of members worldwide and their high level of integration in many societies, are also perceived as normal or conventional religions, although members of one church may attempt to deviantize members of another church. For example, the "deviance dance" between the Christian church and the Islamic church was responsible, in part, for the Crusades—a series of battles lasting from the eleventh century to the sixteenth century.

Sects and cults—which have fewer members, are more isolated from mainstream society, and have doctrine that is more reactionary or oppositional—are the religious groups that are traditionally seen as deviant and in need of social control. In other words, those religious groups that are characterized by high levels of tension with the broader society are perceived as deviant, while those that are characterized by low levels of tension are seen as normal (Stark & Bainbridge, 1996).

The "Deviant" World of Sects and Cults

Although both sects and cults are perceived as deviant, thereby existing in a state of tension with wider society, the deviance of cults is of a greater magnitude than that of sects. Cults are based on novel beliefs, while sects tend to have more traditional belief systems as their foundation, creating some differences in the level of tension that exists with society and the level of social control exerted on the religious groups (Stark & Bainbridge, 1996).

Sects. High levels of commitment are required of members of sects, and their beliefs and life habits are strictly controlled. Members who fail to think or act in accordance with the belief system are punished, and in some sects the most extreme punishment is excommunication from the group (Wilson, 1993; McGuire, 1997; Stark & Bainbridge, 1996).

Although the levels of commitment required of members and the levels of control exerted over members' lives are higher in sects than in churches, there is considerable diversity among sects in these characteristics—that is, some sects have more rigid requirements than others. Similarly, the degree of tension between sects and the wider society also varies. Such tension is fundamental to the social control of sects within society. The level of tension experienced by a particular sect is determined by three factors: (1) the magnitude of the differences between the sect and society; (2) the level of antagonism that the sect feels for society; and (3) the extent to which the sect separates itself from the larger world (Stark & Bainbridge, 1996). Lawson (1995) illustrates this variation by comparing two sects—Seventh-day Adventists and Jehovah's Witnesses. Both sects had similar origins in the seventeenth century, were inspired by apocalyptic visions, and both can now be found in countries around the world. However, since their inception they have followed different trajectories, such that Jehovah's Witnesses experience significantly higher levels of tension with their surrounding societies than do Seventh-day Adventists.

Greater degrees of difference, antagonism, and separation have characterized Jehovah's Witnesses since their inception. They have persistently held to their original apocalyptic vision, although they have had to repeatedly revise their projected dates for the coming apocalypse (past failed dates have caused a drop in membership because of loss of faith). Members face rigid requirements for continued membership, such as attendance at meetings each week, reaching targets for hours spent witnessing (i.e., going door to door in an attempt to draw converts), and following behavioural guidelines (e.g., prohibitions against blood transfusions). Such requirements make the daily lives of members considerably distinct from those who are not a part of that religious group. Their belief system, as reflected in their publications, is antagonistic to other religious groups, the government, and patriotic symbols. Antagonisms toward governments and patriotic symbols in particular have placed them on the receiving end of hostilities during conflicts like the American Civil War, World War I, and World War II.

Because of their beliefs about the wider society, members of the Jehovah's Witnesses live in considerable isolation from it, other than witnessing and participating in the labour force. Labour force participation may be limited, because members are discouraged from pursuing higher education, and jobs are considered secondary to witnessing. When members violate the behavioural requirements of membership, they may be excommunicated from the group, and remaining members are directed to shun them in public. The resulting magnitude of tension has resulted in significant persecution in many countries. Members of the Jehovah's Witnesses have been physically attacked by mobs, arrested, and even put to death for refusing to fight during wartime.

In contrast, Seventh-day Adventists have undergone substantial change over time, which contributes to less tension with the larger society. The belief in a coming apocalypse remains, but it no longer holds the central position that it used to. High levels of commitment are required of members, including not eating certain foods and not consuming certain substances. However, the requirements for membership have relaxed over time as antagonisms and the separation from wider society have declined.

Early in their history, this sect's leaders determined that compromise was necessary to avoid conflicts with the wider society. The sect created schools, universities, businesses, hospitals, and institutions for the elderly in the early twentieth century to "claim an increasing stake in society" (Lawson, 1995, p. 375). Although members are encouraged to use these Seventh-day Adventist resources instead of those outside of the sect, the boundaries with the outside world are permeable. Higher education is common, which has also indirectly contributed to more relaxed requirements and greater diversity of thought among members, further enhancing integration with the wider society. Members of this sect have faced persecution in several countries in the world (e.g., for refusing to fight during wartime). However, the extent of their persecution has been less than that faced by Jehovah's Witnesses.

As a result of the different trajectories the two groups have followed, they are categorized differently. Seventh-day Adventists are frequently labelled a **denominational sect**, suggesting they are verging on being considered a conventional Christian denomination. Jehovah's Witnesses are considered an **established sect** because of the tension that continues to exist with the societies in which they reside.

Seventh-day Adventists and Jehovah's Witnesses are just two of the thousands of sects that exist throughout the world. Because of the similarities in their origins, contrasting these two sects is particularly useful in demonstrating the diversity that exists among sects, as well as the varying degrees of tension between different sects and the larger society. The belief systems and practices of the sects themselves contribute to that level of tension; however, the tension is not solely the result of characteristics of the sects. It is also a product of characteristics of the wider society, such as public attitudes toward the sects and how authorities interact with them. Tension between a sect and society is bidirectional in that a sect may have certain levels of antagonism toward society, but society may have certain levels of antagonism toward a particular sect. Furthermore, existing hostilities in society toward specific religious groups may cause a sect's belief system to become more polarized. When a deviantized group becomes more extreme as a response to hostilities or social control efforts from outsiders, it is referred to as **deviancy amplification** (Becker, 1963).

Although the tensions between different sects and the sociocultural environment vary, some degree of tension must exist for a religious group to be considered a sect rather than a church. Tension is also characteristic of the types of religious groups known as cults. When looking at cults, the tensions with the wider society are typically of an even greater magnitude, especially in the realm of public attitudes. Simply mentioning the word "cult" fuels a flood of images in most people's minds.

Ask Yourself

When you think of cults, what images or ideas come to mind? Who do you see as belonging to cults? What do you imagine their leaders to be like? What actions are carried out within the cults you are thinking about?

Cults. Your thoughts about cults likely draw heavily on the media, particularly news stories about specific cults. When cults are covered in the media, it is usually because of some sensationalistic incident, such as the mass suicides of the Peoples Temple in Guyana in 1978, or the storming of the Branch Davidians' compound in Waco, Texas, by the American government in 1993. These are the kinds of cults typically represented in the media—doomsday suicide cults and cults that engage in various criminal activities.

Wright (1997) explains that the selective coverage of cults arises from (1) a lack of accurate knowledge about cults and the groups in question; (2) the use of biased sources of information (e.g., ex-members of cults rather than social scientists who conduct research on cults); and (3) limited time or financial resources, causing a tendency to over-report sensationalistic stories in the beginning but then ignore later developments. Sensationalist language, used to attract an audience, frequently disparages cult members. For example, after the Heaven's Gate mass suicide in 1997, news stories referred to the leader as "loony" and "crazy," while headlines screamed, "UFO Wackos Blasted Off with Vodka and Pills" (Hoffman & Burke, 1997, p. 63). More than 2000 different cults exist in the United States alone, and of these only a handful have been involved with violence—but each of those received extensive media coverage (Bromley & Melton, 2002). The thousands of other cults in the world—those whose members lead quiet, noncriminal lives—never reach public attention to influence our images of what cults are like (Jenkins, 2000; Wright, 1997).

Consequently, public perceptions are that cults are dangerous to members, to other individuals, and to society (Melton & Bromley, 2002). In the public mind, cults are associated with mind control, violence, mental illness, sexual deviance, and sexual abuse of children. Many people believe that cults carry out mind control using secretive techniques unique to cults, and that as a result cult members may behave uncharacteristically during altered mental states when they are incapable of rational thought (Anthony & Robbins, 1994).

© Eiji Hori/AP Photo/Canadian Press Images

In 1995, 12 people were killed and thousands injured when members of Aum Shinrikyô, a Japanese cult with Christian and Buddhist foundations, released sarin nerve gas in the Tokyo subway. Incidents like this one strongly influence public perceptions about cults.

Violence is commonly perceived as pervasive in cults (Melton & Bromley, 2002), either internally, such as with mass suicides, or externally with acts of mass violence.

The public concerns that emerge from popular images of cults are not entirely unfounded. Behaviours that violate cultural norms do occur in some cults, such as The Family of Love (see Box 9.1) (Lewis & Melton, 1994; Kent, 1994; Bainbridge, 2002). Violence can emerge when beliefs become more polarized, especially when latent tensions between those groups and societal authorities intensify (Bromley, 2002; Hall, 2002). In some groups, the leaders are able to effectively influence members' thoughts (Stark & Bainbridge, 1996) such that members are willing to engage in mass suicide.

Box 9.1

The Family of Love

The Family of Love, formerly known as the Children of God (and now calling itself "The Family") is a group that has been a target of attention for cult watchers for more than 40 years. Its founder, David "Moses" Berg, brought together a group of young hippies in the 1960s based on his revelation from God that he would be the prophet who would play a key role in the second coming of Jesus Christ. Members fully devoted themselves to the group by abandoning all ties with their families, giving up personal possessions, and evangelizing. Although they first lived in several communes across the United States, a revelation that the nation would be destroyed for its impurity led Berg to disperse members throughout the world. There, they continued their attempts to recruit new converts.

Controversy surrounded many of Berg's teachings, such as his concept of flirty fishing. Because Jesus was called a "fisher of men," Berg claimed that the women in the group should also be "fishers of men," seducing and offering sexual favours to men to convert them. Sexual sharing was another component of Berg's doctrine—

sex was to be freely shared among group members, except between two men. Whether sex was freely shared between adults and children is debated. Analyses of the group's newsletters, as well as testimony from former members, point to pedophilia. However, criminal investigations in many countries have not been able to prove these allegations in court; some civil suits have been successful.

In 1987, Berg declared an official prohibition on adult–child sex and decreed that offenders would be excommunicated. Flirty fishing has also been eliminated because of the danger of sexually transmitted diseases. However, some researchers suggest that these practices have only been removed from official documentation to prevent further investigation by authorities, and that the practices continue (e.g., Kent, 1994). Although Berg died in 1994, The Family is alive and well, claiming more than 12 000 members worldwide. They present musical performances at youth shelters and women's shelters free of charge, and bring humanitarian efforts after natural disasters and in developing countries.

Although there is some foundation to the popular images of cults, such as mass sui-cide, violence, mind control, child abuse, and sexual deviance, these qualities are charac-teristic of only a small proportion of the thousands of groups in the world that are considered "cults." Cults, like sects, are characterized by diversity in beliefs and practices, as well as the level of overt tension that exists with society. However, popular images of cults and the resulting public attitudes contribute to more overriding tensions for cults. For both cults and sects, these tensions are played out in the "deviance dance"—the vari-ous means of social control of these deviant religions and the corresponding resistance to those means of control.

TIME TO REVIEW

Learning Objective 1
- What are beliefs and belief systems?
- What are the two ways that deviance can be explored within the context of belief systems?

Learning Objective 2
- What typology has traditionally been used to categorize religious groups, and which groups are socially typed as deviant?

- What factors influence the level of tension between sects and the larger society, and how do these factors vary for Seventh-day Adventists and Jehovah's Witnesses?
- What are cults typically associated with in the public mind?
- Where do these images of cults come from, and are they accurate?
- When is violence more likely to emerge in cults and why?

Cults, Sects, and the "Deviance Dance"

Controlling "Deviant" Religions. The international community has repeatedly declared the importance of religious freedom. Many people see it as the foundation for all human rights. The United Nations Universal Declaration of Human Rights, created in 1948 and signed by more than 100 countries around the world, states that freedom of thought, conscience, and religious belief and practice are fundamental human rights. However, this right is not unbridled. Threats to public health, public order, and infringement on the rights of others constitute valid reasons for governments to violate religious freedom, according to human rights documents themselves. These caveats to freedom of religion serve as the basis for the various measures of social control that target sects and cults.

During the twentieth century, a number of social organizations emerged in response to the perceived problems caused by "deviant" religions. Acting as moral entrepreneurs, they apply measures in their efforts to control "deviant" religions. In particular, during the late 1960s and early 1970s, the **anti-cult movement** materialized (Jenkins, 2000; Bromley

& Shupe, 1993; Shupe & Bromley, 1995). Initially, it consisted of parents whose hippie children had joined new religious groups that were part of the broader countercultural movement. Concerned because their children had severed ties with their families, and fearful that their children would be brainwashed into deviant behaviours, parents coalesced into support groups.

Media stories about violent activities carried out by some of these cults, such as the infamous Tate–LaBianca murders committed by members of the Manson "family" in 1969, seemed to validate their concerns. These support groups later became information networks to make other parents aware of the dangers of these new religious groups. Over time, numerous mental health, legal, and political professionals, along with academic researchers, became involved in anti-cult groups.

Anti-cult groups today, or what Barker (2001) calls **cult awareness groups**, educate people about the dangers of some cults and attempt to control their activities by lobbying governments and other organizations. The anti-cult movement targets only certain religious groups—those considered to be "destructive cults." In fact, the word "cult" is used in this movement to refer specifically to those religious groups that have dangerous or destructive characteristics, as summarized in Box 9.2 (Lalich & Langone, 2006; Fight Against Coercive Tactics Network, 2003; Ontario Consultants on Religious Tolerance, 2003).

Although the anti-cult movement is a relatively recent construction, the **counter-cult movement** is noticeably older, going back more than a century (Bromley & Shupe, 1993; Ontario Consultants on Religious Tolerance, 2003; Cowan, 2001; Melton, 2000;

Box 9.2

Characteristics of Destructive Cults

Although there is some disagreement over precisely what the characteristics of "dangerous" cults are, there are some common warning signs pointed out by various organizations:

- The leader places the group above the law, telling members they are not bound by the same laws as outsiders.

- The leader does not have to follow the same rules as the other members.

- The leader exerts control beyond the realm of religious doctrine, extending control to members' personal lives, education, jobs, or finances.

- "Mind control" techniques are used on members to facilitate indoctrination.

- The group follows a formal or informal policy of deceiving outsiders when recruiting, fundraising, or answering to authorities.

- The group is based on an apocalyptic vision in which the group will play a key role. For example, the group may stockpile weapons to prepare for battle with the outside world when Armageddon arrives.

Barker, 2001). Unlike the anti-cult movement, this movement does not base its philosophy on internationally recognized legitimate limits to religious freedom discussed earlier. In fact, members of the counter-cult movement are overwhelmingly opposed to religious freedom itself. These groups primarily consist of conservative Christians drawn from fundamentalist denominations. They are not concerned about the possibility of brainwashing or abuse in cults, but instead express a theological concern about groups using the "wrong" interpretation of the Bible. Any religious group that does not follow fundamentalist, evangelical Christian doctrine is labelled a cult. Thus, not only are the groups that are commonly categorized as sects or cults targets of the counter-cult movement's control efforts, so are mainstream Christian religions (e.g., Catholicism) and all Eastern religions (e.g., Hinduism, Islam, Buddhism). Franklin Graham (son of the well-known evangelist Billy Graham) referred to Islam as a "wicked and evil" religion, Jerry Vines (former president of the Southern Baptist Convention) called Islam's prophet Muhammad "a demon-possessed pedophile" (Goodstein, 2003), and Pat Robertson blamed poverty in nations like India and Bangladesh on the "demonic cults" of Islam, Buddhism, and Hinduism (Vuijst, 1995).

Counter-cult groups engage in measures to eliminate "deviant" religions in a larger attempt to recruit converts to their own religious groups, including lobbying governments and law enforcement officials to enforce the law harshly against target religions. However, due to some of the negative perceptions that fundamentalist Christian religious groups themselves face in society, their lobbying efforts are not as successful as those of the secular anti-cult movement. Consequently, the counter-cult movement tends to operate on a less formal level inside communities. It also makes extensive use of the Internet to spread its version of the "truth" about deviant religions (Dawson & Henneby, 1999).

In addition to the Internet, the media is fundamental to many of the efforts of both anti-cult and counter-cult groups. The relationship between these groups and the media is bidirectional. At times, groups may use the media as a tool for enhancing their control efforts, but the media may also draw upon the "expertise" of members of these groups when covering news stories that may involve cults (Jenkins, 2000; Crouch & Damphousse, 1992; Bartowski, 1998).

Independent of the anti-cult and counter-cult movements, the media has its own representations of "deviant" religions. The underlying profit motive of the media, with its corresponding need to attract audiences, contributes to distorted and sensationalized coverage of news incidents involving cults or sects (Wright, 1997). The role of the media in the creation of moral panics has been analyzed in the context of the Satanic scare of the 1980s (deYoung, 1998; Jenkins, 2000; Crouch & Damphousse, 1992), the standoff between the Branch Davidians and federal authorities in Waco (Shupe & Hadden, 1996), and the deviantizing of voodoo (Bartowski, 1998).

In addition to having a relationship with the media, anti-cult and counter-cult groups influence governments to create legislation, policies, and programs that will curb the destructive nature of "deviant" religions. When governments do enact legislation or alternative forms of policy, they often do so under the rubric of threats to public health, public order, and the rights of others (Forum 18, 2001; US Department of State, 2010).

Determining at what point governmental measures of control can be enacted without violating the right to religious freedom is an especially grey area in those nations that declare an official separation of church and state.

Thus, in many Western nations, efforts are directed at those religious groups commonly recognized as sects and cults. For example, the Canadian Security Intelligence Service (CSIS) monitors doomsday and apocalyptic cults, those cults whose members may commit mass suicide or inflict mass harm. In the United States, the FBI does the same thing. The actions of some nations, however, are not without controversy. In the late 1990s, the government of France formed the Interministerial Mission in the Fight Against Sects/Cults (MILS) to monitor and control the 173 groups identified as sects or cults in a 1996 government report—groups like the Church of Scientology, Jehovah's Witnesses, Latter-day Saints (Mormons), and doomsday cults. After certain groups were forced to disband and members of other groups were arrested for violating pieces of the new legislation, the European Court of Human Rights overturned many convictions on appeal.

Concerns about violations of religious freedom at the hands of government are of considerable interest to the international community. The US Department of State releases an annual report that documents violations of religious freedom in specific countries and the measures being taken to improve religious freedom in other countries (US Department of State, 2010).

Resisting a Deviant Label.   Anti-cult groups, counter-cult groups, media, and governments all act as social control agents in minimizing the perceived dangers of "deviant" religions. However, their efforts are counteracted to some extent by acts of resistance. The right to religious freedom is an international concept that serves as a nexus for many of these measures of resistance, but the social typing of "deviant" religions is resisted in numerous other ways as well.

Individual religious groups defend themselves against accusations of deviance both inside and outside of court. For example, individuals and groups targeted for control under France's new anti-sect laws have taken their cases all the way to the highest European Court of Human Rights and have frequently won (US Department of State, 2010). During the Waco standoff between the Branch Davidians and federal authorities, Seventh-day Adventists hired public relations people to make it clear to the public that the Branch Davidians were a "cult" that had distorted Seventh-day Adventist teachings and were in no way representative of the larger group (Lawson, 1995). The Family of Love not only defended itself in court cases and child custody hearings against allegations of sexual abuse, it also (1) changed its publications to remove any portions that might be perceived as indicating approval of pedophilia, (2) issued a statement declaring sexual relations between adults and children in the group to be forbidden, and (3) tried to improve the group's image by using its website to highlight humanitarian efforts within the community (Lewis & Melton, 1994; Kent, 1994; Bainbridge, 2002).

One of the most significant forms of resistance to the social typing of "deviant" religious groups comes not from the groups themselves but from academia. The traditional distinction among ecclesia, churches, sects, and cults was used for most of the twentieth century. The distinctions among these different types of religious groups were not questioned, although debates would sometimes emerge about how a specific religion should be categorized. However, as time passed, questions about these distinctions were raised and criticisms grew. Ecclesia were easily recognized in that official state religions are identified in legislation. By contrast, with continued discussion it became evident that the boundaries between churches, sects, and cults may not be as definitive as they seem.

What Are "Deviant" Religions? The Traditional Distinction Reconsidered. As you have read through this chapter thus far, you might have already begun to feel somewhat confused about what religions are actually deviant. We began with academic definitions of cults and sects, but as the chapter progressed we saw that different kinds of religious groups were labelled in this way at various times. The anti-cult movement prefaces the term "cult" with the descriptor "destructive," identifying as cults only those groups that have certain characteristics, such as mind control.

The counter-cult movement uses the term "cult" to refer to the theology of certain religious groups, those which do not adhere to fundamentalist Christian doctrine. We also saw that when media use the word "cult," they usually do so in the context of a distorted image of cults—those religious groups involved in destructive events captured in the news. Finally, we saw that in an international context, any religious groups that a particular government does not approve of are categorized as cults.

The boundaries between churches, sects, and cults become blurred even further when we incorporate a historical perspective. All of the world's major religions, now categorized as churches, began as cults—small groups of highly committed members who followed a single charismatic leader and whose doctrine was oppositional to a society's conventional belief system at the time (Jenkins, 2000; Hadden & Bromley, 1995). As these religious groups became more established, attracted larger numbers of members, and became integrated in a society's power structure, they progressed to being churches.

Even when we temporarily set aside the debates over which groups are cults or sects, the notion of *religion as deviance* crosses all boundaries. Every religious belief system in the world has been considered deviant at some time, in some place. There is no group of religious believers that has not at some moment in history been persecuted or perceived as evil, dangerous, or a threat to the social order. This is evident in looking at the former Soviet Union, where *all* religion was at one time prohibited, but is also apparent when looking at historical events such as the Crusades, the Israel/Palestine conflicts, and the bloodshed between Protestants and Catholics in Europe over hundreds of years.

For all of these reasons, many contemporary academics have abandoned the traditional terminology of ecclesia, churches, denominations, cults, and sects and instead use more encompassing terms, such as "ideological groups." Some scholars distinguish the world's major religions from more recent religious groups by using the term **new religious movements** (Chryssides, 1994; Jenkins, 2000). Although some scholars find the traditional typology valid and, for various reasons, continue to use it, a historical and global perspective shows us that *any* religion can be socially typed as "deviant" and made subject to measures of social control.

TIME TO REVIEW

Learning Objective 3

- In what ways do the anti-cult movement and the counter-cult movement differ in terms of who their members are, which religious groups they target, and their ideologies?

- What is religious freedom and what are its exceptions?

- In what ways have "deviant" religious groups themselves acted in resistance to social typing?

- What limitations are there in the traditional typology that distinguishes between churches, sects, and cults?

Religion as a Social Typer of Deviance

While various religions have been socially typed as deviant at different times and in different places, religious belief systems also play a role in the social typing *of* deviance. That is, their proclamations of truth incorporate moral truths as well, dictums of what is right and wrong. At the individual level, the religious belief systems we adhere to present us with guidelines for our own behaviour, dictate how we should evaluate the behaviours of others, and influence the way we interact with people. For example, adolescents who attend organized religious services are less likely to be sexually active, have stronger relationships with their parents, are more committed to school, and have less permissive attitudes about alcohol use, criminal behaviour, marijuana use, and hard drug use (Good & Willoughby, 2006).

Beyond the individual level, religious belief systems also serve as social typers of deviance at the societal level. This is of particular interest when the boundaries between religious and political belief systems become blurred; that is, when a particular religious belief system becomes institutionalized by the government and serves as the foundation for the construction of governmental policy and law. Those people and behaviours considered deviant according to religious beliefs thereby become the people and behaviours considered deviant at the political level.

Religion and Politics in History

The Witch Persecutions.　From the fourteenth through the seventeenth centuries, the Christian church was essentially the core of government in Europe. It either served as the main governing body itself or acted in a key advisory capacity for governing bodies in most of Europe. Thus, its belief system was the foundation for law and governance. It was in this

Its belief system established as "law," the Christian church was central to the persecution of witches from the fourteenth to the seventeenth centuries.

capacity that the "witch craze" occurred (Anderson & Gordon, 1978; Barstow, 1994; Quaife, 1987).

It is estimated that during this time, between 40 000 and 100 000 "witches" were persecuted, sometimes by being burned at the stake. One of the best-known victims was Joan of Arc, who was convicted of witchcraft and burned at the stake in 1431. Witches were declared to be in league with Satan and responsible for plagues, floods, stillborn babies, infertility, crop failures, and any other unfortunate events in families or communities.

Those accused of witchcraft included a wide range of people, the list growing longer as the witch craze snowballed—followers of the pre-Christian religions, women who were financially independent or who outlived their husbands, midwives who used herbs and other natural techniques to ease the pain of childbirth, village "wise women" who used herbs in healing illness and injury, and peasants. The majority of people prosecuted as witches were women; however, there were considerable regional variations (e.g., in Iceland, 90 percent of the accused were male) (Briggs, 1996). At the peak of the witch craze (1550–1650), just about anyone could be accused of witchcraft.

Once arrested, torture was used to elicit confessions. The torture was so horrendous (e.g., having one's toenails pulled out or being stretched on the rack) that many people did confess. The content of their confessions was virtually guaranteed, given that a handbook (the *Malleus Maleficarum*) had been written in 1486 about how to question and torture witches. The nature of the questions asked typically led to specific types of responses, and torture would progress until that point. Upon being found guilty, the witch was put to death via hanging, decapitation, burning at the stake, or other means. With the invention of the printing press, church documents about the "witch problem" flooded the educated classes. Various witch-hunting manuals, church sermons, and pamphlets made people aware of the extent of the problem, frequently exaggerating the magnitude of persecution to gain more support and strike more fear into the populace.

The witch craze was not a uniform phenomenon. Witch trials occurred more often in some countries than in others, ranging from 26 000 deaths in Germany to four deaths in Ireland (Briggs, 1996). Ben-Yehuda (1980) explains that following the Protestant Reformation, persecutions flourished in the regions of Europe where the Catholic church had weakened (e.g., Germany), while they were rare in those countries where Catholicism continued to hold its traditional power (e.g., Italy); however, both the Catholic and Protestant churches participated in the persecutions, each using the trials to demonstrate their religious dominance.

In some regions, the church was directly responsible for the arrest and trial of witches, while in other regions it was local authorities that searched for and tried them. In these latter instances, even though the church was not directly involved, church doctrine provided the theological foundation for persecution. In some regions, local authorities steered the witch trials, while in other regions it was national authorities. Capital punishment was virtually guaranteed in the former, while in the latter it was possible to hold onto one's life by turning in fellow witches to the authorities. Witch persecutions frequently followed peasant rebellions against the political elite or preceded them in an attempt to distract peasants from rebellion. As Quaife (1987, p. 208) concludes, the witch hunts were the result "of either the godly zeal of the political and religious elite and their peasant allies or the furious rage of her discomforted and ill-fortuned neighbours." As political change progressed, as Christian doctrine was transformed, and as philosophical and scientific ideas grew, the witch hunts faded away. But for those few hundred years, religious belief systems were the foundation of political belief systems, with the end result in this particular instance being the loss of up to 100 000 lives.

Residential Schooling. Following the colonization of North America, European colonizing governments began to establish a long list of laws and policies designed to assimilate Aboriginal people. An integral part of the assimilation process was "Christianizing" natives (Miller, 1996; Milloy, 1999; Fournier & Crey, 1998). Every aspect of Aboriginal culture was perceived as deviant and in need of elimination.

Efforts on this front began when, upon settlement, Christian missionaries were among the first Europeans sent to North America. At a later point, laws prohibiting various Aboriginal spiritual practices were enacted, and spiritual leaders faced up to 30 years in prison for violating some of these laws. In 1879, the Canadian government adopted a **residential schooling** policy that it hoped would guarantee assimilation. Aboriginal children were removed from their homes and families and taken to residential boarding schools where they would be given an education—not only in reading, writing, and arithmetic, but also in Christianity and learning to act "white." Taking children from their homes would remove the cultural influence of their communities and facilitate assimilation. Residential schools were a part of government policy and were funded by the government but were operated by Christian churches. Residential schooling occurred for more than a century, beginning in 1879; the last residential school closed in 1996. Approximately 150 000 children went through these schools.

Parental consent was not necessary, because legislation made all Aboriginals wards of the state. Communities that refused to have their children taken were threatened with the loss of government resources and even arrest. In many of the schools, children received formal teaching for only half of the day. For the remainder of the day, they engaged in physical labour on school grounds or nearby farms. Even more important than education in reading, writing, and math was education in Euro-Canadian beliefs and practices.

Behaviours related to traditional Aboriginal spirituality and culture were prohibited, and children were punished if caught engaging in these behaviours. What was perceived as being normal punishment in that environment, however, is now considered physical abuse. Furthermore, thousands of children were sexually abused in some of these schools. Of the 150 000 children who went to residential schools, 91 000 have reported being physically or sexually abused. The psychological abuse the children experienced is too great to even be estimated. Many children went years without being able to see their parents; some never saw their parents alive again. On a daily basis, many children were told that their parents, having not found God, would burn in hell for eternity—as would they if they did not do as they were told.

In the 1990s, government and religious authorities acknowledged the damage caused by the residential schooling initiative, recognizing the high rates of substance abuse, suicide, and family violence as well as the loss of traditional cultures. The United Church of Canada, Anglican Church of Canada, and Presbyterian Church of Canada have all issued formal apologies to the Aboriginal people of Canada. The Roman Catholic Church (via the Pope) has also apologized for the ethnic and racial injustices inflicted on some groups in the world by members of the Catholic Church, though they have not mentioned residential schools specifically, and their apology is directed to God rather than the victims (Ontario Consultants on Religious Tolerance, 2003). Meanwhile, in 2008 Prime Minister Stephen Harper offered a formal apology on behalf of the government, stating that "there is no place in Canada for the attitudes that inspired the Indian residential schools system to ever again prevail" (CBC News, 2008).

The government and churches have not only issued formal apologies for residential schooling but are also offering restitution. The federal government will give each former residential school student $10 000 plus $3 000 for each year spent in a residential school. In addition, it has invested $10 million in an existing commemoration initiative, will give $125 million to the Aboriginal Healing Foundation, and has established the Truth and Reconciliation Commission to further analyze the legacy of residential schools. A number of churches, in conjunction with Aboriginal communities, are also embarking on various church and community programs to facilitate healing.

Victorian Child-Savers.   At the same time as residential schooling was being implemented in Canada, the Victorian **child-savers movement** was at its apex, another example of religious belief systems influencing political belief systems. During the late nineteenth and early twentieth centuries, this movement played an essential role in child welfare reforms, compulsory education legislation, prohibition, and many other government policies in Canada, the United States, and Britain (Platt, 1977; Jordon, 1998; Valverde, 1991). An aspect of Protestant theology known as the **Social Gospel** informed the child-savers movement, whereby Christian principles were applied in real-world settings to solve social problems (providing humanitarian aid to the less fortunate in society was seen as one way of achieving salvation).

The child-savers were especially interested in social problems that involved children. Children were corrupted by growing up in immoral homes, leading to drunkenness, poverty, and vice. The child-savers believed it was the state's responsibility to provide a moral environment for children whose parents were unwilling or unable to do so. Child abuse and neglect were deviantized, and over time the efforts of the child-savers led to legislation dictating that children whose parents were abusive or neglectful should be removed from their homes. They were placed in foster homes with morally upstanding families who could teach the children the path to good citizenship and salvation.

That path was, however, based on middle-class, Protestant norms. Interpretations of doctrine at the time suggested that material success could be considered a sign of strong morality. Thus, the fact that people of the middle class had material success meant that whatever beliefs and norms they adhered to were the "moral" ones, ordained by God. Members of the lower classes were automatically considered immoral—after all, if they were moral they would have material success and would not be lower class! Consequently, simply being of a lower socioeconomic class was automatically considered deviant, so virtually all of the efforts of the child-savers were directed at lower-class families.

A historical perspective provides excellent examples of blurred boundaries between religious and political belief systems. With the witch craze, residential schooling, and the Victorian child-savers, those

Ask Yourself
Are blurred boundaries between religious and political belief systems relegated only to the past? Where do you see these boundaries potentially being blurred in Canada, the United States, or the rest of the world today?

behaviours, beliefs, and people that were considered deviant within specific religious belief systems came to be socially typed as deviant in political belief systems as well. As components of religious beliefs were incorporated into the political realm, social control shifted to legislation and other forms of government policy.

TIME TO REVIEW

Learning Objective 4

- What role does religion play as a social typer of deviance at the individual level?

- How did religion act as a social typer of deviance during the witch craze?

- What was the nature of religious social typing involved with residential schooling?

- Which groups were socially typed as deviant in the child-savers movement and why?

Ask Yourself

In your own life, what roles are played by the truths proclaimed by the religious belief system you adhere to and scientific belief systems? Which of these belief systems plays a larger role in your life?

Science

Science can be broadly defined as "knowledge or a system of knowledge covering general truths of the operation of general laws especially as obtained and tested through scientific method" (Merriam-Webster, 2013). Belief systems in the sciences are twofold. First, there are claims about the nature of reality, the way the world works. Second, there are ethical and moral claims embedded in the scientific belief system. For example, in cloning research, claims are being made about both the biological or genetic foundations of cloning and the implicit morality of cloning.

Some beliefs are characteristic of science as a whole (e.g., that the truths about nature can be discovered), but other beliefs are specific to each of the disciplines or subdisciplines of science. For instance, biology and sociology each have their own distinct truths based on the specific objects of study.

In the first half of this chapter, we saw that religion is subjected to social control and yet also steers processes of social control—it is socially typed but also socially types others. The same is true for scientific belief systems. Science serves a social control function, dictating to us what is deviant and providing a means for controlling that deviance. It is also made subject to social control itself to prevent and resolve deviance.

Science as Deviance: Scientific Misconduct and Pseudo-Sciences

In the pursuit of the goal to "find, describe, and analyze ... the truth" (Ben-Yehuda, 1990), scientists can be thought of as deviant in two ways. First, scientists may be socially typed when they engage in scientific misconduct. Second, scientists may be considered deviant when they are part of a discipline that is not recognized by the scientific community as being a "real" science.

Scientific Misconduct

In any occupation or profession, some individuals engage in deviant acts. Some elite members of the business world embezzle funds or participate in insider trading, some retail employees steal products from stores, and some police officers use excessive force. Similarly, some scientists engage in acts of scientific misconduct.

Scientific misconduct is used as an umbrella term to refer to fabrication or falsification of data, breaches of ethics, plagiarism, and any other scientific practices deemed unacceptable or inappropriate. Concerns about the nature and extent of scientific misconduct intensified in the late 1970s, partially due to the 1974 Patchwork Mouse incident. This incident involved a researcher who claimed to have grafted skin from a black mouse onto a white mouse, but had actually drawn patches on the white mouse using a black marker (Bleicher, 2003; Judson, 2004). Concerns with how to prevent, detect, and punish scientific misconduct have grown since that time.

The social sciences and other disciplines outside of the hard sciences are not immune to such instances of fraud. Several of the twin studies and adoption studies from the 1970s and 1980s that claimed genetic traits were responsible for various psychological and behavioural characteristics have been accused of scientific misconduct (Joseph & Baldwin, 2000). Cases of fabrication, falsification, and ethical violations have been found in the social sciences, health services (e.g., nursing), and human services (e.g., counselling) (Gibelman & Gelman, 2005). However, misconduct continues to be associated primarily with the hard sciences, especially biomedical research (Gibelman & Gelman, 2005)—not because misconduct is necessarily more common in these fields, but because it is more likely to be looked for and detected.

Ben-Yehuda (1986, p. 18) suggests that deviance is far more likely to be detected in research on hot issues and in breakthrough research because of the interest that is generated—in the twenty-first century, these terms often characterize biomedical research. Furthermore, it is this type of research that receives the most funding from external agencies (Gibelman & Gelman, 2005), and accountability of funds is another factor that stimulates greater interest in potential research misconduct. The US Office for Research Integrity (cited in Langlais, 2006) reports that "the financial cost of gross misconduct in the biomedical fields has been estimated to be as high as $1 million per case" (para. 3). A well-known case of scientific misconduct in a heavily funded breakthrough area of research is the case of scientist Dr. Hwang Woo Suk (see Box 9.3).

The Extent of the Problem. The prevalence of scientific misconduct is difficult to determine (Judson, 2004). A survey of 3200 medical researchers in the United States found that one-third admitted to engaging in at least one of ten "serious" forms of research misconduct, including overlooking "colleagues' use of flawed data," plagiarizing other people's ideas, changing "the design or results of a study under pressure from a funding

Box 9.3

The Rise and Fall of Dr. Hwang Woo Suk

In May 2005, Dr. Hwang Woo Suk, a professor at Seoul National University in South Korea, was a national celebrity and famed international scientist. By the end of that same year, he was under investigation by the university and criminal prosecutors for scientific misconduct and fraud.

He was propelled to fame when he claimed he had successfully cloned human embryos and extracted stem cells from them. His research appeared to be the first step in developing customized cures for various diseases and repairs for spinal cord injuries (Associated Press, 2006; *The Lancet*, 2005; Onishi, 2006). Soon, his research was featured on a Korean postage stamp, Korean Air provided him with free airline travel anywhere in the world, the government provided him with bodyguards and gave him tens of millions of dollars for further research, and the Korean public treated him as a national hero (Onishi, 2006).

However, it wasn't long before anonymous web postings and a call to a television news program claimed he had fabricated at least some of his research

data (Onishi, 2006). An investigation began at Seoul National University, and its final report revealed that the data on human cloning and stem cells had been falsified.

In May 2006, he and five other members of his research team were indicted for embezzlement and bioethics law violations (Associated Press, 2006). He initially denied responsibility for the misconduct, claiming that junior researchers at one of the labs he was working with had provided him with fraudulent data without his knowledge. Since then he has admitted to falsifying data.

Not only has this case received worldwide media attention, it has also stimulated tremendous discussion and debate within the scientific community (*The Lancet*, 2006). Many questions are being asked. For example, how did this fraud fall through the cracks of the peer-review process at the journal that published his articles? Who should hold ultimate responsibility for preventing and detecting scientific misconduct? And how widespread is this problem? Was he simply one "bad apple"? Or is he the "tip of the iceberg"?

source," and ignoring or erasing data "that would have contradicted the results of the research process" (Martinson, cited in Dyer, 2005, p. 1465). Another survey of more than 2000 researchers found that over the previous three years, they had observed 201 cases of suspected misconduct within their own departments; more than one-third of those incidents were never reported to anyone (Titus, Wells, & Rhoades, 2008).

Explanations for Scientific Misconduct.   There are two contrasting explanations for scientific misconduct—**bad apple/person theory** and **iceberg theory** (Ben-Yehuda, 1986; Bechtel & Pearson, 1985; James, 1995). For many years, deviant acts committed by scientists were explained on the basis of individual factors—the *bad apple/bad person theory* of scientific deviance (Ben-Yehuda, 1986; Bechtel & Pearson, 1985). Just as a few "bad" people commit crimes because of psychological disturbances, personality factors, or free choice, a few "bad" scientists commit deviant acts in their work for similar reasons. This theory suggests that we need to find those few bad apples and throw them out so they do not spoil the whole barrel. For example, an editorial in *The Lancet* (2006) about the Hwang Woo Suk incident points out that the structure of science itself is sound: "The fact that Hwang's work has so quickly been shown to be fake is proof that the system of oversight currently in place has the power to self-correct when a transgression occurs" (p. 1).

In contrast, the *iceberg theory* of scientific deviance claims that the structure within which scientists work actually encourages deviance, making it likely to occur (Titus, Wells, & Rhoades, 2008; Nylenna & Simonson, 2006; Ben-Yehuda, 1986). Sleight (2004) proposes that many cases of scientific misconduct "are prompted by ambition/publication pressures" (p. 33). That is, scientists today face an incredible amount of pressure to publish. The number of publications that a scientist has can determine hiring, increases in salary, promotion, likelihood of receiving research grants, and the degree of status within the scientific community. All of these pressures increase the chance that scientists will use deviant means to produce these publications. Furthermore, the institution of science exists within a particular societal context. For instance, an analysis of Hwang Woo Suk's misconduct points out that broader cultural characteristics are reflected within the scientific culture of South Korea: "Knowledge acquisition in South Korea has close connections to hierarchies of status and prestige; and … South Korean work ethos imposes a severe workload on junior researchers" (Kim, 2008, p. 397), creating a foundation upon which this misconduct occurred.

Another factor contributing to scientific misconduct is that it is unlikely to be detected. Most known cases of misconduct are discovered by accident rather than as a function of institutional processes or safeguards (Judson, cited in McCarthy, 2004). In the instances of scientific deviance that Barrett and Jay (2005) have been called upon to investigate, most of the scientists had been engaging in misconduct for five to ten years prior to being caught. Unless research is controversial or about a particularly hot issue, it is unlikely to stimulate questions and efforts at replication, because replicating someone else's research does not add much to the prestige of scientists. Because the chances of being caught are remote, there is little motivation to refrain from deviant acts.

Finally, although organizational structures and committees have been put in place to investigate reports of misconduct, their investigations are often fraught with controversy themselves (e.g., White, 2003), and even if scientists' misconduct is detected, sanctions are not likely to be of sufficient severity to deter other potential offenders. Combined, these characteristics of the scientific community create a structure that actually encourages rather than deters scientific misconduct. After finding that one-third of scientists who were surveyed admitted to engaging in various forms of misconduct, Martinson (cited in Dyer, 2005) concludes the following: "we've shown that it's about more than just fraud, and we shouldn't be looking for a few bad apples. It may be that competition in science in this country has reached dysfunctional levels" (p. 1465).

The scholars who consider the detected cases of scientific misconduct to be just the tip of the iceberg have applied various specific theories that we addressed in Chapter 2 to explain this form of deviance. For example, Ben-Yehuda (1986) proposes that *techniques of neutralization* (Sykes & Matza, 1957) play an important role in scientific deviance. Techniques like *denial of injury* or *denial of responsibility* help scientists justify their actions, convincing themselves or others that what they are doing is not really wrong or that they are not responsible for the misconduct.

We saw this in the case of Korean scientist Dr. Hwang Woo Suk, who initially claimed that junior scientists at another lab had provided him with the fraudulent data and that he had no idea it had been fabricated. Bechtel & Pearson (1985) discuss the usefulness of Robert Merton's *strain theory*. They point out that scientific deviance can be considered an example of the mode of adaptation called *innovation*; that is, the gap between legitimized goals and access to the legitimate means of attaining those goals leads some people to pursue those goals in "innovative" ways. Just as some people who want fancy cars will steal rather than purchase them, some scientists who want career success will engage in misconduct rather than obtain it legitimately.

Gottfredson and Hirschi's (1990) *self-control theory* has not been used to study scientific deviance specifically, but it has been applied to occupational deviance more generally. Research has found that self-control plays a role in occupational deviance, particularly when low self-control is combined with an environment in which co-workers are engaging in deviance (Gibson & Wright, 2001). If co-workers appear to be rewarded for their deviance, such as by receiving promotions or large research grants for their productivity in publishing, the pull toward deviance may be even greater.

Exercise Your Mind

Go back to the various theories discussed in Chapters 2 and 3. Select the *one* theory from each of these chapters that you think best explains scientific misconduct. What makes each of those theories preferable to the others in those chapters?

Misconduct and the Corporatization of Science.   The prevalence and reasons for scientific misconduct are influenced by ties with corporate industry. A growing proportion of scientific research is funded by commercial industry, especially in biomedical fields. These scientist–industry partnerships can result in scientific misconduct that is steered by the funding source, or done by the funded scientists without the funder's knowledge. Corporate funding and the nature of the research results frequently go hand in hand (Born, 2004; Caulfield, 2004).

Martinson (cited in Dyer, 2005) found that 15 percent of 3200 medical researchers surveyed had "changed the design or results of a study under pressure from a funding source" (p. 1465). And resulting publications from industry-sponsored research are far more likely to report positive findings than those sponsored by public (i.e., government) funds (Krimsky, cited in Thompson, Baird, & Downie, 2005). This pattern is most evident in therapeutic/drug research sponsored by pharmaceutical companies. For example, "an analysis of 70 studies of specific cardiac drugs showed that 96 percent of authors with ties to the pharmaceutical company produced favorable results, while only 37 percent of independently funded studies *of the same drugs* showed favorable results" (Stelfox, Chua, O'Rourke, & Detsky, cited in Born, 2004, para. 12).

In many cases, the contracts between pharmaceutical companies and researchers stipulate that the company retains the right to determine which research results do and do not get published (Born, 2004). Even in those instances where the company does not retain the right to publish, the company may delay the publication of negative results (Thompson, Baird, & Downie, 2005), which enables the company to "quickly fund a new study that produces a favorable response and then publish only the positive results" (Born, 1994, para. 14). In addition, most clinical drug research is now done by commercial centres hired by the pharmaceutical companies, compared to 15 years ago when it was done in university research departments, a phenomenon that has been labelled **post-academic science** (Ziman, cited in Montgomery & Oliver, 2009). This creates a structure within which researchers face considerable pressure to obtain the results that will make their funding sources happy, a structure that is conducive to scientific misconduct.

When misconduct is detected, pharmaceutical companies can face economic sanctions. In 2004, the manufacturers of the anti-depressant Paxil (GlaxoSmithKline) settled a lawsuit claiming they had hidden data showing that the drug increased suicidal thoughts in children. They paid a US$2.5 million fine and agreed to make all of their clinical trial data available online; in this way, they were able to avoid criminal charges (Levine, 2005). To most of us, US$2.5 million seems like a large sum of money. However, three years earlier, the very same company had been ordered to pay US$6.4 million to the family of a man who had committed suicide after taking Paxil for only 48 hours. That larger amount of money obviously did not deter the company from future misconduct. In fact, in 2012 GlaxoSmithKline had to pay US$3 billion in fines for multiple forms of misconduct, including publishing articles that misreported data, providing expensive gifts to physicians who prescribed their medications, and failing to report known safety data for a number of drugs (Thomas & Schmidt, 2012).

The profitability of the pharmaceutical industry is such that fines of even millions of dollars seem little more than a proverbial "slap on the wrist" (Levine, 2005, para. 3). By the turn of the twenty-first century, the pharmaceutical industry had become "the most profitable industry in the United States … with an 18.6 percent return on revenues" (Conrad & Leiter, 2004, p. 161). An industry that spends more than $4 billion each year just on public advertising in the United States alone (Mintzes, 2006) is difficult to control with light economic sanctions. Critics state that such corporate scientific misconduct will only cease when executives are held individually responsible and subject to criminal sanctions (Thomas & Schmidt, 2012).

Controlling Scientific Misconduct.   Scientific misconduct can be controlled in a number of ways. Scientists who have engaged in misconduct can face temporary or permanent disbarment from public research funding and from serving on public research bodies, and may face a loss of credibility among their peers. However, preventative social control is even more important. Just as effective efforts to curb binge drinking on university campuses must target the whole environment rather than just those students who are problem drinkers (see Chapter 6), reducing scientific misconduct also requires a population prevention approach (Nylenna & Simonsen, 2006). This approach includes the following: regular informational and educational seminars at research institutions; focusing on misconduct at its broadest level, rather than only on fabrication, falsification, and plagiarism; mentoring of young researchers to transmit guidelines; investigation mechanisms at the national level; and a restructuring of the academic reward system to remove the climate of "publish or perish" (Nylenna & Simonsen, 2006).

Population prevention is a relatively recent approach to controlling scientific misconduct. Montgomery and Oliver's (2009) analysis of the "institutional logics" (p. 139) that govern social control measures directed at scientific misconduct reveals three distinct time periods. Prior to 1975, the institutional logic emphasized science as self-governing, based on the assumption that science was inherently about objectivity and the search for truth. Sociologist Robert Merton (1973) described this as the *normative structure of science*, and listed four norms of science: **communism** (scientists freely give up rights to the knowledge that they create so that this knowledge can be shared by all); **skepticism** (all ideas must be subjected to rigorous scrutiny); **disinterestedness** (scientific work is done in the name of truth rather than for any personal gain or vested interests); and **universalism** (knowledge is free from any biases based on characteristics such as race, gender, or religion). Although Merton himself recognized that not all scientists would necessarily adhere to these norms, the institutional logic of the time suggested that normative pressures within the scientific community would be sufficient to prevent misconduct.

However, with the growing awareness of specific cases of misconduct (such as the Patchwork Mouse incident), it became increasingly clear that the normative structure of science was not sufficient to prevent acts of misconduct. Consequently, from 1975 to 1990 the institutional logic became one of coercive measures to both punish and prevent misconduct. This heralded an era when institutional research boards emerged, and research institutions that received public research funding were required to implement procedures for investigating allegations of misconduct.

Since 1990, the growth of private research funding (through scientist–industry partnerships) has removed some of the power behind the coercive social control mechanisms of the previous time period. It has also subjected scientists to new and different pressures that can increase the likelihood of misconduct.

As a result, the institutional logic has once again shifted from a focus on preventing and punishing misconduct to an emphasis on "promoting research integrity" (Montgomery & Oliver, 2009, p. 146). This entails a cooperative, multifaceted effort among governmental organizations, universities, professional academic societies, credentialing associations, and academic journal editors. It is within this discourse, and its resulting network of stakeholders, that the population prevention approach has emerged.

The history of scientific misconduct is almost as long as the history of science itself (Judson, 2004). But with the proliferation of science over the last century, we have also seen the escalation of scientific misconduct. From the Piltdown Man of 1912 (a hoax where bone fragments were passed off as an early human ancestor) to some of the industry-sponsored research of today, the list of instances of scientific misconduct continues to grow, as does the debate over how to best control it.

TIME TO REVIEW

Learning Objective 5

■ What are some of the forms scientific misconduct?

■ How is misconduct explained by the bad apple/person theory and the iceberg theory?

■ In what way may the relationship between commercial industry and science promote scientific misconduct?

■ How have the institutional logics of social control changed over time?

Science and Pseudo-Science

As we have seen thus far, deviance can occur in science when scientists engage in misconduct. Deviance can also occur in science when a whole discipline of science is perceived as deviant in its entirety and is rejected as a legitimate science (Ben-Yehuda, 1990). An entire science may be socially typed as deviant when its belief system or technologies are significantly called into question. If subject to enough doubt, the belief system or technologies may be determined not to be a science at all; instead, they may be labelled a "non-science." Particular combinations of belief systems and technologies can be thought of as falling along a continuum (Figure 9.1).

At one end of the continuum lie those belief systems, such as astrology, magnetic therapy, and Bible codes (i.e., pseudo-sciences) that have not been supported by empirical research using scientific methods. At the other end of the continuum are those belief systems that have been consistently supported by the most research evidence, such as evolution and quantum mechanics. Falling at various points between these two extreme ends of the continuum is the bulk of other belief systems and technologies (Shermer, 2001).

The media plays an important role in reproducing pseudo-scientific beliefs (Yam, 1997). The stranger the scientific claim, the more likely it is to be reported in the media—unusual scientific claims are sensationalistic and can reliably attract an audience. The media ties into commercialization as well. Belief systems that are frequently labelled as deviant science are often linked to companies selling a marketable product or service related to those claims (Yam, 1997). Astrological charts, magnetic insoles for your shoes, and homeopathic remedies are just some of the services and products available.

Determining what is a pseudo-science may initially appear to be quite straightforward. However, that is not necessarily the case. A science perceived as deviant at one time may

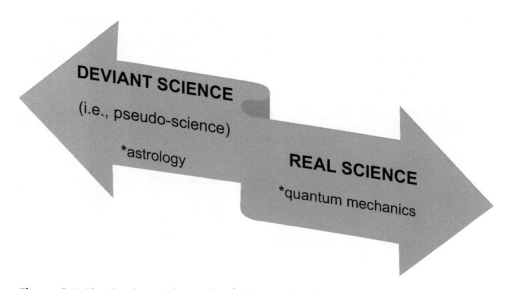

Figure 9.1 The Deviant Science–Real Science Continuum

Based on Shermer's (2001) model of the continuum: Shermer, M. (2001). *The Borderlands of Science: Where Sense Meets Nonsense.* New York: Oxford University Press.

become an accepted science at a later date. This is what happened with radio astronomy in the early twentieth century (Ben-Yehuda, 1986, 1990). Radio astronomy essentially claims that scientists can identify events that are occurring in the solar system by measuring the radio waves the events emit. Those of you who are familiar with this field may ask how radio astronomy can be a deviant science when its claims are entirely accepted in the scientific community. Though this may be true today, it was not always the case. The scientists who argued for the validity of radio astronomy initially faced considerable censure. They had tremendous difficulty finding a research journal willing to publish their article, and for a number of years they were stigmatized in the scientific community. Eventually, other astronomers conducted research and concluded that their claims were, in fact, valid; thus radio astronomy entered the realm of mainstream science.

Because of instances where the claims made by a deviant science eventually came to be adopted by the scientific community, proponents of deviant sciences today claim that the same might eventually become true of their belief systems. They argue that the methods for investigation in mainstream science have not evolved sufficiently to properly evaluate the claims being made (Shermer, 2001). Ben-Yehuda (1986, 1990) points out that one of the reasons that a science may first be considered deviant and later become accepted is the conservative character of the scientific community.

Although scientists pursue innovation via their research efforts, the tendency to resist change can sometimes prevail. Senior scientists who have become well established are usually the members of the scientific community who determine whether new ideas are viewed as valid or not. The cynical view they have developed as part of the scientific worldview (presuming that a claim is *not* true until it is proven beyond a doubt) contributes to this conservative dimension. The conservative aspect of science then increases the likelihood that any claim outside of the mainstream will, at least initially, be looked upon with suspicion.

Just as is the case with religion, science can also be socially typed as deviant and made subject to social control. Sometimes this occurs when scientists engage in specific actions that are considered deviant within the scientific community, such as using data fraudulently, hoaxing, and violating codes of ethics. At other times, the claims about reality or the ethical and moral assumptions of a discipline are called into question themselves. When this happens, the entire science is labelled deviant and made subject to control. However, science also steers the social typing process.

TIME TO REVIEW

Learning Objective 6

■ What is a deviant science?

■ What does the deviant science–real science continuum represent?

■ How have perceptions of radio astronomy changed over time?

■ Why are new scientific claims often regarded as deviant?

Science as a Social Typer of Deviance

In his book *Power/Knowledge*, Michel Foucault (1980) proposed that a relationship exists among knowledge claims, the power of people making those knowledge claims, and the resulting influence those knowledge claims have. Thus, when claims to truth come from locations of institutionalized power, those claims also become institutionalized—people believe the claims being made simply because those claims are coming from "experts." This is the position that science holds in our culture today, such that the social typing done by scientists tends to be effective: "Laypeople generally hesitate to question those who seem to be experts in a mystifying or highly technical field; to do such questioning can feel like asking the clergy if there really is a God" (Caplan, 1995, p. xxii).

Scientific Social Typing in History: Social Darwinism, Eugenics, and the Nazis

Ask Yourself
Where do you see "experts" being used in order to legitimize claims to truth?

Earlier in the chapter, we explored European colonization of North America and the role that religious belief systems played in the government initiative for residential schooling, a policy that caused long-term damage to Aboriginal individuals, their families, and their cultures. European colonization did not occur just in North America, though; it also took place in Africa, Asia, Australia, Central America, and South America.

What all of these instances of colonization have in common is that indigenous populations were encouraged, and usually coerced, into abandoning traditional beliefs and cultural norms and adopting the European beliefs and norms of their colonizers (Abernethy, 2001; Jaimes, 1992). Religious beliefs were central to the push toward colonization, serving as the primary rationalization for several centuries. However, by the end of the nineteenth century, scientific theory also provided a rationale for the last several centuries of European colonization and a justification for government policies regarding indigenous peoples for years to come.

Social Darwinism, exemplified by the work of sociologist Herbert Spencer, applied the Darwinian concept of *evolution* to history and society (Asma, 1993; Jones, 1998). The theory proposed that just as biological species evolve over time, so do human societies, from "primitive" to "civilized." In the nineteenth century, European societies were seen by social Darwinists as the most highly evolved. Thus, the colonization of more "primitive" societies was justified as benefiting indigenous peoples; in other words, European colonizers were seen as helping these cultures to evolve at a more rapid rate than they were doing on their own. Government policies based on the principle of assimilation also justified moving the evolution of indigenous cultures forward.

Social Darwinism was soon popularized as the science of **eugenics** (Asma, 1993; Jones, 1986; Jones, 1998; Kevles, 1995). Similar principles were applied, but to various individuals and groups within particular societies. Recent biological developments were used to support the argument that some social groups were more evolved than, and therefore biologically superior to, other groups. Although eugenics is most often associated with Nazi Germany (Kuhl, 1994), governments in Britain (Jones, 1986), the United States (Seldon & Montagu, 1999), Australia (Jones, 1998) and Canada (McLaren, 1990) also pursued eugenic ideals. According to a 1922 sociology textbook that spoke in favour of eugenics, the goals of eugenics were to ensure that "a larger proportion of superior persons will have children than at present ... the most inferior persons will have no children ... [and] other inferior persons will have fewer children than now" (Popenoe & Johnson, 1922).

Over time, "inferior" persons came to include non-whites, Eastern and Southern Europeans, "mental defectives," criminals, the poor, and the morally suspect (Dennis, 1995; Beaud & Prevost, 1996; McLaren, 1990; Kevles, 1985; Buchanan, 1997). Social activists drawn primarily from the scientific and social reform communities engaged in a number of measures to increase reproduction in "superior" people and decrease reproduction in "inferior" people. In many universities, biology and sociology students studied from eugenics textbooks just like the one quoted above. In churches, ministers presented sermons on eugenic ideals and competed for awards from local eugenics societies (Seldon & Montagu, 1999). Eugenics societies influenced restrictions on immigration policies, legislation enforcing racial segregation and prohibiting interracial marriages, and involuntary sterilization (Seldon & Montagu, 1999; Dennis, 1995; McLaren, 1990).

The history of involuntary sterilization and the eugenics movement reached widespread public attention in Canada in the 1990s, when Leilani Muir launched a lawsuit against the Alberta government for wrongful sterilization. In 1928, the Alberta government set up a eugenics board and instituted the *Sexual Sterilization Act*. The board would evaluate "mental defectives" when they reached puberty, and after an interview of only a few minutes would determine if they should be sterilized. When Muir was a pre-teen, her alcoholic and abusive mother dropped Muir off at the Provincial Training School in Red Deer. Shortly thereafter, she was classified as a "mental defective" and, without her knowledge or permission, was sterilized. After leaving the training school and embarking upon a normal life, she sought medical advice to determine why she had been unable to become pregnant. In the words of Buchanan (1997), "The doctor described her insides as 'being as if she'd been through a slaughterhouse.' Then, when she tried to adopt, she was refused because of the stigma of being a former inmate of Red Deer" (p. 46). Muir won her lawsuit and was awarded an undisclosed amount of money for the pain and suffering she had endured (Whiting, 1996; Buchanan, 1997; Grekul, 2002). Shortly thereafter, the Alberta government introduced legislation to prohibit others from being able to sue the government.

The eugenics board attached the label "mental defective" to an extremely wide range of people—for example, those with low IQs, those who had "immoral" lifestyles (the board presumed that only a "mental defective" would live an immoral lifestyle), immigrants unable to speak English, those who were considered burdens because of their poverty, and poverty-stricken women who dared to have children. In a significant proportion of cases, the "mental defectives" who were sterilized were people who had simply violated social norms (Grekul, 2002). For example, one young woman had been gang raped by local boys and as a result was labelled "sexually immoral" and entered into the juvenile justice system herself. Her father, unable to live with what had happened, placed her in the Provincial Training School, where she was sterilized (Buchanan, 1997).

The *Sexual Sterilization Act* was not repealed until 1978, thus lasting far longer than in other countries that used sterilization in pursuit of eugenic ideals. Even following World War II, at a time when "Nazis were being hung for their eugenic programs, 'lessons from this dark period of human history appeared to have little or no impact on the operation of the Alberta Eugenics Board'" (Wahlstein, cited in Buchanan, 1997, p. 46). Thus, even though governments throughout the world considered the Nazis' pursuit of eugenic ideals to be deviant (Proctor, 1988; Weiss, 1988), the ongoing pursuit of those ideals through sterilization continued to be practised in Canada.

Of course, the Nazis in Germany went much further in their application of eugenics (Proctor, 1988; Weiss, 1988). They sterilized between 350 000 and 400 000 people in the period from Hitler's election in 1933 to the beginning of World War II in the late 1930s. Initially, the world community viewed the size of the Nazi sterilization program in a positive light, setting it as a standard they could attempt to approximate themselves (Proctor, 1988).

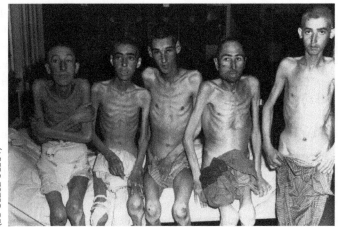

The eugenics movement reached its historical apex in Nazi Germany, with millions of people killed in concentration camps. However, eugenic ideals were also being pursued to lesser degrees in Canada, Britain, Australia, and the United States.

However, as the drive for "racial purity" progressed under the Nazis, genocidal measures were implemented, including the killing of millions in concentration camps—people who were Jewish, Romany, trade unionists, homosexual, or disabled. A large-scale science program was established as well, and significant strides were made in the area of genetics; thus, torturous medical experimentation (e.g., on twins) served as the basis for these scientific advancements (Proctor, 1988).

Today, some scientists continue to make claims about evolutionary differences among the races, such as in terms of intelligence (e.g., Philippe Rushton, founder of the Charles Darwin Research Institute). Their scientific claims are heavily criticized (e.g., Brace, 1996; MacEachern, 2006) as racist and based on faulty science, but are widely used by white supremacist groups to support their ideals. Thus, although history provides us with rather dramatic illustrations of the power of science, the role that science plays in the social typing of deviance is not limited to the past.

Scientific Social Typing Today: Medicalization

Science continues to play a role in the determination and control of deviance. Medical science in particular plays a central role; in fact, some scholars claim that medicine is the form of science that most underlies our culture's dominant moral codes (Conrad, 1992; Turner, 1987). As you have progressed through this textbook, the medicalization of deviance has been one of the central themes. In the chapter on physical appearance, we addressed the role that medical science plays in defining "too fat" and "too thin," and then the various ways that doctors exert social control over those "deviant" populations.

In the chapter on mental disorders, the role of the psychiatric community in the medicalization of deviance was evident. Members of the psychiatric community determine the symptoms that constitute deviance through their revisions of the *Diagnostic and Statistical Manual of Mental Disorders* (American Psychiatric Association, 1994). They then use the manual to diagnose people with those disorders and provide treatment in the amelioration of symptoms. Precisely what mental illness consists of varies over time, as some characteristics are removed from the diagnostic manual (e.g., homosexuality) and new ones are added (e.g., ADHD, gender identity disorder). Therefore, there are ongoing debates over the diagnostic categories of mental deviance, its political nature, and the absolute guardianship that psychiatrists have over it (Caplan, 1995).

In the chapter on youth, we saw that smoking has become successfully medicalized. Direct smoking was the first behaviour to be medicalized, and with medical research as a foundation for their views, anti-smoking activists have had a tremendous impact on society. Their efforts have resulted in warning labels on cigarette packages, bans on cigarette commercials on television, restricted sponsorship of events by tobacco companies, and anti-smoking programs in schools. More recently, secondhand smoking has been medicalized and has resulted in many community bylaws prohibiting smoking in various places.

There is no doubt that medicine is of tremendous importance to people's health throughout the world. Being overweight or underweight *does* increase health risks. Advances in psycho-pharmaceuticals *have* cured many people of mental disorders such as depression and have enabled many people with ongoing mental disorders to lead high-quality, high-functioning lives. Smoking *is* dangerous to smokers and people around them. However, the primacy given to medical science in determining deviance has led to numerous questions and concerns (Conrad, 1992), not the least of which is whether *social* characteristics are being medicalized.

This concern in particular is illustrated by the practice of giving liposuction to patients solely for the purpose of physical appearance, by the categorization of social groups (e.g., immigrants, people who did not follow social norms) as "mental defectives" under the science of eugenics, and by the individualization of social problems in the over-diagnosis of ADHD in North America.

Like religious belief systems, scientific belief systems also have extensive relationships with the concept of deviance. Certain practices that occur in science can be considered deviant, and entire bodies of science can be considered deviant. However, science also serves as a powerful social typer of deviance—perhaps the most powerful social typer in society today. That power does not go unquestioned, and controls are being exerted on the social typing that occurs in science. Both religious and scientific belief systems are governing forces in the lives of billions of people in the world. The truths that they proclaim are a foundation for our own behaviours as well as our judgments of others. But as the quote at the beginning of this chapter suggests, both types of belief systems are socially constructed. The subjective dimension of religion and science means that neither belief system should operate unbridled or without question.

Learning Objective 7

■ What is social Darwinism and how is it related to the social typing of deviance?

■ What is eugenics and what were the goals of the eugenics movement?

■ In what countries were eugenic ideals pursued and how?

■ What are some contemporary examples of how science socially types deviance?

CHAPTER SUMMARY

■ Religion and science both compose belief systems. Belief systems may act *as* deviance, or they may be socially typed as deviant themselves and subjected to social control. (1)

■ Traditionally, the typology distinguishing between ecclesia, churches, sects, and cults has been used to determine which religions are deviant. Within this typology, religious belief systems classified as sects or cults are more likely to be considered deviant. (2)

■ Deviant religions face a wide range of social controls. The anti-cult movement and counter-cult movement are active in reducing the threat they consider cults present. The media exerts control in conjunction with these movements, as well as in their own representations of deviant religions. Governments also exert control over religions they define as deviant. (3)

■ The internationally recognized right to freedom of religion is the foundation for religions to resist a deviant label. Individual religious groups try to demonstrate that they are not deviant. Today, some academics even call into question the traditional distinctions between churches, sects, and cults. (3)

■ At a societal level, religion serves as a social typer of deviance when the boundaries between religious and political belief systems become blurred. Historically, this occurred with the witch persecutions, residential schooling, and the child-savers movement. (4)

■ Various forms of scientific misconduct are possible, ranging from falsifying data to ethical violations. Bad apple/person theories propose that individuals' characteristics are the cause of misconduct. Iceberg theory claims the structure of the scientific community sets the stage for misconduct. The increasing corporatization of science promotes misconduct. The nature of controlling misconduct changes over time, as the institutional logics change. (5)

- Deviant sciences are those where the claims being made about the nature of reality are questioned. What is considered to be a deviant science, or a pseudo-science, changes over time, as happened with radio astronomy; this occurs because of the inherently conservative nature of science (6).

- Science has served as a social typer of deviance in its application of social Darwinism, during the eugenics movement, and in Nazi Germany. The medicalization of deviance in contemporary society also illustrates science's power as a social typer. (7)

MySearchLab®

⊙—Watch · **Go to MySearchLab to watch the video called "Religion and Polarization".**

Apply What You Know: This video suggests that religious belief, at least in the United States, plays a unique role in dividing public opinion about what is and is not acceptable in society. Do you think that particular religious beliefs make people more likely to label others as deviant? If so, what might be the consequences of this for Canadian society?

MySearchLab with eText offers you access to an online interactive version of the text, extensive help with your writing and research projects, and provides round-the-clock access to credible and reliable source material.

Chapter 10
The "Deviance Dance" Continues

© xiver/Shutterstock

Learning Objectives

After reading this chapter, you should be able to

1 Describe how more objective and more subjective approaches to studying deviance have been reflected in the chapters in this textbook.

2 Describe how the notion of the social typing process has been reflected in the topics explored in this textbook.

3 Explain how the importance of power has been addressed in the chapters in this textbook.

4 Explain how the concept of the "deviance dance" has been integrated into the topics explored in this textbook.

5 Cite examples of human rights legislation, and explain how these documents can determine when it is and is not appropriate to attach a deviant label to people, behaviours, or characteristics.

Let's return to some of
the questions raised in
Chapter 1: Who are the
conformists in our soci-
ety and in our world? Is
life easier for them? Are
their thoughts, behav-
iours, and identities limited by their conformity?
Who are the deviants?
Are they really the devi-
ants of our world, or do
they represent some type
of problem that we need
to control? What is it
that differentiates a
"deviant" from a "con-
formist"? How can we
distinguish between
them? Given what you
have learned during the
course and the ideas that
the course material has
stimulated, spend some
time thinking about how
you would answer these
questions now.

This textbook began with two quotations about deviance and conformity. Mason Cooley (2006) stated that "conformity makes everything
easier, if you can still breathe." Television producer David Lee (2006)
pointed out that "you have to be deviant if you're going to do anything
new." The first quotation suggests that conforming will make our lives
run more smoothly; at the same time, it points out that **conformity** is
restricting. The second quotation suggests that we can achieve innovation and change only if we're willing to risk being thought of as **deviant**.
Now that you have reached the last chapter, this is a good time to reflect
upon these concepts. In this chapter, we will look back at some of the
main ideas that were introduced in the first chapter, and explore how
those ideas have been reflected in the various substantive topics that
have been addressed. As you read through this chapter, you will be
asked to do a lot of thinking on your own. This is the time when you can
reflect on the topics you have learned about and the ideas you had during this course.

The Objective–Subjective Continuum

Various researchers approach the study of deviance differently. Although
the differences among researchers have traditionally been characterized
as a dichotomy or dualism (Adler & Adler, 2003; Ben-Yehuda, 1990),
most deviance specialists today combine some aspects of both objective
and subjective approaches. Even looking back at earlier research reveals
that the distinctions between these approaches were not as clear-cut as
has been suggested (e.g., Becker, 1963). Thus, we can think of deviance
research as falling along a continuum, wherein virtually all scholars fit
somewhere between the two extreme ends. Some deviance specialists lean to the more
objective side of the continuum, while others lean to the more subjective side.

Scholars who lean to the more **objective** side of the continuum focus their analytical
spotlight on the deviant act itself. For these scholars, the deviant act exists *a priori* to the
analysis and can be recognized by specific characteristics such as a negative societal reaction, harm, statistical rarity, or a violation of norms. With an overarching **positivist** interest in explaining the variation in human behaviour, they focus on causation—what makes
people act in deviant ways (Ashley & Orenstein, 2001). Due to their focus on explaining
the deviant act, they find that particular types of theories are more useful to them than to
the scholars who lean toward the more subjective side of the research continuum. These
were the theories addressed in Chapter 2: functionalist theories, social learning theories,
and social control theories.

Deviance specialists who lean to the more **subjective** side of the continuum focus their analytical spotlight on the social processes by which certain people, actions, or characteristics come to be perceived as deviant and treated accordingly. They suggest that we cannot recognize deviance in any objective sense, but instead must be taught that certain people, actions, and characteristics are deviant (Becker, 1963). Power is perceived as central to determining what is deviant. Due to their emphasis on explaining the social processes that underlie deviant labels, particular types of theories are more useful to them than to scholars who lean toward the more objective side of the research continuum. These were the theories addressed in Chapter 3: interpretive theories and critical theories (Ashley & Orenstein, 2001).

Combining the results of both the more objective and more subjective research provides us with the most comprehensive understanding of deviance, wherein we learn something about the deviant act (why, when, and how it occurs) and the processes by which that act has come to be perceived and treated as deviant. Throughout this textbook you have seen many instances of each of these areas of emphasis. In the chapter on media and deviance (Chapter 4), we saw that contemporary research on media is both objective (analyzing the effects of media consumption on attitudes and behaviours) and subjective (exploring how the media socially constructs events, issues, and identities, and how those constructions may be affected by changing structures of media ownership).

In the chapter on sexuality (Chapter 5), a historical context surrounded part of our exploration. In looking at the changing sexual cultures in North America before, during, and after industrialization (D'Emilio & Freedman, 1997; Razack, 2002; Valverde, 1991), we saw the various norms (i.e., a more objectivist interest) that shaped people's sexual behaviours. For example, we saw that prior to industrialization, reproduction within marriage was the guiding principle for sexuality. In contemporary society, we explored cultural norms that if violated are considered deviant (e.g., age of the sexual partner). We also saw that the Supreme Court of Canada has shifted the definition of obscenity to one based on social harm.

From a more subjectivist point of view, a historical context also enabled us to look at the culturally specific processes by which certain people, acts, or characteristics come to be labelled as deviant. Our discussion of the tremendous diversity in sexual cultures around the world and throughout history illustrated that what is considered sexually deviant stems not from the acts themselves, but from the evaluations of particular acts based on the dominant moral codes in society at the time.

In the chapter on youth (Chapter 6), the objective and subjective dimensions were reflected in the various topics of youth-related deviance that were addressed—crime, gangs, substance use, and the nature of adolescence itself. An abundance of more objectivist research has been conducted on the causes of youth crime (e.g., Davies, 1994), gang emergence and involvement (e.g., Jankowski, 1991; Grekul & LaBoucane-Benson, 2007; Wortley & Tanner, 2003), smoking, alcohol use, and drug use (e.g., Roberts, McCall, Stevens-Lavigne, Anderson, Paglia, Bollenback, et al., 2001). We explored some of the theoretical and empirical research that explains these "deviant" behaviours. Differential association theory, social control theories, and social learning theories have been applied to understandings of many of these acts, and empirical research reveals the complex web of factors that contributes to them as well. For instance, characteristics of family life (especially the balance of parental expectations and parent–child affection) are consistently found to play an important role in youth crime (Milan, 2000; Brook, Brook, De La Rosa, Whiteman, & Montoya, 1999). Because these behaviours emerge from the interaction of personal, family, school, and community factors, the programs and policies designed to reduce the frequency of these behaviours must address such multilevel factors.

Shifting our focus to the more subjectivist interest in the social processes that underlie the deviantization of youth, we also explored how the gap between the perceptions and actual prevalence of youth crime or the "gang problem" contributes to particular ways of trying to control these problems (Tanner, 2001; Fasiolo & Leckie, 1993). In looking at the way in which youth itself, as a stage in the life cycle, is considered deviant, we saw that adolescents live the lives that we as adults create for them. The exaggerated generation gap of the past may become a reality in the future; however, it is not because of the deviant nature of adolescence, but rather because of the structure of society as created by adults. Even so, the misperceptions that all youth are both troubling and troubled influences the ways that youth are treated in society (Bibby, 2009).

Body size was one of the areas of emphasis for the chapter on physical appearance (Chapter 7), which addressed body images such as "too fat," "too thin," and "ideal." Certain body sizes are indeed associated with significantly higher risks of health problems (World Health Organization, 2010; Health Canada, 2002), and scholars with more objectivist interests have therefore analyzed various biological, psychological, and social factors in their attempts to determine why people become obese or anorexic and what treatments will help them (Caldwell, 2001; McLorg & Taub, 1987). However, scholars with more subjectivist interests reveal that popular social perceptions of "too fat," "too thin," and "ideal" have little to do with health risks and much to do with current cultural standards of beauty—standards that critics say have reached alarmingly thin proportions (Owen & Laurel-Seller, 2000; Spitzer, Henderson, & Zivian, 1999). These standards of beauty vary considerably across cultures and over time, so that what is seen as being a "deviant" body size in twenty-first-century Canada is very different than in twenty-first-century Ghana or even nineteenth-century Canada (Shuriquie, 1999).

Body modification was another area of emphasis in the chapter. More objectivist-based research has explored the motivations for obtaining tattoos or piercings and risk factors with which body modification is associated. From a more subjectivist point of view, scholars have explored what body modification tells us about social interaction (e.g., impression management) and the larger society (e.g., discourses of gender).

Like obesity and anorexia, discussed in Chapter 7, mental disorders are medicalized forms of deviance. In the chapter on mental disorders (Chapter 8), the more objective approach to deviance was reflected in the material on prevalence, causes, and treatments of mental illness. We saw that mental illness affects most Canadians either directly (through their own experiences of mental illness) or indirectly (by having a friend, family member, or co-worker with a mental illness) (Health Canada, 2002). The social and economic costs of mental disorders are tremendous, not only in Canada but throughout the world (Ettner, Frank, & Kessler, 1997; Mental Health Commission of Canada, 2012a; Stephans & Jorbert, 2001). Therefore, a wide range of therapeutic techniques—counselling, medication, and family supports—are used to treat the combined biological and social aspects of mental disorders (World Health Organization, 2002b).

The more subjective approach to deviance is reflected in the research that emphasizes the political and social aspects of diagnosis and treatment. Although there is considerable overlap between North American and international diagnostic tools, scholars point out that there is a political aspect to determining what constitutes psychological deviance (Caplan, 1995). For example, homosexuality is no longer categorized as a mental disorder, but other behaviours (e.g., gender identity disorder) now are. Some critics suggest that *social* problems are being medicalized and treated as illnesses. For example, the high rate of ADHD diagnoses in North America may have more to do with the multitasking that characterizes modern life than with a psychological disorder in particular children (McConnell, 1997; Shute, 2000).

The objective and subjective dimensions of deviance research are reflected in the chapter on religious and scientific belief systems as well (Chapter 9). More objective research on religion is reflected in the search to understand sects and cults. Researchers have explored why "deviant" religious groups form, what conditions foster acts like mass suicides, and what factors contribute to sect or cult violence (Lewis & Melton, 1994; Bromley, 2002; Hall, 2002). Specialists in the study of cults have investigated specific

Marshall Applewhite, founder of the Heaven's Gate cult. Deviance scholars with a more objective approach to research analyze the characteristics of cults.

groups (e.g., "The Family"), testified in court as expert witnesses, and created guidelines for people to use in determining whether a specific religious group may be dangerous (Barker, 2001). Scholars with more subjective interests in deviance have questioned the traditional distinction between churches, sects, and cults and have demonstrated that political factors frequently determine which groups are treated as deviant within a particular society (Jenkins, 2000; Chryssides, 1994). They have also pointed out the power that religion has frequently had as a social typer of deviance—that it dictates to us who or what should be considered deviant—and the potential dangers of the boundaries between religion and politics becoming blurred (Boston, 1996).

Like religion, science now has great influence over what society considers deviant. Chapter 9, therefore, also addresses science as social typer of deviance as well as deviance in science. Researchers with more objective interests have studied "deviant" acts that occur in science, broadly referred to as **scientific misconduct** (e.g., Park, 2000). Many of them have concluded that these acts are more common than might be suspected. Some explanations of "deviant" scientific acts focus on individual factors (the **bad apple/person theory**), but others emphasize that the characteristics of the scientific community itself set the stage for "deviant" acts (**iceberg theory**) (Ben-Yehuda, 1986; Bechtel & Pearson, 1985; James, 1995). In the latter approach, a number of specific theories have been applied, such as differential association theory, Merton's strain theory, and social control theories. The subjective dimension of deviance is explored in the analysis of science as a powerful social typer of deviance, telling us who or what should be considered deviant. When scientists make claims to truth, many of us automatically believe them and would likely never dare question them. Although in many cases the efforts of scientists benefit us all (e.g., regarding the health dangers of obesity and smoking), we must also remember the central role that science played in the eugenics movement and the horrors that occurred in Nazi Germany.

Social Typing, Social Control, and Powerful Groups

The notion of deviance emerges out of the **social typing process** (Rubington & Weinberg, 2008). The first component of social typing is **description**, wherein a label is attached to a person, behaviour, or characteristic. The second component is **evaluation**, in which a judgment is attached to the person, behaviour, or characteristic as a result of the initial label. The last component is **prescription**, where the person is treated in specific ways only because of the label and the judgment that have been attached. This last component of the social typing process refers to measures of **social control** or **regulation**.

Deviance can be met with **informal controls** (through everyday social interactions) or with **formal controls** (at the hands of an institution or organization) (Rubington & Weinberg, 2002). The social control of deviance may be **preventative** (preventing a deviant act in the first place, such as through socialization) or **retroactive** (following a deviant act) (Edwards, 1988). **Self-control** is another form of regulation, wherein we all monitor our own behaviours to prevent and fix our own deviance (Edwards, 1988; Foucault, 1995).

The social typing of deviance is most effective when done by someone who has some institutionalized power in society (Rubington & Weinberg, 2002). Five different groups in society are especially powerful in that they are able to influence our decisions about who or what is "deviant" and to exert potent measures of social control: the media, commercial enterprise, government, religion, and science. At times, these powerful groups act as **moral entrepreneurs** themselves by trying to influence or change society's dominant moral code in relation to a particular issue. At other times, these powerful groups serve as tools used by other groups of moral entrepreneurs in their efforts.

The central role that the media plays in the daily lives of billions of people makes it the locus of claims-making in the struggles over moral codes and deviance. Commercial enterprise is another powerful group involved in the social typing process. Its efforts are intertwined with the media in two different ways. First, although there is a small nonprofit element in Canadian broadcasting, the media are predominantly a form of commercial enterprise—that is, an industry that is driven by the profit motive. Second, commercial enterprise uses the media as a tool for selling its products, via advertising, commercials, and product placement in television shows, movies, or video games.

Another group using the media is, of course, politicians and government, who have ultimate power vested in them. In their hands lies the power to create or revoke legislation, to construct social policies that will be implemented through various means, and to influence the enforcement of society's dominant moral codes. Politicians may act as moral entrepreneurs or may be lobbied by interest groups acting as moral entrepreneurs. The work of politicians also exists in a bidirectional relationship with the media, where the media follow the work of politicians, and politicians use media to influence the public mind.

Ask Yourself

Social typers frequently rationalize the labelling of certain people, actions, or characteristics as deviant on the basis of notions of statistical rarity, social harm, negative societal reaction, or normative violation. As you read through the review of how social typing was addressed in the substantive topics in this textbook, consider the rationales that were used for the social typing of deviance in each of the various instances.

There are two other groups of moral entrepreneurs, however: religion and science. Religious institutions have played a vital role in the creation of dominant moral codes throughout history, maybe more so in the past than today. Finally, the power of scientists in the social typing process is perhaps granted more legitimacy than any other group. Science is seen by many people as a purely objective discipline, such that its claims to truth are frequently considered unaffected by political, religious, or commercial interests.

Chapter 5, on sexuality, revealed that in any given culture at any particular time in history, certain sexual behaviours are socially typed as deviant and made subject to social control measures. Following European colonization, Aboriginal sexuality was socially controlled through religion (e.g., the teachings of local missionaries) and government (e.g., through legislation banning polygamy) (Newhouse, 1998; Razack, 2002).

Over the past several hundred years, what has been socially typed as deviant sexuality has varied based on the cultural norms of the time (D'Emilio & Freedman, 1997). When sexuality was perceived as solely for the purpose of procreation, any nonprocreative sexual acts (e.g., heterosexual coitus involving contraceptive use, homosexuality, masturbation) were socially typed as deviant. This is considerably different from society today, wherein personal fulfillment is perceived as the purpose of sexuality.

Although there is more freedom in sexual norms today than in the past, certain sexual acts are still socially typed as deviant (e.g., sex with a minor, having sex "too frequently," or being "kinky") (Goode, 1997). The way that sexuality is socially controlled has changed as well. During the sixteenth and seventeenth centuries, sexual deviance was primarily a religious and familial concern; for example, sexual deviance could result in excommunication from the church, and fathers would enforce "shotgun" weddings following premarital pregnancy. Today, religion has lost its hold over sexuality and has been succeeded by a diversity of social control measures. We have legislation that governs certain aspects of sexuality (e.g., degree of consent and age), medicalization (e.g., encouraging "safer" sex and the designation of "sexual disorders" as mental disorders), social organizations that try to encourage abstinence and contraceptive use in adolescents, and the pervasiveness of sexuality in all forms of the media.

In Chapter 6, on youth, we saw that certain behaviours and characteristics of youth are socially typed as deviant and made subject to social control. Youth crime is defined and controlled by government and the criminal justice system. Youth gangs are considered a widespread social concern, which is reflected in media reports of youth street gangs, specialized law enforcement units to monitor gang members, as well as various educational programs that discourage gang membership (Fasiolo & Leckie, 1993; Tanner, 2001, 2010).

The science of "risk management" attempts to intervene with youth who are seen as "at risk" of gang membership, criminal involvement, homelessness, substance abuse, teen pregnancy, and more. Law enforcement, social workers, psychologists, educators, health professionals, government, and social organizations all participate in such "risk management" (Bessant, 2001). Youth substance use is socially typed as deviant, seen as both a medical and a social problem. Public service campaigns via the media, education and intervention programs within various social organizations, and medical treatment are all means by which substance use is controlled (Roberts et al., 2001). Binge drinking in university is controlled through diverse programs that include peer education and support, university policies, and in some cases even "dry" campuses (Keeling, 2000, 2002).

Chapter 7 addressed how certain types of voluntary and involuntary physical appearances are socially typed as deviant. Those who choose particular hairstyles, makeup, and clothing (e.g., "goths") may find it difficult to find employment because of employers' attitudes and biases. Body modification that may be considered acceptable in some groups may be considered unacceptable in others (e.g., in physicians). People who stray beyond the "ideal" body size are socially typed as "too fat" or "too thin," although there is much more leeway for thinness before a deviant label is attached.

Body size is regulated in the realms of medicine for health reasons, but is controlled in other arenas as well. The media is a powerful social typing and social control agent for "too fat," with media imagery having a significant influence on people's perceptions of body size, feelings about themselves, and efforts at weight loss (Stice & Shaw, 1994; Garner, 1997). Commercial industry permeates social control over "too fat." Books, magazines, videos, pills, potions, and patches all promise to help us lose weight and look great. In the realm of everyday interaction, people who are considered "too fat" are controlled through stigmatization (e.g., name-calling), prejudicial attitudes, and overt discrimination (e.g., in employment) (Puhl & Heuer, 2009; Puhl & Brownell, 2001). Government programs target people who are overweight or out of shape, trying to encourage people to adopt healthier lifestyles (e.g., Health Canada, 2005c). Even some schools are attempting to reduce the proportion of children who are overweight by instituting daily fitness activities (DeMont, 2002).

Chapter 8 discussed the social typing of psychological deviance as mental illness, which occurs at both formal and informal levels. Mental illness today is highly medicalized. The fields of psychiatry and psychology are intimately involved in social typing, determining what the "descriptions" are (e.g., "depression"), what the evaluation is (i.e., "ill"), and what the treatments should be (e.g., therapy, medication, hospitalization).

In the past, mental illness was perceived quite differently. For example, for several centuries people who are now seen as "mentally ill" were instead perceived as being possessed by the devil or guilty of witchcraft. Control measures included religious rituals to exorcise the devil (in the case of possession) or, in the case of witchcraft, executions carried out by religious or governmental authorities. Over the last several decades, the **deinstitutionalization** movement has characterized most Western nations, with a shift from hospital-based treatments to community-based ones. Deinstitutionalization has worked very well for those people who have strong support networks and who live in communities with sufficient resources. However, for people lacking support networks and community resources, deinstitutionalization has meant a lack of medical treatment (Krieg, 2001; Sullivan, Jackson, & Spritzer, 1996). People with mental illnesses who do not receive medical treatment frequently end up being socially controlled as homeless persons or criminals (Belcher, 1989; Hodgins, 1993).

In Chapter 9, on religious and scientific belief systems, we saw that many different religious groups are socially typed as deviant by governments, scientific "experts," or other religious groups. For example, the government of Germany labels Scientology as deviant and does not hire its adherents (Forum 18, 2001).

The **anti-cult movement** socially types certain religious groups as deviant, emphasizing those groups thought to use mind control techniques and authoritarian leadership. Organizations that are part of this movement provide information on cult awareness, support groups for parents of cult members, and in some cases deprogramming services for

Ask Yourself

An important aspect of social typing is who benefits from the social typing process—the social typers themselves, particular groups in society, society as a whole, or sometimes even the people who have been socially typed. Select one specific issue from each of the substantive topics covered in the textbook —sexuality, youth, physical appearance, mental illness, religion, or science—and ask yourself who has benefited from the social typing in that instance.

former cult members (Barker, 2001). The **counter-cult movement** consists of certain fundamentalist Christian groups that identify all nonfundamentalist Christians and all non-Christian religions as deviant. They spread their messages via the Internet, at church meetings, and through publications that teach members how to convince adherents of specific cults to leave those groups (Bromley & Shupe, 1993).

One of the ways that social typing, social control, and power made themselves evident in relation to science is in the concept of deviant sciences or pseudo-sciences (Shermer, 2001). The scientific community itself determines which belief systems are not "real" sciences, such as astrology. Although the scientific community is the most qualified entity to evaluate scientific claims being made by others, some scholars suggest that its inherent conservatism often leads it to automatically rejecting anything that is new or too different from the status quo (Ben-Yehuda, 1990). This is particularly apparent in those instances where claims that were initially rejected as deviant later come to be accepted. The astronomy community socially typed the first radio astronomers as deviant; consequently, they had difficulty getting their work published and became outcasts in the astronomy community. At a later point, however, that same scientific community determined that radio astronomy was a "real" science after all (Ben-Yehuda, 1990).

The "Deviance Dance"

Another theme throughout this textbook is the notion of the "**deviance dance**." This refers to the idea that with any particular person, action, or characteristic that has been socially typed as deviant, there will be differing points of view, debate, and resistance. The dance surrounding deviance is sometimes uniform (like a country line dance), with virtually everyone agreeing on the issue and what should be done with it; everyone moves in the same direction in pursuit of the same goal. At other times, the dance is more waltz-like, where various groups work toward the same goal, but everyone is not taking the same steps to reach that goal. At yet other times, the dance is more like a mosh pit, with groups pushing, shoving, and slamming into each other to reach their own particular goals.

Every substantive topic we have looked at involves the "deviance dance." In Chapter 5 on sexuality, we see debates over various aspects of sexuality, such as how often is "too often," whether exotic dancers are victims of violence in a patriarchal society versus legitimate workers, the purported harms caused by pornography, and social policies governing prostitution. We can even see resistance to legislation that prohibits sexual contact between adults and children; despite the fact that such behaviours are widely abhorred in Canadian society, the North America Man/Boy Love Association (NAMBLA) tries to convince people that consensual sexual relationships between adults and children are not harmful (NAMBLA, n.d.).

In Chapter 6 on youth, we also see differing opinions, a number of debates, and acts of resistance. For example, critics say that virtually every adolescent ends up being perceived

At times, the struggle over deviance is characterized by intense debate and conflict.

as "at risk" within the knowledge and practices of "risk management" (Bessant, 2001; Ericson & Haggerty, 2001). That is, adolescence itself has become defined as a time of inherent risk. The "deviance dance" is also apparent in the debates that occur between politicians or interest groups that proclaim youth crime to be out of control and in need of tougher legislation, and those groups that point out that the public image of youth crime is tremendously overblown. Differing points of view are present with regard to problems that *are* generally recognized, as well. For example, although most university administrators see binge drinking among students as problematic, they can have very different approaches to controlling it (Wechsler, Lee, Kuo, Seibring, Nelson, & Lee, 2002). The most controversial approach has been the "dry campus," where all alcohol is prohibited. This has met with resistance from students who oppose university alcohol programs or policies that are directed *at* them rather than created *with* them. It has also been criticized by a number of substance abuse experts, who claim that prohibitionist approaches are ineffective and simply move binge drinking off campus (Keeling, 2002).

The topic of body size embodies differing views and resistance as well (Chapter 7). Although the cultural ideal of thinness continues to be perpetuated in the media and public opinion, various organizations are trying to change cultural ideals to accommodate a wider range of body sizes and are lobbying the media to integrate more realistic representations of the female body. Anorexia is an extremely dangerous disorder that frequently requires immediate medical intervention. However, media images (e.g., of *Playboy* centrefolds) actually promote anorexic ideals, and "Ana" websites even provide tips to people with anorexia to enable them to continue their pursuit of weight loss. Like the behaviours of these lobbyists and even the "Ana" websites, body modification may also be seen as a form of resistance to social typing. For example, women may get tattoos to reject traditional discourses of gender in society (Atkinson, 2002), and straightedgers use their bodies as statements against the hedonism and self-indulgence of the modern world (Atkinson, 2003b).

In the chapter on mental disorders (Chapter 8), the "deviance dance" is evident in a number of ways, such as the stigma management strategies of **deflecting** and **challenging** that some people with mental disorders use. The deviance dance is particularly apparent in debates surrounding specific diagnostic categories contained in the American Psychiatric Association's *Diagnostic and Statistical Manual of Mental Disorders* (e.g., Caplan, 1995). For example, in contemporary society, debates over the extent to which ADHD is being diagnosed in North America are common. However, some groups have even gone a step further, suing the American Psychiatric Association for "manufacturing" a mental illness (Shute, 2000; Peck, 2001). Debates over whether gender identity disorder is a mental illness are also common today. Some scholars resist the medicalization of mental disorders even more profoundly, by arguing that the concept of mental illness itself is a "myth" (Szasz, 1994).

The deviance dance is perhaps at its most obvious in situations involving religion (see Chapter 9)—those in which particular groups have been socially typed as being sects or cults, and then the ways that they actively resist those labels. In France, more than 100 groups have been socially typed in this way by the French government. Some members of these groups have taken their cases all the way to the European Court of Human Rights, where the judges' decisions have frequently opposed the claims made by the French government (US Department of State, 2010). Throughout the world, as Jehovah's Witnesses resist the "deviant" label that has been attached to them (and the discriminatory actions they have faced as a result, including arrest), they also claim that all religious groups other than their own are deviant (Lawson, 1995).

Difference, debate, and resistance are even evident in the world of science. Ongoing debates have characterized scientific claims in relation to the tobacco industry. For example, the industry's scientists label the work of their opposition as **junk science**, while scientists whose research shows the dangers of smoking launch similar claims at the industry (Rampton & Stauber, 2000; Ong & Glantz, 2001). Historically, although the eugenics movement had considerable influence in Canada, the United States, Britain, and Germany, there were also scientists and social organizations in each of those nations who were critical of eugenic ideals. In contemporary society, while some groups of scientists proclaim the benefits that genetic testing and manipulation will bring to the world, others disagree, and some claim that modern genetics is nothing more than eugenics in twenty-first-century clothing (Ward, 1993; Carlson & Stimeling, 2002).

TIME TO REVIEW

Learning Objective 1

■ How have more objective research interests been reflected in the chapters of this textbook?

■ How have more subjective research interests been reflected in the chapters of this textbook?

Learning Objective 2

■ What are some examples of how social typing and social control are evident

with each of the substantive topics explored in the textbook?

Learning Objective 3

■ How are notions of power embedded in the chapters of the textbook?

Learning Objective 4

■ In what ways are the "deviance dance" apparent in the topics we have looked at?

The Search for Standards

Throughout this textbook, we have seen that, to some extent, "deviance" is in the eye of the beholder. That is, there is far more to the concept of deviance than the inherent nature of the person, act, or characteristic. The cross-cultural and historical examples that we have looked at show us that power is fundamental to determining what or who will be considered deviant in society. Actions considered criminal in certain cultures at specific historical moments are seen as acceptable actions in other cultures and at other historical times. For example, homosexual acts were seen as criminal throughout North America a century ago, but today they are not considered criminal in Canada, although they are criminalized in some other regions of the world.

Conversely, during most of the nineteenth century, child abuse and spousal abuse were seen as legally, socially, and morally acceptable, but today are considered crimes in much of the world. The sexual relationships between boys and adult men in Sambian society would constitute pedophilia according to Canadian standards. Adultery, while merely frowned upon in North America, is considered criminal in other nations (Mackay, 2000). A half-century ago, youth (but not adults) could run afoul of the criminal justice system for misbehaviours like truancy, sexual promiscuity, and incorrigibility; today, the list of criminal offences is identical for youth and adults.

Historically, acts that were carried out by societal authorities with wide support from the rest of the community would be considered deviant by contemporary standards. The witch persecutions that swept much of Europe for centuries are now looked upon with disdain as an instance of religious and political authorities preying on the superstitious populace to further their own goals of power. Residential schooling is perceived as a regrettable event in Canadian history, even by those societal institutions that participated in it—that is, the federal government and several church bodies. Formal apologies have been issued, reparations are underway, and programs have been instituted to assist Aboriginal communities in beginning the healing process (Ontario Consultants on Religious Tolerance, 2003).

Social Darwinism and the subsequent eugenics movement, popular in Canada, the United States, Britain, and other nations during the late nineteenth and early twentieth centuries, targeted numerous social groups for forced sterilization. The eugenics movement itself is now looked upon as a deviant use of science and politics. The apex that the eugenics movement reached in the Holocaust is widely perceived as one of the most horrific events in human history; however, it is important to remember that for several years during the 1930s, the rest of the world (including Canada) looked upon the success of Nazi eugenics with admiration.

After exploring cross-cultural and historical variations, as well as the debate and differing points of view that exist within a single society at any given time, some people may understandably begin to think that there are no transcendent standards by which people, behaviours, or characteristics can be evaluated—and that no group has the right to impose its subjective standards of behaviour on any other group. Because deviance is in the eye of the beholder, "anything goes." Of course, if that belief were fully realized, anarchy would reign in society. So how can balance be achieved? How can we determine whether it is appropriate to socially type specific groups of people as deviant and subject them to measures of social control?

To some extent, subjectivity will always be involved in the social typing of deviance. Regardless of what norms, policies, programs, or legislation exist, there will always be some people (no matter how few) who will be in opposition. However, one place to begin a search for possible universal standards is with documents that emphasize the notion of human rights.

The Universal Declaration of Human Rights, adopted by the member states of the United Nations on December 10, 1948, is the foundational document for other modern human rights policies, programs, and legislation throughout the world (including the Canadian Charter of Rights and Freedoms). A larger sample of human rights documents can be found in Box 10.1.

A number of themes run through the range of human rights documents that can be found in countries around the world. One of these is the right to **human dignity**, which is the right to be treated with respect. Numerous issues that have been addressed in this textbook can be considered in relation to this human right. The way that certain social groups were targeted by the eugenics movement can certainly be considered a violation of human dignity, as can the Nazis' racial hygiene program. European colonization and residential

The United Nations is one international body that develops universal human rights standards.

Box 10.1

A Sample of Human Rights Documents

- The Magna Carta (see the British Library website for scanned pages of the original Magna Carta and an English translation, at *www.bl.uk/treasures/magnacarta/*)

- Declaration of the Rights of Man and of the Citizen (from the French Revolution)

- Universal Declaration of Human Rights

- Canadian Charter of Rights and Freedoms

- Convention on the Rights of the Child

- International Covenant on Civil and Political Rights

- International Covenant on Economic, Social, and Cultural Rights

- European Convention on Human Rights

- Universal Declaration of Sexual Rights

- Universal Declaration on the Human Genome and Human Rights

- Declaration on the Elimination of All Forms of Intolerance and of Discrimination Based on Religion or Belief

- Declaration on the Rights of Disabled Persons

- Principles for the Protection of Persons with Mental Illness and for the Improvement of Mental Health Care

- Convention Concerning Indigenous and Tribal Peoples in Independent Countries

All of these documents can be found in their entirety on the Internet using any search engine.

schooling also involved infringements on the dignity of Aboriginal peoples. The notion of human dignity underlies other international documents as well, such as the Universal Declaration of Sexual Rights (World Association for Sexology, 1999), and UNESCO's Universal Declaration on the Human Genome and Human Rights (UNESCO, 1997). The former document emphasizes that consensual adult sexual activities should not be deviantized, and that freedom to sexual expression must prevail. The latter document suggests that certain genetic traits should not be considered superior or inferior to other traits; that is, individuals with specific genetic traits should not be deviantized.

Another theme in human rights documents is the prohibition of differential treatment on the basis of group membership (i.e., **discrimination**). The characteristics that are commonly listed in relation to this right are race, sex, ethnicity, colour, nation of origin, religion, political membership, and language; however, other categories (e.g., sexual orientation) are included in some human rights documents as well. The Canadian Charter of Rights and Freedoms and various pieces of provincial human rights legislation address the notion of discrimination in Canadian society. The World Health Organization's constitution declares that the right to physical, mental, and social health applies to all social groups, such as those just listed (World Health Organization, 2003). The Universal Declaration on the Human Genome and Human Rights prohibits discrimination on the basis of genetic characteristics (UNESCO, 1997).

Historically, the right to freedom from discrimination was infringed upon in the eugenics movement and during European colonization. In contemporary society, people who are considered "too fat" face discrimination in employment, housing, health care, and education (Puhl & Brownell, 2001). Members of certain religious groups are discriminated against in several countries, such as the groups identified by the government of France as cults (e.g., Jehovah's Witnesses, Scientology) (US Department of State, 2010).

Security of person and property are also prevalent in human rights documents. Violent crimes (e.g., assault) and property crimes (e.g., theft) violate security of the person and property. The World Health Organization's constitution declares that the universal right to physical, mental, and social health is necessary for peace and security, not specifically for individuals but in societies and throughout the world (World Health Organization, 2004b); thus, the failure to provide the necessary means for achieving health for any group is seen as unacceptable. The involuntary sterilization of "mental defectives," the torture and death involved in the Holocaust, the abuse suffered by tens of thousands of Aboriginal children in residential schools, and the witch persecutions (wherein witches were not only executed but also had their property seized to pay for their persecution) can all be seen as infringements on the right to security of the person and of property. When the Canadian government defined Japanese-Canadians as "enemy aliens" during World War II, it placed thousands of Japanese-Canadian citizens in internment camps and subsequently seized their property and auctioned it to the highest bidder. Security of person and security of property were again violated by the Canadian government.

Human dignity, freedom from discrimination, and security of person and property are three of the core themes that are integrated into various types of human rights policies and legislation. Given the influence of subjectivity and power that has been involved in the social typing of deviance across cultures and throughout history, human rights policies represent some basic standards that we may be able to apply in determining whether it is appropriate to label anyone or anything as deviant. However, a level of subjectivity also exists in determining whether human rights have been violated in any particular instance. Human rights documents themselves state that there are circumstances where someone's human rights may legitimately be violated; typically, this is when there are threats to social order, public health, or other people's human rights. For example, although freedom of religion is a basic human right, many governments monitor, regulate, and even ban specific religious groups that are perceived as a threat to social order (Forum 18, 2001; US Department of State, 2010).

Although freedom of expression is a universal human right, Canada, the United States, and numerous other countries have hate crime or human rights legislation that prohibits spreading hatred or advocating the genocide of identifiable social groups. For instance, some leaders and members of white supremacist groups have been charged with spreading hatred, even though charging them with that offence is a violation of their right to freedom of expression. International human rights documents condone this as a legitimate violation of that freedom, based on threats to the social order and violations of other people's human rights.

If you are interested in learning more about human rights, see the information contained in Box 10.2.

Box 10.2

Are You Interested in Human Rights?

If you want to learn more about human rights, or wish to become active in the pursuit of human rights, you may find the following organizations and information centres useful:

- Human Rights Watch (*www.hrw.org*)
- Amnesty International (*www.amnesty.org*)

- International Gay and Lesbian Human Rights Commission (*www.iglhrc.org*)
- Women's Human Rights Resources Programme (*www.law-lib.utoronto.ca/diana*)

CHAPTER SUMMARY

- Certain ideas that were introduced in Chapter 1 represent themes that have been carried through the various chapters in the textbook. One of these themes is the blending of *objective* and *subjective* approaches to the study of deviance. In various chapters, the *positivist* interest in causation that characterizes more objective approaches was explored, such as in explanations of youth crime and substance use. (1)

■ The *interpretive* and *critical* interests in the social processes by which deviance is assigned, which characterize more subjective approaches, was addressed throughout the chapters, as well. For example, we looked at the *moral panics* surrounding youth crime and gangs, and the social standards that define "too fat." (1)

■ A second theme throughout this book is the notion of the *social typing process*. Power plays a critical role in determining who or what will be considered deviant and what social control measures are directed at them. Governments, the media, religious institutions, scientists, and commercial industry are all intimately involved in the social typing and social control of various aspects of deviance. (2, 3)

■ The *deviance dance* can be seen throughout this book as well. Regardless of the specific issue in question, various individuals and groups have differing points of view on whether something or someone is deviant, how deviant they are, and what the most effective means of social control will be. (4)

■ Given the role of subjectivity in understanding deviance, does that mean "anything goes"? Does it mean that we cannot legitimately socially type anyone or anything as deviant? The concept of *human rights* is one place where we can begin looking at whether any standards can be applied. Numerous international human rights documents exist, and they give some indication of criteria that may be used to determine who should and should not be deviantized. (5)

MySearchLab®

⊙-[Watch] Go to MySearchLab to watch the video called "Grievances, Anger, and Hope".

Apply What You Know: Think about the idea of hope as the central element in the civil rights movement, a social movement that fundamentally altered what people in the United States thought was normal and acceptable. How do you think social movements like the civil rights movement are related to the "deviance dance"? Can you think of other social movements that have changed what we consider to be deviant behaviour?

MySearchLab with eText offers you access to an online interactive version of the text, extensive help with your writing and research projects, and provides round-the-clock access to credible and reliable source material.

Glossary

absolute others Individuals who are presented (through the media) as inherently evil.

adapting Body projects that involve removing or repairing aspects of one's body.

affirmative postmodernism A form of postmodern theory that deconstructs master narratives, overarching theories, or knowledge and focuses analysis on the local and specific.

androcentric bias A bias toward the experiences of males, whereby female experiences are ignored; a critique of functionalist theories.

anomie (1) In Durkheim's functionalist theory, a state of normlessness. (2) In Merton's functionalist theory, a state where society's institutionalized goals are emphasized more than the legitimate means of attaining those goals.

anorexia nervosa A mental disorder characterized by being significantly below the ideal body weight according to scientific standards in conjunction with several additional physical and psychological characteristics.

anti-cult movement Individuals that educate people about dangerous or destructive cults and attempt to control their activities by lobbying governments and other organizations; also known as *cult awareness groups*.

appealing to higher loyalties A technique of neutralization that rationalizes one's deviant behaviour as serving a higher purpose.

atavists In early criminological theories, the view that criminals were evolutionary throwbacks whose biology prevented them from conforming to society's rules.

at-risk youth Youth who have been identified as having a greater likelihood of negative outcomes.

attachment In social bonds theory, the bond characterized by one's emotional attachment to others.

atypical anorexia A mental disorder characterized by satisfying some but not all of the diagnostic criteria for anorexia nervosa.

back-stage self In the dramaturgical approach, individuals' identities and behaviours when they are no longer in front of any audience, but rather are alone or with those who are closest to them.

bad apple/person theory A theory that claims acts of scientific misconduct are rare.

belief Any proposition that an individual considers to be true, regardless of whether it is true or not.

belief systems Organized sets of interrelated beliefs.

berdache A derogatory term used by European explorers to refer to biological males who assumed female roles in some Aboriginal cultures.

binge drinking The consumption of five or more drinks (for males) or four or more drinks (for females) in one drinking session.

body mass index (BMI) A calculation of height and weight that determines an individual's level of risk for a variety of health problems.

body projects The ways that people adapt, change, or control characteristics of their bodies.

bourgeoisie In Marxist conflict theory, the owners of the means of economic production.

camouflaging Body projects that reflect normative processes learned through socialization.

career contingencies In the theory of the deviant career, significant turning points that influence the directions that people take at various points in the deviant career.

chaining In terrorist networks, the process by which an individual can only join the network after being introduced and recommended by an existing member.

challenging A stigma management technique in which individuals actively fight back against an external stigmatizing force, such as through confronting or educating others.

child pornography Any representation of someone under the age of 18 engaged in explicit sexual activity or any representation of someone under the age of 18, "the dominant characteristic of which is the depiction, for a sexual purpose, of a sexual organ or the anal region."

child-savers movement During the Victorian era, middle-class church groups who thought it was the state's responsibility to provide a moral environment for children whose parents were unwilling or unable to do so.

churches Large and powerful religious groups that are well established in society and highly bureaucratized.

commitment In social bonds theory, the bond characterized by one's vested interest in the conforming world.

commitment to the community A motivation for gang membership that involves continuing a family or neighbourhood tradition.

communism The assumption that scientists freely give up rights to the knowledge that they create so that this knowledge can be shared by all; part of the normative structure of science.

concentration The trend toward a small number of corporations owning the majority of the market share.

condemnation of the condemners A technique of neutralization that shifts the focus from the deviant's own behaviour to the deviant behaviour of others, especially people from the social groups that have pointed to this person's deviance.

conflict frame A frame used in the news media that emphasizes conflicts between nations, institutions, groups, or individuals.

conflict gangs In differential opportunity theory, gangs who engage in violent conflict with other gangs in pursuit of status and power.

conflict theories Critical theories that claim social rules emerge out of conflict and are made by the powerful to serve their own interests, that the powerful are less likely to break social rules, and that the powerless are more likely to break the social rules.

conflict view (of law) The view that laws are created by the powerful to serve their own interests.

conformity (1) A person, behaviour, or characteristic that is considered normal and acceptable; the opposite of *deviance*. (2) In Merton's strain theory, the mode of adaptation that involves acceptance of both the institutionalized goals and the legitimate means of attaining those goals.

conglomeration The trend toward companies merging, or some companies purchasing other companies to form large multinational conglomerates.

consensual view (of law) The view that suggests society's laws emerge out of consensus.

consent One of the criteria used to judge deviant and normal sexual activity, based on some level of agreement between the two sexual partners.

contextual constructionism A form of social constructionism that emphasizes the processes by which certain social phenomena come to be perceived and reacted to in particular ways in a given society at a specific time in history; also known as *soft constructionism*.

convergence The trend toward media companies owning multiple forms of media; for example, a single corporation owning not only several television stations, but also the cable companies that deliver the service.

counter-cult movement Fundamentalist Christian groups that express concerns about other religious groups they consider to be based on "wrong" theologies.

criminal gangs In differential opportunity theory, gangs whose activities are economic in nature.

criminologists Scholars who exclusively study criminalized forms of deviance.

critical theories Theories that focus on the power relations that underlie the creation of social rules, and that have an interest in emancipation and social justice.

cult awareness groups Individuals that educate people about dangerous or destructive cults and attempt to control their activities by lobbying governments and other organizations; also known as *the anti-cult movement*.

cults Small religious groups characterized by a highly oppositional and reactionary doctrine, extremely high levels of commitment required of members, and a single, charismatic leader.

cyberbullying Bullying behaviours that use information and communication technologies.

cyberdeviance Deviant acts that are committed using computer technology.

cyberterrorism Forms of hacking that use computer viruses and malware to attack societal infrastructure.

dancers Female exotic dancers who have considerable training in dance and who enjoy the artistic and creative expression of the industry.

date rape drugs Odourless, tasteless drugs that when mixed with alcohol, cause intense drowsiness and memory impairment.

deflecting A stigma management technique in which individuals block an external stigmatizing force by distancing themselves from the labels they have been given.

deinstitutionalization The social control of people with mental illnesses in community-based programs rather than in institutions.

denial of injury A technique of neutralization that argues one's behaviour does not hurt anybody.

denial of responsibility A technique of neutralization that acknowledges one's behaviour but shifts the larger blame to someone or something else.

denial of the victim A technique of neutralization that argues the victim of one's behaviour was deserving of that behaviour.

denominational sect A religious sect that has become increasingly integrated into the larger society, such that it is on the verge of being considered a denomination of a larger church.

denominations Religious subgroups of larger churches.

description The first component of the social typing process, whereby a label is attached to a particular person, behaviour, or characteristic.

deviance A person, behaviour, or characteristic that is socially typed as deviant and subjected to measures of social control.

deviance dance The interactions, negotiations, and debates among groups with different perceptions of whether a behaviour or characteristic is deviant and needs to be socially controlled and, if so, how.

deviance specialists Scholars who study criminalized or non-criminalized forms of deviance.

deviancy amplification The process by which a deviantized group becomes more extreme as a response to hostilities or social control efforts from outsiders.

deviant career An interpretive theory of deviance that claims deviance emerges, progresses through stages, and changes over time, similar to the developmental stages of a career.

deviantize To subject a person, behaviour, or characteristic to the complete social typing process.

differential association The process by which individuals learn deviant or conforming techniques and motives.

digital piracy The illegal downloading of music, software, or video.

discourse A body of knowledge, or all that is "known" about a particular phenomenon.

discrimination Differential treatment on the basis of group membership; a violation of human rights.

discrimination paradigm A view of mental illness that emphasizes the role that stigmatization plays in the daily experiences of people with mental illnesses and seeks to reduce those experiences.

disease paradigm A view of mental illness that emphasizes the symptoms of the disorder that distress and impair individuals' functioning and seeks to ameliorate those symptoms.

disintegrative shaming The process by which deviantized persons are rejected by the community.

disinterestedness The assumption that scientific work is done in the name of truth rather than for any personal gain or vested interests; part of the normative structure of science.

divide their social worlds A stigma management technique that involves carefully managing who is and is not permitted to know about one's stigmatized behaviour or characteristic.

dominant moral codes The "lists" of right/ wrong, appropriate/inappropriate, moral/immoral that predominate in a particular society at a given time in history and that are enforced in multiple ways.

dramatization of evil In Tannenbaum's labelling theory, the judgment that it is no longer a particular behaviour that is deviant, but rather it is the person her or himself that is deviant.

dramaturgy The interpretive school of thought that suggests social life is similar to performing in the theatre, wherein individuals have *front-stage selves* and *back-stage selves*.

ecclesia State religions that are sanctioned by the government and adopted as a nation's official religion.

economic consequences frame A frame used in the news media that highlights material costs and benefits for countries, regions, groups, or individuals.

ego-psychological theories (of anorexia) Theories that explain anorexia nervosa in terms of impaired psychological functioning emerging from the child–mother relationship.

endocrinological theories (of anorexia) Theories that explain anorexia nervosa in terms of hormonal defects.

established femininity A form of femininity that embodies the dominant cultural constructions of what a female body should look like.

established sect A religious sect that retains a high level of tension with the larger society.

ethnographic research Research in which the researcher embeds her or himself with the groups being studied for an extended period of time.

eugenics Practices to increase sexual reproduction among individuals believed to be genetically superior while decreasing (or eliminating) sexual reproduction among those believed to be genetically inferior.

evaluation The second step of the social typing process, whereby a person, behaviour, or characteristic has judgments attached based on the label applied during the description component.

exhibitionists People who enjoy having sex in places where others might see them (i.e., public places).

extending Body projects that attempt to overcome physical limitations.

false consciousness In conflict theories, the false sense of freedom held by powerless groups.

family systems theories (of anorexia) Theories that explain anorexia in terms of emotionally enmeshed, rigid, overly controlling families.

feminine touch A media frame that portrays women as caressing or stroking an object, person, or themselves.

folkways Norms that govern informal everyday behaviours.

formal regulation Forms of social control that emerge from organizations or institutions; also known as *formal social control*.

formal social control Forms of social control that emerge from organizations or institutions; also known as *formal regulation*.

framing The overall way that an issue is depicted in the media, which influences what we notice about reality.

front-stage self In the dramaturgical approach, the social roles people play when in front of a variety of audiences.

functional definition (of pornography) Forms of media or popular culture used by an individual for the purposes of sexual arousal.

functionalist theories Positivist theories that explain the causes of behaviour in terms of the various structures that fulfill important functions for society.

gang A debated term that frequently refers to "any denotable ... group [of adolescents or young adults] who (a) are generally perceived as a distinct aggregation by others in the neighbourhood, (b) recognize themselves as a denotable group (almost invariably with a group name), and (c) have been involved in a sufficient number of [illegal] incidents" (Sanday cited in Chatterjee, 2006).

gang problem The socially constructed representations of gangs that are communicated through the media.

generalized other In symbolic interactionist theory, our perception of the viewpoints of generic "people" in society.

generation gap The perception that conflicts are inherent between the adult and youth generations.

genre definition (of pornography) Media or popular cultural products created for the purposes of arousing the consumer.

hackers People who access computer systems without authorization and sometimes use that access for malicious purposes.

harm An objective definition of deviance that claims a person, behaviour, or characteristic is deviant if it causes harm.

hegemony In conflict theories, the dominant way of seeing and understanding the world, as determined by the ideology of powerful groups and then taught to citizens as common sense.

high-consensus deviance Forms of deviance about which there are high levels of agreement in society.

human dignity The right to be treated with respect; a fundamental human right.

human interest frame A frame used in the news media that focuses on human life stories and emotions.

human trafficking Illegal trade in human beings for the purposes of sexual exploitation, forced labour, or slavery.

iceberg theory A theory that claims the acts of scientific misconduct that are detected are only a small proportion of all of the instances of misconduct that are actually occurring.

identity management Techniques used by individuals to manage their stigmatization; also known as *impression management*.

ideology In conflict theories, the worldview held by society's powerful groups.

impression management Techniques used by individuals to manage their stigmatization; also known as *identity management*.

infantilization A media frame that portrays women in little-girl poses, such as peeking from behind an object.

informal regulation Forms of social control that emerge from everyday social interaction; also known as *informal social control*.

informal social control Forms of social control that emerge from everyday social interaction; also known as *informal regulation*.

innovation In Merton's strain theory, the mode of adaptation that involves accepting society's institutionalized goals but rejecting the legitimate means of attaining those goals.

institutionalized goals In Merton's strain theory, the goals that are culturally exalted, including wealth, status/power, and prestige.

interactionist view (of law) The view of law that suggests that society's powerful define the law at the behest of interest groups, who appeal to those with power to rectify a perceived social ill.

instrumental Marxism A form of Marxism that proposes social rules are created to serve the interests of the powerful, becoming tools to control the proletariat.

interpretive theories Theories that draw attention to people's intersubjective understandings of the world around them, other people, and themselves.

involvement In social bonds theory, the bond characterized by the time one spends involved in conventional activities.

junk science Ungrounded claims of people with little or no scientific background, or people using their scientific credentials alone to convince people of the validity of their claims.

labelling definitions (of pornography) Sexually explicit materials deemed obscene according to community standards.

labelling theories Interpretive theories that describe the process by which individuals are labelled as deviant, which then has implications for how others treat them and their own subsequent behaviours and identities.

latent functions In functionalist theories, those functions that are unintentionally served by society's structures.

learning theories Positivist theories that explain the causes of behaviour in terms of the learning processes that people are subjected to.

least restrictive alternative Legislation stating that involuntary admission to psychiatric institutions can occur only if there are no reasonable noninstitutional alternatives.

legitimate means In Merton's strain theory, socially acceptable ways of attaining the institutionalized goals in society.

les femmes du pays Country wives, or Aboriginal women who formed intimate relationships with male European fur traders and settlers.

LGBT An acronym that represents individuals or communities that are lesbian, gay, bisexual, or transgendered.

licensed withdrawal A media frame that portrays women as not paying attention or with their eyes glazed over.

looking-glass self According to symbolic interactionist theory, the process by which our assumptions about what other people think of us influences what we think about ourselves and how we look or act.

low-consensus deviance Forms of deviance about which there are low levels of agreement in society.

manifest functions In functionalist theories, those functions that are intended to be fulfilled by society's structures.

master status A core characteristic by which others identify a person.

material incentives A motivation for gang membership involving the desire to make more, or more consistent, money.

McDonaldization of society The routinization of activities in contemporary capitalism, characterized by efficiency, predictability, control, and calculability.

mechanical solidarity In Durkheim's functionalist theory, preindustrial societies in which people were bonded together by their similarity to one another.

media Any form of communication that targets a mass audience in print or electronic format.

mental disorder "Alterations in thinking, mood or behaviour ... associated with significant distress and impaired functioning" (Health Canada, 2002, p. 7).

microanomie A state wherein an individual's self-transcendence values are exceeded by self-enhancement values.

middle-class measuring rod In status frustration theory, the middle-class norms that permeate the school system and against which all students are compared.

moral entrepreneurs Individuals or groups who manufacture public morality by bringing a social problem to public awareness and then attempting to affect change in society's dominant moral codes.

moral panic An exaggerated and sensationalized concern over a particular phenomenon, characterized by heightened concern, hostility toward the offending group, a certain level of consensus that there is a real threat, disproportionality, and volatility.

moral regulation In Durkheim's functionalist theory, the extent to which norms are enforced in society.

mores Norms that are considered to be the foundation of morality in society.

motives In differential association theory, the rationales for deviance or conformity.

muscle dysmorphia A psychological disorder that involves a preoccupation with being too thin or small and results in an obsession with weightlifting accompanied by anxiety or mood disorders, extreme body dissatisfaction, distorted eating attitudes, and anabolic steroid use.

mutual conversion The way in which lower-class boys join with similar others in response to status frustration.

nadleeh In some Aboriginal cultures, masculine female-bodied or feminine male-bodied members of the community.

nature of the sexual act One of the criteria for determining deviant and normal sexuality, which identifies certain sexual activities as being acceptable or unacceptable.

nature of the sexual partner One of the criteria for determining deviant and normal sexuality, which identifies certain sexual partners as being acceptable or unacceptable.

negative affect In Agnew's general strain theory, the negative emotions that mediate the relationship between strain and deviance.

new religious movements A term used by some scholars in place of the terms *sect* or *cult*.

nonconformists Female exotic dancers who come from privileged, educated backgrounds and who have the freedom to enter and leave the industry as they wish.

normative violation An objective definition of deviance that claims a person, behaviour, or characteristic is deviant if it violates society's norms.

obese A person that has a body mass index (BMI) between 25.0 and 29.9.

objective The view of deviance as being characterized by a single, common, clearly identifiable characteristic; also known as *objectivist*.

organic solidarity In Durkheim's functionalist theory, industrial societies in which people are bonded together by their interdependence.

overweight (1) According to scientific standards, a person that has a body mass index (BMI) 30.0 and higher. (2) According to social standards, a body that is larger than current cultural ideals.

Panopticon A prison design that enabled guards to observe prisoners at all times and yet did not allow prisoners to definitively know whether they were being watched or not.

parens patriae Parent of the country, or the child welfare approach to youth crime that was embodied in the Juvenile Delinquents Act.

parenting style An overall approach to parenting, including supervision, parental control, and emotional ties between parent and child.

physical protection A motivation for gang membership involving increased safety from the known dangers of the neighbourhood.

place of refuge and camouflage A motivation for gang membership involving a level of anonymity, removing a sense of personal responsibility for illegal activities.

pornography Forms of media or popular culture that include explicit sex.

positivist (theories of deviance) Theories that attempt to explain the causes of behaviour.

post-academic science A term that refers to the predominance of scientific research occurring in commercial centres rather than university environments.

praxis The Marxist view that social scientists have a responsibility to use their work in pursuit of practical, emancipatory goals.

prescription The third component of the social typing process, whereby measures of social control are directed at a person, behaviour, or characteristic because of the previously attached label and judgment.

preventative social control Forms of social control intended to prevent a deviant behaviour or characteristic from emerging in the first place.

prevention paradox The growing efforts to help "problem" drinkers on university campuses have not reduced the extent of harm caused by alcohol consumption, because most of the harms are caused by low- to moderate-risk drinkers.

primary deviance In Lemert's labelling theory, the occasional rule breaking everyone engages in, which is seldom noticed and rarely caught.

primary prevention (of anorexia) Efforts to prevent eating disorders from occurring in the first place.

proletariat In Marxist conflict theory, the employees of the owners of the means of production.

racialize The process by which representations of social phenomena become associated with specific racial or ethnic groups.

radical constructionism A form of social constructionism that claims the world is characterized by endless relativism; also known as *strict constructionism.*

reaction formation In status frustration theory, the oppositional standards that are developed by lower-class boys in the school system.

rebellion In Merton's strain theory, the mode of adaptation that involves replacing society's institutionalized goals and legitimate means with new sets of goals and means.

recreation A motivation for gang membership involving opportunities for entertainment and socializing.

redesigning Body projects that involve fundamental, lasting reconstructions of bodies.

reintegrative shaming Individuals are temporarily stigmatized for their deviant acts, but then accepted back into the community.

religion as deviance Deviant acts that occur within accepted religions, or religious belief systems that are socially typed as deviant.

residential schooling A policy of the Canadian government that removed Aboriginal children from their communities and placed them in boarding schools run by various Christian churches.

resistant femininity A form of femininity that opposes dominant ideals of what the female body should look like.

retreatism In Merton's strain theory, the mode of adaptation that involves rejecting both society's institutionalized goals and the legitimate means of attaining those goals.

retreatist gangs In differential opportunity theory, gangs whose activities revolve around substance use.

retroactive social control Forms of social control intended to punish, fix, or cure deviance that has already occurred.

risk society A society in which knowledge experts warn us that risks that must be identified and managed are everywhere around us.

ritualism In Merton's strain theory, the mode of adaptation that involves rejecting society's institutionalized goals but continuing to accept the legitimate means of attaining those goals.

ritualization of subordination A media frame that portrays women lying on a bed, off-balance, or beneath men.

role taking In symbolic interactionist theory, the process by which we vicariously place ourselves in the roles of others in order to see the world from their points of view, which then influences our own attitudes and actions.

schema A cognitive, or mental, framework that helps us organize and interpret information.

science "Knowledge or a system of knowledge covering general truths of the operation of general laws especially as obtained and tested through scientific method" (Merriam-Webster, 2013).

science of risk The processes by which a variety of professionals are trained to identify populations that are "at risk" of various negative outcomes and implement programming that will manage those risks.

scientific misconduct An umbrella term used to refer to fabrication or falsification of data, breaches of ethics, plagiarism, and any other scientific practices deemed unacceptable or inappropriate.

secondary deviance A lifestyle and identity based on chronic rule breaking.

secondary prevention (of anorexia) Identifying those young men and women who may be in the very early stages of an eating disorder to provide early intervention.

sects Smaller religious groups that have usually broken away from larger churches and which have more rigid doctrine and higher levels of commitment required of members.

security of person and property A fundamental human right that protects individuals' physical well-being and entitles them to control over their own property.

self-control (1) Forms of social control that one directs at oneself; also known as *self-regulation*. (2) In self-control theory (also known as the general theory of crime), the factor that prevents most people from engaging in deviance.

self-regulation Forms of social control that one directs at oneself; also known as *self-control*.

self-stigma The process of stigmatizing oneself for a particular behaviour or characteristic.

sex hygiene movement During the Victorian era, moral entrepreneurs who equated social purity with sexual purity and who sought to solve problems such as prostitution, divorce, and illegitimacy; also known as the *social purity movement*.

sexting Sending nude or partially nude photos of oneself using forms of electronic communication.

sick role The role that ill individuals may be assigned, under certain conditions, in which they are given a temporary reprieve from some of life's responsibilities and are not blamed for their conditions.

significant others In symbolic interactionist theory, people who are personally important to us.

skeptical postmodernism A form of post-modern theory that postulates knowledge is not possible and only chaos and meaninglessness exist.

skepticism The assumption that all ideas must be subjected to rigorous scrutiny; part of the normative structure of science.

social causation hypothesis The proposal that more life stresses and fewer resources characterize the lives of the lower class, contributing to the emergence of mental disorders.

social constructionism The perspective proposing that social characteristics are creations or artifacts of a particular society at a specific time in history, just as objects are artifacts of that society.

social control theories Positivist theories that explain the causes of conforming behaviour rather than the causes of deviant behaviour.

social Darwinism The application of the Darwinian concept of evolution to history and societies.

social gospel A theology that informed the work of the child-savers movement during the Victorian era, whereby Christian principles were applied in real-world settings to solve social problems.

social integration In Durkheim's functionalist theory, the level of cohesion or social bonds in society.

social purity movement During the Victorian era, moral entrepreneurs who equated social purity with sexual purity and who sought to solve problems such as prostitution, divorce, and illegitimacy; also known as the *sex hygiene movement*.

social selection hypothesis The proposal that people with mental disorders fall into lower economic strata because of their difficulties in daily functioning.

social typing The process by which some people come to be perceived as deviant and others as normal.

societal reaction An objective definition of deviance that claims a person, behaviour, or characteristic is deviant if society's masses react to it negatively.

sociocultural theories (of anorexia) Theories that explain anorexia nervosa in terms of social norms emphasizing thinness, media images, and social learning or modelling.

soft constructionism A form of social constructionism that emphasizes the processes by which certain social phenomena come to be perceived and reacted to in particular ways in a given society at a specific time in history; also known as *contextual constructionism*.

spoiled identity In the dramaturgical approach, the stigmatization faced when an individual assumes a deviant role on the front stage.

statistical rarity An objective definition of deviance that claims a person, behaviour, or characteristic is deviant if it is statistically rare.

status frustration In status frustration theory, the strain experienced by lower-class boys who are unable to live up to the middle-class standards of the school system.

stigmatization The process of exclusion that follows a deviant master status.

stigmatized others Individuals who are presented (through the media) as threats to the way of life of decent people.

strain The structural gap that exists between institutionalized goals and the legitimate means of achieving those goals for people located in some parts of the social structure.

strict constructionism A form of social constructionism that claims the world is characterized by endless relativism; also known as *radical constructionism*.

structural Marxism A form of Marxism that proposes social rules are created to protect the capitalist economic system and may then be applied to members of the proletariat or bourgeoisie.

sturm und drang Storm and stress, perceived by G. Stanley Hall as being inherent during adolescence.

subjective The view of deviance as being the result of processes of social construction such that a person, behaviour, or characteristic is deviant "if enough important people say so"; also known as *subjectivist*.

survivors Female exotic dancers who have extensive histories of childhood abuse and who feel forced into the industry because of few available alternatives.

symbolic interactionism The theoretical perspective that describes society as composed of social interaction, which occurs via communication through symbols; the foundation for all interpretive theories.

tagging In Tannenbaum's labelling theory, the deviant label that we initially attach to an individual's behaviour.

tautological A circular argument, in which the latter part of the argument merely restates the former part of the argument; a critique of functionalist theories.

techniques In differential association theory, the skills that are required for deviance or conformity.

techniques of neutralization Self-rationalizations for deviant behaviour.

teleological An argument that proposes the existence of a phenomenon lies in the functions that it serves; a critique of functionalist theories.

tertiary deviance Following a person's transition to secondary deviance, his or her efforts to resist a deviant label and instead redefine normal in a way that includes the deviantized behaviour or characteristic.

time to resist A motivation for gang membership that involves a statement of rejection to society, a rejection of the type of lives being offered.

troubled youth Youth who are considered to be primarily a threat to themselves, such as through substance use.

troubling youth Youth who are considered to be primarily a threat to others or to society, such as through criminal activity.

trying to pass A stigma management technique that involves hiding the behaviour or characteristic that is stigmatized.

underweight (1) According to scientific standards, a person that has a body mass index (BMI) of 18.4 or lower. (2) According to social standards, a body that is thinner than current cultural ideals.

universalism The assumption that scientific knowledge is free from any biases based on characteristics such as race, gender, or religion; part of the normative structure of science.

workers Female exotic dancers primarily from working-class backgrounds who become exotic dancers because of the money they can earn.

young offenders Individuals under the age of 18 who commit criminal acts.

youth A transitional time in life between childhood and maturity.

References

Abernethy, D. B. (2001). *The dynamics of global dominance: European overseas empires, 1415–1980.* New Haven, CT: Yale University Press.

Accordino, M. P., Porter, D. F., & Morse, T. (2001). Deinstitutionalization of persons with severe mental illness: Context and consequences. *Journal of Rehabilitation Medicine, 67*(2), 16–21.

Adherents.com. (2007). Major religions of the world by number of adherents. Retrieved from www.adherents.com.

Adlaf, E. M., Demers, A., & Gliksman, L. (Eds.). (2005). *Canadian campus survey 2004.* Toronto, ON: Centre for Addiction and Mental Health.

Adlaf, E. M., Gliksman, L., Demers, A., & Newton-Taylor, B. (2001). The prevalence of elevated psychological distress among Canadian undergraduates. *Journal of American College Health, 50*(2), 67–72.

Adlaf, E. M., & Paglia-Boak, A. (2007). *Drug use among Ontario students, 1977–2007.* CAMH Research Document Series No. 21. Toronto, ON: Canadian Association for Mental Health.

Adler, P. A., & Adler, P. (2003). *Constructions of deviance: Social power, context, and interaction* (4th edition). Belmont, CA: Wadsworth.

Adler, P. A., & Adler, P. (2006a). *Constructions of deviance: Social power, context, and interaction* (5th ed.). Toronto, ON: Thomson Wadsworth.

Adler, P. A., & Adler, P. (2006b). The deviance society. *Deviant Behavior: An Interdisciplinary Journal, 27*(2), 129–148.

Agliata, D., & Tantleff-Dunn, S. (2004). The impact of media exposure on males' body image. *Journal of Social and Clinical Psychology, 23*(1), 7–22.

Agnew, R. (1992). A foundation for a general strain theory of crime and delinquency. *Criminology, 30,* 47–87.

Agnew, R. (1998). A general strain theory of crime and delinquency. In F. T. Cullen & R. Agnew (Eds.), *Criminological Theory: Past to Present* (pp. 152–156). Los Angeles, CA: Roxbury.

Agnew, R. (2001). Building on the foundation of general strain theory: Specifying the types of strain most likely to lead to crime and delinquency. *Journal of Research in Crime and Delinquency, 38*(4), 319–361.

Agnew, R. A. (2006). *Pressured into crime: An overview of general strain theory.* Los Angeles, CA: Roxbury.

Agnew, R., Cullen, F., Burton, V., Evans, T. D., & Dunaway, R. G. (1996). A new test of classic strain theory. *Justice Quarterly, 13,* 681–704.

Akers, R. L. (1977). *Deviant behavior: A social learning approach.* Belmont, CA: Wadsworth.

Akers, R. L. (1991). Self-control as a general theory of crime. *Journal of Quantitative Criminology, 7,* 201–211.

Akers, R. L. (1998). *Social learning and social structure: A general theory of crime and deviance.* Boston, MA: Northeastern University Press.

Akers, R. L. (2000). *Criminological theories: Introduction, evaluation, and application* (3rd ed.). Los Angeles, CA: Roxbury.

Akers, R. L. (2006). *Social learning and social structure: A general theory of crime and deviance.* Boston, MA: Northeastern University Press.

Alberta Alliance on Mental Illness & Mental Health. (2003). Homepage. Retrieved from www.aamimh.ca.

Alberta Mental Health Act. (n. d.). Retrieved from www.qp.alberta.ca/574.cfm?page=M13.cfm&leg_type=Acts&isbncln=9780779741168.

American Psychiatric Association. (1994). *Diagnostic and statistical manual of mental disorders–IV*. Washington, DC: Author.

Anderson, A., & Gordon, R. (1978). Witchcraft and the status of women: The case of England. *British Journal of Sociology, 29*, 171–184.

Anderssen, E. (2012, March 2). Disney closes exhibit over criticism for stigmatizing overweight kids. *Globe and Mail*. Retrieved from www.theglobeandmail.com.

Angus Reid. (2012, November 29). Most Americans and Canadians are ready to legalize marijuana. Retrieved December 9, 2012, from www.angus-reid.com.

Anthony, D., & Robbins, T. (1994). Brainwashing and totalitarian influence. In S. Ramachandran (Ed.), *Encyclo-pedia of human behavior* (Vol. 1, pp. 457–471). San Diego, CA: Academic Press.

Arkins, B. (1994). Sexuality in fifth-century Athens. *Classics Ireland, 1*, 1–8.

Armstrong, L. (1993). *And they call it help: The psychiatric policing of America's children*. Reading, MA: Addison-Wesley.

Armstrong, M. L., Roberts, A. E., Owen, D. C., & Koch, J. R. (2004). Toward building a composite of college student influences with body art. *Issues in Comprehensive Pediatric Nursing, 27*, 277–295.

Arnett, J. (1992). Reckless behavior in adolescence: A developmental perspective. *Developmental Review, 12*, 339–373.

Arnett, J. J. (1999). Adolescent storm and stress reconsidered. *American Psychologist, 54*(5), 317–326.

Aronson, E., Wilson, T. D., Akert, R. M., & Fehr, B. (2013). *Social Psychology* (5th Canadian ed.). Toronto, ON: Pearson Education Canada.

Aseltine, R. (1995). A reconsideration of parental and peer influences on adolescent deviance. *Journal of Health and Social Behavior, 3*(6), 103–121.

Ashley, D., & Orenstein, D. M. (2001). *Sociological theory: Classical statements* (5th ed.). Boston, MA: Allyn & Bacon.

Asma, S. T. (1993). The new social Darwinism. *Humanist, 53*(5), 10–12.

Associated Press. (2006, May 21). Disgraced Korean cloning scientist indicted. *New York Times*. Retrieved from www.nytimes.com.

Atkinson, M. (2001). Flesh journeys: Neo primitives and the contemporary rediscovery of radical body modification. *Deviant Behavior, 22*, 117–146.

Atkinson, M. (2002). Pretty in ink: Conformity, resistance, and negotiation in women's tattooing. *Sex Roles, 47*(5/6), 219–235.

Atkinson, M. (2003a). *Tattooed: The sociogenesis of a body art*. Toronto, ON: University of Toronto Press.

Atkinson, M. (2003b). The civilizing of resistance: Straightedge tattooing. *Deviant Behavior: An Interdisciplinary Journal, 24*, 197–220.

Attwood, F. (2011). The paradigm shift: Pornography research, sexualization and extreme images. *Sociology Compass, 5*(1), 13–22.

AuCoin, K. (2005). Children and youth as victims of violent crime. *Juristat, 25*(1). Statistics Canada Catalogue No. 85002XIE.

Bagdikian, B. H. (2004). *The new media monopoly*. Boston, MA: Beacon Press.

Bailey, S., & Bronskill, J. (2007, January 30). Prison warehouses, 'open-air asylums' are home to the mentally ill. *Edmonton Journal*. Retrieved from www.canada. com.

Bainbridge, W. S. (2002). *The endtime family: Children of God*. New York, NY: State University of New York Press.

Baird, A. L., & Grieve, F. G. (2006). Exposure to male models in advertisements leads to a decrease in men's body satisfaction. *North American Journal of Psychology, 8*(1), 115–122.

Ball, R. A. (2012). Changing images of deviance: Nineteenth-century Canadian anti-prostitution movements. *Deviant Behavior, 33*(1), 26–39.

Bandura, A. (1986). *Social foundations of thought and action: A social cognitive theory*. Englewood Cliffs, NJ: Prentice Hall.

Bandura, A., Ross, D., & Ross, S. A. (1961). Transmission of aggression through imitation of aggressive models. *Journal of Abnormal and Social Psychology, 63*, 575–582.

Bandura, A., Ross, D., & Ross, S. A. (1963). Imitation of film-mediated aggressive models. *Journal of Abnormal and Social Psychology, 66*, 3–11.

Barker, E. (2001). Watching for violence: A comparative analysis of the roles of five types of cult-watching groups. Paper presented at the annual meeting of the Center for Studies in New Religions.

Barman, J. (1997/1998). Taming Aboriginal sexuality: Gender, power, and race in British Columbia, 1850–1900. *BC Studies, 115/116*, 237–266.

Baron, S. W. (1989). Canadian west coast punk subculture: A field study. *Canadian Journal of Sociology, 14*(3), 289–316.

Barrett, J., & Jay, P. (2005). Clinical research fraud: A victimless crime? *Applied Clinical Trials, 14*(2), 44–46.

Barsley, M. (1967). *The other hand: An investigation into the sinister history of left-handedness*. New York, NY: Hawthorn Books.

Barstow, A. L. (1994). *Witchcraze*. San Francisco, CA: Pandora.

Bartowski, J. P. (1998). Claimsmaking and typifications of voodoo as a deviant religion: Hex, lies, and videotape. *Journal for the Scientific Study of Religion, 37*(4), 559–579.

Bassett, H., Lampe, J., & Lloyd, C. (1999). Parenting: Experiences and feelings of parents with a mental illness. *Journal of Mental Health, 8*(6), 597–604.

Baumrind, D. (1991). Parenting styles and adolescent development. In R. Lerner, A. Peterson, & J. Brooks-Gunn (Eds.), *Encyclopedia of adolescence*. New York, NY: Garland Publishing.

Beaman, L. G. (2000). *New perspectives on deviance: The construction of deviance in everyday life*. Toronto, ON: Prentice Hall.

Beaud, J. P., & Prevost, J. G. (1996). Immigration, eugenics, and statistics: Measuring racial origins in Canada, 1921–1941. *Canadian Ethnic Studies, 28*(2), 1–23.

Beaver, W., & Paul, S. (2011). Internet pornography: Variables related to use among traditional-aged college students. *Sociological Viewpoints, Fall*, 25–38.

Bechtel, K., & Pearson, W. (1985). Deviant scientists and scientific deviance. *Deviant Behavior: An Interdisciplinary Journal, 6*, 237–252.

Beck, M. (2001, November). Embracing your inner brat. *O Magazine*, 69.

Beck, U. (1992). *Risk society: Towards a new modernity*. London, UK: Sage.

Beck, U. (1999). *World risk*. Cambridge, UK: Polity Press.

Becker, H. (1963). *Outsiders: Studies in the sociology of deviance*. New York, NY: Free Press.

Beckford, M. (2007, February 15). Sister of tragic 'size zero' model found dead. *The Telegraph*. Retrieved from www.telegraph.co.uk.

Belcher, J. R. (1989). On becoming homeless: A study of chronically mentally ill persons. *Journal of Community Psychology, 17*, 173–185.

Bell, B. T., & Dittmar, H. (2011). Does media matter? The role of identification in adolescent girls' media consumption and the impact of different thin-ideal media on body image. *Sex Roles, 65*, 478–490.

Bell, S., Cossman, B., Ross, B. L., Gottell, L., & Janovicek, N. (1998). Bad attitude/s on trial: Feminism, pornography, & the Butler decision. *Journal of Canadian Studies, 33*(1), 163–172.

Bell, S. J. (2002). *Young offenders and juvenile justice: A century after the fact* (2nd ed.). Toronto, ON: Nelson Thomson.

Benard, B. (1991). *Fostering resilience in kids: Protective factors in the family, school, and community.* Portland, OR: Northwest Regional Educational Laboratory.

Benda, B. B. (1994). Testing competing theoretical concepts: Adolescent alcohol consumption. *Deviant Behavior: An Interdisciplinary Journal, 15*, 375–396.

Benson, M. (1985). Denying the guilty mind: Accounting for involvement in white-collar crime. *Criminology, 23*(4), 589–599.

Ben-Yehuda, N. (1980). The European witch craze of the 14th to 17th centuries: A sociologist's perspective. *American Journal of Sociology, 86*(1), 1–31.

Ben-Yehuda, N. (1986). Deviance in science. *British Journal of Criminology, 26*(1), 1–27.

Ben-Yehuda, N. (1990). *The politics and morality of deviance: Moral panics, drug abuse, deviant science, and reversed stigmatization.* Albany, NY: State University of New York Press.

Beres, M. A. (2007). 'Spontaneous' sexual consent: An analysis of sexual consent literature. *Feminism & Psychology, 17*(1), 93–108.

Berger, B. (1963). Adolescence and beyond. *Social Problems, 10*, 294–408.

Bernberg, J. G., & Krohn, M. D. (2003). Labeling, life chances, and adult crime: The direct and indirect effects of official intervention in adolescence on crime in early adulthood. *Criminology, 41*(4), 1287–1318.

Bessant, J. (2001). From sociology of deviance to sociology of risk: Youth homelessness and the problem of empiricism. *Journal of Criminal Justice, 29*, 31–43.

Best, J. (2003). Constructionism in context. In E. Rubington & M. S. Weinberg (Eds.), *The study of social problems: Seven perspectives* (6th ed., pp. 351–356). New York, NY: Oxford University Press.

Bibby, R. W. (2001). *Canada's teens: Today, yesterday, and tomorrow.* Toronto, ON: Stoddart.

Bibby, R. W. (2009). *The emerging millenials: How Canada's newest generation is responding to change and choice.* Lethbridge, AB: Project Canada Books.

Bissell, K., & Hays, H. (2011). Understanding anti-fat bias in children: The role of media and appearance anxiety in third to sixth graders' implicit and explicit attitudes toward obesity. *Mass Communication and Society, 14*(1), 113–140.

Bleicher, P. (2003). Is change afoot? 21 CFR 11 in transition. *Applied Clinical Trials, 12*(6) 34–36.

Bloch, E. (2001). Sex between men and boys in classical Greece: Was it education for citizenship or child abuse? *Journal of Men's Studies, 9*(2). Retrieved from Expanded Academic ASAP database.

Blumer, H. (1986). *Symbolic interactionism: Perspective and method.* Berkeley, CA: University of California Press.

Born, L. (2004). Fast-tracking the plague: Drugging America to death. *International Socialist Review, 33.* Retrieved from www.isreview.org.

Bortner, M. (1988). *Delinquency and justice: An age of crisis.* Toronto, ON: McGraw-Hill.

Boston, R. (1996). *The most dangerous man in America? Pat Robertson and the rise of the Christian Coalition.* Amherst, NY: Prometheus Books.

Bostrom, M. (2001). *The 21st century teen: Perception and teen reality.* Washington, DC: Frameworks Institute.

Bourget, B., & Chenier, R. (2007). *Mental health literacy in Canada: Phase one report mental health literacy project.* Ottawa, ON: Canadian Alliance on Mental Illness and Mental Health.

Bourgois, P. (1995). *In search of respect: Selling crack in El Barrio.* Cambridge, UK: Cambridge University Press.

Boyce, W. F. (2004). *Young people in Canada: Their health and well-being.* Ottawa, ON: Health Canada.

Boyce, W. F., King, M. A., & Roche, J. (2008). *Healthy settings for young people.* Ottawa, ON: Public Health Agency of Canada.

Brace, C. L. (1996). Racialism and racist agendas. *American Anthropologist, 98*(1), 176–177.

Braithwaite, J. (2000). Shame and criminal justice. *Canadian Journal of Criminology, 42*(3), 281–298.

Brennan, S. (2012, July). Police-reported crime statistics in Canada, 2011. *Juristat.* Ottawa, ON: Author. Catalogue No. 85-002-X.

Brezhnev, L. I. (2006). The Quotations Page. Quoted in V. Rich, (1977). *Nature, 270,* 470–471. Retrieved August 24, 2006, from www.quotationspage.com.

Briggs, R. (1996). *Witches and neighbors: The social and cultural context of European witchcraft.* New York, NY: Viking Penguin.

British Columbia Eating Disorders Association. (2003). Homepage. Retrieved from webhome.idirect.com/~bceda/index.html.

British Fashion Council. (2007). *The report of the model health inquiry.* Retrieved from www.modelhealthinquiry.com.

Bromley, D. G. (2002). Dramatic denouement. In D. G. Bromley & J. G. Melton (Eds.), *Cults, religion, and violence* (pp. 11–41). Cambridge, UK: Cambridge University Press.

Bromley, D. G., & Melton, J. G. (Eds.). (2002). *Cults, religion, and violence.* Cambridge, UK: Cambridge University Press.

Bromley, D. G., & Shupe, A. D. (1993). Organized opposition to new religious movements. In D. G. Bromley & J. K. Hadden (Eds.), *The handbook of cults and sects* (pp. 177–198). Greenwich, CT: JAI Press.

Brook, J. S., Brook, D. W., De La Rosa, M., Whiteman, M., & Montoya, I. D. (1999). The role of parents in protecting Colombian adolescents from delinquency and marijuana use. *Archives of Pediatrics & Adolescent Medicine, 153*(5). Retrieved from Expanded Academic ASAP database.

Brounstein, P. J., & Zweig, J. M. (1999). *Understanding substance abuse prevention: Toward the 21st century: A primer on effective programs.* Rockville, MD: US Department of Health and Human Services.

Brower, A. M. (2002). Are college students alcoholics? *Journal of American College Health, 50*(5), 253–255.

Brower, R. (1999). Dangerous minds: Eminently creative people who spent time in jail. *Creative Research Journal, 12*(1). Retrieved August 6, 2001, from Academic Search Premier database.

Brown, F. L., & Slaughter, V. (2011). Normal body, beautiful body: Discrepant perceptions reveal a pervasive "thin ideal" from childhood to adulthood. *Body Image, 8,* 119–125.

Bruinsma, G. J. N. (1992). Differential association theory reconsidered: An extension and its empirical test. *Journal of Quantitative Criminology, 8,* 175–187.

Buchanan, E. (1997). A school for sterilization. *World Press Review,* June, 46.

Burger, T. D., & Finkel, D. (2002). Relationships between body modifications and very high-risk behavior in a college population. *College Student Journal, 36*(2), 203–213.

Burgess, R., & Akers, R. (1966). A differential association reinforcement theory of criminal behavior. *Social Problems, 25,* 128–147.

Burton, V. S., & Cullen, F. T. (1992). The empirical status of strain theory. *Journal of Crime and Justice, 15,* 1–30.

Burton, V., & Dunaway, R. G. (1994). Strain, relative deprivation, and middle-class delinquency. In G. Barak (Ed.), *Varieties of criminology: Readings from a dynamic discipline* (pp. 79–96). Westport, CT: Praeger.

Buzzell, T. (2005). Holiday revelry and legal control of fireworks: A study of neutralization in two normative contexts. *Western Criminology, 6*(1), 30–42.

Caldwell, W. (2001). *Obesity sourcebook.* Detroit, MI: Omnigraphics.

Caliendo, C., Armstrong, M. L., & Roberts, A. E. (2005). Self-reported characteristics of women and men with intimate body piercings. *Journal of Advanced Nursing, 49*(5), 474–484.

Canadian Centre on Substance Abuse. (2011). *Cross-Canada report on student alcohol and drug use.* Ottawa, ON: Author.

Canadian Living. (2006, August). Your teenager: An owner's manual (for the bewildered parent), pp. 159–162.

Canadian Mental Health Association (2013). *Facts About Eating Disorders.* Retrieved August 15, 2013 from www.cmah.ca.

Canadian Paediatric Society. (2004). Dieting in adolescence. Position statement AH-2004-01. Retrieved from www.cps.ca.

Canadian Press. (2012, July 19). RCMP arrest Alberta man who U.S. says is a suspect in international cyber crime. Retrieved from www.canada.com.

Caplan, P. J. (1995). *They say you're crazy: How the world's more powerful psychiatrists decide who's normal.* Reading, MA: Perseus Books.

Carlson, R. J., & Stimeling, G. (2002). *The terrible gift: The brave new world of genetic medicine.* New York, NY: PublicAffairs.

Carroll, L., & Anderson, R. (2002). Body piercing, tattooing, self-esteem, and body investment in adolescent girls. *Adolescence, 37*(147), 627–637.

Carroll, S. T., Riffenburgh, R. H., Roberts, T. A., & Myhre, E. B. (2002). Tattoos and body piercings as indicators of adolescent risk-taking behaviors. *Pediatrics, 109*(6), 1021–1027.

Caulfield, T. (2004). The commercialisation of medical and scientific reporting. *PLoS Medicine, 1*(3), 178–179.

CBC News. (2001, June 8). PM blasts MP for blocking Mandela honour. *CBC News.* Retrieved from www.cbc.ca/canada/story/2001/06/07/Mandela_mp010607.html.

CBC News. (2007). Same-sex rights: Canada timeline. *CBC News Indepth.* Retrieved from www.cbc.ca/news/background/samesexrights/timeline_canada.html.

CBC News. (2008, June 11). Prime Minister Stephen Harper's statement of apology. Retrieved from www.cbc.ca/anada/story/2008/06/11/pm-statement.html.

CBC News (2012a, January 31). Homosexuality an "illness." *CBC Digital Archives*. Retrieved from www.cbc.ca/archives/categories/politics/rights-freedoms/trudeaus-omnibus-bill-challenging-canadian-taboos/homosexuality-an.html.

CBC News. (2012b, October 16). Negative Amanda Todd post costs man his job. *CBC News*. Retrieved from www.cbc.ca/news/canada/calgary/story/2012/10/16/calgary-airdrie-woman-website-comment.html.

CCTV User Group (2008). How many cameras are there? Retrieved from www.cctvusergroup.com.

Center on Alcohol Marketing and Youth. (2004). *Clicking with kids: Alcohol marketing and youth on the Internet*. Washington, DC: Author.

Chambliss, W. J., & Seidman, R. (1982). *Law, order and power* (2nd ed.). Reading, MA: Addison-Wesley.

Chappell, A. T., & Piquero, A. R. (2004). Applying social learning theory to police misconduct. *Deviant Behavior*, 25, 89–108.

Chatterjee, J. (2006). *A research report on youth gangs: Problems, perspectives, and priorities*. Ottawa, ON: Research and Evaluation Branch, RCMP. Toronto, ON: Harper-Collins.

Chettelburgh, M. (2007). *Young thugs: Inside the dangerous world of Canadian street gangs*. Toronto, ON: HarperCollins.

Childress, S. A. (1991). Reel "rape speech": Violent pornography and the politics of harm. *Law & Society Review*, 25(1), 177–214.

Chryssides, G. D. (1994). New religious movements—some problems with definition. *Diskus: Web Edition*, 2(2). Retrieved from web.uni-marburg.de/religionswissenschaft/journal/diskus/chryssides.html.

Claes, L., Vandereycken, W., & Vertommen, H. (2005). Self-care versus self-harm: Piercing, tattooing, and self-injuring in eating disorders. *European Eating Disorders*, 13, 11–18.

Clark, W., & Schellenberg, G. (2006). Who's religious? *Canadian Social Trends* (Summer), 2–9. Ottawa, ON: Statistics Canada. Catalogue No. 11-008.

Clinard, M. B., & Meier, R. F. (2001). *Sociology of deviant behavior* (11th ed.). Fort Worth, TX: Harcourt College Publishers.

Cloward, R. A., & Ohlin, L. E. (1960). *Delinquency and opportunity: A theory of delinquent gangs*. New York, NY: Free Press.

Cohen, A. J. (1955). *Delinquent boys*. New York, NY: Free Press.

Cohen, S. (1973). *Folk devils and moral panics*. London, UK: MacGibbons and Kee.

Columbia World of Quotations. (1996). Chinese Proverb. Retrieved from www.bartleby.com.

Complex Magazine. (2011, June 22). The 25 funniest celebrity Twitter hacks. Retrieved from www.complex.com.

comScore. (2012). *Canada digital future in focus, 2012*. Retrieved from www.comscore.com.

Conrad, P. (1992). Medicalization and social control. *Annual Review of Sociology*, 18, 209–232.

Conrad, P., & Leiter, V. (2004). Medicalization, markets and consumers. *Journal of Health and Social Behavior*, 45(Extra Issue), 158–176.

Conservative Party of Canada. (2006). *Stand up for Canada: Conservative Party of Canada election platform 2006*. Retrieved August 10, 2006, from www.conservative.ca.

Coontz, S. (1992). *The way we never were: American families and the nostalgia trap*. New York, NY: Basis Books.

Cooley, M. (2006). In *Columbia World of Quotations, City Aphorisms, Fourteenth*

Selection. Retrieved August 23, 2006, from www.bartleby.com.

Costin, C. (1999). *The eating disorder sourcebook*. Los Angeles, CA: Lowell House.

Covarrubias, I., & Han, M. (2011). Mental health stigma about serious mental illness among MSW students: Social contact and attitude. *Social Work, 56*(4), 317–325.

Cowan, D. E. (2001). From parchment to pixels: The Christian countercult on the Internet. Paper presented at the 2001 Conference of the Center for Studies on New Religions, April 20, London.

Cromwell, P., & Thurman, Q. (2003). The devil made me do it: The use of neutralization by shoplifters. *Deviant Behavior, 24*(6), 1–16.

Cronin, T. A. (2001). Tattoos, piercings, and skin adornments. *Dermatology Nursing, 13*(5), 380–383.

Crouch, A., & Degelman, D. (1998). Influence of female body images in printed advertising on self-ratings of physical attractiveness by adolescent girls. *Perceptual & Motor Skills, 87*(2), 585–586.

Crouch, B. M., & Damphousse, K. R. (1992). Newspapers and the anti-Satanism movement. *Sociological Spectrum, 12*, 1–20.

Cullen, F. T., & Agnew, R. (1998). *Criminological theory: Past to present*. Los Angeles, CA: Roxbury.

Das Gupta, T. (2000). Families of native people, immigrants, and people of colour. In N. Mandell & A. Duffy (Eds.), *Canadian families: Diversity, conflict, and change* (2nd ed., pp. 146–187). Toronto, ON: Nelson Thomson.

Davidson, L., Hoge, M. A., Godleski, L., Rakfeldt, J., & Griffith, E. I. H. (1996). Hospital or community living? Examining consumer perspectives on deinstitutionalization. *Psychiatric Rehabilitation Journal, 19*(3), 49–58.

Davies, J. (1996). The future of "no future": Punk rock and postmodern theory. *Journal of Popular Culture, 29*(4), 3–25.

Davies, K. A. (1997). Voluntary exposure to pornography and men's attitudes toward feminism and rape. *Journal of Sex Research, 34*(2), 131–137.

Davies, L. (1994). In search of resistance and rebellion among high school drop-outs. *Canadian Journal of Sociology, 19*(3), 331–350.

Dawson, L. L., & Henneby, J. (1999). New religions and the Internet: Recruiting in new public space. *Journal of Contemporary Religion, 14*(1), 17–39.

Degher, D., & Hughes, G. (2003). The adoption and management of a "fat" identity. In P. A. Adler & P. Adler (Eds.), *Constructions of deviance: Social power, context, and interaction* (pp. 211–221). Belmont, CA: Wadsworth.

Delaney, T. (2005). *American street gangs*. Upper Saddle River, NJ: Prentice Hall.

De Maio, F. (2010). *Health and social theory*. New York, NY: Palgrave Macmillan.

DeMello, M. (2000). *Bodies of inscription: A cultural history of the modern tattoo community*. Durham, NC: Duke University Press.

D'Emilio, J., & Freedman, E. B. (1997). *Intimate matters: A history of sexuality in America* (2nd ed.). Chicago, IL: University of Chicago Press.

DeMont, J. (2002, August 5). Growing up large. *Maclean's, 115*(31), 20–26.

Dennis, R. M. (1995). Social Darwinism, scientific racism and the metaphysics of race. *Journal of Negro Education, 64*(3), 243–252.

Dennis, A., & Martin, P. J. (2005). Symbolic interactionism and the concept of power. *The British Journal of Sociology, 56*(2), 191–213.

Deschesnes, M., Demers, S., & Finès, P. (2006). Prevalence and characteristics of body piercing and tattooing among high school students. *Canadian Journal of Public Health, 97*(4), 325–329.

Deshotels, T. H., & Forsyth, C. J. (2008). Sex rules: The edicts of income in exotic dancing. *Deviant Behavior, 29,* 484–500.

Deshotels, T. H., Tinney, M., & Forsyth, C. J. (2012). McSexy: Exotic dancing and institutional power. *Deviant Behavior, 33,* 140–148.

Desmond, R. J., & Carveth, R. (2007). The effects of advertising on children and adolescents: A meta-analysis. In R. Preiss, B. Gayle, N. Burrell, M. Allen, & J. Bryant (Eds.), *Mass media effects research: Advances through meta-analysis* (pp. 169–179). Mahwah, NJ: Lawrence Erlbaum.

Des Rosiers, N., & Bittle, S. (2004). Introduction. In the Law Commission of Canada (Ed.) *What is a crime? Defining criminal conduct in contemporary society* (pp. vii–xxv). Vancouver, BC: UBC Press.

Deutschmann, L. B. (2002). *Deviance and social control* (3rd ed.). Toronto, ON: Nelson Thomson Learning.

deYoung, M. (1998). Another look at moral panics: The case of Satanic day care centers. *Deviant Behavior: An Interdisciplinary Journal, 19,* 257–278.

Dobson, R. (1996, November 30). Mentally ill people face discrimination. *British Medical Journal, 313*(7069), 1352.

Doherty, T. (1988). *Teenagers & teenpics: The juvenilization of American movies in the 1950s.* Boston, MA: Unwin Hyman.

Dohrenwend, B. P., Levav, I., Shrout, P. E., & Schwartz, S. (1992). Socioeconomic status and psychiatric disorders: The causation selection issue. *Science, 255,* 946–952.

Downes, D., & Rock, P. (2003). *Understanding deviance* (4th ed.). New York, NY: Oxford University Press.

Dukes, R. L., & Stein, J. A. (2011). Ink and holes: Correlates and predictive associations of body modification among adolescents. *Youth and Society, 43*(4), 1547–1569.

Dunleavey, M. P. (2001, April). Would you have surgery to lose weight? *Self,* 172–175, 199–200.

Durkheim, E. (1933). *The division of labor in society.* New York, NY: Free Press.

Durkheim, E. (1951). *Suicide.* New York, NY: Free Press.

Dyer, O. (2005). US survey shows extent of research misconduct. *British Medical Journal, 330,* 1465.

Eaton, W. W. (2001). *The sociology of mental disorders.* Westport, CT: Praeger Publishing.

Edmonton Police Service. (2003). *Who are your children hanging with? A resource guide on youth & gangs.* Edmonton, AB: Author.

Edmonton Police Service. (2009). Traits of gang members. Retrieved from www.edmontonpolice.ca.

Edwards, A. R. (1988). *Regulation and repression: The study of social control.* Sydney, Australia: Allen & Unwin.

Egan, R. D. (2003). I'll be your fantasy girl, if you'll be my money man: Mapping desire, fantasy and power in two exotic dance clubs. *JPCS: Journal for the Psychoanalysis of Culture & Society, 8(1),* 109–120.

Elliot, D., Huizinga, D., & Ageton, S. (1985). *Explaining delinquency and substance use.* Beverly Hills, CA: Sage.

England, J. (2004). Disciplining subjectivity and space: Representation, film and its material effects. *Antipode, 36,* 295–321.

Entman, R. M. (1993). Framing: Toward clarification of a fractured paradigm. *Journal of Communication, 43*(4), 51–58.

Erickson, K. G., Crosnoe, R., & Dornbusch, S. M. (2000). A social process model of adolescent deviance: Combining social control and differential association perspectives. *Journal of Youth and Adolescence, 29*(4), 395–425.

Ericson, R. V., & Haggerty, K. D. (2001). Governing the young. In R. C. Smandych (Ed.), *Youth justice: History, legislation, and reform* (pp. 104–123). Toronto, ON: Harcourt.

Erikson, K. (1966). *Wayward Puritans*. New York, NY: Wiley.

Eron, L. D., Huesmann, L. R., Lefkowitz, M. M., & Walder, L. O. (1996). Does television cause aggression? In D. F. Greenberg (Ed.), *Criminal careers: The international library of criminology, criminal justice, and penology* (Vol. 2, pp. 311–321). Aldershot, UK: Dartmouth Publishing Company Limited.

Esala, J. J. (2013). Communities of denial: The co-construction of gendered adolescent violence. *Deviant Behavior, 34*(2), 97–114.

Essex County Diversion Program. (2012). Teen girls warned of sexting consequences. Retrieved from www.youtube.com.

Ettner, S. L., Frank, R. G., & Kessler, R. C. (1997). The impact of psychiatric disorders on labor market outcomes. *Industrial and Labor Relations Review, 51*(1), 64–83.

Fasiolo, R., & Leckie, S. (1993). *Canadian media coverage of gangs: A content analysis*. Ottawa, ON: Solicitor-General Canada.

Fass, P. S. (1979). *The damned and the beautiful: American youth in the 1920s*. New York, NY: Oxford University Press.

Featherstone, R., & Deflam, M. (2003). Anomie and strain: Context and consequences of Merton's two theories. *Sociological Inquiry, 73*(4), 471–489.

Fekete, D. J. (2012, November 28). Commentary: New movie present skewed view of bipolar disorder. *Edmonton Journal*.

Retrieved from www.edmontonjournal.com.

Fernea, E. W. (1998). *In search of Islamic feminism*. New York, NY: Anchor Books.

Ferreira, V. S. (2009). Youth scenes, body marks and bio sociabilities. *Youth, 17*(3) 285–306.

Fight Against Coercive Tactics Network. (2003). Homepage. Retrieved from www.factnet.org.

Fischer, B., Ala-Leppilampi, K., Single, E., & Robins, A. (2003). Cannabis law reform in Canada: Is the "saga of promise, hesitation and retreat" coming to an end? *Canadian Journal of Criminology and Criminal Justice, 45*(3), 265–297.

Fischer, P., & Greitemeyer, T. (2006). Music and aggression: The impact of sexual-aggressive song lyrics on aggression-related thoughts, emotions, and behavior toward the same and the opposite sex. *Personality and Social Psychology Bulletin, 32*, 1165–1176.

Flannery, D. J., Huff, C. R., & Manos, M. (2001). Youth gangs: A developmental perspective. In R. C. Smandych (Ed.), *Youth crime: Varieties, theories, and prevention* (pp. 206–229). Toronto, ON: Harcourt.

Fleming, A. T. (1999, January). The new ideal: What makes a body beautiful? *Women's Sports and Fitness, 2*(2). Retrieved from Expanded Academic ASAP database.

Fleras, A., & Kunz, J. L. (2001). *Media and minorities: Representing diversity in multicultural Canada*. Toronto, ON: Thompson Educational Publishing.

Forbes, G. B., Adams-Curtis, L. E., Holmgren, K. M., & White, K. B. (2004). Perceptions of the social and personal characteristics of hypermuscular women and the men who love them. *The Journal of Social Psychology, 144*(5), 487–506.

Ford, J. A., & Schroeder, R. D. (2009). Academic strain and non-medical use of prescription stimulants among college students. *Deviant Behavior: An Interdisciplinary Journal, 30,* 26–53.

Forum 18. (2001). Freedom of religion: A report with special emphasis on the right to choose religion and registration systems. Retrieved from www.forum18.org.

Foucault, M. (1978). *The history of sexuality, volume I: An introduction.* New York, NY: Vintage Books.

Foucault, M. (1980). *Power/knowledge: Selected interviews and other writings 1972–1977* (1st American ed.). C. Gordon, L. Marshall, J. Mepham, & K. Super (Trans.). New York, NY: Pantheon Books.

Foucault, M. (1995). *Discipline and punish: The birth of the prison* (2nd ed.). (A. Sheridan, Trans.). New York, NY: Vintage Books. (Original work published 1977.)

Fournier, S., & Crey, E. (1998). *Stolen from our embrace.* Berkeley, CA: Roundhouse Publishing.

Frailing, K., & Harper, D. W. (2010). The social construction of deviance, conflict and the criminalization of midwives, New Orleans: 1940s and 1950s. *Deviant Behavior, 31,* 729–755.

Frederick, C. M., & Bradley, K. A. (2000). A Different Kind of Normal? Psychological and motivational characteristics of young adult tattooers and body piercers. *North American Journal of Psychology, 2*(2), 380–393.

Freedhoff, Y. (2012, February 23). Disney's horrifying new interactive child obesity exhibit at Epcot. Retrieved from www.weightymatters.ca.

Free Press. (2011). *Who owns the media? The "big six" companies.* Washington, DC: Free Press and the Free Press Action Fund. Retrieved from www.freepress.net/resources/ownership.

Freud, S. (1999). The social construction of normality. *Families in Society: The Journal of Contemporary Human Services,* 80(4), 333–339.

The Futurist. (2004, July/August). Western lifestyles and South African women. *The Futurist, 38*(4), 2

Gabbidon, S. L. (2003). Racial profiling by store clerks and security personnel in retail establishments: An exploration of "shopping while black." *Journal of Contemporary Criminal Justice, 19*(3), 345–364.

Gackenbach, J., & Snyder, T. (2012). *Play reality: How video games are changing everything.* Calgary, AB: Authors.

Gardner, C. B. (1991). Stigma and the public self: Notes on communication, self, and others. *Journal of Contemporary Ethnography, 20*(3), 251–252.

Garner, D. M. (1997, January/February). The 1997 body image survey results. *Psychology Today,* 31–44, 75–84.

Gater, R., Tnasella, M., Korten, A., Mavreas, V. G. & Olatawura, M. O. (1998). Sex differences in the prevalence and detection of depressive and anxiety disorders in general health care settings. *Archives of General Psychiatry, 55,* 405–413.

Gerbner, G., Gross, L., Morgan, M., Signorielli, N., & Shanahan, J. (2002). Growing up with television: Cultivation processes. In J. Bryant & D. Zillman (Eds.), *Media effects: Advances in theory and research* (2nd ed., pp. 43–67). Mahwah, NJ: Lawrence Erlbaum Associates.

Gibelman, M., & Gelman, S. R. (2005). Scientific misconduct in social welfare research: Preventive lessons from other fields. *Social Work Education, 24*(3), 275–295.

Gibson, C., & Wright, J. (2001), Low self-control and co-worker delinquency: A research note. *Journal of Criminal Justice, 29,* 483–492.

Giesbrecht, N. (2000). Roles of commercial interests in alcohol policies: Recent developments in North America. *Addiction, 95* (suppl. 4), S581–S595.

Godfrey, T. (2012, July 22). Strip clubs set to recruit high school students. *The Barrie Examiner*. Retrieved from www.thebarrieexaminer.com.

Goffman, E. (1959). *The presentation of self in everyday life*. Garden City, NY: Doubleday-Anchor.

Goffman, E. (1961). *Asylums: Essays on the social situation of mental patients and other inmates*. Garden City, NY: Anchor Books.

Goffman, E. (1963). *Stigma: Notes on the management of spoiled identity*. Englewood Cliffs, NJ: Prentice Hall.

Goffman, E. (1979). *Gender advertisements*. New York, NY: Harper & Row.

Gomme, I. M. (1985). Predictors of status and criminal offences among male and female adolescents in an Ontario community. *Canadian Journal of Criminology, 27*, 157–159.

Good, M., & Willoughby, T. (2006). The role of spirituality versus religiosity in adolescent psychological adjustment. *Journal of Youth and Adolescence, 35*(1), 41–55.

Goode, E. (1997). *Deviant behavior* (5th ed.). Upper Saddle River, NJ: Prentice Hall.

Goode, E., & Ben-Yehuda, N. (1994). *Moral panics: The social construction of deviance*. Cambridge, UK: Blackwell.

Goodstein, L. (2003, May 27). Seeing Islam as an evil faith, Evangelicals seek converts. *New York Times*. Retrieved from www.nytimes.com.

Gordon, R. A. (2000). *Eating disorders: Anatomy of a social epidemic*. Malden, MA: Blackwell.

Gordon, R. M. (1993). Incarcerated gang members in British Columbia: A preliminary study. Victoria, BC: Ministry of the Attorney-General.

Gordon, R. M. (1995). Street gangs in Vancouver. In J. Creechan & R. Silverman (Eds.), *Canadian delinquency* (pp. 311–320). Toronto, ON: Prentice Hall.

Gordon, R. M. (2001). Street gangs and criminal business organizations: A Canadian perspective. In R. C. Smandych (Ed.), *Youth crime: Varieties, theories, and prevention* (pp. 248–265). Toronto, ON: Harcourt.

Goring, C. (1919). *The English convict*. London, London, UK: H. M. Stationery Office.

Gottfredson, M. R., & Hirschi, T. (1990). *A general theory of crime*. Stanford, CT: Stanford University Press.

Government of Canada. (2006). *The human face of mental health and mental illness 2006*. Ottawa, ON: Author.

Grasmick, H. G., Tittle, C. R., Bursik, R. J., & Arneklev, B. J. (1993). Testing the core empirical implications of Gottfredson and Hirschi's general theory of crime. *Journal of Research in Crime and Delinquency, 30*(1), 47–54.

Greco, A. N. (1995). The first amendment, freedom of the press, and the issues of "harm": A conundrum for publishers. *Publishing Research Quarterly, 11*(4), 39–57.

Greenberg, B. S., Eastin, M., Hofschire, L., Lachlan, K., & Brownell, K. D. (2003). Portrayals of overweight and obese individuals on commercial television. *American Journal of Public Health, 93*(8), 1342–1348.

Greenleaf, C., McGreer, R., & Parham, H. (2006). Physique attitudes and self-presentational concerns: Exploratory interviews with female aerobic exercisers and instructors. *Sex Roles, 54*(3/4), 189–199.

Greer, C., & Jewkes, Y. (2005). Extremes of otherness: Media images of social exclusion. *Social Justice, 32*(1), 20–31.

Gregoire, L. (2003). Alberta teens face smoking fines, price of cartons tops $70. *Canadian Medical Association Journal,* 168(7), 888.

Grekul, J. M. (2002). *The social construction of the feebleminded threat: Implementation of the Sexual Sterilization Act in Alberta, 1929–1972.* Unpublished doctoral dissertation, University of Alberta, Edmonton, AB.

Grekul, J., & LaBoucane-Benson, P. (2007). *An investigation into the formation and recruitment processes of Aboriginal gangs in Western Canada.* Ottawa, ON: Aboriginal Corrections Policy Unit, Public Safety Canada.

Grob, G. N. (1994). *The mad among us: A history of the care of America's mentally ill.* New York, NY: Free Press.

Ha, T. T. (2012, November 12). Denmark sheds its maligned fat tax. *Globe and Mail.* Retrieved from www.theglobeandmail.com.

Hackler, J. C. (2000). Strain theories. In R. Linden (Ed.), *Criminology: A Canadian perspective* (4th ed., pp. 270–300). Toronto, ON: Harcourt Canada.

Hadden, J., & Bromley, D. (Eds.). (1995). *The handbook of cults and sects in America.* Greenwich, CT: JAI Press.

Hagedorn, J. M. (2007). Introduction: Globalization, gangs, and traditional criminology. In J. M. Hagedorn (Ed.), *Gangs in the global city: Alternatives to traditional criminology* (pp. 1–10). Chicago, IL: University of Illinois Press.

Hagmann, M. (2001). Alcohol takes its toll on Europe's youth. *Bulletin of the World Health Organization,* 79(4), 380.

Haldane, J. B. S. (1927). "Science and technology as art-forms," in *Possible worlds and other essays.* London, UK: Chatto & Windus. Retrieved from www.bartleby.com.

Hall, G. S. (1904). *Adolescence* (Vol. I). Englewood Cliffs, NJ: Prentice Hall.

Hall, J. (2002). Mass suicide and the Branch Davidians. In D. G. Bromley & J. G. Melton (Eds.), *Cults, religion, and violence* (pp. 149–169). Cambridge, UK: Cambridge University Press.

Hall, S. (2009). The work of representation. In Stuart Hall (Ed.), *Representation: Cultural representations and signifying practices* (pp. 1–11). Thousand Oaks, CA: Sage Publications.

Hamilton, S. N. (2010). Considering critical communication studies in Canada. In L. R. Shade (Ed.), *Mediascapes: New patterns in Canadian communication* (3rd ed.). Toronto, ON: Nelson Education.

Hannigan, B. (1999). Mental health care in the community: An analysis of contemporary public attitudes towards, and public representations of, mental illness. *Journal of Mental Health,* 8(5), 431–440.

Harkin, A. M., Anderson, P., & Goos, C. (1997). *Smoking, drinking and drug taking in the European region.* Copenhagen, DK: World Health Organization.

Harrison, M. L., Jones, S., & Sullivan, C. (2008). The gendered expressions of self-control: Manifestations of non-criminal deviance among females. *Deviant Behavior: An Interdisciplinary Journal,* 29(1), 18–42.

Hathaway, A. D., & Atkinson, M. F. (2001). Tolerable differences revisited: Crossroads in theory on the social construction of deviance. *Deviant Behavior: An Inter-disciplinary Journal,* 22, 353–377.

Hawdon, J. E. (1996). Deviant lifestyles: The social control of daily routines. *Youth & Society,* 28(2), 162–188.

Hawdon, J. E., Ryan, J., & Agnich, L. (2010). Crime as a source of social solidarity: A research note testing Durkheim's assertion. *Deviant Behavior,* 31, 679–703.

Hawkes, D., Senn, C. Y., & Thorn, C. (2004). Factors that influence attitudes toward women with tattoos. *Sex Roles, 50*(9/10), 593–604.

Hay, C., & Meldrum, R. (2010). Bullying, victimization, and adolescent self-harm: Testing hypotheses from general strain theory. *Journal of Youth and Adolescence, 39*, 446–459.

Hayden-Wade, H. A., Stein, R. I., Ghaderi, A., Saelens, B. E., Zabinski, M. F., & Wilfley, D. E. (2005). Prevalence, characteristics, and correlates of teasing experiences among overweight children vs. non-overweight peers. *Obesity Research, 13*(8), 1381–1392.

Health Canada. (1999). *Trends in the health of Canadian children.* Ottawa, ON: Author.

Health Canada. (2002). *A report on mental illness in Canada.* Ottawa, ON: Author.

Health Canada. (2005a). *2002 youth smoking survey: Technical report.* Ottawa, ON: Author.

Health Canada. (2005b). *Evaluation of retailers' behaviour towards certain youth access-to-tobacco restrictions. Final Report Findings 2005.* Ottawa, ON: Author.

Health Canada. (2005c). *The integrated pan-Canadian healthy living strategy.* Ottawa, ON: Author.

Hefley, K. (2007). Stigma management of male and female customers to a non-urban adult novelty store. *Deviant Behavior: An Interdisciplinary Journal, 28*(1), 79–109.

Heltsley, M., & Calhoun, T. C. (2003). The good mother: Neutralization techniques used by pageant mothers. *Deviant Behavior: An Interdisciplinary Journal, 24*, 81–100.

Herdt, G. (1984). Ritualized homosexuality in the male cults of Melanesia, 1862–1982: An introduction. In G. Herdt, (Ed.), *Ritualized homosexuality in Melanesia* (pp. 1–81). Berkeley, CA: University of California Press.

Herman, N. J. (1995). Introduction. In N. J. Herman (Ed.), *Deviance: A Symbolic Interactionist Approach* (pp. 1–6). Lanham, MD: General Hall.

Herman, N. J., & Miall, C. E. (1990). The positive consequences of stigma: Two case studies of mental and physical disability. *Qualitative Sociology, 13*, 251–269.

Hersch, P. (1998). *A tribe apart: A journey into the heart of American adolescence.* New York, NY: Ballantine Books.

Hicinbothem, J., Gonsalves, S., & Lester, D. (2006). Body modification and suicidal behavior. *Death Studies, 30*, 351–363.

Hier, S. P. (2002). Raves, risks and the ecstasy panic: A case study of the subversive nature of moral regulation. *Canadian Journal of Sociology, 27*(1), 33–57.

Higgins, G. E., Wolfe, S. E., & Marcum, C. D. (2008). Digital piracy: An examination of three measurements of self-control. *Deviant Behavior: An Interdisciplinary Journal, 29*(5), 440–460.

Hinduja, S., & Higgins, G. E. (2011). Trends and patterns among music pirates. *Deviant Behavior, 32*(7), 563–588.

Hinduja, S., & Patchin, J. W. (2008). Cyberbullying: An exploratory analysis of factors related to offending. *Deviant Behavior, 29*(2), 129–156.

Hirschi, T. C. (1969). *Causes of delinquency.* Berkeley, CA: University of California Press.

Hodgins, S. (1993). The criminality of mentally disordered persons. In S. Hodgins (Ed.), *Mental disorder and crime.* Newbury Park, CA: Sage.

Hoek, H. W. (2007). Incidence, prevalence, and mortality of anorexia and other eating disorders. *Current Opinion in Psychiatry, 19*(4), 389–394.

Hoffman, B., & Burke, C. (1997). *Heaven's Gate cult: Suicide in San Diego*. New York, NY: HarperCollins.

Hollinger, R. (1991). Neutralizing in the workplace: An empirical analysis of property theft and production deviance. *Deviant Behavior, 12*, 169–202.

Holt, T. J., & Copes, H. (2010). Transferring subcultural knowledge online: Practices and beliefs of persistent digital pirates. *Deviant Behavior, 31*(7), 625–654.

Holt, T. J., & Turner, M. G. (2012). Examining risks and protective factors of on-line identity theft. *Deviant Behavior, 33*(4), 308–323.

Hope, T. L., & Chapple, C. L. (2005). Maternal characteristics, parenting, and adolescent sexual behavior: The role of self-control. *Deviant Behavior, 26*, 25–45.

Hotton, T., & Haans, D. (2004). Alcohol and drug use in early adolescence. *Health Reports, 15*(3), 9–19. Statistics Canada Catalogue No. 82003XIE.

Hudson, J. I., Hiripi, E., Pope, H. G., & Kessler, R. C. (2007). The prevalence and correlates of eating disorders in the national comorbidity survey replication. *Biological Psychiatry, 61*(3), 348–358.

Human Resources and Skills Development Canada. (2012, July 4). Government of Canada takes action to protect temporary foreign workers. Canada News Centre. Retrieved from news. gc.ca.

Humphreys, A. (2012, March 26). Ontario Court of Appeal greenlights brothels, sweeps aside many of Canada's anti-prostitution laws. *National Post*. Retrieved from www.news.nationalpost.com.

Hunt, A. (1998). The great masturbation panic and the discourses of moral regulation in nineteenth- and early twentieth-century Britain. *Journal of the History of Sexuality, 8*(4), 575–615.

Hunt, P. (2010). Are you kynd? Conformity and deviance within the jamband subculture. *Deviant Behavior, 31*, 521–551.

Interactive Advertising Bureau of Canada. (2011). *2010 Canadian media usage trends study*. Retrieved from www. iabcanada.com.

International Size Acceptance Association. (2003). Homepage. Retrieved from www. size-acceptance.org.

Investopedia. (2011, December 16). Where are advertisers spending their money? Retrieved from www.investopedia.com.

Ipsos-Reid. (2012). *Socialogue: Hello, my virtual friend!* Retrieved from www. ipsos.ca.

Irwin, D. (1999). The straight edge subculture: Examining the youths' drug-free way. *Journal of Drug Issues, 29*, 365–380.

Irwin, K. (2003). Saints and sinners: Elite tattoo collectors and tattooists as positive and negative deviants. *Sociological Spectrum, 23*, 27–57.

Jafari, S., Copes, R., Baharlou, S., Etminan, M., & Buxton, J. (2010). Tattooing and the risk of transmission of hepatitis C: A systematic review and meta-analysis. *International Journal of Infectious Disease, 14*(11), 928–940.

Jaimes, M. A. (1992). *The state of Native America: Genocide, colonization, and resistance*. Cambridge, MA: South End Press.

James, R. (2009, December 9). Top 10 Disney controversies. *Time Magazine*. Retrieved from www.entertainment. time.com.

James, W. H. (1995). Frauds and hoaxes in science. *Nature, 377*(6549), 474.

Jang, S. J.. & Smith, C. A. (1997). A test of reciprocal causal relationships among parental supervision, affective ties, and delinquency. *Journal of Research in Crime and Delinquency, 34*(3), 307–336.

Jankowski, M. S. (1991). *Islands in the street: Gangs and American urban society.* Berkeley, CA: University of California Press.

Janz, T. (2012). Current smoking trends. *Health at a Glance.* Ottawa, ON: Statistics Canada. Catalogue No. 82-624-X.

Jenkins, P. (2000). *Mystics and messiahs: Cults and new religions in American history.* New York, NY: Oxford University Press.

Jernigan, *Alcohol and young people.* Geneva, CH: D. H. (2001). *Global status report:* World Health Organization.

Jhally, S. (Writer, Director). (2009). *The codes of gender: Identity and performance in pop culture.* Retrieved from Media Education Foundation, www.mediaed.org.

Jiwani, Y. (2010). Race(ing) the nation: Media and minorities. In L. R. Shade (Ed.), *Mediascapes: New patterns in Canadian communication* (3rd ed.). Toronto, ON: Nelson Education.

Johnson, C. A. (2009, February 11). Cutting through advertising clutter. *Sunday Morning.* Retrieved from www.cbsnews.com.

Johnson, J. G., Cohen, P., Smailes, E. M., Kasen, S., & Brook, J. (2002). Television viewing and aggressive behavior during adolescence and adulthood. *Science, 295,* 2468–2471.

Jones, G. (1986). *Social hygiene in twentieth-century Britain.* London, UK: Croom Helm.

Jones, L. (1998). Social Darwinism revisited. *History Today, 48*(8). Retrieved from Expanded Academic ASAP database.

Jones, S., & Quisenberry, N. (2004). The general theory of crime: How general is it? *Deviant Behavior, 25,* 401–426.

Jordon, T. E. (1998). Victorian child savers and their culture: A thematic evaluation (Mellon Studies in Sociology, Vol. 19). Lewiston, NY: Edwin Mellon Press.

Joseph, J., & Baldwin, S. (2000). Four editorial proposals to improve social sciences research and publication. *International Journal of Risk & Safety in Medicine, 13,* 109–116.

Josephson, W. L. (1987). Television violence and children's aggression: Testing the priming, social script, and disinhibition predictions. *Journal of Personality and Social Psychology, 53*(5), 882–890.

Judson, H. F. (2004). *The great betrayal: Fraud in science.* Orlando, FL: Harcourt.

Katz, J. (1999). From the film *Tough Guise,* produced by Sut Jhally. Available from the Media Education Foundation, www.mediaed.org.

Katzmarzyk, P. T., & Janssen, I. (2004). The economic costs associated with physical inactivity and obesity in Canada: An update. *Canadian Journal of Applied Physiology, 29*(1), 104.

Kaufman, J. M. (2009). Gendered responses to serious strain: The argument for a general strain theory of deviance. *Justice Quarterly, 26*(3), 410–444.

Kaufman, M. R. (2009). "It's just a fantasy for a couple of hours": Ethnography of a nude male show bar. *Deviant Behavior, 30,* 407–433.

Keeling, R. P. (2000). The political, social, and public health problems of binge drinking in college. *Journal of American College Health, 48*(5), 195–198.

Keeling, R. P. (2002). Binge drinking and the college environment. *Journal of American College Health, 50*(5), 197–201.

Kendall, D., Murray, J. L., & Linden, R. (2007). *Sociology in our times* (4th Canadian ed.). Toronto, ON: Thomson Nelson.

Kent, S. A. (1994). Lustful prophet: A psychosexual history of the Children of

God's leader, David Berg. *Cultic Studies Journal, 11*(2), 135–188.

Kent, S. L., & Jacobs, D. (2004). Social divisions and coercive control in advanced societies: Law enforcement strength in eleven nations from 1975 to 1994. *Social Problems, 51*(3), 343–361.

Kessler, R. C., McGonagle, K. A., Zhao, S., Nelson, C. B., Hughes, M., Eshleman, S., et al. (1994). Lifetime and 12-month prevalence of DSM-III-R psychiatric disorders in the United States. *Archives of General Psychiatry, 51*, 8–19.

Kevles, D. (1995). *In the name of eugenics: Genetics and the uses of human heredity.* Berkeley, CA: University of California Press.

Kim, L. (2008). Explaining the Hwang scandal: National scientific culture and its global relevance. *Science as Culture, 17*(4), 397–415.

Kinsey, A. (2006). In *Rand Lindsly's Quotations.* Retrieved from www.quotationspage.com.

Kinsmen, G., & Gentile, P. (2009). *The Canadian war on queers: National security as sexual regulation.* Vancouver, BC: UBC Press.

Kitsuse, J. I. (1980). Coming out all over: Deviants and the politics of social problems. *Social Problems, 28*(1), 1–12.

Kitsuse, J. I., & Dietrick, D. C. (1979). Delinquent boys: A critique. In H. L. Voss (Ed.), *Society, delinquency, and delinquent Behavior* (pp. 238–245). Boston, MA: Little, Brown.

Klauer, (2005). *How the rich get thin.* New York, NY: St. Martin's Press.

Koch, J. R., Roberts, A. E., Cannon, J. H., Armstrong, M. L., & Owen, D. C. (2005). College students, tattooing, and the health belief model: Extending social psychological perspectives on youth culture and deviance. *Sociological Spectrum, 25*, 79–102.

Kong, T. S. K. (2009). More than a sex machine: Accomplishing masculinity among Chinese male sex workers in the Hong Kong sex industry. *Deviant Behavior, 30*, 715–745.

Konty, M. (2005). Microanomie: The cognitive foundations of the relationship between anomie and deviance. *Criminology, 43*(1), 107–131.

Kosut, M. (2006). An ironic fad: The commodification and consumption of tattoos. *The Journal of Popular Culture, 39*(6), 1035–1048.

Krashinsky, S. (2012, April 19). Canadian Club on the rocks? Far from it, thanks to *Mad Men. Globe and Mail.* Retrieved from www.theglobeandmail.com.

Krieg, R. G. (2001). An interdisciplinary look at the deinstitutionalization of the mentally ill. *Social Science Journal, 38*, 367–380.

Kroska, A., & Harkness, S. K. (2006). Stigma sentiments and self-meanings: Exploring the modified labeling theory of mental illness. *Social Psychology Quarterly, 69*(4), 325–348.

Kubrin, C. E., Stucky, T. D., & Krohn, M. D. (2009). *Researching theories of crime and deviance.* New York, NY: Oxford University Press.

Kuhl, S. (1994). *The Nazi connection.* New York, NY: Oxford University Press.

Kuhns, E. (2003). *The habit: A history of the clothing of Catholic nuns.* New York, NY: Doubleday.

Lalich, J., & Langone, M. D. (2006). Characteristics associated with cultic groups—Revised. Retrieved from www.icsahome.com/infoserv_articles/langone_michael.checklis.htm.

The Lancet. (2006, January 7). Editorial: Writing a new ending for a story of scientific fraud. Retrieved from www.thelancet.com.

Langlais, P. J. (2006). Ethics for the next generation. *Chronicle of Higher Education, 52*(19). Retrieved from Expanded Academic ASAP database.

Larsen, N. (2000). Prostitution: Deviant activity or legitimate occupation? In L. G. Beaman (Ed.), *New perspectives on deviance: The construction of deviance in everyday life* (pp. 50–66). Toronto, ON: Prentice Hall.

Larson, R., & Richards, M. H. (1994). *Divergent realities: The emotional lives of mothers, fathers, and adolescents.* New York, NY: Basic Books.

Latner, J., & Stunkard, A. (2003). Stigmatization of obese children. *Nutrition Research Newsletter, 22*(4), 12.

Lauritsen, J. L. (1994). Explaining race and gender differences in adolescent sexual behavior. *Social Forces, 72*(3), 859–884.

Laursen, B. (1995). Conflict and social interaction in adolescent relationships. *Journal of Research on Adolescence, 5,* 55–70.

Laursen, B., Coy, K. C., & Collins, W. A. (1998). Reconsidering changes in parent-child conflict across adolescence: A meta-analysis. *Child Development, 69,* 817–832.

Law, C., & Labre, M. P. (2002). Cultural standards of attractiveness: A thirty-year look at changes in male images in magazines. *Journalism & Mass Communication Quarterly, 79*(3), 697–711.

Lawrie, S. M., Martin, K., McNeill, G., Drife, J., Chrystie, P., Reid, A., et al. (1998). General practitioners' attitudes to psychiatric and medical illness. *Psychiatric Medicine, 28,* 1463–1467.

Lawson, R. (1995). Sect–state relations: Accounting for the differing trajectories of Seventh-day Adventists and Jehovah's Witnesses. *Sociology of Religion, 56*(4), 351–378.

Lazarsfeld, P. F. (1941). Remarks on administrative and critical communication research. *Studies in Philosophy and Social Science, 9* (1), 2–16.

Lee, D. (2006). In *Rand Lindsly's Quotations.* Retrieved August 23, 2006, from www. quotationspage.com.

Lemert, E. M. (1951). *Social pathology: A systematic approach to the study of sociopathic behavior.* New York, NY: McGraw-Hill.

Leon, J. S. (1977). The development of Canadian juvenile justice: A background for reform. *Osgoode Hall Law Journal, 15,* 71–106.

Leone, J. E., Sedory, E. J., & Gray, K. A. (2005). Helping athletes: Recognition and treatment of muscle dysmorphia and related body image disorders. *Journal of Athletic Training, 40*(4), 352–359.

Levenkron, S. (2000). *Anatomy of anorexia.* New York, NY: W.W. Norton.

Levine, B. (2005). Behind the Paxil scandals. *Z Magazine, 18*(4). Retrieved from web.uni-marburg.de/ religionswissenschaft/journal/diskus/ chryssides.html.

Levine, M., & Maine, M. (2005). Eating disorders can be prevented. National Eating Disorders Association. Retrieved from www.nationaleatingdisorders.org.

Levy, L. D. (2000). *Conquering obesity.* Toronto, ON: Key Porter Books.

Lewis, J., & Melton, J. G. (1994). *Sex, slander, and salvation: Investigating The Family/Children of God.* Stanford, CA: Center for Academic Publication.

Li, Q. (2010). Cyberbullying in high schools: A study of students' behaviors and beliefs about this new phenomenon. *Journal of Aggression, 19,* 372–392.

Lianos, M., with Douglas, M. (2000). Dangerization and the end of deviance. *British Journal of Criminology, 40,* 261–278.

Liazos, A. (1972). The poverty of the sociology of deviance: Nuts, sluts, and perverts. *Social Problems, 20,* 102–120.

Linden, R. (Ed.). (2000). *Criminology: A Canadian perspective* (4th ed.). Toronto, ON: Harcourt Canada.

Lindsay, C. (2008). Canadians attend weekly religious services less than 20 years ago. *Matter of Fact, No. 3.* Ottawa, ON: Statistics Canada. Catalogue No. 89-630-X.

Liska, A., & Reid, M. (1985). Ties to conven-tional institutions and delinquency. *American Sociological Review, 50,* 547–560.

Liu, C. M., & Lester, D. (2012). Body modification sites and abuse history. *Journal of Aggression, Maltreatment and Trauma, 21*(1), 19–30.

Lock, J. (2001). *Treatment manual for anorexia nervosa: A family-based approach.* New York, NY: Guilford Press.

Löfgren-Mårtenson, L., & Månsson, S.-A. (2010). Lust, love, and life: A qualitative study of Swedish adolescents' perceptions and experiences with pornography. *Journal of Sex Research, 47*(6), 568–579.

Lombroso, C. (1911). *Crime, its causes and remedies.* Boston, MA: Little, Brown.

Longshore, D., Chang, E., Hsieh, S., & Messina, N. (2004). Self-control and social bonds: A combined control perspective on deviance. *Crime & Delinquency, 50*(4), 542–564.

Loring, M., & Powell, B. (1988). Gender, race and DSM-III. *Journal of Health and Social Behavior, 29,* 1–22.

Lyman, S. (2000). Accounts: Roots and foundations. In C. D. Bryant (Ed.) *Encyclopedia of criminology and deviant behavior.* Philadelphia, PA: Brunner-Routledge.

MacEachern, S. (2006). Africanist archaeology and ancient IQ: Racial science and cultural evolution in the twenty-first century. *World Archaeology, 38*(1), 72–92.

Mackay, J. (2000). Global sex: Sexuality and sexual practices around the world. Paper presented at the 5th Congress of the European Federation of Sexology, June 29–July 2, 2000, Berlin.

Macnamara, J. R. (2006). *Media and male identity: The making and remaking of men.* New York, NY: Palgrave MacMillan.

Mandell, N., & Momirov, J. (2000). Family histories. In N. Mandell & A. Duffy (Eds.), *Canadian families: Diversity, conflict, and change* (2nd ed., pp. 17–47). Toronto, ON: Nelson Thomson.

March, P. A. (1999). Ethical responses to media depictions of mental illness: An advocacy approach. *Journal of Humanistic Counseling, Education, & Development, 38*(2), 70–79.

Marcos, A. C., Bahr, S. J., & Johnson, R. E. (1986). Test of a bonding/association theory of adolescent drug use. *Social Forces, 65,* 135–161.

Marcum, C. D., Higgins, G. E., & Ricketts, M. L. (2010). Potential factors of online victimization of youth: An examination of adolescent online behaviors utilizing routine activity theory. *Deviant Behavior, 31*(5), 381–410.

Markowitz, F. E., Angell, B., & Greenberg, J. S. (2011). Stigma, reflected appraisals, and recovery outcomes in mental illness. *Social Psychology Quarterly, 74*(2), 144–165.

Marshall, B. L. (2006). The new virility: Viagra, male aging and sexual function. *Sexualities, 9*(3), 345–362.

Martin, N., & Johnston, V. (2007). *A time for action: Tackling stigma and discrimination: Report to the Mental Health Commission of Canada.* Calgary, AB: Mental Health Commission of Canada.

Marvasti, A. (2008). Being Middle Eastern American: Identity negotiation in the context of the war on terror. In E. J. Clarke (Ed.), *Deviant behavior: A text-reader in the sociology of deviance* (pp. 648–671). New York, NY: Worth.

Massey, J. L., & Krohn, M. D. (1986). A longitudinal examination of an integrated social process model of deviant behavior. *Social Forces, 65,* 106–134.

Matthews, D. D. (2001). *Eating disorders sourcebook.* Detroit, MI: Omnigraphics.

Mattson, K. (2001). Did punk matter? Analyzing the practices of a youth subculture. *American Studies, 42*(1), 69–97.

Matusitz, J. (2008). Similarities between terrorist networks in antiquity and present-day cyberterrorist networks. *Trends in Organized Crime, 11,* 183–199.

Maugham, W. S. (1998). In *W. Somerset Maugham's Birthday: January 25, 1874.* Retrieved from www.quotationspage.com.

Mayers, L. B., & Chiffriller, S. H. (2008). Body art (body piercing and tattooing) among undergraduate university students: "Then and now". *Journal of Adolescent Health, 42,* 201–203.

McCaghy, C. H., Capron, T. A., & Jamieson, J. D. (2003). *Deviant behavior: Crime, conflict, and interest groups* (6th ed.). Boston, MA: Allyn & Bacon.

McCarthy, M. (2004). Lies, damn lies, and scientific research. *The Lancet, 364,* 1657–1658.

McConnell, H. (1997, January 21). ADHD just doesn't add up to Brit psych society. *Medical Post.* Retrieved from mentalhealth.com.

McCray, K., Wesely, J. K., & Rasche, C. (2011). Rehab restrospect: Former prostitutes and the (re)construction of deviance. *Deviant Behavior, 32*(8), 743–768.

McGovern, C. M. (1985). *Masters of madness: Social origins of the American psychiatric profession.* Hanover, NH: University Press of New England.

McGuire, M. B. (1997). *Religion: The social context* (4th ed.). Belmont, CA: Wadsworth.

McKee, M. (2002). Substance use and social and economic transition: The need for evidence. *International Journal of Drug Policy, 13,* 453–459.

McKeen, S. (2002, March 24). An XXX-ray of our psyche: Basic instinct or debauchery? *Edmonton Journal,* D6.

McIlroy, A. (2012, September 20). Home, sweet home gives hope to mentally ill. *Globe and Mail.* Retrieved from www.theglobeandmail.com.

McLaren, A. (1990). *Our own master race: Eugenics in Canada 1885–1945.* Toronto, ON: McClelland & Stewart.

McLorg, P. A., & Taub, D. E. (1987). Anorexia, bulimia, and developing a deviant identity. *Deviant Behavior: An Interdisciplinary Journal, 8,* 177–189.

Media Education Foundation. (n.d.). *10 reasons why media education matters.* Retrieved from www.mediaed.org.

Melton, D. E. (2000). Emerging religious movements in North America: Some missiological reflections. *Missiology: An International Review, 27*(1), 85–98.

Melton, J. G., & Bromley, D. (2002). Challenging misconceptions about the new religion-violence connection. In D. G. Bromley & J. G. Melton (Eds.), *Cults, religion, and violence* (pp. 42–56). Cambridge, UK: Cambridge University Press.

Menn, J. (2012, July 12). Can social media ever be made safe from sex predators? *Globe and Mail.* Retrieved from www.theglobeandmail.com.

Mental Health Commission of Canada. (2008). The homeless and mental illness: Solving the challenge. Presentation by the Honourable Michael Kirby, Chair, Mental Health Commission of Canada at the "Collaboration for Change Forum," Vancouver, BC, April 28, 2008. *MHCC TV*. Retrieved from www.mentalhealthcommission.ca.

Mental Health Commission of Canada. (2009). *Toward recovery and well-being: A framework for a mental health strategy for Canada. Draft: For public discussion.* Calgary, AB: Author.

Mental Health Commission of Canada. (2012a). *Why investing in mental health will contribute to Canada's economic prosperity and to the sustainability of our health care system. Background. Key facts.* Calgary, AB: Author.

Mental Health Commission of Canada. (2012b). *Changing directions: The mental health strategy for Canada.* Calgary, AB: Author.

Merriam-Webster. (2013). Deviant. *Merriam-Webster's Online Dictionary.* Retrieved from www.merriam-webster.com.

Merriam-Webster. (2013). pornography. *Merriam-Webster's Online Dictionary.* Retrieved from www.merriam-webster.com.

Merriam-Webster. (2003). Science. *Merriam-Webster's Online Dictionary.* Retrieved from www.merriam-webster.com.

Merton, R. K. (1938). Social structure and anomie. *American Sociological Review, 3,* 672–682.

Merton, R. K. (1968). *Social theory and social structure.* New York, NY: Free Press.

Merton, R. K. (1973). *The Sociology of science: Theoretical and empirical investigations.* Chicago, IL: University of Chicago Press.

Merton, R. K. (1995). Opportunity structure: The emergence, diffusion, and differentiation of a sociological concept, 1930s–1950s. In F. Adler and W. S. Laufer (Eds.), *The legacy of anomie theory* (pp. 3–78). New Brunswick, NJ: Transaction Publishers.

Messner, S. F., & Rosenfeld, R. (2001). *Crime and the American dream.* Belmont, CA: Wadsworth.

Mestemacher, R. A., & Roberti, J. W. (2004). Qualitative analysis of vocational choice: A collective case study of strippers. *Deviant Behavior, 25,* 43–65.

Miech, R. A., Caspi, A., Moffitt, T. E., Wright, B. R. E., & Silva, P. A. (1999). Low socioeconomic status and mental disorders: A longitudinal study of selection and causation during young adulthood. *American Journal of Sociology, 104*(4). Retrieved from Expanded Academic ASAP database.

Milan, A. (2000). One hundred years of families. *Canadian Social Trends, 56,* 2–12. Statistics Canada Catalogue No. 11-008.

Millanvoye, M. (2001). Teflon under my skin. *The UNESCO Courier, July/August,* 57.

Miller, J. (1996). *Shingwauk's vision.* Toronto, ON: University of Toronto Press.

Miller, J. M. (2011). Becoming an informant. *Justice Quarterly, 28*(2), 203–220.

Miller, J. M., Wright, R. A., & Dannels, D. (2001). Is deviance "dead"? The decline of a sociological research specialization. *American Sociologist, 32*(3), 43–59.

Milloy, J. S. (1999). *A national crime: The Canadian government and the residential school system, 1879–1986.* Winnipeg, MB: University of Manitoba Press.

Mintzes, B. (2006). *What are the public health implications? Direct-to-consumer advertising of prescription drugs in Canada.* Toronto, ON: Health Council of Canada.

Monahan, J. (1992). Mental disorder and violent behavior: Perceptions and evidence. *American Psychologist, 47,* 511–521.

Montgomery, K., & Oliver, A. L. (2009). Shifts in guidelines for ethical scientific conduct: How public and private organizations create and change norms of research integrity. *Social Studies of Science,* 39(1), 137–155.

Moon, B., Hays, K., & Blurton, D. (2009). General strain theory, key strains, and deviance. *Journal of Criminal Justice, 37,* 98–106.

Moon, D. (2008). Culture and the sociology of sexuality: It's only natural? *The Annals of the American Academy of Political and Social Science,* 619(1), 183–205.

Morrow, L. C. (2012). Cyclical role-playing and stigma: Exploring the challenges of stereotype performance among exotic dancers. *Deviant Behavior,* 33(5), 357–374.

Mosher, C. E. (2002). Impact of gender and problem severity upon intervention selection. *Sex Roles,* 46(3/4), 113–119.

Mosher, J. F., & Johnsson, D. (2005). Flavored alcoholic beverages: An international marketing campaign that targets youth. *Journal of Public Health Policy,* 26(3), 326–342.

Mostert, M. P. (2002). Useless eaters: Disability as genocidal marker in Nazi Germany. *Journal of Special Education,* 36(3), 155–168.

Murphy, E. F. (1973 [1922]). *The Black Candle.* Toronto, ON: Coles Publishing.

Murray, J. L., & Lopez, A. D. (1996). *The global burden of disease: A comprehensive assessment of mortality and disability from diseases, injuries, and risk factors in 1990 and projected to 2020: Summary.* Boston, MA: Harvard School of Public Health/ World Health Organization.

Nakhaie, M. R., Silverman, R. A., & LaGrange, T. C. (2000). Self-control and resistance to school. *Canadian Review of Sociology and Anthropology,* 37(4), 443–460.

NAMBLA. (n.d.). Homepage. Retrieved from www.nambla.org.

NAMBLA Controversy. (n.d.). Let us first dispell the conservative myth on NAMBLA being supported by the gay community, paragraph 1. Retrieved from www.network54.com/ Forum/114969/message/1007273804.

Nanda, S. (2000). *Gender diversity: Crosscultural variations.* Chicago, IL: Waveland Press Inc.

Nathanson, C., Paulhus, D. L., & Williams, K. M. (2005). Personality and misconduct correlates of body modification and other cultural deviance markers. *Journal of Research in Personality,* 40, 779–802.

National Eating Disorders Association. (2003). Homepage. Retrieved from national-eatingdisorders.org.

National Eating Disorder Information Centre. (2008). Statistics. Retrieved from www.nedic.ca/knowthefacts/ statistics.html.

National Eating Disorder Information Centre (2012). *Definitions.* Retrieved August 15, 2013 from www.nedic.org.

National Institutes of Mental Health (2011). *What Are Eating Disorders?* Retrieved August 15, 2013 from www.nimh.nih. gov.

Nelson, A. (2006). *Gender in Canada* (3rd ed.). Toronto, ON: Pearson Prentice Hall.

Nelson, E. D., & Robinson, B. W. (2002). *Gender in Canada.* Toronto, ON: Prentice Hall.

Neumark-Sztainer, D., Story, M., & Faibisch, L. (1998). Perceived stigmatization among overweight African-American and Caucasian adolescent girls. *Journal of Adolescent Health,* 33(5), 264–270

Neumark-Sztainer, D. R., Wall, M. M., Haines, J. I., Story, M. T., Sherwood, N. E., & van den Berg, P. A. (2007). Shared risk and protective factors for overweight and disordered eating in adolescents. *American Journal of Preventative Medicine, 33*(5), 359–369.

Newhouse, D. (1998). Magic and joy: Traditional Aboriginal views of human sexuality. *Canadian Journal of Human Sexuality, 7*(2), 183–187.

Newman, A. W., Wright, S. W., Wrenn, K. D., & Bernard, A. (2005). Should physicians have facial piercings? *Journal of General Internal Medicine, 20*(3), 213–218.

Newman, G. (2008). *Comparative deviance: Perception and law in six cultures.* New Brunswick, NJ: Transaction Publishers.

Nietzsche, F. (2004 [1886]). *Beyond good and evil.* I. Johnston (Trans.). Retrieved from www.mala.bc.ca/~Johnstoi/Nietzche/beyondgoodandevil4.htm.

Nylenna, M., & Simonsen, S. (2006). Scientific misconduct: A new approach to prevention. *The Lancet, 367,* 1882–1884.

Obesity Association. (2003). Homepage. Retrieved April 4, 2003, from www.obesity.org.

Ofori-Atta, A. (2012, March 6). Disney's black princess sells watermelon candy. *The Root.* Retrieved from www.theroot.com.

Ong, E. K., & Glantz, S. A. (2001). Constructing "sound science" and "good epidemiology": Tobacco, lawyers, and public relations firms. *American Journal of Public Health, 91,* 1749–1757.

Onishi, N. (2006, January 22). In a country that craved respect, stem cell scientist rode a wave of Korean pride. *New York Times.* Retrieved from www.nytimes.com.

Ontario Consultants on Religious Tolerance. (2003). Homepage. Retrieved from www.religioustolerance.org.

Orend, A., & Gagné, P. (2009). Corporate logo tattoos and the commodification of the Body. *Journal of Contemporary Ethnography, 38,* 493–517.

Oselin, S. S. (2010). Weighing the consequences of a deviant career: Factors leading to an exit from prostitution. *Sociological Perspectives, 53*(4), 527–549.

Owen, P. R., & Laurel-Seller, E. (2000). Weight and shape ideals: Thin is dangerously in. *Journal of Applied Social Psychology, 30*(5), 979–990.

Owens, E. W., Behun, R. J., Manning, J. C., & Reid, R. C. (2012). The impact of Internet pornography on adolescents: A review of the research. *Sexual Addiction & Compulsivity: The Journal of Treatment and Prevention, 19*(1–2), 99–122.

Overton, S. L., & Medina, S. L. (2008). The stigma of mental illness. *Journal of Counseling & Development, 86,* 143–151.

Parents Television Council. (2012). Family guide to prime-time television. Retrieved from www.parentstv.org.

Park, K. (2002). Stigma management among the voluntarily childless. *Social Perspectives, 45*(1), 21–45.

Park, R. (2000). *Voodoo science: The road from foolishness to fraud.* New York, NY: Oxford University Press.

Parnaby, P. F., & Sacco, V. F. (2004). Fame and strain: The contributions of Mertonian deviance theory to an understanding of the relationship between celebrity and deviant behavior. *Deviant Behavior, 25*(1), 1–26.

Parsons, T. (1951). *The social system.* Glencoe, IL: Free Press.

Parsons, T., & Bales, R. F. (1955). *Family, socialization, and interaction process.* Glencoe, IL: Free Press.

Parsons, T., & Smelser, N. J. (1956). *Economy and society: A study in the integration of economic and social theory.* Glencoe, IL: Free Press.

Patel, V., Araya, R., deLima, M., Ludermir, A., & Todd, C. (1999). Women, poverty and common mental disorders in four restructuring societies. *Social Science & Medicine, 49*, 1461–1471.

Peace, K. A., Beaman, L. G., & Sneddon, K. (2000). Theoretical approaches to the study of deviance. In L. G. Beaman (Ed.), *New perspectives on deviance: The construction of deviance in everyday life* (pp. 2–17). Toronto, ON: Prentice Hall.

Pearson, G. (1983). *Hooligan: A history of respectable fears.* London, UK: MacMillan Press.

Peck, R. L. (2001). What's new with ADHD? *Behavioral Health Management* (November/December), 26–29.

Penrose, L. S. (1939). Mental disease and crime: Outline of a comparative study of European statistics. *British Journal of Medical Psychology, 18*, 1–15.

Perry, B. L. (2011). The labeling paradox: Stigma, the sick role, and social networks in mental illness. *Journal of Health and Social Behavior, 52*(4), 460–477.

PFLAG Canada. (2009). PFLAG Canada homepage. Retrieved from www. pflagcanada.ca.

Pfohl, S. (1994). *Images of deviance and social control: A sociological history.* New York, NY: McGraw-Hill.

Piccinelli, M., & Homen, F. G. (1997). *Gender differences in the epidemiology of affective disorders and schizophrenia.* Geneva, CH: World Health Organization.

Piquero, N. L., Tibbets, S. G., & Blankenship, M. B. (2005). Examining the role of differential association and techniques of neutralization in explaining corporate crime. *Deviant Behavior, 26*, 159–188.

Platt, A. M. (1977). *The child savers: The invention of delinquency.* Chicago, IL: University of Chicago Press.

Pongonis, A., & Snyder, R. (1998). Links between body size, food, and perceptions of morality. Paper presented at the Annual Meeting of the American Psychological Association, August 14–18, San Francisco.

Popenoe, P., & Johnson, R. H. (1922). *Applied eugenics.* New York, NY: Macmillan.

Potts, A., & Tiefer, L. (Eds.). (2006). Introduction. *Sexualities, 9*(3), 267–272.

Pratt, T. C., et al. (2010). The empirical status of social learning theory: A meta-analysis. *Justice Quarterly, 27*(6), 765–802.

Price, J. H., Desmond, S. M., Krol, R. A., Snyder, F. F., & O'Connell, J. K. (1987). Family practice physicians' beliefs, attitudes, and practices regarding obesity. *American Journal of Preventative Medicine, 3*(6), 339–345.

Price, V. D., Tewkesbury, D., & Powers, E. (1997). Switching trains of thought: The impact of news frames on readers' cognitive responses. *Communication Research, 24*(5), 481–506.

Priebe, S., et al. (2005). Reinstitutionalization in mental health care: Comparison of six European countries. *British Medical Journal, 330*, 123–126.

Proctor, R. N. (1988). *Racial hygiene: Medicine under the Nazis.* Cambridge, MA: Harvard University Press.

PRweb. (2011, May 9). *U. S. weight loss market worth $60.9 billion.* Retrieved from www.prweb.com.

Puhl, R., & Brownell, K. D. (2001). Bias, discrimination, and obesity. *Obesity Research, 9*, 788–805.

Puhl, R. M., & Heuer, C. A. (2009). The stigma of obesity: A review and update. *Obesity, 17*, 941–964.

Puhl, R. M., & Latner, J. (2007). Obesity, stigma, and the health of the nation's children. *Psychological Bulletin, 133*, 557–580.

Quaife, G. R. (1987). *Godly zeal and furious rage: The witch craze in early modern*

Europe. New York, NY: St. Martin's Press.

Quinney, R. (1977). *The problem of crime: A critical introduction to criminology* (2nd ed.). New York, NY: Harper & Row.

R. v. Butler. (1992). Canadian Legal Information Institute. Retrieved from www.canlii.org.

R. v. Sharpe. (2001). Canadian Legal Information Institute. Retrieved from www.canlii.org.

Rabak-Wagener, J., Eickhoff-Shemek, J., & Kelly-Vance, L. (1998). The effect of media analysis on attitudes and behaviors regarding body image among college students. *Journal of American College Health, 47*(1). Retrieved from Expanded Academic ASAP database.

Rampton, S., & Stauber, J. (2000). How big tobacco helped create "the junkman." *PR Watch, 7*(3), 5–9.

Razack, S. H. (2002). *Race, space, and the law: Unmapping a white settler society*. Toronto, ON: Between the Lines.

Read, J., & Harre, N. (2001). The role of biological and genetic causal beliefs in the stigmatisation of 'mental patients.' *Journal of Mental Health, 10*(2), 223–235.

Regioli, R., & Hewitt, J. (1994). *Delinquency in society: A child-centered approach*. New York, NY: McGraw-Hill.

Reid, S. (2003). *Crime and criminology* (10th ed.). Toronto, ON: McGraw-Hill.

Reitsma-Street, M. (1989–1990). More control than care: A critique of historical and contemporary laws for delinquency and neglect of children in Ontario. *Canadian Journal of Women and the Law, 3*(2), 510–530.

Reuters. (2012, March 20). Israel bans use of ultra-skinny models. Retrieved from www.reuters.com.

Reyns, B. W., Henson, B., & Fisher, B. S. (2012). Stalking in the twilight zone: Extent of cyberstalking victimization and offending among college students. *Deviant Behavior, 33*(1), 1–25.

Richardson, J. T., Best, J., & Bromley, D. G. (1991). *The satanism scare*. New York, NY: Aldine de Gruyter.

Rideout, V. J., Foehr, U. G., & Roberts, D. F. (2009). *Generation M2: Media in the lives of 8–18 year olds*. Report by the Kaiser Family Foundation. Retrieved from www.kff.org.

Ritzer, G. (2006). *McDonaldization: The reader* (2nd ed.). Thousand Oaks, CA: Pine Forge Press.

Ritzer, G., & Goodman, D. J. (2004). *Sociological theory* (6th ed.). New York, NY: McGraw-Hill.

Roberts, G., McCall, D., Stevens-Lavigne, A., Anderson, J., Paglia, A., Bollenbach, S., et al. (2001). *Preventing substance abuse problems among young people: A compendium of best practices*. Ottawa, ON: Health Canada.

Roberts, G. L., Lawrence, J. M., Williams, G. M., & Raphael, B. (1998). The impact of domestic violence on women's health. *Australia and New Zealand Journal of Public Health, 22*, 796–801.

Roberts, J. (2003). Introduction: Commentaries on policing in Toronto. *Canadian Journal of Criminology and Criminal Justice, 45*(3), 343–346.

Roberts, T. A., & Ryan, S. A. (2002). Tattooing and high-risk behavior in adolescents. *Pediatrics, 110*(6), 1058–1063.

Robinson, C. M. (2008). Order in chaos: Security culture as anarchist resistance to the terrorist label. *Deviant Behavior: An Interdisciplinary Journal, 29*, 225–252.

Robinson, T., Callister, M., & Jankoski, T. (2008). Portrayal of body weight on children's television. *Body Image, 5*, 141–151.

Roehling, M. (1999). Weight-based discrimination in employment: Psychological and legal aspects. *Personnel Psychology,*

52(4). Retrieved from Expanded Academic ASAP database.

Rosenau, P. M. (1992). *Postmodernism and the social sciences*. Princeton, NJ: Princeton University Press.

Rosenhan, D. L. (1973). Being sane in insane places. *Science, 179*, 250–258.

Ross, K. (2010). *Gendered media: Women, men and identity politics*. Plymouth, UK: Rowman and Littlefield.

Rothman, D. J. (1971). *The discovery of the asylum: Social order & disorder in the new republic*. Baltimore, MD: Johns Hopkins University Press.

Rubington, E., & Weinberg, M. S. (2002). *Deviance: The interactionist perspective* (8th ed.). Boston, MA: Allyn & Bacon.

Rubington, E., & Weinberg, M. S. (2008). *Deviance: The interactionist perspective* (10th ed.). Boston, MA: Pearson Education.

Sacco, V. F. (1992). *Deviance, conformity and control in Canadian society*. Toronto, ON: Prentice Hall.

Salvatore, C., & Taniguchi, T. A. (2012). Do social bonds matter for emerging adults? *Deviant Behavior, 33*(9), 738–756.

Sandbek, T. J. (1993). *The deadly diet: Recovering from anorexia & bulimia* (2nd ed.). Oakland, CA: New Harbinger Publications.

Sanders, C. (1989). *Customizing the body: The art and culture of tattooing*. Philadelphia, PA: Temple University Press.

Sands, E. R., & Wardle, J. (2003). Internalization of ideal body shapes in 9–12-year-old girls. *International Journal of Eating Disorders, 33*(2), 193–204.

Sareen, J., Cox, B. J., Afifi, T. O., Yu, B. N., & Stein, M. B. (2005). Mental health service use in a nationally representative Canadian survey. *Canadian Journal of Psychiatry, 50*(12), 753–761.

Saxe, J. G. (1873). *The poems of John Godfrey Saxe*. Boston, MA: James R. Osgood and Company. Retrieved from rack1.ul.cs.cmu.edu/is/saxe.

Sayce, L. (2000). *From psychiatric patient to citizen: Overcoming discrimination and social exclusion*. New York, NY: St. Martin's Press.

Scheff, T. J. (1966). *Being mentally ill*. Chicago, IL: Aldine Publishing.

Schildkrout, E. (2004). Inscribing the body. *Annual Review of Anthropology, 33*, 319–344.

Schissel, B. (1997). *Youth crime, moral panics, and the politics of hate*. Halifax, NS: Fernwood.

Schissel, B. (2001). Youth crime, moral panics, and the news: The conspiracy against the marginalized in Canada. In R. C. Smandych (Ed.), *Youth justice: History, legislation, and reform* (pp. 84–103). Toronto, ON: Harcourt.

Schreck, C., Stewart, E., & Fisher, B. (2006). Self-control, victimization, and their influence on risky lifestyles: A longitudinal analysis using panel data. *Journal of Quantitative Criminology, 22*(4), 319–340.

Schwartz, M. B., Vartanian, L. R., Nosek, B. A., & Brownell, K. D. (2006). The influence of one's own body weight on implicit and explicit anti-fat bias. *Obesity, 14*(3), 440–447.

Sefiha, O. (2012). Bike racing, neutralization and the social construction of performance-enhancing drugs. *Contemporary Drug Problems, 39*, 213–245.

Seib, C., Fischer, J., & Najman, J. (2009). The health of female sex workers from three industry sectors in Queensland, Australia. *Social Science and Medicine, 68*, 473–478.

Seidman, S. (2002). *Beyond the closet: The transformation of gay and lesbian life*. New York, NY: Routledge.

Seldon, S., & Montagu, A. (1999). *Inheriting shame: The story of eugenics and racism in America*. New York, NY: Teachers College Press.

Seligson, S. V. (2001). Wacky weight-loss products. *Good Housekeeping, 232*(4), 58–61.

Sellin, T. (1938). *Culture conflict and crime.* New York, NY: Social Science Research Council.

Shade, L. R. (Ed.). (2010). *Mediascapes: New patterns in Canadian communication* (3rd ed.). Toronto, ON: Nelson Education.

Shade, L. R., & Lithgow, M. (2010). The cultures of democracy: How ownership and public participation shape Canada's media systems. In L. R. Shade (Ed.), *Mediascapes: New patterns in Canadian communication* (3rd ed.). Toronto, ON: Nelson Education.

Sharp, S. F., Terling-Watt, T. L., Atkins, L. A., & Gilliam, J. T. (2001). Purging behavior in a sample of college females: A research note on general strain theory and female deviance. *Deviant Behavior: An Interdisciplinary Journal, 22,* 171–188.

Shavitt, S. (1990). The role of attitude objects in attitude functions. *Journal of Experimental Social Psychology, 26,* 124–148.

Shea, B. C. (2001). The paradox of pumping iron: Female bodybuilding as resistance and compliance. *Women and Language, 24*(2), 42–46.

Shermer, M. (2001). *The borderlands of science: Where sense meets nonsense.* New York, NY: Oxford University Press.

Shields, M. (2005). The journey to quitting smoking. *Health Reports, 16*(3), 19–37. Statistics Canada Catalogue No. 82003XIE.

Shilling, C. (1993). *The body and social theory.* London, UK: Sage.

Shirpak, K. R., Maticka-Tyndale, E., & Chinichian, M. (2007). Iranian immigrants' perceptions of sexuality in Canada: A symbolic interactionist approach. *The Canadian Journal of Human Sexuality, 16*(3/4), 113–128.

Shoenberger, N., Heckert, A., & Heckert, D. (2012). Techniques of neutralization theory and positive deviance. *Deviant Behavior, 33*(10), 774–791.

Shupe, A. D., & Bromley, D. G. (1995). The evolution of modern American anti-cult ideology. In T. Miller (Ed.), *America's alternative religions* (pp. 401–409). Albany, NY: State University Press.

Shupe, A., & Hadden, J. K. (1996). Copes, new copy and public opinion: Legitimacy and the social construction of evil in Waco. In S. Wright (Ed.), *Armageddon in Waco* (pp. 177–202). Chicago, IL: University of Chicago Press.

Shuriquie, N. (1999). Eating disorders: A transcultural perspective. *Eastern Mediterranean Health Journal, 5*(2), 354–360.

Shute, N. (2000, October 2). Pushing pills on kids? *U S. News & World Report, 129*(13), 60.

Siegel, K., Lune, H., & Meyer, I. H. (1998). Stigma management among gay/bisexual men with HIV/AIDS. *Qualitative Sociology, 21*(1), 3–24.

Siegel, L. J., & McCormick, C. (2003). *Criminology in Canada: Theories, patterns, and typologies* (2nd ed.). Toronto, ON: Nelson Thomson.

Silverstone, R. (2007). *Media and morality: On the rise of the Mediapolis.* Cambridge, UK: Polity Press.

Simon, R. W. (2002). Revisiting the relationships among gender, marital status, and mental health. *American Journal of Sociology, 107*(4), 1065–1098.

Simoni-Wastila, L. (2000). The use of abusable prescription drugs: The role of gender. *Journal of Women's Health and Gender Based Medicine, 9,* 289–297.

Sleight, P. (2004). Where are clinical trials going? Society and clinical trials. *Journal of Internal Medicine, 255,* 151–158.

Sloan, L., & Wahab, S. (2004). Four categories of women who work as topless dancers. *Sexuality & Culture, 8*(1), 18–43.

Smetana, J. G. (1988). Adolescents' and parents' conceptions of parental authority. *Child Development, 59*(2), 311–335.

Solivetti, L. M. (2003). Structural features, diffusion of addiction and addicts' social traits: The case of Italy. *International Review of Sociology, 13*(1), 39–66

Spector, M. (1981). Beyond crime: Seven methods to control troublesome rascals. In L. Ross (Ed.), *Law and deviance* (pp. 127–148). Beverly Hills, CA: Sage Publications.

Spitzer, B. L., Henderson, K. A., & Zivian, M. T. (1999). Gender differences in population versus media body sizes: A comparison over four decades. *Sex Roles, 40*, 545–565.

Springhall, J. (1999). *Youth, popular culture and moral panics: Penny gaffs to gangsta rap, 1830–1997.* New York, NY: Palgrave Macmillan.

Stark, C. A. (1997). Is pornography an action? The causal vs. the conceptual view of pornography's harm. *Social Theory & Practice, 23*(2), 277–306.

Stark, R., & Bainbridge, W. S. (1996). A *theory of religion.* New Brunswick, NJ: Rutgers University Press.

Statistics Canada. (n. d.). Adult and youth charged, by detailed offences, annually (number). Table 252-0014. Using CHASS (distributor). Retrieved from http://dc1.chass.utoronto.ca/chasscansim.

Statistics Canada. (1992). Crime trends in Canada, 1962–1990. *Juristat, 12*(7). Catalogue No: 85002XIE.

Statistics Canada. (2006). Smoking and diabetes care: Results from the CCHS cycle 3.1 (2005). Catalogue No. 82621XIE.

Statistics Canada. (2008). Victims and persons accused of homicide, by age and sex (accused). CANSIM Table 253-0003.

Statistics Canada. (2011a, January 19). Canadian health measures survey: Physical activity of youth and adults. *The Daily.* Ottawa, ON: Author. Catalogue No. 11-001-X.

Statistics Canada. (2011b, May 25). Canadian Internet use survey. *The Daily.* Ottawa, ON: Author. Catalogue No. 11-001-X.

Statistics Canada. (2012a). Body composition of Canadian adults 2009 to 2011. *Health Fact Sheet.* Catalogue No. 82-625-X.

Statistics Canada. (2012b). Overweight and obesity in children and adolescents: Results from the 2009 to 2011 Canadian Health Measures Survey. *Health Reports, 23*(3). Catalogue No. 82-003-XPE.

Stebbins, R. A. (1996). *Tolerable differences: Living with deviance.* Toronto, ON: McGraw-Hill Ryerson.

Steinmetz, K. F., & Tunnell, K. D. (2013). Under the pixelated Jolly Roger: A study of online pirates. *Deviant Behavior, 34*(1), 53–67.

Stephans, T., & Jorbert, N. (2001). The economic burden of mental health problems in Canada. *Chronic Diseases in Canada, 22*(1), 18–23.

Stephey, M. J. (2009, December 9). Top 10 Disney controversies. *Time Magazine.* Retrieved from www.entertainment.time.com.

Stice, E., & Shaw, H. E. (1994). Adverse effects of the media-portrayed thin-ideal on women and linkages to bulimic symptomatology. *Journal of Social and Clinical Psychology, 13*(3). Retrieved from Expanded Academic ASAP database.

Stip, E., Caron, J., & Lane, L. J. (2001). Schizophrenia: People's perceptions in Quebec. *Canadian Medical Association Journal, 164*(9), 1299–1300.

Stirn, A. (2003). Body piercing: Medical consequences and psychological motivations. *The Lancet, 361*, 1205–1215.

Stoppe, G., Sandholzer, H., & Huppertz, C. (1999). Gender differences in the recognition of depression in old age. *Maturitas, 32*, 205–212.

Stylianou, S. (2002). Control attitudes toward drug use as a function of paternalistic and moralistic principles. *Journal of Drug Use, 32*(1), 119–152.

Sullivan, G., Jackson, C. A., & Spritzer, K. L. (1996). Characteristics and service use of seriously mentally ill persons living in rural areas. *Psychiatric Services, 47*(1), 57–61.

Sumner, C. (1994). *The sociology of deviance: An obituary.* New York, NY: Continuum.

Sumner, W. G. (1906). *Folkways: A study of the sociological importance of usages, manners, mores, and morals.* Boston, MA: Ginn and Co.

Sutherland, E. H. (1947). *Principles of criminology.* Philadelphia, PA: J. B. Lippincott.

Sutherland, N. (1976). *Children in English-Canadian society: Framing the twentieth-century consensus.* Toronto, ON: University of Toronto Press.

Swami, V., & Furnham, A. (2007). Unattractive, promiscuous and heavy drinkers: Perceptions of women with tattoos. *Body Image, 4*, 343–352.

Symbaluk, D. G., & Bereska, T. M. (2013). *Sociology in action: A Canadian perspective.* Toronto, ON: Nelson Education.

Sykes, G., & Matza, D. (1957). Techniques of neutralization: A theory of delinquency. *American Sociological Review, 22*, 664–670.

Szasz, T. (1994). Mental illness is still a myth. *Society, 31*(4), 34–39.

Tait, G. (1999). Rethinking youth cultures: The case of the gothics. *Social Alternatives, 18*(2), 15–20.

Tannenbaum, F. (1938). *Crime and the community.* New York, NY: Ginn.

Tanner, J. (1992). Youthful deviance. In V. Sacco (Ed.), *Deviance, conformity and control in Canadian society* (2nd ed.). Toronto, ON: Prentice Hall.

Tanner, J. (2001). *Teenage troubles: Youth and deviance in Canada* (2nd ed.). Toronto, ON: Nelson Thomson.

Tanner, J. (2010). *Teenage troubles: Youth and deviance in Canada* (3rd ed.). Toronto, ON: Oxford University Press.

Tanzman, B. (1993). An overview of surveys of mental health consumers' preferences for housing and support services. *Hospital and Community Psychiatry, 44*(5), 450–455.

Taylor, A. (2011). *Social media as a tool for inclusion.* Ottawa, ON: Human Resources and Skills Development Canada.

Taylor, N. L. (2011). Negotiating popular obesity discourses in adolescence. *Food, Culture and Society, 14*(4), 587–606.

Taylor-Butts, A., & Bressan, A. (2008). Youth crime in Canada, 2006. *Juristat, 28*(3). Statistics Canada Catalogue No. 85002XIE.

Thio, A. (1983). *Deviant behavior* (2nd ed.). Boston, MA: Houghton Mifflin.

Thoits, P. A. (2011). Resisting the stigma of mental illness. *Social Psychology Quarterly, 74*(1), 6–28.

Thomas, K., & Schmidt, M. S. (2012, July 12). Glaxo agrees to pay $3 billion in fraud settlement. *New York Times.* Retrieved from www.nytimes.com.

Thompson, J., Baird, P. A., & Downie, J. (2005, December 3). The Olivieri case: Context and significance. *Ecclectica.* Retrieved from www.ecclectica.ca.

Thompson, W. E., Harred, J. L., & Burks, B. E. (2003). Managing the stigma of topless dancing: A decade later. *Deviant Behavior, 24*, 551–570.

Thornberry, T., Lizotte, A., Krohm, M., Farnworth, M., & Jang, S. (1991). Testing interactional theory: An examination of reciprocal causal relationships among family, school and delinquency. *Journal of Criminal Law and Criminology, 82*(1), 3–33.

Tiefer, L. (2006). The Viagra phenomenon. *Sexualities, 9*(3), 273–294.

Tittle, C. R., & Paternoster, R. (2000). *Social deviance and crime.* Los Angeles, CA: Roxbury.

Titus, S. L., Wells, J. A., & Rhoades, L. J. (2008). Commentary: Repairing research integrity. *Nature, 453,* 980–982.

Tjepkema, M. (2005). *Measured obesity: Adult obesity in Canada: Measured height and weight.* Statistics Canada Catalogue No. 82620MWE2005001.

Todd, P. (2001, October). Veiled threats? *Homemakers,* October, 45–53.

Tsoukala, A. (2008). Boundary-creating processes and the social construction of threat. *Alternatives, 33*(2), 137–152.

Turk, A. (1969). *Criminality and legal order.* Chicago, IL: Rand McNally.

Turner, B. S. (1987). *Medical power and social knowledge.* London, UK: Sage.

Turner, R. J., Wheaton, B., & Lloyd, D. A. (1995). The epidemiology of social stress. *American Sociological Review, 60*(1), 104–127.

Tylka, T. L., & Calogero, R. M. (2011). Fiction, fashion, and function finale: An introduction and conclusion to the special issue on gendered body image. *Sex Roles, 65,* 447–460.

Tyyskä, V. (2001). *Long and winding road: Adolescents and youth in Canada today.* Toronto, ON: Canadian Scholars' Press.

Ullman, S. R. (1997). *Sex seen: The emergence of modern sexuality in America.* Berkeley, CA: University of California Press.

UNESCO. (1997). *Universal Declaration on the Human Genome and Human Rights.* Paris, FR: Author.

US Attorney's Office. (2012, June 26). Manhattan U.S. attorney and FBI assistant director-in-charge announce 24 arrests in eight countries as part of international cyber crime takedown. Retrieved from www.justice.gov/usao/nys.

US Department of Health and Human Services. (2000). *Healthy people 2010: Understanding and improving health.* Washington, DC: US Government Printing Office.

US Department of State. (2010). *Report on international religious freedom 2010.* Washington, DC: Bureau of Democracy, Human Rights, and Labor.

Valpy, M. (1998, March 7). Cleaning out the cuckoo's nest. *Globe and Mail,* p. D1.

Valverde, M. (1991). *The age of light, soap, and water: Moral reform in English Canada, 1885–1925.* Toronto, ON: McClelland & Stewart.

Vancouver Police Department. (2012). "1040 charges against 315 rioters." Retrieved from riot2011vpd.ca.

van der Meulen, E. (2011). Sex work and Canadian policy: Recommendations for labor legitimacy and social change. *Sex Research and Social Policy, 8,* 348–358.

Van Rassel, J. (2009, March 14). The evolution of Calgary's deadly gang war. *Calgary Herald.* Retrieved May 11, 2009, from www.calgaryherald.com.

Vanston, D. C., & Scott, J. M. (2008). Health risks, medical complications and negative social implications associated with adolescent tattoo and body piercing practices. *Vulnerable Children and Youth Studies, 3,* 221–233.

Venkatesh, S. (2003). A note on social theory and the American street gang. In L. Kontos, D. Brotherton, and L. Barrios (Eds.), *Gangs and society: Alternative perspectives.* New York, NY: Columbia University Press.

Victor, J. (1992). The search for scapegoat deviants. *Humanist, 52*(5), 10–13.

Victor, J. S. (2004). Sluts and wiggers: A study of the effects of derogatory labeling. *Deviant Behavior, 25,* 67–85.

Vold, G. (1958). *Theoretical criminology.* New York, NY: Oxford University Press.

Vowell, P. R., & Chen, J. (2004). Predicting academic misconduct: A comparative test of four sociological explanations. *Sociological Inquiry, 74,* 226–249.

Vuijst, F. (Director & Producer). (1995). *Onward Christian soldiers.* United States: Green Room Productions. Available from Filmakers Library, 124 East 40th Street, NY, NY 10016.

Wahl, O. F. (1992). Mass media images of mental illness: A review of the literature. *Journal of Community Psychology, 15,* 285–291.

Wahl, O. F. (1999). Mental health consumers' experience of stigma. *Schizophrenia Bulletin, 25,* 467–478.

Wahl, O. F. (2003). Depictions of mental illness in children's media. *Journal of Mental Health, 12*(3), 249–258.

Wai Ting Cheung, N., & Cheung, Y. W. (2010). Strain, self-control, and gender differences in delinquency among Chinese adolescents: Extending general strain theory. *Sociological Perspectives, 53*(3), 321–345.

Wallace, C., & Alt, R. (2001). Youth cultures under authoritarian regimes: The case of the swings against the Nazis. *Youth and Society, 32*(3), 275–302.

Walsh, P., & Dauvergne, M. (2009). Police-reported hate crime in Canada, 2007. *Juristat, 29*(2), 1–6. Statistics Canada Catalogue No. 85002X.

Want, S., Vilkers, K., & Amos, J. (2009). The influence of television programs on appearance satisfaction: Making and mitigating social comparisons to *Friends. Sex Roles, 60*(9/10), 642–655.

Ward, D. E. (1993). Gene therapy: The splice of life. *USA Today Magazine, 121*(2572), 63–66.

Ward, D. A., Carter, T. J., & Perrin, R. D. (1994). *Social deviance: Being, behaving,* *and branding.* Boston, MA: Allyn & Bacon.

Warschburger, P. (2005). The unhappy obese child. *International Journal of Obesity, 29,* 127–129.

Weber, M. (1946). *Essays in sociology.* Translated and edited by H. H. Gerth and C. Wright Mills. New York, NY: Oxford University Press.

Weber, T. (1999). Raving in Toronto: Peace, love, unity, and respect in transition. *Journal of Youth Studies, 2*(3), 317–336.

Wechsler, H., & Kuo, M. (2000). College students define binge drinking and estimate its prevalence: Results of a national survey. *Journal of American College Health, 49*(2), 57–64.

Wechsler, H., Lee, J. E., Kuo, M., Seibring, M., Nelson, M. S., & Lee, H. (2002). Trends in college binge drinking during a period of increased prevention efforts: Findings from four Harvard School of Public Health College alcohol student surveys: 1993–2001. *Journal of American College Health, 50*(5), 203–217.

Wechsler, H., & Nelson, T. F. (2008). What we have learned from the Harvard School of Public Health College alcohol study: Focusing attention on college student alcohol consumption and the environmental conditions that promote it. *Journal of Studies on Alcohol and Drugs, 69*(4), 481–490.

Wechsler, H., Seibring, M., Liu, M. T. S., & Ahl, M. (2004). Colleges respond to student binge drinking: Reducing student demand or limiting access. *Journal of American College Health, 52*(4), 159–168.

Wegs, R. (1999). Youth delinquency & "crime": The perception and the reality. *Journal of Social History, 32*(3). Retrieved from Expanded Academic ASAP database.

Weinberg, M. S. (1967). Nudist camp: Way of life and social structure. *Human Organization, 26*, 91–99.

Weiss, S. F. (1988). *Race hygiene and national efficiency: The eugenics of Wilhelm Schallmayer.* Berkeley, CA: University of California Press.

Weitzer, R. (2010). The mythology of prostitution: Advocacy research and public policy. *Sex Research and Social Policy, 7*, 15–29.

Weitzman, E. R., & Nelson, T. F. (2004). College student binge drinking and the "prevention paradox": Implications for prevention and harm reduction. *Journal of Drug Education, 34*(3), 247–266.

Wells, E., & Rankin, J. (1991). Families and delinquency: A meta-analysis of the impact of broken homes. *Social Problems, 38*, 71–93.

Wertheim, E. H., Paxton, S. J., Schutz, H. K., & Muir, S. L. (1997). Why do adolescent girls watch their weight? An interview study examining sociocultural pressures to be thin. *Journal of Psychosomatic Research, 42*(4), 345–355.

Wesely, J. K. (2003). "Where am I going to stop?" Exotic dancing, fluid body boundaries, and effects on identity. *Deviant Behavior, 24*, 483–503.

West, G. (1991). Towards a more socially informed understanding of Canadian delinquency legislation. In A. Leschied, P. Jaffe, & W. Willis (Eds.), *The Young Offenders Act: A revolution in Canadian juvenile justice.* Toronto, ON: University of Toronto Press.

West, W. G. (1984). *Young offenders and the state: A Canadian perspective on delinquency.* Toronto, ON: Butterworths.

Westbrook, M. T., Legge, V., & Pennay, M. (1993). Attitudes towards disabilities in a multicultural society. *Social Science & Medicine, 36*(5), 615–623.

Wheeler, S. (1960). Sex offenses: A sociological critique. *Law and Contemporary Society, 25* (Spring), 258–278.

White, C. (2003). Environmentalist accused of scientific dishonesty. *British Medical Journal, 326*(7381), 120.

Whiting, G. (1996). *The sterilization of Leilani Muir* [videorecording]. Available from the National Film Board of Canada.

Whorton, J. (2001). The solitary vice. *The Western Journal of Medicine, 175*(1). Retrieved January 24, 2002, from Expanded Academic ASAP database.

Williams, D. R., & Takeuchi, D. T. (1992). Socioeconomic status and psychiatric disorder among blacks and whites. *Social Forces, 70*(5), 179–194.

Wilson, B. (2002). The Canadian rave scene and five theses on youth resistance. *Canadian Journal of Sociology, 27*(3), 373–412.

Wilson, B. R. (1993). Historical lessons in the study of sects and cults. *Religion and the Social Order, 3A*, 53–73.

Wilson, T. D., & Brekke, N. C. (1994). Mental contamination and mental correction: Unwanted influences on judgments and evaluations. *Psychological Bulletin, 116*, 117–142.

Windecker, J. (1997). The prostitution of native women on the north coast of British Columbia. *British Columbia Historical News, 30*(3), 29–33.

Withey, E. (2012, October 1). Tattoos offer parents permanent tributes to their children, says Edmonton artist. *Edmonton Journal.* Retrieved from www.edmonton-journal.com.

Wohlrab, S., Stahl, J., & Kappeler, P. M. (2006). Modifying the body: Motivations for getting tattooed and pierced. *Body Image, 4*, 87–95.

Wolff, N. (2007). The social construction of the costs of mental illness. *Evidence & Policy, 3*(1), 67–78.

Wood, R. (1999). Nailed to the X: A lyrical history of the straightedge youth subculture. *Journal of Youth Studies, 2,* 133–151.

Wood, R. (2001). *Straightedge youth: Subculture, genesis, permutation, and identity formation.* Unpublished doctoral dissertation, University of Alberta, Edmonton, AB.

World Association for Sexology. (1999). *The Universal Declaration of Sexual Rights.* Retrieved from www.worldsexology.org/about_sexualrights.asp.

World Health Organization. (2001). Costs of mental illness. *Fact Sheet No. 218.* Retrieved from www.who.int.

World Health Organization. (2002a). Homepage. Retrieved from www.who.int.

World Health Organization. (2002b). *Mental Health Global Action Programme.* Geneva, CH: Author.

World Health Organization. (2003). *WHO Constitution.* Retrieved from www.who.int.

World Health Organization. (2004a). Estimates of global prevalence of childhood underweight in 1990 and 2015. *Global Database on Child Growth and Malnutrition.* Retrieved from www.who.int.

World Health Organization. (2004b). *Constitution of the World Health Organization.* Retrieved from www.who.int/governance/en.

World Health Organization (2010). Mental health: Strengthening our response. *Fact Sheet No. 220.* Retrieved from www.who.int.

World Health Organization (2012). Obesity and overweight. *Fact Sheet No. 311.* Retrieved from www.who.int.

World Psychiatric Association. (2003). Program against stigmatization and discrimination because of schizophrenia. Retrieved from www.wpanet.org.

Wortley, S. S., & Tanner, J. (2003). Data, denials, and confusion: The racial profiling debate in Toronto. *Canadian Journal of Criminology and Criminal Justice, 45*(3), 367–389.

Wright, S. A. (1997). Media coverage of unconventional religion: Any "good news" for minority faiths? *Review of Religious Research, 39*(2), 101–115.

Wroblewska, A. M. (1997). Androgenic anabolic steroids and body dysmorphia in young men. *Journal of Psychosomatic Research, 42,* 225–234.

Yam, P. (1997). The media's eerie fascination. *Scientific American, 276*(1), 100–101.

Youngblut, S. (2012, January 4). Do these childhood obesity ads go too far? *Globe and Mail.* Retrieved from www.theglobeandmail.com.

Zamaria, C., & Fletcher, F. (2007). *Canada online! The Internet, media and emerging technologies: Uses, attitudes, trends and international comparisons—year two report. Report by the Canadian Internet Project.* Retrieved from www.ciponline.ca.

Zeman, K., & Bressan, A. (2008). Factors associated with youth delinquency and victimization in Toronto, 2006. *Crime and Justice Research Paper Series.* Statistics Canada Catalogue No. 85561M, No. 14.

Index

stigma management, male prostitution 74
strain theories, modifications of 50
General Strain Theory 46–47, 50
Generalized other 70, 196
Genetic science 295, 299
Globalization 51
Group conflict theory 81–82

H

Hacking, computer 110–112
Hegemony 83, 106
High-consensus deviance 14, 20, 110, 112
Hippies 45, 55
  see also Family of Love
Homework drugs 47
Homicide
  absolutist view of deviance 12
  consequences of marijuana use, historical
    perceptions 8–9
  Criminal Code of Canada 14
  offenders, by age and gender
    156–157
  Manson family murders 259
  normative violation 14
  Shepard, Matthew 55
  see also capital punishment
Homosexuality
  aboriginal cultures 124
  absolute others, media 96–97
  as a crime 13, 296
  criminal victimization 138
  cyberbullying 114
  harm, definition of deviance 7
  hate crimes 138
  identity 122
  in the *DSM* 240, 281, 288
  legislation, changes in 137–138
  mores 12
  Nazi persecution 280
  pornography, Butler decision 148
  same-sex marriage 11, 19
  social construction 17
  Shepard, Matthew 55
  stigmatization 117, 130, 137–138
  Stonewall Inn uprising 137
Human rights policy 297–300
Human trafficking 145

I

Iceberg theory 270–271, 289
Identity management 73–74, 196, 236–237,
  287, 295
Ideology 82–83, 98, 106
Impression management. *See* identity
  management
Institutional anomie theory 43
Instrumental conditioning 57
Interactionist view of law 14
Interpretive theories
  body modification 196
  critiques of 76–79
  digital piracy 113
  gangs 161–163
  integration with positivist theories 77–78
  link to interactionism 68
  media research, critical 98
  mental illness 222
  relationship to subjective views of
    deviance 64, 286
  sexuality 121–122, 151
  social construction 64, 67–68
  see also deviant career
  see also identity management
  see also labelling theories

J

Jamband subculture 54
Jazz, deviantization of 117
Joan of Arc 6–7, 264
Juvenile Delinquents Act 167

K

King, Martin Luther, Jr. 45

L

Labelling theory 70–75, 77–79, 113, 163,
  217, 228, 244–245
Latent functions 37
Left-handedness 6
Location of sex as deviant 140
Low-consensus deviance 14, 20, 110, 112